I0024786

The Call of Self
Psychosynthesis Life Coaching

Edited by Dorothy Firman, Ed.D,

Synthesis Center Press
Amherst, Massachusetts
www.synthesiscenter.org
© 2018

All authors retain copyright to their individual chapters

ISBN 978-0-9909590-1-4

Cover & interior design and technical editor: Ted Slawski
Set in Adobe™ Jenson Pro & ITC Legacy Sans

Praise for The Call of Self

In their book, *The Call of Self: Psychosynthesis Life Coaching*, thirty authors, from around the world, discuss the fields of coaching, psychology, and psychosynthesis, and the unique way in which these practices combine to support clients in their inner and outer growth and development.

While traditional coaching emphasizes the setting and achieving of external goals, it neglects to take into account aspects of personhood which may influence the goal or task at hand. Psychosynthesis sheds light on all aspects of human existence in both personal and spiritual development, allowing inner and outer goals to be addressed, deeply and effectively. The authors are life coaches with expertise ranging from body work to trauma to social activism to the practice of accessing transpersonal realities and they are business coaches deeply steeped in corporate, executive and work world practices.

As a coach myself, I highly recommend this book and will use much of the material within it, in my own work. It offers a wonderful overview of psychosynthesis coaching and its application in a multitude of situations.

—Jill Becker, MD, Empowerment Coach

By drawing upon the writings of cutting edge psychosynthesis academics, researchers and practitioners, Dorothy Firman has compiled a wealth of information in a one-stop volume. Everyone who supports others in their personal growth will benefit from understanding the historical evolution of psychosynthesis, as well as the many insights offered into breakthrough practices and emerging techniques of life coaching. This, indeed, is a rich treasury of Psychosynthesis paradigms and perspectives.

—Mark L. Smith, MBA,
CERTIFIED FINANCIAL PLANNER™

Foreword

The collection of wisdom and various techniques and strategies present-ed in this volume is such an exciting addition to the field of professional life coaching and purposeful living. As a leadership and life coach myself (for three decades), and someone who has written many books and articles about coach-ing as well as a leader in credentialing organizations, I am happy to welcome such a book.

I had the pleasure of learning Psychosynthesis in 1976 as part of my doctoral degree in Transpersonal Psychology and Counseling. Assagioli, the founder of psychosynthesis was a colleague of Freud early on but broke away, as did Carl Jung, to pursue a more teleological and future oriented approach to living optimally. The goal is to manifest the art and science of human develop-ment and personal transformation, and to do so creatively. The psychosynthesis life coach uses many methods and techniques to assist those clients, who seek the next step of inner and outer development in their lives. As stated in the first chapter of this book:

"Any method that assists in the personal evolution of a human being is a method useful in psychosynthesis. To be maximally effective, we clearly must have a broad range of methods and techniques to meet the needs presented by different situations and people."

The Call of Self: Psychosynthesis Life Coaching is a comprehensive and rich collection from 30 different authors, with a broad array of theory and practical application to special uses for psychosynthesis techniques. The reader might think that the term, psychosynthesis, sounds esoteric and scientific...and in a way, that is partly true, as much of the wisdom was not really published until 40 years after first postulated by Roberto Assagioli. However, it had been prac-ticed in Italy and spread through Europe and America over many years with no published book, but many archives of articles and essays. It still blossoms more than one hundred years after Dr. Assagioli first wrote about his conception of the synthesis of the psyche: psychosynthesis!

Psychosynthesis is truly a great word for blending and synthesizing the conscious and unconscious aspects of being a human. A full and comprehen-sive psychological and educational approach to whole person development in-evitably utilizes information from wisdom cultures and traditions from our past, as well as from current practical and scientific knowledge.

Transpersonal Psychology embraces a holistic view of Eastern and Western disciplines, of ways to live fully and with purpose. Eastern disciplines are viewed as emphasizing the spiritual aspect of being and approaches in the Western cultures have usually been more focused on the scientific and behavioral discussion of personality and psychological processes. Of the four major forces in psychology: psychoanalytic, behavioral, humanistic and transpersonal psychology, psychosynthesis places itself firmly in the transpersonal dimension.

It offers an assumption of a centered "Self" with an invitation to be actively involved in the relationship with the various levels of the unconscious, even so far as including the realm of a collective consciousness and universal energy (as Jung did) that we can tap into. Psychosynthesis, then, is a blending of all Eastern and Western, ancient and modern, philosophical, spiritual, psychological and practical wisdom, that will aid in the integration and full development of a human being while they live in a world of paradox, conflict, and the beauty and mystery of human life.

The extensive array of knowledge, theory, and yet practical applications in this impressive volume is a welcome addition to the books available to practicing coaches today. To be a human being, living optimally, encompasses individual growth, living with relationships, the world of work, and even the role of the individual in society and life on this planet.

You will want this book on your shelf, avail yourself of practical learning from the authors and thereby become a powerful vehicle for your clients (and yourself) to live the best life possible.

Enjoy the journey…why not?

Patrick Williams, Ed.D,
    Master Certified Coach, Board Certified Coach
    Author of *Therapist as Life Coach: Transforming Your Practice; Becoming a Professional Life Coach: Lessons from the Institute for Life Coach Training;* and *Total Life Coaching: 50+ Life Lessons, Skills, and Techniques to Enhance your Practice and Your Life.* See more at https://DrPatWilliams.com

PREFACE

I am, at this moment, sixty-eight years old and I have been involved with psychosynthesis since I was twenty-four. I was first introduced to psychosynthesis by my cousin John Firman (eternal gratitude), sitting around my living room, with my young son, jumping from lap to lap. I "got it," as my life's call, in that first conversation. I have never turned back. From that moment, through 3 academic degrees, 2 more children, licensure as a mental health counselor, training center director, graduate psychology professor, psychotherapist, author, certified life coach…and all the rest of life, my professional life has been built on psychosynthesis principles. Likewise, my own personal development has always been anchored around the practices from within the psychosynthesis model.

It is also true that all our authors are steeped in psychosynthesis theory, practice and personal and professional engagement. They are life or business coaches, with an orientation in psychosynthesis, as Psychosynthesis Life Coaches (PLC), Board Certified Coaches (BCC), International Coach Federation coaches (ICF) and with other designations in the field of coaching. Beyond that, each one comes with extensive life experience, amazing training in a variety of fields, deep commitment to the well-being of our world and they come with something to say.

We have written this book for life coaches, helping professionals and seekers on any path. It offers a deep view into the philosophy, theory and practice of psychosynthesis, complete with exercises, from time to time, offered by authors who want their readers to experience psychosynthesis, while reading this book.

The book itself, each of the thirty-three chapters, delves into an orientation or perspective on life itself. Psychosynthesis practitioners are hopeful, creative and dedicated people, called in a soulful way to be in this work. And that will be clear in every chapter. Readers will visit psychosynthesis coaching through a variety of lenses that will allow a deep and vast overview of this field, along with clear opportunities to expand skills as a life coach or helping professional, and to travel into inner and outer development as a human being on the path of life.

This book might be read cover to cover, or skipped through by section or chapter, based on the reader's interest. While there is so much here, it is also true that there is so much more: in the field of psychosynthesis coaching, in all psychosynthesis practices, in every wisdom tradition and every field of endeavor. And there is so much more in each life. May we continue to live into our evolution. —Dorothy Firman, Editor

Acknowledgements

In honoring the transpersonal nature of the work of psychosynthesis, I want to gratefully acknowledge all beings, each in the process of evolution. May all know safety and peace.

Individually, there are too many people to thank, but you know who you are, so thanks!

Gratitude goes to all my teachers, both in psychosynthesis and in the whole of my life. Thank you to my colleagues in psychosynthesis, in all parts of the world, who continue to enrich this theory and practice, both professionally and personally, carrying it forward to yet a new generation. Particular warm-hearted appreciation goes to the people who have created psychosynthesis centers, from the seeds of their training at the Synthesis Center. And to my students and clients, a deep bow of gratitude, for you have been the real gift.

There are those who have specifically helped in the creation of this book and I thank each of you. And a grand Thank You to the amazing authors, all 28 of you, who worked with me from start to finish to make this happen.

And to Ted, thank you forever.

Dorothy Firman, Summer 2018

Contents

Part 1

Psychosynthesis Life Coaching: The Goodness of Fit

From a still wider and more comprehensive point of view universal life itself appears to us as a struggle between multiplicity and unity—a labor and an aspiration towards union. We seem to sense that—whether we conceive it as a divine Being or as cosmic energy—the Spirit working upon and within all creation is shaping it into order, harmony and beauty, uniting all beings (some willing, but the majority as yet blind and rebellious) with each other through links of love, achieving—slowly and silently, but powerfully and irresistibly—the Supreme Synthesis.

—Roberto Assagioli

Editor's Note:
Welcome to the practice of psychosynthesis life coaching, a powerful field of work designed to support the evolution of individuals, groups, and all beings. If you are new to psychosynthesis, this first section will be important for grounding into the core theory of the field. For those who are familiar with psychosynthesis, I invite you to visit the current thinking, the questions that emerge in the field, the inherent possibilities for growth based on this work, and the ultimate Goodness of Fit that inspires the integration of psychosynthesis into the field of coaching. A special chapter invites us to see our roots in this work, as the chapter by Martha Crampton (1933-2009), takes us to the earliest writing, in the US, on psychosynthesis and coaching.

Chapter 1

Psychosynthesis: A Brief Overview

by Dorothy Firman
with reference to the words of Dr. Roberto Assagioli

Let us feel and obey the urge aroused by the great need of healing the serious ills which at present are affecting humanity. Let us realize the contribution we can make to the creation of a new civilization characterized by an harmonious integration and cooperation, pervaded by the spirit of synthesis.

—*Roberto Assagioli*

In its most basic sense, psychosynthesis is simply a name for the process of personal growth: the natural tendency in each of us to harmonize or synthesize our various aspects at ever more inclusive levels of organization. In its more specific sense, psychosynthesis is a name for the conscious attempt to cooperate with the natural process of personal development. All living things contain within them a drive to evolve, to become the fullest realization of themselves. This process can be supported consciously, and psychosynthesis is one means to do this. Cooperating effectively with this process can be assisted by a conceptual understanding of the nature of this evolution, and by practical techniques. Psychosynthesis provides these and integrates them into an inclusive and ever-growing framework designed to support the individual, groups, and the planet in their process of unfolding.

In one of his letters Freud said, "I am interested only in the basement of the human being." Psychosynthesis is interested in the whole building. We try to build an elevator which will allow a person access to every level of his personality. After all, a building with only a basement is very limited. We want to open up the terrace where you can sun-bathe or look at the stars. Our concern is the synthesis of all areas of the

3

personality. That means psychosynthesis is holistic, global and inclusive. It is not against psychoanalysis or even behavior modification but it insists that the needs for meaning, for higher values, for a spiritual life, are as real as biological or social needs. We deny that there are any isolated human problems. (Sam Keen interview of Assagioli, *Psychology Today*, 1974)

As an inclusive approach to human growth, psychosynthesis dates from 1911 and the early work of Roberto Assagioli, an Italian psychiatrist, whose biography appears later in this book. Though one of the pioneers of psychoanalysis in Italy, Assagioli maintained that Freud had not given sufficient weight to the "higher" aspects of the human personality, and recognized a need for a more comprehensive concept of humanity. From this beginning, Assagioli and an increasing number of psychotherapists, educators, physicians, social workers, clergy, and others have worked to develop and refine this inclusive view of human growth. The task is considered to be an open one, one that will never be finished. Each year, new discoveries in psychology, neuropsychology, new developments in education, religion, anthropology, physics, new fields such as life coaching, energy medicine, hospice work, and other disciplines add to the principles and to the techniques of psychosynthesis. Psychosynthesis, by its very nature, is always open to new approaches to human development.

Over the past 100 + years, a number of conceptual points and a number of methods have proven themselves to be fundamental. These provide a working structure for psychosynthesis and will be explored throughout this book. The work of Psychosynthesis Life and Business Coaching represent a growing next step, with a concurrent development and expansion of original psychosynthesis theory.

A Synthesis Of Many Traditions

Psychosynthesis may also be considered as the individual expression of a wider principle, of a general law of interindividual and cosmic synthesis. Indeed, the isolated individual does not exist; every person has intimate relationships with other individuals which make them all interdependent. (Assagioli, 1965, pp.30-31)

Any comprehensive psychological and educational approach to the development of the whole person must draw from many traditions. While Eastern disciplines often have tended to emphasize the spiritual side of being,

Western approaches usually have focused on the personality level. The "four forces" of psychology also orient themselves towards one dimension or another: psychoanalytic, behavioral, humanistic and transpersonal psychology. But humanity must be viewed as a whole and each aspect accorded its due importance. Psychosynthesis recognizes that we have a transpersonal essence, and at the same time holds that the individual's purpose in life is to manifest this essence, or Self, as fully as possible in the world of everyday personal and social existence. Beyond the integration and inclusion of a wide variety of perspectives, psychosynthesis holds to its own center point: the experience and realization of the Self, a center of content-less awareness and will.

> In my opinion, the direct experience of the self, of pure self-awareness independent of any 'content' of the field of consciousness and of any situation in which the individual may find himself—is a true 'phenomenological' experience, an inner reality which can be empirically verified and deliberately produced through appropriate techniques. (Assagioli, 1965, p.5)

> Let us realize thoroughly the full meaning and immense value of the discovery of the will. In whatever way it happens, either spontaneously or through conscious action, in a crisis or in the quiet of inner recollection, it constitutes a most important and decisive event in our lives. (Assagioli, 2010, p.8)

Stages In Psychosynthesis

> *A living human being is not a building for which the foundations must be laid, then the walls erected and, finally, the roof added. The carrying out of the vast inner program of psychosynthesis may be started from various points and angles at the same time, and the different methods and activities can be wisely alternated through shorter or longer cycles, according to circumstances and inner conditions. (Assagioli, 1965, p. 29)*

Every person is an individual, and the psychosynthesis of each person follows a unique path. At the same time, the overall process of psychosynthesis can be divided into two stages: personal and transpersonal (or spiritual). In personal psychosynthesis, the integration of the personality takes place around the personal self, and the individual attains a level of functioning in terms of work, relationships, and general living that is experienced as satisfactory and meaningful, and which might be termed "healthy" by current standards.

In the transpersonal stage the person learns to achieve alignment with and to work through the energies of the transpersonal or "Higher" Self, manifesting such qualities as responsibility, the spirit of cooperation, global perspective, love, peace, creativity and more, in service of life's purpose. Having access to one's own inner guidance and wisdom; an internal unifying center, that is not limited by conditioning, each person or group is able to hear their unique Call of Self.

The two stages overlap and may, in fact, be considered intertwined elements, each working hand in hand with the other to support conscious evolution. Personal and spiritual integration become both the process and the outcome.

Methods Employed In Psychosynthesis

Moreover, psychosynthesis utilizes many techniques of psychological action, aiming first at the development and perfection of the personality and then at its harmonious coordination and increasing unification with the Self. These phases may be called respectively "personal" and "spiritual" psychosynthesis. (Assagioli, 1965, p. 30)

According to the various fields of activity in which it is used, and the different purposes which it may serve, psychosynthesis is or may become:
1. A method of psychological development and Self-realization for those who refuse to remain the slaves of their own inner phantasms or of external influences, who refuse to submit passively to the play of psychological forces which is going on within them, and who are determined to become the master of their own lives.
2. A method of treatment for psychological and psychosomatic disturbances when the cause of the trouble is a violent and complicated conflict between groups of conscious and unconscious forces, or when it is due to those deep-seated and tormenting crises (not generally understood or rightly judged by the patient himself) which often precede a phase of Self-realization.
3. A method of integral education which tends not only to favor the development of the various abilities of the child or of the adolescent, but also helps him to discover and realize his true spiritual nature and to build under its guidance an harmonious, radiant and efficient personality. (Assagioli, 1965, p. 30)

Any method that assists in the personal evolution of a human being is a method useful in psychosynthesis. To be maximally effective, we clearly must have a broad range of methods and techniques to meet the needs presented by different situations and people. As each person must be treated as an individual, an effort must be made to choose the methods best suited to each person's existential situation, psychological type, goals, desires and path of development. Some of the methods more commonly used include purpose based inquiry, self-reflection, values clarification, guided imagery, self-identification, creativity, meditation, will development and manifestation of goals, symbolic art work, journal keeping, ideal models, the development of intuition and other psychological functions, and many more. The emphasis is on fostering an ongoing process of growth that can gain momentum and bring a more joyful and balanced actualization to our lives.

As this process goes on, we gain the freedom of choice, the power of decision over our actions, and the ability to regulate and direct many of the personality functions. This entails developing the personal will—the will of the personal self. Through this development, we free ourselves from helpless or pre-programmed reactions to inner impulses and external situations and expectations. We become truly "centered" and gradually become able to follow our own path, guided by our inner knowing, our true Self.

As we reach toward the transpersonal Self, we can liberate and encourage the synthesizing energies that organize and integrate the personality. We can make ever-increasing contact with the will of our transpersonal Self, which provides clearer and clearer meaning and purpose in our personal lives and our social tasks. We become able to function in the world more serenely and effectively, in a spirit of cooperation and good will. Psychosynthesis is a powerful and effective mode of growth. It is a positive and dynamic framework from which to view the evolution of our planet.

The Core Maps In Psychosynthesis

As a rule, we live life more or less as it comes. Yet the business of living is in reality an art and should be the greatest of all the arts. (Assagioli, 1973, p.1)

You will see these two maps mentioned at various times throughout the book, as well as hearing more about the theory behind each map. At the same time, you will see visionary practitioners of psychosynthesis coaching elaborate and enliven these maps. For your convenience, they are here, as originally represented and described by Roberto Assagioli, with permission for reprinting given by the publisher.

1. The Lower Unconscious
2. The Middle Unconscious
3. The Higher Unconscious
   or Superconscious
4. The Field of Consciousness
5. The Conscious Self, or I
6. The Transpersonal Self
7. The Collective Unconscious

The "egg" or oval diagram of the psyche, points to the levels of the unconscious and the role of consciousness and the s(S)elf.

The lower unconscious, sometimes also referred to as the "pre-personal" dimension, holds fundamental drives and urges; complexes, scripts and stories that have been internalized in our younger lives, often with trauma or intense emotion; and experiences from the past, both negative and positive, that have yet to be integrated. The middle unconscious ("personal" dimension) holds psychological elements that are easily accessible to the conscious mind. This includes everything from facts that are not currently in consciousness, to awareness of some of our patterns of behavior that we would be able to accurately predict. The higher unconscious ("transpersonal" dimension) carries our ethical imperatives, our transpersonal qualities (love, creativity, wisdom, etc.) and our inherent sense of purpose, meaning and values. The collective unconscious is the delineated but not divided access to the archetypes and collective knowing.

The field of consciousness is just that, the area of awareness and experience that we are conscious of in any given moment, while the "I" (also called personal self or conscious self) is the point of pure self-awareness and will, freed of attachment to the contents of consciousness and personality presentation. This is the "un-storied" self, centered, in and of the world. The higher (or transpersonal) Self carries the same qualities and aspects as the personal self, while connected to the experience of the universal nature of being. The personal self may be considered our truest self, at the kitchen sink, immanent and living within the world we inhabit, while the higher Self sits at the mountaintop. It points to peak experiences, connection with our transcendent capacities, and our experience of unity consciousness. And this "apparent" duality is only one of awareness, in any given moment. "The Self is one; it manifests in different degrees of awareness and self-realization" (Assagioli, 2012, p. 17).

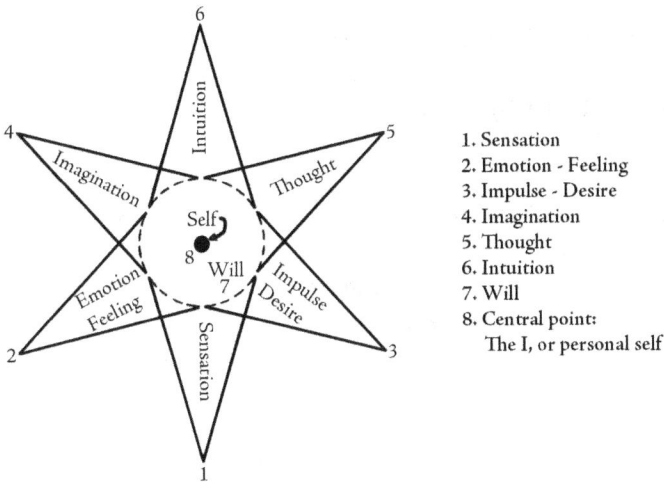

1. Sensation
2. Emotion - Feeling
3. Impulse - Desire
4. Imagination
5. Thought
6. Intuition
7. Will
8. Central point:
   The I, or personal self

The map of the psychological functions (or star diagram) invites a consideration of the psychological structures through which the human being has access to experiencing the world. These various functions: thinking, impulse-desire, sensation, emotions, imagination and intuition, work either to serve or derail us. Noting the same centered presence of the Self, functioning through awareness and will, the psychological functions become our means to taking in information and expressing ourselves in the world. "The relationships among these functions are complex, but there are two kinds of interactions: first, those that take place spontaneously, one might say mechanically; second, those that can be influenced, governed, and directed by the will" (Assagioli, 2010, p.37).

It is the ongoing intention of the work of psychosynthesis to bring consciousness and will to bear on the unfolding of a life. By attention to the psychological functions and their interplay, we can move from scripted and unconscious experiences that may stem from any psychological function, towards the creation of active allied resources and ways of knowing, to be used in service of the search for self-realization.

As you will discover, this brief introduction invites you, the reader, into a wide and vast world of psychosynthesis theory, practice and experience, viewed through the lens of the rapidly emerging field of psychosynthesis coaching. Whether you read the book from cover to cover, or jump to chapters with specific appeal, you will be reading the work of wise, experienced and forward thinking psychosynthesis practitioners, from throughout the world. We all wish you a joyful and productive journey.

References

Assagioli, R. (1965). *Psychosynthesis: A manual of principles and techniques.* New York: Hobbs, Dorman & Company, Inc.

Assagioli, R. (1973). *Life as a game and stage performance.* New York: Psychosynthesis Research Foundation.

Assagioli, R. (1973). *The act of will.* New York: The Viking Press.

Assagioli, R. (2010). *The act of will.* Amherst, MA: Synthesis Center Press.

Assagioli, R. (2012). *Psychosynthesis: A collection of basic writings.* Amherst, MA: The Synthesis Center, Inc.

Keen, S. (1974, December). The golden mean of Roberto Assagioli. *Psychology Today,* 97-107.

Chapter 2

Introduction to Psychosynthesis Coaching

by Roger H. Evans

The author's central thesis is that the current coaching models, such as the GROW Model (Whitmore, 1996), and the CLEAR Model, developed by Hawkins (1980), while very useful, are either incomplete, or unbalanced. Much coaching is based on 'winning' or gaining high performance through 'goal setting'. The effectiveness of this approach is now being questioned. I believe that coaches increasingly need to include the question 'Why?' in relation to setting goals and achieving success (not the 'why because' in terms of history, rather 'Why, what is trying to emerge?') so that their clients seek answers, which are informed by their own values and purpose for how they want to live their lives. For some this may mean working with explicit existential issues and dilemmas and for others a need to live a 'more spiritual life'. In short, by holding Trifocal Vision (Where is the client now? Where do they want to go? What is the gap between these?), the coach can work with both emergence and evolution. This call appears to correlate well with the parallel 'Spiritual Intelligence' movement (Zohar & Marshall 2000).

The Evolving World of Coaching

History and Development of Coaching

Coaching started as a radical new approach to helping people learn and originated in the mid 70s in California, through the work of Timothy Gallwey, who applied emergent humanistic psychology to learning skills (like tennis) and later to development at work. Humanistic Psychology distinguishes itself by identifying an intrinsic growth need in people and by regarding people as responsible beings who decide and choose their actions freely and so it seeks to empower people to maximize growth during their life journey. He called his approach the 'Inner Game'.

11

In his book, *The Inner Game of Tennis* (1975) Gallwey, a former tennis expert, described his new and radical approach to helping people learn to play tennis. Instead of telling people what to do, he helped people learn from their own experiences—a radical departure from the instructor as expert, who gave advice and suggestions to people who were regarded as 'empty vessels'. Instead, Gallwey focused on people's innate ability to learn, grow and actualize their potential and evoked this through a non-directive approach: asking questions, so that the performer learned from experience. In this way, the instructor transforms into a coach, facilitating the performers to self-observe, express their inherent potential and be the source of their own answers. This context is a defining aspect of coaching.

Coaching, as an approach to development, can therefore be considered, on a surface level, as a manifestation of a very different, non-directive approach to learning, and, on a deeper level, a reflection of the shift from a more mechanistic perception of people (who can be 'instructed' like a machine to produce particular outcomes), towards a more holistic perspective, where the inherent potential in each of us, and the urge to actualize this, is acknowledged. In order to manifest this potential, we need to become more observant and aware of ourselves. A coach facilitates this process of self-discovery in order to help us take action based on the awareness we gain.

Sir John Whitmore (1937-2017) has been one of the foremost spokesmen of coaching. He was an early pioneer in bringing Gallwey's 'Inner Game' to business in the UK. His definition is of coaching as an activity: "Coaching is concerned with unlocking a person's potential to maximise their own performance. It is helping them to learn rather than teaching them" (Whitmore, 1996, p. 10). The key principles of coaching he defines as "building awareness and responsibility."

There is agreement that coaching is concerned with actualizing potential and possibilities, with personal (and organizational) growth and change being an integral part of this process. In psychosynthesis coaching we consider this the purpose (WHAT FOR) of coaching and a key reflection of its humanistic foundations.

Whitmore (1996) further emphasized the importance of building self-belief as a cornerstone of coaching activity so that people become more self-reliant and less dependent on the coach. This process inevitably supports personal growth and change.

We can extrapolate that coaching as an activity, is distinct in its approach by helping people to learn, to self-reflect, to define their own measures for success and direction, rather than being taught along pre-determined parameters.

We believe this is a defining aspect of coaching: enabling self-learning and self-leadership. Difficult as it may sometimes be, this requires that the coach acts predominantly as a facilitator rather than an expert/teacher. It requires from the coach a lived, enacted, not just intellectually espoused, trust in clients' capacity to discover and unfold their potential in the way that is best for them. This does not preclude the coach from giving suggestions or even teaching concepts, once in a while, in order to spark fresh insights or help promote self-awareness, but this is not the main focus, as it might be for a conventional skills trainer for example.

Finally, the focus of coaching interactions is goal oriented, helping clients to realize a future that motivates them. In the process of coaching clients towards these goals, there will be attention on addressing the obstacles that get in the way of expressing more of their potential, be that limiting beliefs or lack of skills.

The Relevance of Psychosynthesis Coaching Today

I believe that psychosynthesis coaching is important across the vast scope of applications, and very relevant at this time for everyone desiring change and for all leaders, in any context, who are responsible for other people in environments interwoven with great complexity and change. Many of these leaders are struggling with their own issues about balancing their own personal needs with those of the organization, family or group. They may shun the need for a 'balance' until a personal relationship or health crisis emerges and they find they are without the psychological skills to handle this. Many of these highly intelligent, hardworking people are also—given the stage in their lives—facing existential ('mid-life') or transitional crises which for many have remained 'under wraps' with the consequence of unconscious 'acting out'.

The relevance of psychosynthesis as a context for coaching in today's organizational, as well as personal, world should not be underestimated. In these troubling times of antagonism and polarization, political leaders and social change agents, as well as our business, group and cultural leaders, face the call for transparency, honesty, social responsibility and environmental concern. These leaders' values are being rigorously challenged. These are the issues that our psychosynthesis coaches are able to work with. Given the context of Self that they hold, they are ideally prepared to work with people committed to self-reliance and evolution, in many different situations.

The Coach's Toolkit—an Overview of Contemporary Models of Coaching

Introduction

There are many, many models of coaching. My intention here is to focus on a few that can provide coaches with a useful framework for their work within a clear psychosynthesis context.

Goal Setting

Goal setting, in itself, is probably the most fundamental tool used by coaches. The theory is based on creating specific achievable targets. Hence, most coaches will quickly work with clients to identify what they wish to achieve based on SMART principles, where S.M.A.R.T. stands for Specific and detailed, Measurable, Achievable, Realistic aiming high, but within the realms of possibility and Time Framed, with target dates.

GROW Model

The GROW Model is one of the best known and widely used coaching models. It provides a simple and powerful framework for navigating each coaching session. Described by Whitmore (1996) GROW is an acronym for Goal, current Reality, Options and Will, which are seen as the four key elements of a coaching session. So, a session must firstly have a goal, target or outcome to be achieved. The goal should be as specific as possible and it must be possible to measure whether it has been achieved, or not. Questions like 'How will you know that you have achieved that goal?' are useful here.

As well as knowing the goal, the starting point is important, hence the current Reality. Often this is the key part of a coaching session. Exploration of the current reality with careful open questions may open up a deeper awareness in the client about what is truly going on. The 'W' is often taken to stand for a number of other elements of a session. Downey (2003) suggests it stands for 'Wrap-up', while others have it standing for "What, Where, Why, When and How". I believe at this stage there needs to be motivation to reach the goal and from a psychosynthesis framework the 'W' is best seen as Will, which in this context means assessing the readiness of the client to reach a goal. GROW is presented sequentially, but in practice, it is much less linear, starting anywhere and revisiting each of the stages several times. GROW is easily understood, straightforward to apply and when used, very thorough.

CLEAR Model

The CLEAR Model (Hawkins, 1980) provides a different perspective on what to focus on in a coaching session. CLEAR is an acronym for: Contracting, which involves opening the discussion, setting the scope, establishing the desired outcomes, and agreeing on the ground rules; Listening, in which active listening and catalytic interventions by the coach helps the client develop their understanding of the situation and generate personal insight; Exploring, which is both helping the client to understand the personal impact the situation is having on them and challenging the client to think through possibilities for future action in resolving the situation; Action, which is supporting the client in choosing a way ahead and deciding the next step; and lastly Reviewing, which involves closing the intervention, reinforcing ground covered, decisions made and value added. The coach also encourages feedback from the client on what was helpful about the coaching process, what was difficult and what they would like to be different in future coaching sessions.

CLEAR makes explicit the importance of not just having a goal (as in GROW model) but also of the wider contracting issues, encouraging questions like 'How would you like me to coach you today?', 'What helps you learn?' and 'What blocks your learning?' It also emphasizes the importance of reviewing the session. This is a powerful tool since in GROW, the wrap-up (W) suggests that the session is finished and is complete. By introducing a review at the end of each session and the start of the next, sessions start to become linked and a stronger picture emerges for the client to work with.

Life Coaching

Much life coaching theory (Harrold, 2001) expects clients to set a very clear linear direction in relation to envisioned set of goals. The writer's experience is that this may not be always appropriate. 'A to Z' life coaching may be possible with some clients, but it could follow different forms. Given the Trifocal model that we (at the Psychosynthesis Institute in London) use as the context for psychosynthesis coaching, it provides our coaches with a natural starting point for clients who want to consider the next and emerging steps for their lives and want to use a coach to help them do so. Within this context we consider the wheel of life a useful model where the client is asked to map out on the diagram the areas of their life in which they may seek change or improvement. Typically, this is used in life coaching, but can be used in executive coaching, especially where issues of work-life balance emerge.

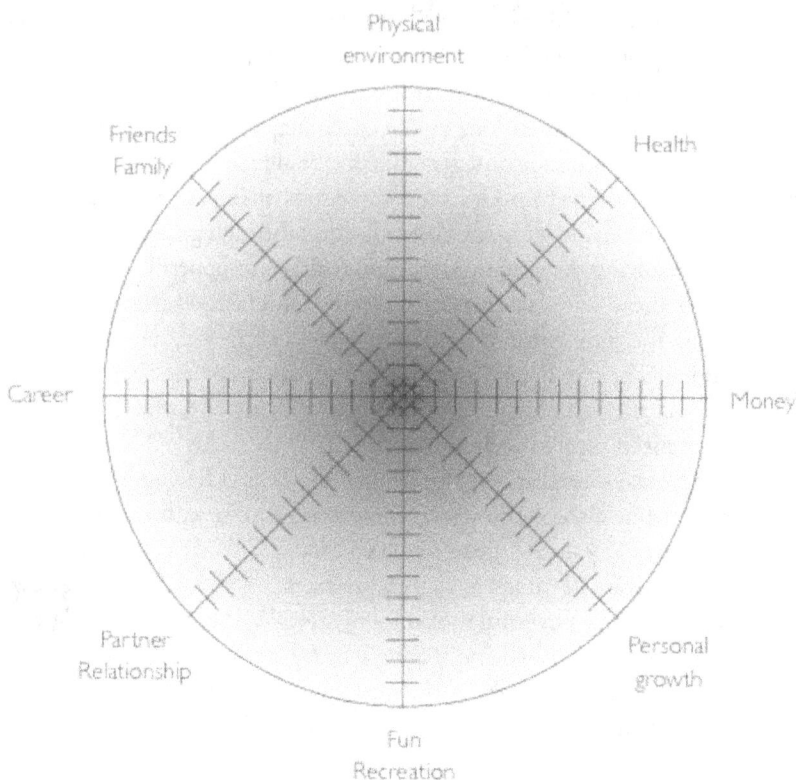

Physical environment · Health · Money · Personal growth · Fun Recreation · Partner Relationship · Career · Friends Family

A Psychosynthesis Context for Coaching – a Powerful Way of Evoking and Working with the Will in a Focused Series of Small Steps

Tri-focal Vision

The theory and practice of psychosynthesis coaching rests upon the idea that Self is always seeking to express itself; speaking through the client's symptoms—the difficulties and suffering experienced in the personality, which bring them to coaching—is the urge to wholeness, to expression and realization of Self.

Assagioli (1965) emphasized the existence of two realms of energy impacting upon the experience of the individual: the unconscious drives and conflicts that bring about symptoms, and the pull of the Self. Firman and Vargiu (1977) describe two dimensions of human growth, the personal and transpersonal.

If our work as coaches is only to relieve and 'fix' symptoms and achieve personal goals, that is to say, to work only with the personal and the neurotic to the exclusion of the spiritual (the transpersonal and existential) then we deny the Self and repress the urge to wholeness. Not only do we miss the soul of the client, but, also, we waste the potential resource of the Self which is available as the source of creativity. The personality is only a vehicle. The symptoms exist because the Self's intention is frustrated. They tell us something about this intention. In this sense, symptoms are messages to be understood rather than problems to be solved.

Critically, psychosynthesis coaching works with clients who can best be described as 'healthy neurotics'. That is to say clients who have sufficient ego strength, have a sense of their own identity and are looking to actualize and express more of themselves in their lives. They may not be doing that and instead struggling with the existential frustration and confusion that being stuck brings. Implicit in these clients is that there is a sense of 'I' and some level of will available to them as they have previously demonstrated in living their lives.

Basic Coaching Frame

In order to work in depth within a Trifocal context and given the basic pre-condition of 'healthy neurotic client'—determined at the initial coaching interview—the psychosynthesis coach uses a simple and basic framework to work within. In a six-session model, for example, the sessions can be used as a series of six sessions over a shorter or longer period, as appropriate. Let's consider how this framework of six sessions works. At the initial interview, maybe session one or before session one, the client and coach determine as best they can, and as realistically as they can, where the client wants to get to by session six. We could call this the client's goal for the six sessions. This is a crucial step because it provides the backdrop for the work in each subsequent session. Once this goal is agreed, the coach then helps the client think through and determine a mini-goal, a next step, in relation to the six-session goal. In this way, the client has a very focused container to do a specific piece of work and within which time they are able both to assess their readiness/willingness to achieve their desired outcomes but also, importantly, are able to build self-belief in achieving a number of small steps.

The importance of this frame cannot be stressed enough, because within it lies the possibility of small scale transformation and of both coach and client developing an understanding of what it is going to take, time and energy-wise to build or transform where the client is, into where the client wants to be.

Significantly, from a psychosynthesis point of view, this process enables the coach to use a very direct and focused way to work with the available will of the client. And in doing so it provides the client not only the wherewithal to conduct an act of will but also to disidentify and free the will at the appropriate level. We will unpack this process more fully as we explore in the following paragraphs. Before we do so, let us look at the two dimensions that Assagioli (1965) uses to hold the Self and the personality.

Two central and interrelated themes of psychosynthesis are personal psychosynthesis, which addresses a healthy, integrated personality and spiritual psychosynthesis, which addresses the soul level of existence and acknowledges Self. Hence, unlike many other contexts, psychosynthesis addresses the very core of Being, as well as holding the presenting physical, emotional, or mental issues. What then are the key components to establishing a Psychosynthetic Coaching Alliance? The first relates to the purpose of the alliance itself. Assagioli beautifully describes the purpose, which is: "To release, or let us say to help release, the energies of the Self. Prior to this the purpose is to help integrate, to synthesize, the individual around the personal self and then later to effect the synthesis between the personal ego and the Self" (1965 p. 65).

Hence as a coach, we are simultaneously looking to hold the presenting issues in the immanent here and now, as well as holding the emergent call of the Self. In doing so, the immediate conflict and suffering and presenting symptoms can be seen as the call to Purpose, Meaning and Value through the 'eyes' of the coach.

Trifocal Vision: Psychosynthesis Coaching Context—Managing The Gap

Working with Trifocal Vision

Let us now look at the Trifocal Vision, how to use it and how to work with the client to assess their readiness, their available Will, in each session to reach their stated goal or outcome. This is the underlying context for all psychosynthesis coaching work we do that involves others, whether as individuals, groups or the whole system.

When the psychosynthesis coach holds and uses Trifocal Vision, they are looking to 'see' the Being/the Self that is the client—'who this person is most essentially at this time'. So, for the coach there is both this Self in potential, and at the same time there is also the client's personal life and issues, (that is the sum total of how this person has learned to function in the world till now). When the coach holds both, they also experience the gap between these two dimensions and the pain of that 'gap'. How coaches manage the process of dealing with (or 'bridging') this gap is the substance of psychosynthesis coaching. When the client first comes for coaching this 'gap' is often too large and trying to resolve it may be experienced by the client as, too hard, too difficult or painful.

The skill and work of the psychosynthesis coach is thus to help the client not only understand the gap but also to assess what is a realistic next step along the road to the goal for the sessions, thus reducing the gap and helping the client and the coach get a sense of where the Self is most available at this point in time. To the best they can, the coach then asks the client how ready they are to make that small next step they have articulated. We often say to them; "On a scale from 0-5 where 5 is totally ready, how ready are you?" and ask them to score themselves. In the energy and the score they give themselves, the experienced coach can get a very clear sense of the available will. If you get an unrealistic reading you challenge it—both ends of the scale—and go on to explore why. If it seems realistic, then set with the client the time frame to see that it happens, hopefully before the next session. In that sense working within the realistic gap is about helping the client access their will and build and strengthen their ability to will—like building links in the chain. These steps need to be big enough to be challenging and small enough to be achievable. So, we see step 1, step 2, and so on, each step becoming a context for the next level of work.

If this trifocal context is held and worked with in this way, then you are working directly with where the client is most available and with their will. In doing so the client begins to see the effect of building towards the goal and increasing their self-belief. The thrust of the work, over time, is to help the client develop inner skills of personal mastery and thereby learn to manage the gap and, in that sense, their will and express as much of their Selves as is available.

In the preceding paragraphs, we have spoken of individuals, but the same concepts of trifocal vision and bridging the gap underlie group and whole systems as well as individual coaching work. This is because these wider spheres of influence involve individuals and the same principles apply.

The Critical Role of Coach Development through Supervision & Spiritual Practice

Many coaches fail to have appropriate supervision for their work, and/or fail to follow a regular spiritual praxis. With psychosynthesis coaches, I believe this is potentially limiting for a number of reasons.

Firstly, working with the energies of the will and in the context of Self needs containment and mirroring plus a deep understanding of the personal and interpersonal psychological dynamics at play. I believe it is therefore important that all psychosynthesis coaches working in this area have another qualified person to talk to, who can formally provide a mirror to the relationships between coach and client. In this way, the coach can keep their practice psychically as 'clean' as possible, become aware of the issues surrounding transference and countertransference and have a second opinion on how to best help clients. Without such containment, it is possible that the coach may either become 'burned out' or become unclear about the boundaries with their clients. In short, coaches need supervision to become disidentified from their coaching alliances with clients. Another vital dimension of the need for pragmatic supervision has to do with the different boundary conditions encountered by coaches working with different forms of coaching.

In addition, for psychosynthesis coaches working with deep existential and psychospiritual issues around spiritual emergence and emergency it is essential, I believe, that they are rooted within a spiritual tradition and practice. Without being prescriptive, I think it is important that the Self of the coach is held, nourished and supported in this way, by the coach, as an act of will and a commitment to their own purpose, meaning and values.

Conclusion

This chapter considers the relevance of psychosynthesis coaching within a fast moving and burgeoning coaching market. I have considered a few contemporary coaching models that can be used effectively within a psychosynthesis context for coaching—Trifocal Vision. In doing so, the centrality of evoking and working with the will within the focused coaching framework is illuminated.

This paper has been adapted from the *Evans & Elliott in Essays on the Theory and Practice of a Psychospiritual Psychology*, page 190, Volume 1, 2013

References

Assagioli, R. (1965). *Psychosynthesis: A manual of principles and techniques.* London: Turnstone Books.

Downey, M. (2003). *Effective coaching: Lessons from the coaches' coach.* London: Texere Publishing.

Firman, J. & Vargiu, J. (1977). Dimensions of Growth. *Synthesis Journal.*

Gallwey, T. (1975). *The inner game of tennis.* New York: Vintage.

Harrold, F. (2000). *Be your own life coach.* London: Coronet Books.

Hawkins, P. (1980). Coaching supervision. *OCM Coach and Mentor Journal.* UK: OCM Group Limited.

Whitmore, J. (1996). *Coaching for performance.* UK: Nicholas Brearley.

Zohar, D. & Marshall, I. (2000). *Spiritual Intelligence: The ultimate intelligence.* London: Bloomsbury Publishing.

Chapter 3

Empowerment of the Will through Life Coaching

by Martha Crampton

Editor's Note: More than twenty years ago, Dr. Martha Crampton, a student of Roberto Assagioli, and a key trainer of psychosynthesis in North America, began her exploration of the field of life and business coaching and its relationship to psychosynthesis. Martha had been teaching and writing extensively about psychosynthesis since the 1960's, shortly after psychosynthesis came to the United States. This article, written in 2000, represents our earliest psychosynthesis orientation to the field of coaching. To my knowledge, she is the first psychosynthesis practitioner, in the U.S, to write about this new field. Martha was my primary psychosynthesis teacher and a valued mentor. She died in 2009. It is with great appreciation that I share this piece, which also moved my work towards this powerful integration of psychosynthesis and coaching.

Introduction

The emerging profession of personal and business coaching is an exciting new arena in which to study the will and to cultivate this vital function in the life of humanity. The will has an even more central and explicit role in coaching than it does in psychotherapy. The rich understanding of the will that psychosynthesis offers can, I believe, make an important contribution to the field. In this paper, I will introduce the coaching paradigm and discuss some ways in which the will is used in coaching.

The field of coaching came into its own in the final years of the 1990's (Ellis, 1998; Fortgang, 1998; Whitworth, Kinsey-House, & Sandahl, 1998).

Enthusiasts believe that having a personal coach will soon be viewed as a necessity by anyone who aspires to a life of success and fulfillment. At the present time, it is estimated that there are about 3,000 trained coaches with 100,000 clients. The numbers are growing by leaps and bounds. At the time of this writing, one of the popular books in the field, *Take Time for your Life*, by Cheryl Richardson (1999) just made the New York Times Best Seller List; and Fortune (February 1, 2000) recently featured an article on executive coaches which stated that the "hottest thing in management" is the executive coach.

Coaching has roots in disciplines such as counseling, consulting, and organizational development. In the last few years it has begun to articulate itself as a discipline in its own right with professional organizations and standards of practice.

Personal coaches often liken their work to that of a sports coach. Just as an Olympic coach prepares athletes to reach for the gold medal, so a personal coach partners with clients to bring out their best in their personal and business lives. The International Coach Federation defines coaching as an ongoing relationship which focuses on clients taking action toward the realization of their visions, goals, or desires. The definition goes on to state, "Coaching uses a process of inquiry and personal discovery to build the client's level of awareness and responsibility and provides the client with structure, support, and feedback. The coaching process helps clients both define and achieve professional and personal goals faster and with more ease than would be possible otherwise." (ICF brochure, n.d)

There are various specialty areas within the field such as executive coaches; career coaches; relationship coaches; coaches for children, entrepreneurs, and almost any conceivable market niche. Coaching that addresses all areas of a person's life is usually called "personal coaching" or "life coaching."

Coaches work in a variety of formats. Most commonly, coaching takes place by telephone for weekly sessions of 30 minutes. Between sessions, clients take action steps toward goals they define with the assistance of their coach. Progress is reported at the following session. Communication may occur between sessions by e-mail, fax, or brief telephone calls. Tele-classes in which clients call in to a common bridge number are frequently used for group coaching. Our virtual-age technologies now enable us to work very effectively at a distance. I find it exciting to be able to work with people from around the world from my home office, free from the constraints of geography.

A Dream About Coaching

Recently I woke up in the night from a dream that movingly portrays my vision of coaching. In the dream, a woman was walking along a road, an archetypal life path. I was struck by the unusual quality of her energy. She had an amazing clarity of purpose and her intent was unwavering, as though she was carrying out a sacred mission. I felt that nothing could deter her from her purpose, yet she was not driven in an ego-based way. Her energy was peaceful and balanced. She walked with ease, grace, and quiet confidence, in what could be described as a "flow state." She appeared to receive strength and be moved along her path by an energy that came from beyond herself, as though from a higher power. I was inspired by her presence and remarked to my companion in the dream, "This woman must have a coach."

As I reflect on this dream, several points strike me as significant from a coaching perspective:

- The person is connected to her life purpose or spiritual mission.
- She is able to stay on track with this and not get sidetracked.
- She is so aligned with higher will that this power moves through her without resistance, propelling her forward in a seemingly effortless way.

The sections that follow will discuss how coaching addresses these various aspects of the will.

Coaching and the Higher Will: The Spiritual Connection

As a spiritually-based coach, my aim is to help people connect with their higher Self and live a soul-infused life. Though I hold this ideal as a psychotherapist, I find it to be a more explicit focus in coaching. Since coaching clients tend to be more self-actualizing than the average psychotherapy client, they tend to focus on the life they want to create rather than on fixing what's wrong. This naturally leads to an exploration of their higher purpose.

Establishing the Essence Connection

I deeply believe that the most important way I can support clients in building their spiritual connection is to connect with their essence myself. This bond is an energetic one. It is a silent appreciation and affirmation of who that person is as a being. It invites their essence to come forth and take its place in the world.

Most of us suffer from the primal childhood wound of not having been recognized as a sovereign and unique spiritual being. Instead, we have been manipulated by conditional love to fit in with someone else's idea of who we should be. The coach's unconditionality and honoring attitude helps to heal this wound. One of the best-known life coaches looks at a picture of each of his clients several times a day to help him maintain this kind of connection. When a person feels held in this way, they feel safe to come out of hiding and express the will of their true Self in the world.

Holding Sacred Space

The second most important thing we can do is to "hold sacred space" for the client. This too is something that happens at an energetic level. It is based on affirming and trusting the client's process. It involves intentionality toward the ability of the client to connect with their wisdom nature and to find the answers they need from within. It involves deep and respectful listening to what is trying to happen in the client's life. This attitude of invocation calls forth the client's deepest truth and inner resources.

Enabling Processes to Clarify Vision, Core Values, and Life Purpose

Coaches often suggest exercises to clients to help clarify their vision, core values, and life purpose. When people make choices based on their core values, their passion and genius are released. Typically, I use a values exercise in which the client lists peak experiences which have given them a sense of deep fulfillment. The person then explores the personal qualities, skills, and values operative in these experiences. Common threads are found and a list of five or six core values is made based on these common threads.

"The Future Self" guided imagery exercise is also widely used in coaching (Whitworth et al, 1998). It takes the client on a journey into the future in which they meet a fulfilled version of themselves. The Future Self shares with the present-day self how he or she got from where the client is today to that future state. In a related exercise, the client imagines the Future Self on a stage in front of an audience. The Future Self speaks to the audience in a way that is profoundly moving and changes people's lives. Exercises of this kind can provide useful clues to the client's core values, essence qualities, and spiritual mission.

Coaches also use more conscious processes to explore their clients' visions for their lives. This could include asking questions such as:

- What do you want your life to look like five (10, 20) years from now?
- What contribution do you want to make to the world?
- What do you want your legacy to be?
- How do you want to be remembered?

Providing Intuition and Spiritual Practice Training

Some coaches teach clients skills to develop their intuition and strengthen their spiritual connection. It is common to suggest a meditation or relaxation practice. One spiritually-oriented coach has clients identify the "clair" skill that works best for them, be it clairaudience. clairvoyance, clairsentience, or claircognizing. The coach then supports the person in paying attention to this channel. Intuition can be accessed in many other ways, as well, allowing the client a clear path to inner knowing.

I may ask clients to get an image or a felt sense in their body when they focus on a particular issue. The classic psychosynthesis technique of having the client confer with a wisdom figure or inner advisor also lends itself well to coaching. Depth techniques of this kind bring fresh perspectives from beyond the surface mind. These depth approaches enable the client to access their internal guidance system and often inspire highly creative ideas. Dream work is also quite powerful in the coaching context.

At times, I use my own intuitive skills to assess what is going on with a client. I have been trained in a process of energy diagnosis (Stillpoint.org) which provides a useful "x-ray" of the psyche based on the chakra system. This helps me to understand where the will of the higher Self is being directed, as well as issues the person may be facing with their personal will. Ways of helping a client to find inner guidance are countless.

I find that centering awareness in the heart is one of the most rapid and effective ways to access the wisdom nature. A simple technique that lends itself well to coaching invites the person to place a hand over their heart while focusing on an issue and sensing the heart's message about this issue. This is easy to do while talking on the telephone, in group process or in person. In an instant, this simple technique can shift a person from being identified with a negative mindset to an expanded state in which they experience clarity, compassion, and release of healthy will functions.

An example of the "hand on heart" technique in telephone coaching took place in a session I conducted this week. My client, who serves on the Board of a community group, was about to resign over a disagreement she had with the group director. Though reluctant to give up her membership on the Board, which she valued, she felt unable to resolve the conflict. She feared losing control of her rage if she had to interact with this person. When she placed her hand on her heart, she experienced an immediate shift in perspective. This enabled her to see that she herself had a part in creating the conflict so she could choose to forgive the other person. She made a plan to work on this during the week and agreed to meet with this person as soon as she felt ready to approach the meeting in a healing spirit. Through connecting with the wisdom of her heart, she was able to step back from the victim stance and align her will with resolving the conflict.

Another effective method for focusing awareness in the heart is the "freeze-frame" technique (Childre & Martin, 1991), developed by the Heartmath Institute. In this approach, the heart is activated by breathing into it (imaging sending your breath to your heart) and evoking memories of open-hearted experiences in the past.

Connecting with the Higher Will

There are many methods to help clients connect with their higher will. It seems important that the coach have a personal connection with the method being used so he or she can hold the thought-form with greater clarity of intention. It is also important, of course, that the method be suited to the client's own temperament and preference.

One method I find particularly useful is providing feedback about the client's energy when talking about a topic. When people are connected to their higher purpose, I experience a sense of excitement, a kind of electric charge. When they are doing something because they think they "should" do it, there is a heavy energy with no life. Reflecting this back to the person can increase their awareness of what they really want. In this way, the conversation and reflection support the will of the client's true Self.

Related approaches that have become quite popular among life coaches are "attraction coaching" and "radical self-care". The aim of attraction coaching is to help people shift from struggling to get what they want to opening up to possibilities. There are two basic rules:

+ eliminate what drains your energy, and
+ add what gives you energy.

The premise is that by eliminating "energy-drainers" (e.g, clutter, un-finished business, a missing button on your coat, or neglected finances), you become more open and willing to create space in your life for good things to come in. The traditional psychosynthesis view, seen in the last stage of the act of will, "manifestation," elaborates this process of orienting towards purpose and "clearing" the way for opening to creating next, meaningful steps (Assagioli, 1973/1999).

The "radical self-care" idea is attributed to Shirley Anderson, former coach to Cheryl Richardson (1999). Coaches working in the self-care mode can be very helpful to people on the burnout track. They encourage clients to lead balanced lives, establish healthy boundaries, and do what nurtures them. The assumption is that overwork and stress diminish our creativity and effectiveness. Through radical self-care, well-being and health improvement, relationships flourish, and clients actually become more, not less, productive.

The self-care and attraction approaches are based on treating oneself as a person whose life has value for its own sake, rather than as an expendable machine. Perhaps these ideas are arising to counter the self-abuse so prevalent in our workaholic culture. In any case, they open up a fresh perspective on the will. They suggest that there may be a gentler and easier way to get things done than by laborious striving. Could it be that uncluttering our lives, eliminating self-sabotage, and honoring our true needs creates sacred space in which the will of the Self can more easily manifest? Can deeply valuing ourselves raise our vibration to a point where the power of our intention is vastly amplified? The coaching field may be fertile ground for researching the principles of "manifestation".

Coaching and the Personal Will: Setting Goals, Priorities, and Boundaries

Coaches differ in their emphasis on personal and transpersonal will. Spiritually-based coaches tend to begin by exploring the client's values and higher purpose. This provides the context for establishing specific goals. When a person's goals express core values, passion and creativity are released. Personal will becomes aligned with carrying out the will of the higher Self.

Establishing an Agreement

A "coaching agreement" is usually drawn up which establishes the client's desired areas of focus. Some people have a specific concern such as finding a new job or dealing with a particular crisis. Others want to consider all areas of their lives, including such things as health, relationships, finances, and their environment. Having explored their core values, clients work with their coach to develop goals that express these values in the various areas of their lives. It is crucial that the goals be those of the client and that the coach avoid a parental or nagging role.

The coach assists the person to envision possibilities, expand options, establish time lines and priorities, and commit to realistic goals within a specific time frame. Each coaching session reviews the client's progress with goals established in prior sessions and new goals are created for the following week. Clients may recommit to existing goals or revise plans made at an earlier date. In the parlance of coaching, "requests" are made by the coach (often developed collaboratively with the client) for specific action steps to forward the client's goals between sessions. The client is free to accept, renegotiate, or decline a request.

Reflection on One's Goal-Setting Process

I often explore with clients how they make choices and set goals in their lives. We do this when they set goals for the period ahead and when they report on what they accomplished between sessions. It is helpful to look at what part of a person is drawn to particular choices. There is frequently a subpersonality or complex involved like the pleaser, the rebel, the driven person, the martyr, or the one who feels inadequate. Belief systems such as "I can't have what I really want" or "It's selfish to focus on my own needs" may come into play. Clients are often tempted to set goals they believe they "should" accomplish rather than goals with intrinsic value. One of the most useful interventions a coach can make is to let clients know when "should" energy is present and, on the contrary, when they light up with authentic joy and passion.

Other will problems that frequently show up are tendencies to over-commit, to give up, to lack boundaries, or to set one's sights too high or too low. Subpersonality integration may help to align a client's will behind their goals.

Inquiry About Actions Taken or Not Taken

When a client fails to accomplish goals they have chosen, a wonderful opportunity for learning is present. Coaches need to protect clients from their inner critic (both the coach's and their own) at such times, cultivating an attitude of neutral observation. It is important that they model an accepting attitude, with unconditional regard and belief in the client.

I find the following questions helpful in guiding the client's reflection:

External Action Taken
* What steps did you take and what were the results?
* If you did not accomplish certain goals you intended to, what do you know about this?

Internal Experience
* What was your experience of doing this?
* Did you feel confidence, anxiety, joy, guilt, resistance, etc.?
* What beliefs generated these feelings?
* Were all parts of you aligned behind your goals?

Processing the Experience
* How have you been processing what happened?
* Can you witness it from a neutral place without self-judgment?

+   What did you learn about yourself?
+   What do you conclude from this experience?

Processing from a Higher Self or Wisdom Perspective
(Using a centering process, such as meditative, heart-centered, or imagery techniques, view the situation from an expanded perspective.)
+   What learnings or new options does this reveal?

Next steps
+   Based on the above, what next steps would you like to plan?

If the process is handled with sensitivity, it can be just as valuable to reflect on goals not achieved as to actually accomplish the goals. For example, a client who is an aspiring actress had set a goal of going to three auditions. She noticed that she resisted doing this and in fact had not done so when she came to the next coaching session. In discussing this, she became aware that she envied her friends who had agents and didn't have to waste time on auditions. She realized that she really wanted an agent herself and could probably get one. She made the important shift from compliant behavior to empowerment by clarifying what she wanted and setting her intention to achieve it. The following week she focused her will on taking steps toward finding an agent.

Setting Boundaries
Most people have difficulty in setting healthy boundaries. Even prominent coaches say, that without their own coach, they lose their way. They become side-tracked, over-committed, and over-stressed, making self-sabotaging decisions that undermine their true interests.

In our culture, it is rare indeed that a person's real Self has been acknowledged and supported. Instead, there is pressure to conform to other peoples' perceptions and agendas. Listening to one's own needs is not a highly encouraged skill. To the contrary, children all too frequently get the message that it is selfish to think about their own needs and presumptuous to want too much happiness or success for themselves. Not surprisingly then, as adults, we often feel on shaky ground when it comes to making decisions on our own behalf. When we lack a foundation of unconditional love in our lives, we seek to validate ourselves by pleasing, impressing, or taking care of others. A coach provides needed permission and support for people to dream big dreams and to follow through on them.

I had an interesting experience recently in helping a client set boundaries. She had been offered a job as executive director of a human service organization where she had worked as a volunteer teacher. Though she disliked administrative work, she felt she should take the job. She wanted to please the other staff members and liked the validation of a salary. I helped her listen to her real feelings about this and encouraged her to stand by what she really wanted. To her surprise, she was able to negotiate the job of her dreams, doing what she loved without having to handle the administrative tasks. Through taking this stand to be true to herself, she was able to access deeper resources within her being. She entered a period of intense communion with her higher Self in which she felt that her steps were divinely guided. Shortly thereafter, she received what she believes is her life mission. This has unleashed an incredible passion in her that is inspiring to behold. The moral: when we set boundaries that honor our true nature, we create space for the higher Self to enter our lives.

Use of Therapeutic Techniques to Free the Will in Coaching

When clients reach an impasse in using their will, the coach needs to decide to what extent he or she is comfortable addressing "therapeutic" issues in a coaching context. Opinion differs within the coaching field about whether a coach should attempt to deal with deep emotional issues. Some prefer to avoid this area altogether. Others freely draw on a therapeutic background to help clients resolve issues that get in the way of creating desired results. Still others work easily in deep spaces, due to their own coach training. There is, none-the-less, a fine line to be maintained between doing therapy and doing coaching while using therapy-like techniques. In contrast to psychotherapy clients, who seek to alleviate pain or dysfunction, coaching clients want to go beyond the ordinary, to fulfill their highest potentials. A coach must not lose sight of this context in dealing with emotional issues.

I find that certain tools from my therapist's tool kit lend themselves well to the coaching work, while others do not. In the last few years, new methods that vastly accelerate the processing and release of unhealthy patterns have entered the field of psychotherapy. Referred to as the "power therapies" or "energy psychotherapies," they produce remarkable breakthroughs in freeing the will. Within the past year, the Association for Comprehensive Energy Therapies (www.energypsych.org) was formed, providing an umbrella for practitioners interested in these and related methods.

The best known of the energy therapy methods is EMDR (Eye Movement Desensitization and Reprocessing). This method, widely used in trauma treatment, has the client focus on a disturbing thought, feeling, or incident, while receiving bilateral stimulation through eye movements or binaural sound. I often use this highly effective process when working with a client face to face, though it is not recommended for telephone work.

Some of the energy techniques are more appropriate for telephone coaching. These methods have the client gently press or tap certain points on the acupuncture meridians while focusing on the undesired thought, pattern, or emotional state. Typically, and often within a few minutes, the emotional charge on the issue dissipates, the client gains insight into the problem, and is able to disidentify from the beliefs which underlie it. This process combines intention with balancing the energy system to achieve results so rapidly it sometimes appears miraculous.

The meridian-based therapies I prefer are the Emotional Freedom Technique (EFT) and Tapas Acupressure Technique (TAT) because of their simplicity and ease of use. I recently used EFT in a coaching session with a man whose work involved public speaking. This individual suffered so deeply from feelings of inadequacy when making presentations that he almost quit his job. In a five-minute round of the EFT process, he saw how he created his own anxiety. He perceived how his imagination turned others into judges so that he then felt he must bend himself out of shape to accommodate them. He realized that he could view the other people, not as judges, but as team members, helping one another to solve the problem. He said, "I've chosen to put myself in a maze, but nothing stops me from walking out of it." By the end of our telephone call, his will was committed to success in that firm. He immediately felt confident in making his presentations and within the week was offered a promotion.

Summary

The emerging profession of life coaching seems destined to play a significant role in the future, providing support for relatively healthy people to realize their full potentials. It is a discipline which assigns a central role to the will, drawing on both personal and spiritual levels of this core psychological function. In contrast to psychotherapy, coaching assumes that clients have sufficient emotional integration to function in self-responsibility, at least as an ideal, and that they can use their will with some degree of effectiveness. This would imply basic levels of good, strong and skillful will, in psychosynthesis terminology. In this context, Assagioli's (1999) profound insights into the nature and functioning of the will, so far ahead of their time, will likely find a receptive audience.

References

Assagioli. R. (1999). *The act of will.*, England: David Platts Publishing Company.

Childre. D.L. & Martin. H. (1999). *The Heartmath Solution.* San Francisco, CA: Harper.

Ellis. D. (1998). *Life coaching: A new career for helping professionals.* Rapid City, SD: Breakthrough Enterprises.

Fortgang, L. (1998). *Take yourself to the top.* New York: Warner Books.

Morris, Betsy. (2000, February 21). Executive coaches. *Fortune.* 144ff.

Richardson, Cheryl. (1999). *Take time for your life.* New York: Putnam.

Whitworth, L., Kinsey-House, H., & Sandahl, P. (1998). *Co-active coaching.* Palo Alto: Davies Black Publishing.

Chapter 4

Therapy and Coaching: Challenging the Orthodoxy

by Aubyn Howard

Introduction

When running courses on coaching, we (at the Institute of Psychosynthesis, London) frequently are asked questions about the relationship, boundaries, and differences between therapy or counseling and coaching. This topic is fraught with difficulty and complexity and is prone to trite or superficial treatment, so this chapter, developed from an article posted on *LinkedIn* (Howard, 2018), is intended to shed some light on it and set it within the larger context of shifting sands within the therapy and coaching worlds.

If you Google "what is the difference between therapy or counseling and coaching?" or something similar, you will find plenty of mostly superficial answers to the question that seek to delineate territory in ways that end up limiting the scope of both counseling and coaching to fit the author's agenda (disclaimer—I too have an agenda for this piece! See later).

Michael Bader, in a *Psychology Today* Blog (2009), identifies this problem pretty well from stories he often hears from coaches. For example, they work with the future and therapists with the past, coaches work to make healthy clients better, therapists work with pathology and problems, etcetera. He suggests, "that this is a mythic narrative that aims to insulate coaching—a profession in its infancy—from claims that it's therapy without a license. It seeks to protect the egos and wallets of coaches while appeasing therapists on the same grounds". He goes on to lay some of the blame for this at the door of the therapy profession for practicing "a model of psychotherapy that is so ridiculously narrow and theory-driven".

A good example of this 'dodgy' narrative can be found on Tony Robbins' website (n.d.)—*life coach vs therapist, learn the difference*, in which, although he acknowledges overlaps, he then proceeds to define coaching in very narrow terms of client agendas (for example, working to improve communication skills or work-life balance) that fit his target market of "ambitious achievers" (see Laloux's [2014] *Achievement paradigm*).

Even worse offenders (whom I won't name) of this dodgy narrative make sweeping distinctions (in addition to the common **future** and **past** delineation), along the lines that coaching deals with the conscious mind, rational behaviors, measurable goals, involves positive thinking and focusing on solutions (that is, all the good stuff), whereas therapy or counseling works with the unconscious mind, with emotions, subjective goals, pathologies and problems (that is, all the murky stuff). This narrative is usually espoused by coaching schools that offer a very prescriptive method for young or inexperienced coaches on the basis that if they follow the method this will keep them (and their client) safe from straying off the path and into deep waters. The problem with this very delineated approach (this belongs to coaching, that belongs to counseling) is that people (that is, all clients) are whole human beings who bring the good stuff as well as the murky stuff with them, their light and their dark, their conscious goals and their unconscious drives, whether to coaching or counseling. There is another fundamental problem with any attempt to separate rational and emotional domains—all the recent neuropsychological research (such as Daniel Kahneman's [2012] *Thinking Fast and Thinking Slow*) points towards a much greater role of the unconscious and our emotions in all our behavior and decision making than previously acknowledged by the modern western worldview. Particularly in business and organizational life, where the rational and individual agency has been elevated at the expense of the emotional and the human system, a new awareness is beginning to be established.

Some better approaches (from my google search) tackle the distinction by working through themes such as: the objectives, agendas, or focus (of the activity); education, training, and qualification (required of practitioners); ethics and governance (of the profession); approaches and methods (for example, psychologies) used. The most useful commentary I found along these lines is at South African College of Applied Psychology (2014) which describes the relationship between professional counselors and coaches as comparable to that of stepsiblings. The author goes on,

> The emphasis in a coaching relationship is on goals, action and accountability, although an experienced coach will know when to look at the past should it inform the present and help pinpoint limiting belief systems. So, while counseling is geared towards understanding and resolving the past for healing, coaching works with functional people and uses the past only insofar as it provides a context in which future goals can be set.

This goes some way to teasing out the subtleties needed, but is still part of a static approach and as such has limitations

A Dynamic Practitioner Framework – the Four C's

I suggest a more dynamic approach for differentiating counseling and coaching that will help us understand differences within coaching and counseling practice as well as between coaching and counseling and also help coaches and counselors alike to think critically about how they frame the work they do. Here is an orienting framework called the Four C's:

The dynamic Practitioner Framework

✦ **Context** – what is the context of the relationship? How has it come about? What is the wider systemic context? Are other parties involved?

✦ **Contract** – what formal or informal goals or outcomes are the focus of the work? How is the relationship structured and what agreements are made? What is the understanding between practitioner and client?

✦ **Client** – what needs, issues and agendas are they bringing? What is their ego strength and stability? What is their level and depth of personal development, self-awareness and self-responsibility?

✦ **Capability** – what is the coach's level of education and training, professional and personal development? What is their experience and level of confidence of working in different domains or dimensions or with different types of client?

This framework further breaks into two parts:

Part One: Context and Contract determine the nature of the professional relationship or the '*container*'—whether counseling or coaching—or what kind of coaching, for example, life coaching within an individual or personal context or leadership coaching within an organizational context, along with a more complex multi-party contract.

Context and contracting are all important in any practitioner relationship. We are not just saying that coaching and counseling will have different contexts, but that the practitioner needs to be aware and able to hold the context of the relationship and needs the skills to contract with the client (or client system) in a way that is congruent with the context. This does not mean that everything should be written down and formally agreed, but the practitioner and client relationship does need a level of clarity or problems may occur. Having established these principles, we can start to distinguish how the context and contract might differ between coaching and counseling. This is where we will generally characterize the coaching context as forward looking and outcome oriented in purpose, although this can involve working across temporal dimensions, past, present and future.

I like to hold Sir John Whitmore's (2017) principles of **awareness** and **responsibility** as part of my coaching context with clients. There is something of paradox here, in that the coach can take responsibility for holding the context while the client is responsible for their own process, actions and outcomes. One thing I stress as a possible difference with counseling is that the coach doesn't need to diagnose the client's issues, rather they are helping the client reach an understanding or diagnosis for themselves with a view to finding solutions or taking actions. As psychosynthesis coaches our focus is on Self (who is this being most essentially and what is emergent for them?) and finding available Will—what small steps or actions will take the client forwards and release more will? Something we notice with counselors making the transition to coaching is the tendency to over psychologize and want to fully diagnose the client's issues for themselves (and therefore spend too long in sessions working on their understanding rather than the client's self-understanding). This does not mean the coach should not be curious or formulate hypotheses, but they should hold these lightly and leave the primary responsibility for understanding with the client.

Contracting is a major topic in itself. Most coaching contracts involve regular monthly or bi-monthly meetings and work with repeatable contractual cycles (for example, six sessions or three months) but leadership coaching can also allow for ad-hoc meetings or calls in response to emergent situations or crises. Counseling contracts tend to involve more frequent meetings (for example, weekly), at the practitioner's premises and be open-ended in terms of duration. But again, there are no hard and fast rules, providing there is congruence across the four C's.

Part Two: Client and Capability define the scope and nature of the work that can potentially take place within the professional relationship, the 'contents'—as determined by the openness, development, and availability of the client as well as the nature of the needs and issues they bring, coupled with the professional capability and personal capacity of the coach. Different coaches can work at a greater or lesser level of depth, involving emotional, personal, and psychological ground, depending upon their training, skills, and experience.

The key boundary concerning the client that we hold in coaching, is that we only work with functioning people with sufficient ego strength. Another way of saying this is that we work with people who are able to function in the world (that is, get to work, hold down relationships, pay their bills). However, this does not mean that successful people do not have psychological problems or pathologies—increasingly our clients bring issues of anxiety, stress, addiction or depression alongside their personal development and stated agendas. This does not mean we should not work with them or we should pack them off to a therapist as soon as one of these issues emerges. Nor does it mean that we will work with them as a therapist would in the area of the past traumas and unresolved history. The coach can help clients become aware of how past trauma and mirrors of the past are influencing or impeding their objectives, and help them take responsibility for healing or resolving these. The key here is that the coach is helping the client find their own strategy and way forward to dealing with their past at the level of the prepersonal unconscious (or psychodymanic). Sometimes this can involve referral to a counselor or therapist for specific work alongside the coaching, sometimes working with the coach in a boundaried context (if the coach has the experience and training), as well as engagement with all manner of other personal development and therapeutic resources or solutions (for example, group work, somatic work, systemic work, healing, retreats, etcetera).

I draw from Julia Vaughan Smith's APECS paper (2015) to add insight into how the coach can work in relationship to past trauma:

> Coaches with understanding and experience of this field (trauma and personality splits) can bring something additional to the coaching work, a greater transitional space between the inner and outer worlds, which allows for deep transformation without working directly with the traumatised self or with the past. It needs a slightly different tool kit, perhaps, particularly for those clients who are clearly under the control of their survival strategies, if they wish to address some underlying issues within the boundaries of the coaching relationship and contract. (p. 10)

Mapping the Territory

So, how do we describe the nature and the scope of the work that takes place with a coach or counselor in an inclusive and expansive way, that then allows for specific emphasis to be made between counseling and coaching and between different approaches within these?

In psychosynthesis coaching, we make the distinction between the client's inner and outer worlds and agendas that they might bring to coaching. Alongside this, we can map the different temporal domains of past, present and future, with a further distinction between near and far future.

37

Below we map out the territory more explicitly using these distinctions:

Orientation and domain	Inner world and agenda/ Being	Outer world and agendas/ Doing
Past	Healing Trauma, reflection, understanding (prepersonal)	Resolution Sense making, acceptance. completion
Present	Inner crisis and change Self, personality, awareness (personal)	Outer crisis and change Systems, relationships solutions
Near future	Personal development Will, capacity, growth	Performance development Behaviors, skills, actions
Far future	Self-realization Purpose, meaning, values (transpersonal)	Self actualization Potential, career, leadership

In simple terms, we might expect conventional behavioral coaching to lean to the right-hand side/outer world and counseling/therapy to the left-hand side/inner world and focus more on the past than the future. As psychosynthesis coaches we seek to hold awareness of all these domains and are open and free to work across them as needed in response to the Four C's: the context we hold, the contract we establish, the client's needs and issues, and our capability and skills.

However, it is extremely important to add that our capability and effectiveness to work across these domains is predicated on drawing upon a core coaching psychology (or combination of psychologies) that is holistic, one that enables practitioners to work with both the inner and outer lives of their clients, navigating the past, present and future. This translates into prepersonal, personal, and transpersonal levels, which are embraced within psychosynthesis psychology.

Choices and Challenges

Let us remind ourselves why this topic (of distinctions between and within coaching and counseling) is important. It is key for the choices of both people seeking help from these professions, as well as those seeking to train and develop in these professions, i.e. for both potential coachees and coaches. With this in mind I want to challenge two conventional assumptions or orthodoxies:

1. 'That coaches need to train as therapists if they want to work at depth'—twenty years ago it was assumed that any organizational practitioner who was serious about working at the most meaningful and important levels with their clients would need to go down the arduous route of therapy training. Besides the time and cost commitment, the practitioner also then needs to deal with the baggage that comes with the therapeutic paradigm.

2. 'That leaders need to go into therapy if they want to heal and resolve their past'—rather we need more coaches that are equipped to help clients frame the healing and resolution of their past within wider context of ongoing personal and leadership development, and can support leaders to take responsibility for their own healing process, whichever resources they might draw upon.

Let me back this up this with a quote from my supervisor, Fiona Adamson, in response to a previous piece I wrote on a related theme:

"What is so fascinating is that some coaches are training to become therapists as they sense they need more theory and practice of working at depth. Until coaching courses can bring the methods and practices for coaches to work at depth then this will continue. So great that your course for coaches is already attending to this focus."(personal communication, nd)

Shifting Sands Between Coaching and Therapy

A recent Forbes article (Whittaker Dunlop, 2017) estimates coaching to be a two billion dollar global industry and growing (not that financial exchange is necessarily the best measure for assessing the growth of our profession). Meanwhile, in the mental health industry, the use of psychotherapy, at least relative to other solutions, is reported to be in decline. What about the middle ground, where many might choose from a spectrum of options to support themselves in their personal and professional development? Data is hard to find, but anecdotal evidence suggests that there seems to be a long-term shift taking place from therapy or counseling to coaching in both the life/personal as well as the leadership/organizational environment. Many people find coaching more acceptable, accessible and available than counseling or therapy.

My view is that the coaching profession needs to respond to this opportunity and find ways to develop and enable coaches to broaden their spectrum and deepen their reach. The Institute of Psychosynthesis in London, as well as other organizations world-wide are beginning to offer comprehensive training for coaches, often associated with master's level academic degrees, as a viable next step in creating fully prepared coaches.

Interestingly, there now seems to be a healthy organic exchange taking place between the coaching and therapy professions, as they find ways to learn from each other. Psychotherapy is looking to learn from coaching how to make itself more relevant and effective (see the Michael Bader [2009] post as an example). Over time, coaching and therapy appear to be moving towards each other at the same time as maintaining clear contextual distinctions. There are, of course, major differences in the professional qualification and regulatory environments that the two professions operate within. Although there are wide national variations, we can generalize; therapy might be seen as over rigorous and restrictive in placing daunting hurdles for potential practitioners to clear (I know some therapists who have taken seven years to become qualified), whereas the coaching profession is often criticized for being under regulated and inconsistent in terms of standards of practice.

In practice, the coaching profession has an advantage over psychotherapy because it is at greater liberty to respond to the emerging challenges and changing needs of clients. At the same time, we must seek ways to professionalize and increase confidence in the coaching profession, without limiting the depth and breadth of the work through ill-conceived boundary drawing, as discussed in this chapter. I hope the dynamic practitioner framework I have outlined here might contribute to the professionalization challenge, as well as helping psychosynthesis coaches to reflect seriously and deeply upon our practice.

References

Bader, M. (2009, April 15). The difference between coaching and therapy is greatly overstated. *Psychology Today*. Available at www.psychologytoday.com/us/blog/what-is-he-thinking/200904/ the-difference-between-coaching-and-therapy-is-greatly-overstated.

Howard, A. (2018, January 10). Therapy and coaching — challenging the orthodoxy. Available at: https://www.linkedin.com/pulse/coaching-therapy-challenging-orthodoxy-aubyn-howard/.

Kahneman, D. (2012). *Thinking fast and slow*. London: Penguin Group.

Laloux, F. (2014) *Reinventing organisations; A guide to creating organisations inspired by the next generation of human consciousness*. Belgium: Nelson Parker.

Robbins, T. (n.d.). Life coach vs therapist. *Tony Robbins*. Available at: https://www.tonyrobbins.com/coaching/life-coach-vs-therapist/.

South African College of Applied Psychology. (2014, November 20). What's the difference between counseling and coaching? *Blog*. Available at: https://www.sacap.edu.za/blog/coaching/whats-difference-counselling-coaching/.

Vaughan Smith, J. (2015). What has trauma got to do with coaching? Or coaching to do with trauma? [Presentation]. *Paper presented at APECS Symposium 2015—The future for executive coaching—Evolving professional practice*. Available at: https://www.juliavaughansmith.co.uk/uploads/9/7/1/9/97199636/trauma_and_coaching.pdf

Whitmore, J. (2017). *Coaching for performance: The principles and practice of coaching and leadership* (5th ed.). UK: Nicholas Brealey Publishing.

Whittaker Dunlop, C. (2017, October 5). The success and failure of the coaching industry. *Forbes.com*. Available at: https://www.forbes.com/sites/forbescoachescouncil/2017/10/05/the-success-and-failure-of-the-coaching-industry/#1bfe1c9a6765.

Chapter 5

New Stories, New Possibilities through Psychosynthesis Coaching

by Kirsten Ireland

Introduction

"This is an extraordinary time full of vital, transformative movements that could not be foreseen. It's also a nightmarish time. Full engagement requires the ability to perceive both" (Solnit, 2005, p.33).

It is currently a time where many people are feeling an increasing sense of misplacement, a disconnection that is rapidly gaining potency as the world around us changes. Many of us hold a deep need to find our own space for belonging, a new future that carries with it feelings of meaning, nourishment, vitality, wholeness, and relationship.

Psychosynthesis is an invitation to support us in this searching. "As a holistic, transpersonal, psychological orientation" (Firman, 2016, p.3), it offers a model, maps, and tools for use when "contemplating the messy complexity of experience" (Clandinin & Connelly, 1994, p.2). Psychosynthesis coaching and guiding, in particular, assist in our navigation and offer ways of exploring where we are now and informing our future focus, action, and experience of life. As a person-centered approach that recognizes that individuals have the answers within themselves, working in collaboration with a psychosynthesis coach is about "discovering, harnessing, and expanding on strengths and tools" individuals already possess (Williams & Menendez, 2015, p.6).

It provides a way to look inward (in the sense of feelings, intuition, dreams, aesthetic reactions, inner dialogues and stories, embodied sensations); outward (in the sense of paying attention to existential conditions); backwards and forwards (our childhood, our past experiences, choices and interests, and our desires, goals and vision for ourselves and for the world we live in). A coaching session centers on the principles of supporting individuals to actualize their potential and focuses on "values, alignment to potential, eliciting information, self-empowerment (self-belief), a holistic approach (importance of mind, body, emotions, spirit) and emergence and learning about oneself" (Whitmore, 2014, p.198).

So whatever life is calling us to in this moment, we are presented with an opportunity to look at what is brought up in us and to notice the stories we are telling about what is happening in us and the world. To become aware of how we are responding. To ask, "How can we deepen into what is meaningful for us in this moment?" To stay curious, and ask ourselves how we can honor and support what is emerging. Be with what is, and at the same time actively cooperate with our own development and be supported to move towards new behaviors, and new stories that deepen and enrich our lives. "The world as it is, bubbling and swirling, unreasonable and uncertain, is a story fountain" (Bateson, 2016, p.66).

The significance of story in our lives is fundamental and constant. The stories we tell ourselves shape how we interpret and respond to any experience. It is by and through stories that individuals and communities think and perceive. "Coming in and out of our conscious minds, as the warp and weave of what we see as real, is the story we tell ourselves about our lives" (O'Dea, 2010, p.95). We live by our shared framing stories, and we are at a time where many of us are yearning for a more hopeful and worthwhile story.

Archetypal, cultural, and familial stories, and their defining characteristics, shape the narratives we are told, roles we play and stories we hold of ourselves. These stories often do not reflect our unique deeper sense of meaning, purpose and values. As we come into adulthood, there are stories and roles that have worked well in our childhood, but as we develop, we move out into a more expansive view of ourselves. Often the inherited stories and the self-crafted, sense-making stories are limiting; stuck in patterns that reflect a lack of attunement and mirroring as children, trauma of all kinds, and unconscious limiting beliefs that we have internalized, but do not know we have.

A defining principle of psychosynthesis coaching is that it requires us as coaches and guides, and clients and travelers, to know ourselves beyond the everyday stories or 'content' that is presenting to us 24 hours a day, seven days a week. It invites us to discern and connect from a place that feels like our most authentic and expansive selves rather than our most limiting stories, our most neurotic self or most distressing story. By living in these stories, our choices are driven by these aspects and subpersonalities (a constellation of behaviors, habits, feelings, and thoughts) and don't allow us to connect with our deepest desires, sense of purpose in this moment, this day or lifetime.

At the center of the psychosynthesis egg diagram is a place of contentless awareness—at the place of 'I' (or personal self and transpersonal Self) we are not our stories, not our thoughts, not our belief systems, not our cultures, not our bodies. We are able to step out of our stories and disidentify from content, to become consciousness and connect to what gives us meaning. However most of us are operating from our subpersonalities—the "small I's" that speak for the part rather than the whole (Brown, 2004) and limit, confine, and prevent us from experiencing our complete story; our deepest and fullest sense of ourselves. This results in an illusory or partial reality, and operating from unconscious beliefs. We are immersed so deeply in our incessant internal thought and ideas that we are driven by limiting stories that block us from living the story we want to author and to unfold in our lives.

In the holding environment of a coaching relationship there is an opportunity to be witnessed and 'seen'; for the client to be still and tune in to a deeper 'Call of Self'—"the assumption that each individual has the capacity to tune in, deeply, to a sense of life purpose" (Firman, 2016, p.4), and listen to those stories. As guides, we invite our clients to be curious about who is telling the story. Who is responding? Is it an old story? Are they holding old shoulds and old messages? By bringing awareness, presence, and compassion to these stories, and often to younger parts of ourselves, there is an opportunity to update them, to reflect a deeper truth, so that we may consciously participate in a life of meaning, purpose, and aliveness.

The five-phase map (Vargiu, 1974, p.8) is a tool used in psychosynthesis to support the process of helping clients to identify those parts of themselves (subpersonalities) that are creating a limiting story and from which they are habitually acting; supporting them to disidentify from this and move towards greater integration and Self-identification:

1. **Recognition:** Knowing it is there, experiencing its existence as a subpersonality.
2. **Acceptance:** Breaking polarization with it, coming to identify with, understand, and accept it. This is easier when it fits our self-image. Resistance to acceptance is by another subpersonality.
3. **Co-ordination:** Through acceptance, the subpersonality changes, to become able to work with the rest of the personality. "I" works on discovering and fulfilling real need.
4. **Integration:** Becomes able to work as a harmonious part of the whole personality. Negotiation for fulfillment: conflict resolution, time-sharing, co-operation, etc. The subpersonality grows up.
5. **Synthesis:** No longer exists as an autonomous subpersonality, but is experienced as a quality, or skill or attribute that is accessed through "I".

45

In practice, the five phases are not necessarily linear and generally overlap, each doing part of the work of the others. The work moves along a continuum moving from a split-off position, through being a separate part of the whole, to integration into the whole. As coaches and guides, our goal is to support the client to get to the most "I" they can and to anchor that "I." However, the "I" is not an end point, rather a process and a life's work.

Another commonly used technique in psychosynthesis coaching is the use of autonomous placement to act out different subpersonalities. We support our client to get in touch with one subpersonality at a time by creating the space where they can act it out, using techniques of improvised dialogue, body awareness, and symbolic movement or gesture, imagery and drawing to gain a fuller understanding of how this subpersonality is experienced. Borrowing from the 'empty chair' technique in Gestalt therapy (Yeomans, 2003), our client sits on a seat designated as the observer, or the "center" or "I," through which they are able to disidentify from the subpersonality and gain a different perspective. The "center" speaks to the subpersonalities involved, inquiring into the dynamics of what is happening and offering new ways in which they might co-operate better and meet their needs more effectively.

Unless the subpersonalities are fully accepted, they do not feel 'heard' or understood, and this will cause them to 'shout louder' and they will resist anything that challenges their needs. Each subpersonality has an important message, a need that is attempting to be met, and if we ignore this aspect of ourselves it will continue to dominate our stories and dictate our behavior. As the subpersonalities are given a chance to express themselves, the "center" (a stepping out of the identified subpersonality), is able to listen to their concerns, fears, needs etc. and respond and reassure to address these—helping to support an integration and eventually synthesis. The co-operation at the integration stage allows the qualities and polarities of many of the subpersonalities to come together and gives access to the valuable potential that each of them has to offer.

Choice Follows Awareness

As we work with clients to become more aware, they have an opportunity to gain a 'new' experience of their lived reality and re-construct their own stories. It can feel uncomfortable, but it also offers space to go deep enough to gather 'data' from which to move towards a new sense of self and life goals.

As coaches and guides, we are seeking to support our clients in becoming more than their limiting stories by reflecting on their language in a session; consistently pushing them back into self/Self; noticing and grasping hold of qualities and purpose and directing them into the session; noticing images and using them. We invite more story, and help clients accept the 'yes' or the 'no' that comes up as we delve in to their habitual stories and move towards new goals or 'stories.' We help our clients to deepen into self/Self-identification, checking in to our client's experience through all psychological functions (thinking, feeling, body-sensation, impulse-desire, imagination, intuition); moving the client from inside the story to outside of it.

The very nature of becoming aware brings a new quality, an unpeeling of layers. It offers clients a choice to use their will—what Roberto Assagioli described as "the central power of our individuality, the innermost essence of ourself," (Assagioli, 1966, p.4) to heal and strengthen the parts of ourselves that limit us, so that we "gradually become more coherent and creative instruments for expression of our true Selves" (Yeomans, 2003, p.1).

Clients can begin to notice patterns emerging, to understand more clearly the relationships and the wider context. They can move from day-to-day experiences into a more extended form which seeks to include a wider 'life context,' seeking to capture the relationship of themselves with others and the wider world. "People live stories and in the telling of them reaffirm them, modify them and create new ones" (Clandinin & Connelly, 1994, p.7).

As guides, we support our clients in moving towards self-empathy, helping them to build the capacity to hold all feelings and emotions, in one totality of experience. The coaching structure, and techniques and maps, all work to support transformation. We must also have the ability to support and nourish, and to provide direction—trusting the process and creating the process. It means being present (a synthesis of the two qualities/functions of love and will) and having available to us our listening and open mind, our feelings, our receptivity, our reflective abilities, an embodiment, and our ability to challenge and encourage.

For our clients, 're-storying' and creating more 'appreciative' images can become an action of will to interrupt the messages and stories they have told themselves. Our role is to "support the Act of Will and the client as 'willer,' both empowering purpose, and inviting, even requiring deliberation, to check the clarity of purpose" (Firman, 2013, p.8). We seek to support our clients to "enliven their act of will from purpose and deliberation into affirmation, choice, planning and realization (manifestation)" (Firman, 2013, p.9). Firman also elaborates the stages in the act of will in a training document.

1. **Purpose**, evaluation, motivation (why?) – Gain clarity on what this is, not just the presenting issue, why is this important? Maybe it is symbolic of something else, of something the client wants to work on, or we might find out it is really important. The client is able to

gain a sense of power of purpose, and then we can work with the client;

2. **Deliberation** (pros and cons) – pros and cons, going deeper, where all subpersonalities need to get considered; If a subpersonality isn't an ally it will be our enemy. Looking at subs and also sometimes purpose, isn't always overt. These are often embedded (and often unconsciously) in the stories clients live. Clients may need to ask how to go for purpose in a different way, or in many ways. The purpose is a quality or experience we want to have and we want to explore with our clients what form this might take;

3. **Choice** (yes or no) – yes or no; an overt choice is made;

4. **Affirmation** (energize your choice) – energize the choice, yes or no;

5. **Planning and Programming** (How? When? Where? With What?) – work with the client to develop a clear: how, when, where, why;

6. **Manifestation** (Do it now) – execution of the action

It is through the use of questions, active listening, attention, and holding presence that as coaches we are able to act as an external unifying center, holding what is emerging in the moment while at the same time the potential; to give space to allow the client access to hidden or untapped potential, and through their own will, to generate new possibilities.

Listen Carefully to the Invitation

The invitation is to know ourselves in the largest possible context, the most expansive story of who we are. The limiting stories, including the internal and external messages, block the ability to allow us to be whoever we want to be, even if we do not have the language to describe it. We have a choice and we experience the constant challenge of setting our own boundaries through 'composing' our own life, against allowing others to put those limitations on to us. Most ways that the cultures we live in want to categorize us are not nearly big enough to describe who we are. Psychosynthesis allows us to be all of who we are, with all our qualities acknowledged, included, and celebrated.

Echoing the words from Rebecca Solnit's *Field Guide to Getting Lost* (2006), an exploration of being lost and the uses of the unknown:

The things we want are transformative, and we don't know or only think we know what is on the other side of that transformation. Love, wisdom, grace, inspiration—how do we go about finding these things that are in some way about extending the boundaries of the self into unknown territory?" (p.5)

Through a deepening into our selves, listening and responding to our "Call of Self," we allow ourselves to become more of who we really are.

Untold Stories and New Possibilities

"We illuminate the road to freedom each time we make a conscious choice to stay out of our stories. The road gets easier to see in the light of each pause" (Wheatley, 2010, p.66).

Through working in an I-thou relationship with a coach, there is a change in the form of storytelling and an opportunity to test a newly forming relationship with ourselves. A coaching relationship supports the cultivation of a skillful and strong will in individuals. With a clear destination in mind, one that has an emotional connection to a number of gains and benefits, there will be the motivation (or will) to work out what it takes to get there, and then to get started. Without a goal, there is nothing to aim for and our old stories, habits, and patterns can stifle the will.

The GROW (Goal, Reality, Options, What next or Will) model is a simple structure to use to frame a coaching session. The value of a GROW conversation also helps us, as coaches, to discern what can best be supported in the session. More often than not, the presenting story is masking a deeper issue, but this simple model can help focus the conversation around a key issue as well as support the client with a manageable goal and a clearer way forward:

Goal: Purpose
Reality: Context
Options: Consideration
What next?: Conclusion (Gribben, 2016, p.87)

In a psychosynthesis coaching relationship, the context is created for clients to discover and uncover their own will. Assagioli (1966, p.3) argued "the simplest and most frequent way in which we discover our will lies in determined action and struggle." However, even this can be a distorted view through the stories we shape around it.

As we support our clients in unpacking old stories, we need them first to identify with the old story or subpersonality that is telling the story before we work with them to change the negative scripts. We welcome the precious and difficult scripts that our clients carry around with them, but we do not need to stay there. We support our clients from the pull of an old identification in to "what next?"

"The Future Self" guided imagery exercise is a useful technique (Whitworth et al, 1998, p.219) that allows a client to step into the future in which they meet a more integrated, fulfilled version of themselves. The future self/Self shares with the present-day self/Self how they got from where the client is today to that future state. Similarly, Assagioli's ideal model (2000, pp.147-148) exercise invites us to create a realistic vision of that which we can and truly want to become—a clear viewing of the emerging self.

As coaches, we work particularly with the qualities of the will (strong, skillful, and good), always aware that there is no right or wrong. Using their own will, we support our clients to make choices about who they are as a self/Self to manifest in the world. Together with our clients, we uncover what is most alive and meaningful for them—the call of the Self, and support them in manifesting it in their lives through acts of will by setting actionable goals. As we work together, we can look again beyond their self-dialogue and step out towards new stories.

Dissolving Ourselves to Embody New Stories

"The symbols of the self arise in the depth of the body." (C G Jung as cited in Johnson & Grand, 1998, p.149)

As psychosynthesis coaches and guides, we recognize that there are not only two psyches in the room, but also two souls, in two bodies. We want to delve into and work through, and with, all of the functions, but it is often in the body where unresolved emotional and physical trauma is held. "We live in stories. We embody our stories" (Strozzi-Heckler, 2014, p.47). In bodies, a re-storying can be catalyzed.

Our feelings and emotions influence directly the physical body and our sense of self. Through somatic awareness we can start to bring attention to sensations in our body and notice where we have numbed, disassociated from feelings, or feel most alive. In working with the body, we can support clients to move beyond old, limiting stories. In our clients "we notice a complexity of holding and releasing, of pulsing out and collecting in, of bewilderment and clarity, of locality and universality. Feeling is a catalyst for new, unexpected images and narratives" (Strozzi-Heckler, 2014, p.48).

Working through the somatic lens/function, psychosynthesis coaching includes the "physical world of sensations, temperature, weight, movement, streaming, pulsation and vibrations, as well as images, thoughts, attitudes, yearnings, dreams and language" (Strozzi-Heckler, 2014, p.33). As coaches, we are supporting clients to become more aware and 'visible' to themselves, and then to support them towards a more grounded transformation that is purpose-driven and a movement into wholeness.

To go deeper with awareness out of the habitual patterned and looping narrative and into our somatic experience is difficult for many people however, but through the embodied presence of the coach, clients are supported in a safe and holding environment, to explore these stories. Our stories are sacred, and can be re-authored and retold, but from a place of calm, of presence, of curiosity, and of care. We can come back to the story and offer a more integrated vision once we have metabolized the emotions and feelings from a place of empathic presence.

We may ask our clients to bring attention to their body, to know themselves in their body as a breather, to become aware and appreciate their body. For example, it has given the gift of life, has transported us, travelled, it is the container that holds spirit and self, it is the embodied us. We encourage them to make the connection as who they are as a physical body from head to toe. Appreciate different parts of their body; all of the organs that carry oxygen, circulate blood, digest food, process waste. Appreciate the amazing automatic, super computer that is their brain. Appreciate that they have this body, yet at the same time recognizing that while they have a body, they are more than just a physical being.

Assagioli's disidentification exercise (1999) can be used to support clients in appreciating and acknowledging their bodies, their emotions, and thoughts, while knowing they are more than that at any time:

I have a body but I am not my body. ...
I have emotions, but I am not my emotions. ...
I have a mind but I am not my mind. ...
I recognize and affirm that I am a center of pure self-consciousness. I am a center of will, capable of observing, directing, and using all psychological processes and my physical body. (pp. 214-216)

As coaches and guides, we can engage our clients in becoming more aware of their own bodily responses and invite them to notice what sensations they are aware of in their body. Encouraging and inviting them to 'tune in' to what they are experiencing internally at that moment, for example, the quality of their breathing, tone of voice, speech, posture, gestures, and other qualities. It is a continuing invitation to pay attention to and re-inhabit themselves. We may ask: "If this image, incident, dream or story were 'living' or residing anywhere in your body where would it be?"(Hanlon, Johnson & Grand, 1998, p.159). Although the sensations are constantly changing, the one observing, the "I", remains the same.

We work from intention and respond to the unfolding in the session, letting go of outcomes. In relationship, clients learn to open up to a quality of inquiry while not allowing self-dialogue to mask the ability to notice and respond to other senses. In relationship with a 'holding other,' psychosynthesis coaching allows clients to conceive new ways of understanding their connection to themselves. It invites a broader way of 'knowing' themselves, not just through the mental stories, but also through the embodied stories, the sensations, the feelings, dreams, and unconscious stories, a deeper knowing through intuition.

> Right in the core of the very hot, panicky, and claustrophobic sensations — erupting through your belly, your heart, and your throat—the unmet ones have come again. They will never give up on you, for they are emissaries of love, come this time in a wrathful form to remind you of wholeness and of how full-spectrum the journey of the heart really is. (Licata, 2016)

An Aesthetic Engagement and Connectivity

Through accepting the invitation that psychosynthesis offers us to open ourselves to different ways of knowing ourselves, we have an opportunity to cultivate new qualities to support us in more hopeful stories, bringing a deeper connectivity to the body, mind, feelings, soul, and a knowing that we are more than that at any time. Cultivating an aesthetic engagement with qualities of beauty, joy, and relationship, among others, can help us to embrace multi-dimensional ways of knowing and support us to experience glimpses of our interconnectedness and a new wholeness.

David Whyte (2015) describes beauty as "the harvest of presence" (p.139). As a core transpersonal quality in psychosynthesis, it can open us to a learning based on a different kind of awareness. In the sacred space of the coaching session, we can support individuals in attuning to their senses and body rhythms. The presence of the coach can help clients develop a new sensory knowing and sensory perception to re-discover their true nature, beyond their stories. Nurturing the glimpses of 'wholeness,' builds a resilience and relationship to ourselves, which places us in a broader context of meaning, and gives us choices from which to be in the world. It deepens our access to our innate qualities and enables us to explore parts of ourselves, and it also challenges our continually forming notion of self/Self and supports a 're-storying.'

The Courage to Create a New Collective Story

There is great courage in being willing, not just to explore and honor our own stories, but also to participate open-heartedly in life, to be part of a wider collective story. Courage is a central quality of psychosynthesis coaching work, as clients and travelers make conscious those things that are felt and held deeply.

The challenge is to refuse to categorize ourselves. We do not have to take sides or define ourselves. We have the opportunity to experience all of our feelings, the 'both... and,' the paradox and the mystery of the unfolding of our lives. The goal of this work is not to 'get rid of our story,' but to have a more flexible relationship with it.

When people feel held in the sacred space of the coaching relationship, they feel safe to come out of hiding and express the will of their true self/Self in the world. As coaches, we continually seek to affirm and trust the client's process. It involves deep and respectful listening to what is trying to happen in the client's life. Likewise, families, communities, organizations, and cultures have the potential for responding to what is truly important, through reflection, deeper presence, open and respectful listening, and meaningful conversations to support healthier and more fulfilled people, families, communities—a new story.

Human beings are storytellers. Go ahead. Tell one. And then listen carefully as the characters, the sub-plots, and the narratives share their longing to be authored in more integrated forms. With curiosity, openness, acceptance, and love, you can practice intimacy with your story, touching the beauty, the pain, the joy and the heartbreak of your life as it is. (Licata, 2017)

What is the story that we want for ourselves and our collective future?

References

Assagioli, R. (1966). *The training of the will.* Amherst, MA: Synthesis Center Press.

Assagioli, R. (1999). *The act of will.* U.K: David E. Platts & Associates.

Assagioli, R. (2000). *Psychosynthesis: A collection of basic writings.* Amherst, MA: Synthesis Center Press.

Bateson, N. (2016). Small arcs of larger circles, framing through other patterns. England: Triarchy Press.

Brown, M. Y. (2004). *Unfolding self: The practice of Psychosynthesis.* New York: Allworth Press.

Clandinin, D. J., & Connelly, F. M. (1994). Personal experience methods. In N. K. Denzin & Y. S. Lincoln (Eds.), *Handbook of qualitative research* (pp. 413-427). London: SAGE Publications Inc.

Firman, D. (2016, June). Supporting the future of Psychosynthesis: Coaching as a path to self-realization. [Presentation].

Firman, D. (2013). *Supporting the future of Psychosynthesis: Coaching as a path to self-realization.* Amherst, MA: Synthesis Center Press.

Gribben, S. (2016). *Key coaching models, the 70+ models every manager and coach needs to know.* UK: Pearson Education Limited.

Johnson, D.H., & Grand, I. J. (1998). *The body in psychotherapy—inquiries in somatic psychology.* Berkeley, CA: North Atlantic Books.

Licata, M. (2016, February 21). *At the precipice of a new world.* Retrieved from http://alovinghealingspace.blogspot.co.uk

Licata, M. (2017, May 6). *Pure imagination.* Retrieved from http://alovinghealingspace.blogspot.co.uk

O'Dea, J. (2010). *Creative stress, a path for evolving souls living through personal and planetary upheaval.* Ross, CA: Pioneer Imprints.

Solnit, R. (2005). *Hope in the dark: Untold histories, wild possibilities.* Melbourne, Australia: Text Publishing Company.

Solnit, R. (2006). *A field guide to getting lost.* (Kindle version). London: Penguin Books. Retrieved from www.amazon.co.uk.

Strozzi-Heckler, R. (2014). *The art of somatic coaching: Embodying skillful action, wisdom, and compassion.* Berkeley, CA: North Atlantic Books.

Vargiu, J. (1974). "The realization of the self" in *Synthesis Journal*, v.1. Redwood City, CA: The Synthesis Press.

Wheatley, M.J. (2010). *Perseverance.* San Francisco: Berrett-Koehler Publishers.

Whyte, D. (2015). *Consolations: The solace, nourishment and underlying meaning of everyday words.* Langley, WA: Many Rivers Press.

Whitmore, D. (2014). *Psychosynthesis counselling in action* (Counselling in Action series), 4th Ed. London: SAGE Publications Inc.

Whitworth, L., Kimsey-House, H., & Sandahl, P (1998). *Co-active coaching*, 1st Ed. Palo-Alto, CA: Davies Black.

Williams, P., & Menendez D.S (2015). *Becoming a professional life coach*, 2nd Ed. New York: W.W. Norton & Company.

Yeomans, T. (2003). Psychosynthesis practice, Vol. 1, Psychosynthesis Exercises for Personal and Spiritual Growth. Amherst, MA: Synthesis Center Press.

Part 2

Transpersonal Coaching: The Call of Purpose, Meaning and Values

The awakening of the soul, that first blinding flash of new spiritual consciousness which transforms and regenerates the whole being, is an event of fundamental importance and has incomparable value for our inner life.

—Roberto Assagioli

Editor's Note:
The experience of working in the transpersonal dimension is a cornerstone of psychosynthesis work. It is here that we touch into core truths and values and find resonance with a sense of life purpose. And it is that alignment with purpose that anchors all coaching work. The client's unfolding purpose may be, in itself, of a spiritual nature, allowing the work to be enfolded in the transpersonal dimension. And, as often, the client's needs are of a personal nature, where psychosynthesis coaching brings the best of a transpersonal orientation to the lived experience of life every day. Be it the transcendence of knowing Self in Unity, or the immanence of knowing Self in particularity, all psychosynthesis coaching touches the dimension where each human being holds closest to their own purpose, meaning and values.

Chapter 6

I Am a Psychosynthesis Coach

by Cristina Pelizzatti

I am a psychosynthesis life coach and a trainer of psychosynthesis coaches. I have practiced in the field of psychosynthesis for 10 years. The following is a brief presentation of the experience that I have in doing this work and references the foundation of understanding that I carry in my work.

We truly believe, as coaches and guides, that all humans have immeasurable resources of energy, wisdom, love, intelligence and ability, waiting to be discovered and used to co-create the life we want, faster and more easily, utilizing these resources to facilitate change and realize our potential.

We believe that clients contain within them all their answers, talents and strengths and we assist them, with trust and confidence, in the process of self-discovery, grounding and anchoring this awareness through deep presence and powerful questions, to increase awareness and bring that awareness into actionable steps to reach the clients' chosen goals.

We focus on the present and future, on the clients' strengths, on life purpose and goals, working with clients to create new possibilities to fulfill their lives. We visit the past, when it is called for, in the present, knowing that it holds much that we need to examine, integrate and heal. We are professional helpers, supporting a natural evolutionary process, by honoring the past and living fully in the present with open minds, open hearts, and open Wills toward the emerging possibilities of the future. Through Presence, we activate generative listening, with an emphasis on the client's "Call of the Self". We work in partnership with our clients to free their highest human potentials and maximize their success in achieving their meaningful goals.

We help our clients to name and become more and more aware of the field of infinite possibilities, that they have already felt throughout their lives, whether they have been able to acknowledge this or not. This call is present as an un-named (content-less) experience, and then, by accessing this transpersonal dimension, naming it, grounding it, and, through affirmation and practice, anchoring these energies into daily life as empowerment toward meaningful living.

With patience and determination, we encourage our clients to listen, to discover and to live their life's purpose; to grow in perspective, attitude, and mindset; to raise their own standards, first to design the life they want; and then to bring out their own brilliance and resources to achieve excellence. Thus, they are invited and encouraged to create purposeful, extraordinary lives.

The necessary first phase of the psychosynthesis process is the creation of clarity and space for the "I" as director of the whole personality (personal psychosynthesis). This is followed by a second phase involving movement toward the realization, grounding, and utilization of the higher potentials within everyday life (spiritual psychosynthesis).

Psychosynthesis coaching moves the client into action, accelerating their progress by providing greater focus and awareness of all the possibilities which exist as "I", which by definition is content-less awareness and will, the "who" that they are beyond their limiting stories. Immediately we share their goals of creating fulfilling lives and setting healthy boundaries, instead of creating comfort zones, that while seeming safe, block the movement of Self.

In the coaching conversation we work, in particular, with the "I" by expanding the limiting identifications, by exploring the old and constricted beliefs of a comfort zone—pushing the edges with empathy. Our goal is to reach the deepest, truest needs, often barred by the patterns of the subpersonalities. As value based needs emerge, we help clients find motivation for these needed changes, through awareness and will, opening to the realization of a profound sense that the personal self or "I" exists as a relational emanation of the Self, forever linked to It. The bond between "I" and Self is never lost nor broken, but each person has a different level of awareness about this relationship, and some may be completely blind to it, until, in life, or in coaching, this deep relationship is awakened.

The transpersonal path includes the sequence of getting beyond the personality, through a process of energy transmutation toward the depths and heights of excellence and back into the personality, thereby becoming fully human, in action, as the meaningful co-creator of life.

Psychosynthesis coaching, as a transpersonal process, recognizes developmental stages (though not simply linear) and states of consciousness: Prepersonal, Personal, and Transpersonal. All of this is within a structure involving a transpersonal orientation, client content, and processes involving specific methodologies, strategies and ways of knowing. As coaches, we are the experts in the strategies and skills and the client is the expert in knowing their own story: the content that they bring to coaching. The transpersonal orientation is the worldview that the coach holds, creating the environment for unfolding, based on the coach's own psychosynthesis (and transpersonal) perspective.

We guide clients to loosen the rational mental dimension, opening up a space to the intuitive mind, grounding and anchoring the awareness of transpersonal contents into the "I" and using them as a motivator for chosen goals, by maintaining the awareness of the unbroken relationship of "I and Self" throughout the journey of life, allowing an expanded experience of responses and solutions to presenting issues that come into the coaching office. With this "lived" connection, the client is encouraged to move forward and commit to realistic goals, within a specific time frame, in a way that they can bring transpersonal resources into daily life as a driver of change.

We predispose ourselves, as guides, with empathy, presence, beginner's mind, unconditional positive regard, bereft of judgmental attitude, and awareness of the self-actualizing tendency of human beings. All transpersonal qualities that the coach brings into the session are a mirror with which clients may see themselves and recognize the presence of these same qualities (and others) within them.

We allow ourselves to become an external unifying center, holding the "I- Self" space as a transpersonal setting, moved by the energy of the Self. The "I-Thou" becomes a "Self-to-Self" relationship, and the transpersonal process occurs, emphasizing the client's awareness of the "here and now" as a Self, accessing awareness and will.

As a coach, we assist clients in the process of human development, inviting the deeper resources already existing dormant in each person, allowing these resources to ground, anchor, and create awareness of new potentialities. From this, clients naturally manifest the inherent capacities of who they truly are, beyond the "normal" understanding of a limited self-story, thus becoming "more" and claiming their own internal unifying center.

The awakening of these reserves empowers the person with self-care skills, generating new perspectives on professional or personal life direction and future choices. These perspectives are potentially world-changing as clients gain access to the resources of wisdom, innate creativity, and spirituality that we all have within us, and which we need when we are to confront the many challenges we face as human beings.

The experience of reaching the awareness of our infinite nature as a Self, and then bringing back the subtle transpersonal energies into the personal "I", conditioned by the limits of the form we wear, requires training and the humility and courage to recognize and therefore deal with our vulnerability.

Psychosynthesis coaches support the creation of the sacred space, the space in which clients can permit themselves to let go of the many masks they are carrying throughout everyday life. In this process, they start to realize and show their vulnerability, the core of themselves, the content-less Self. This Self is not vulnerable in substance, but in the form that covers the Self: the personality. This realization enables clients to reach the freedom of being who they really are and allows them to find the courage to be that Self in action, facing whatever shows up in everyday life, gathering and using deep inner resources, while also accepting human limitations.

Working on the inevitable human vulnerability awakens and leads the client to the power of resilience as an inherent capacity of a human being to learn from crisis, personal history, and primal wounds, in the process becoming stronger and more flexible. Thanks to inner resources, personal skills, and strategies in line with purpose, meaning and values, as motivators toward chosen goals, clients often experience passing from a state of powerlessness to one of being empowered.

The ability of the coach to be fully present (through love and will), allows the client to be vulnerable during the coaching conversation. In this sacred space, the client experiences the quality of this mutual presence: the I-Thou relationship, where the client feels not only seen, but profoundly understood, contained, supported, and guided toward the solution they have chosen.

Three fundamental steps along this transpersonal path are:
1. **Identification** of contents and players (subpersonalities) within the personality;
2. **Disidentification**, leading into the space between the I and the contents, becoming the observer, noting the contents of experience as they arise in consciousness, with the power of choosing where to direct the attention;
3. **Self-Identification**, the process of gaining the awareness of being the "I- Self". The "I" is not a place to go or a goal to attain. It is the experience of being the observer, aware of the contents of consciousness and having the power of choice (awareness or mindfulness and will).

The experience of unity as "I-Self", allows the acceptance of the existence of a multiplicity of subpersonalities (diversity), through the phases of knowing, possessing, and transforming. The client is moved into the experience of unity in diversity, the "both-and" of being many diverse parts and existing ultimately as "I-Self", a nondual reality. From here the client acts as a coordinating center (director), from the energetic space of content-less awareness and will, co-creating the future in line with purpose, meaning and values.

As coaches, we assist and guide people into the process of Self-actualization, a transformational way to become more of who they are by expanding and stepping out of the usual, limited mindset. This process occurs in dynamic tension, not by rejecting any lived reality or pattern. There is no dismissal or shame about "who we are and what we did", but there builds an understanding of who we really are, thanks, in part, to the "everything we did". This leads to a compassionate forgiveness about the past and creates the capacity to become the "more" that is always waiting to emerge.

We, coaches, listen with intuition, with open hearts and open minds to the emerging future possibilities, and we can share our intuition, while inviting the client's own intuition, because the relationship of the coach and client is an I-Thou or Self-Self partnership. From this place of deep presence, full acceptance, open invitation and purpose infused guiding, clients learn to listen to themselves, through the transpersonal process in which we guide them.

During coaching sessions, we guide clients along the path of self discovery, to become more and more self-confident while experiencing the deepest and highest regions of the unconscious, gaining knowledge of the many parts which live within and the dynamics of their interactions. This leads to an increase in awareness and confidence in stepping out of the safety of the "comfort zone", recognizing the "I" in its freedom, as the new comfort zone to inhabit. From there, we invite the many parts, stories, partial truths, experiences, both good and bad, as welcome guests, empowering the "I" to be the holding environment for all that is.

The transpersonal coaching process is the search for meaning and the movement of Self-actualization and Self-realization; the process of becoming more and more true to the Self, manifesting Self internally and externally, while living the deepest truths of existence.

I am a psychosynthesis coach, dedicated to supporting this evolution in all beings.

Chapter 7

A Transpersonal Orientation: Psychosynthesis in the Coach's Office

by Dorothy Firman

Introduction

Defining transpersonal as simply that which goes beyond the individual or personal, it could be hypothesized that all coaches are, at least in part, transpersonal in their orientation. The transpersonal (or spiritual) dimension, is, almost inevitably, part of a coach's possible arena of concern, because it is so often (perhaps always) part of the concern of people in general.

The movement to bring transpersonal psychology into the mainstream and into research and training, started officially in 1969, with the advent of the *Journal of Transpersonal Psychology* and the first definition thereof. Sutich, editor for that first journal, defined transpersonal psychology as follows:

Transpersonal Psychology is the title given to an emerging force in the psychology field by a group of psychologists and professional men and women from other fields who are interested in those ultimate human capacities that have no systematic place in positivistic or behavioristic theory ("first force"), classical psychoanalytic theory ("second force"), or humanistic psychology ("third force"). The emerging Transpersonal psychology ("fourth force") is concerned specifically with the empirical, scientific study of, and responsible implementation of the findings relevant to becoming, individual and species-wide meta-needs, ultimate values, unitive consciousness, peak experiences, B-values, ecstasy, mystical experience, awe, being, self-actualization, essence, bliss, wonder, ultimate meaning, transcendence of self, spirit, oneness, cosmic awareness, individual and species-wide synergy, maximal interpersonal encounter, sacralization of everyday life, transcendental phenomena, cosmic self-humor and playfulness, maximal sensory awareness, responsiveness and expression, and related concepts, experiences and activities (p.16).

In that same issue was an article, *Symbols of Transpersonal Experience*, by Roberto Assagioli, founder of psychosynthesis (1969). Assagioli's own work towards the creation of a transpersonal psychology began much earlier. He had coined the term **psychosynthesis** as early as 1911 (Hardy, 1987) and by the advent of the *Journal of Transpersonal Psychology* he had published, in his language of origin, Italian, hundreds of articles and in English, the book *Psychosynthesis* (1965) had been published, to be followed in a few short years by *The Act of Will* (1973). And even earlier, in 1907, he had written an essay "where his life-long habit of approaching theory through both Western and Eastern psychological wisdom is introduced" (Sliker, p.12).

More than 100 years later, psychosynthesis continues to present in the world of psychology as one of the most comprehensive transpersonal theories and one uniquely suited for the field of coaching. Beyond the very broad stroke definition offered by a fledgling journal in the 1960's, there are well matured, professionally tried and tested descriptions and pointers towards the field of transpersonal psychology that orient the psychosynthesis coach in a current and relevant way. Vaughan (1980) noted that transpersonal psychology is "an open-ended endeavor to facilitate human growth and expand awareness beyond limits implied by most traditional Western models of mental health" (p. 182). More recently Walsh and Vaughan (1993) make clear that transpersonal psychology is not simply concerned with transpersonal experience. Personal level realities, issues and needs, might be supported by being viewed through the lens of a larger (transpersonal) model. Transpersonal psychology becomes, then, a holistic perspective, focusing on the whole spectrum of human experience, with an eye towards holding a wider view, one that sees spiritual issues with equal relevance to personality and family of origin issues.

Psychosynthesis, a Transpersonal Psychology

Psychosynthesis was at the forefront of the transpersonal psychology movement, not only by its early theoretical orientation in that direction, but even more importantly by the creation of a methodology by which a transpersonal orientation could be put into place. Battista (1996) in his article, *Abraham Maslow and Roberto Assagioli: Pioneers of Transpersonal Psychology*, states Assagioli's prominent role quite simply.

Whereas Maslow explored fundamental issues in transpersonal psychology, Roberto Assagioli pioneered the practical application of these concepts in psychology. Assagioli proposed a transpersonal view of personality and discussed psychology in terms of the synthesis of personality at both the personal and spiritual levels. He dealt with the issue of spiritual crises and introduced many active therapeutic techniques for the development of a transcendent center of personality (1996, p. 52).

Psychosynthesis concerns itself with the arena of the transpersonal, first and foremost, through an ongoing consideration of meaning, purpose and values in the individual's life. This defining characteristic of the practice of psychosynthesis points to the whole spectrum of coaching inquiry, since the accessing and manifesting of purpose, meaning and values is as likely to take the client back to family of origin issues as it is to take them into transpersonal content areas. Psychosynthesis expects the coach to work within this whole spectrum, while orienting towards the purview that is that of a coach, not that of a psychotherapist.

The regions of the lower, middle and higher unconscious (see map below) will all be largely or partially explored, based on goals that the client presents. Assagioli notes that this exploration will serve the client in many ways.

In that way, we shall discover in ourselves hitherto unknown abilities, our true vocations and our higher potentialities which seek to express themselves but which we often repel and repress through lack of understanding, prejudice or fear. We shall also discover the immense reserve of udifferentiated psychic energy latent in every one of us; that is, the plastic part of our unconscious which lies at our disposal, empowering us with an unlimited capacity to learn and to create. (2009, p.19)

In looking at the template of movement in the coaching relationship, from a transpersonal orientation, psychosynthesis has articulated the stages of work that client and coach may move through. The stages are not considered to be a simple, linear ladder-like progression, but a synthetic movement between stages and through all stages, in a multi-layered experience of self-inquiry. The first stage is that exploration of who we are, what we carry, what our strengths and needs are, while the second stage is considered the period of coming into right relationship with these same elements that the client has come to discover in the first stage. Where psychosynthesis begins to show its transpersonal colors most fully is in the 'last' stage of work. Firman and Gila (2002) note that these stages "describe how we may then become conscious of, and respond to, the deeper motivations and meanings in our lives, the source of which is termed the **Self**" (p.45). Assagioli (2000) referred to these stages as "realization of one's true Self".

It is the consideration of Self; an emphasis on meaning; and the ultimate goal of synthesis of the psyche that anchor psychosynthesis deeply into the tradition of transpersonal psychology. Purpose, meaning and values are touchstone concepts in psychosynthesis, pointing to the ever-present transpersonal orientation. For whatever the work being done in the office is, that work is predicated upon and guided by an intention to understand the client's purpose, what has meaning for the client and what the client values. This will inevitably define coaching work as transpersonal, no matter what the presenting issues and goals may be.

Map of the Psyche

Psychosynthesis posits a division of the psyche into its component levels of unconsciousness. These are the lower unconscious, middle unconscious and higher unconscious or superconscious. Similar to Wilber's prepersonal, personal and transpersonal dimensions, (1982, 1983) these states point to the wide experience of humanness from family and culture of origin experience, to the life of the personality, in present time, with real-life concerns to the arena of meaning, purpose and values, spirituality and the realm of the transpersonal dimension.

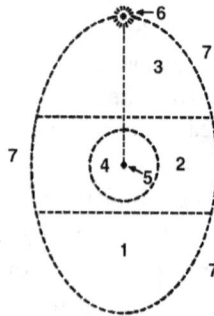

1. lower unconscious
2. middle unconscious
3. higher unconscious or superconscious
4. field of awareness
5. I or self (small "s")
6. higher Self or Self ("capital "S")
7. collective unconscious (Assagioli, 2000, p.15)

Every client entering a coach's office will potentially need to work at all levels. And healing, transforming, "fixing" any one will, of course, have impact on all the others. Key here is the coach's ability to see with wide vision, what has been called bifocal and trifocal vision in psychosynthesis (Whitmore, 2004; Assagioli, 2010). Bifocal vision invites the coach to see the client through the lens of that client's presenting issues, while at the same time seeing that person as a soul in search of realization. As such, each client brings to the coaching encounter all the qualities of their essential, unwounded nature; all the unique aspects of their being; and all the transpersonal qualities and potential named in that first definition of transpersonal psychology so many years ago. Trifocal vision assumes that same orientation adding **the awareness** of the next step to be taken (Assagioli, 2010). Holding this inclusive vision invites a willingness to see what is calling and the movement between those.

Some of the simplifications in both the "new age" and the "old way" have been a disservice to the field of transpersonal psychology. Among these include the tendency, in some forms of "healing," to assume that all healing takes place at the transpersonal level, that spirit cures all, and that, as one bumper sticker puts it, "It's never too late to have a happy childhood". The opposite distortion, sometimes seen in traditional psychotherapy, is that everything that ails the client is prepersonal in origin. Wilber elaborates this insidious dilemma in much of his writing, referring to it as the pre-trans fallacy.

The essence of the pre/trans fallacy is easy enough to state. We begin by simply assuming that human beings do in fact have access to three general realms of being and knowing—the sensory, the mental, and the spiritual. These three realms can be stated in any number of different ways: subconscious, self-conscious and super-conscious, or prerational, rational, and transrational, or prepersonal, personal and transpersonal. The point is simply that, for example, since prerational and transrational are both, in their own ways nonrational, then they appear quite similar or even identical to the untutored eye. Once this confusion occurs—the confusion of "pre" and "trans"—then one of two things inevitably happens: the transrational realms are reduced to prepersonal status, or the prerational realms are elevated to transrational glory. Either way a complete and overall world view is broken in half and folded in the middle, with one half of the real world (the "pre" or the "trans") being thus profoundly mistreated and misunderstood (1983, p.202).

Thus, the psychosynthesis coach is always alert to (and trained in), assessing both prepersonal and transpersonal, as well as personal levels of need. And the stages of psychosynthesis work support that movement through all three aspects of the being, without falling prey to the pre-trans fallacy.

The completed description of the map of the psyche, points to the remainder of the key psychosynthesis concepts. The I or self (small "s") is defined as a center of pure awareness and will, independent of any content of consciousness. The Self (capital "S") is the same Self, anchored at the border of the transpersonal and the universal. Alternate versions of this map remove the "higher" Self, attributing the transpersonal aspects of the Self to the very ground of being, or place that same star at the bottom, middle and top of the map, indicating that same ever-present reality of Self.

The outer dotted line indicates the collective unconscious, a significant nod to Jung's seminal work in that field (1938) and an indication in Assagioli's understanding, that the individual is not only connected transpersonally to the larger universe, but collectively and archetypally, as well. Both Jung and Assagioli (1967) envision this realm as the large and all-encompassing unconscious from which stems much of human creativity, experience and connection.

Identification and Disidentification

As the coach conceives of clients as more than their presenting issues and views them through the lens of purpose, meaning and values, techniques and strategies must support that orientation. One of the key principles and active techniques in psychosynthesis is the principle of **disidentification**. Literally the principle is a practice of identification, disidentification and Self-identification. Assagioli (2000) says, "We are dominated by everything with which our self becomes identified. We can dominate and control everything from which we disidentify ourselves" (p.19).

For the modern reader, it is important, parenthetically, to remember that Assagioli was born in the 19th century and wrote as a psychiatrist in Italian or in English as a second language. His sometimes-archaic language easily translates beyond the time and place of his historical location to the real work in the field today. The concept of control and domination actually point to the experience of contentless-ness and disidentification (or non-attachment) and not to the experience of **power over**.

In the reality of people's lives, the way identifications are known can be enduring or transient. The most difficult identifications are scripted messages from childhood that stick through thick and thin. These nearly intractable self-concepts can define a lifetime, eliminating possibilities that inherently exist in that person, by the sheer weight of the experience of **this is who I am**. Identification asks clients to fully know how they experience themselves: in body, feelings, mind, self-concepts, beliefs and the like. And by so knowing—consciously—the boundaries of that experience, whatever it may be, an almost inevitable movement towards disidentification becomes apparent. For who is it that knows this identification? Every identification has its use and its limits. The so-called empty-nest syndrome points to an identification held for too long. The field abounds with catch phrases to describe the various identifications that don't work: the ways people know and experience themselves that limit them. These very limiting identifications are often the motivation for coaching.

The weight of early identifications, based on the experiences of a child, are the hardest to step beyond. But when a client has the experience of knowing, **I have that wounded child and I am more than that child** or any variation of identification and the subsequent disidentification that follows, that person moves one step closer to Self-identification and becomes, incrementally more connected to the experience of being Self. The client, in this moment of disidentification, is more.

The **I am more** is a key theoretical underpinning of psychosynthesis. It points to the assumption of Self. The core principles of psychosynthesis that define it as a transpersonal psychology include this assumption of a center of consciousness (and will) that is content-less. This essential concept implies a potential way of Self-knowing that is not simply, or perhaps at all, defined by personal history. The principle of identification (disidentification and Self-identification) aims towards that end point. The exercise, practice or ongoing assumption looks something like this: "I have content, personal history, trauma, strengths, weaknesses, personality inclinations. I have this body, this age, these beliefs. And I am more that that." Or as this principle was first articulated by Assagioli, **I have these things but I am NOT these things** (2000).

Not this, not that! the Zen Master cries to the hapless student, who is clinging to an identify as some thing, any thing, any one. Eastern religions frequently point to concepts of the **Not** that we are, by way of directing identification away from the passing contents of consciousness to the one (Self) who is conscious. St. Francis (pointing to similar truths in the essential or esoteric underpinnings of many Western religions) said, "That which we are looking for, is that which is looking."

The implications for this orientation are profound both philosophically and psychologically. To know oneself beyond content, is to transcend or experience oneself outside of the story of one's life. Disidentification (**I am not this**) steps us back from content and story. Self-identification anchors us into the experience of being the one who is aware (and the one who chooses).

Classic meditation practices, especially those using mindfulness-based techniques (Goleman, 1977) lead to this same point of reference. But in coaching, the potential of this experience is that the client, having accessed the experience of being the one who is aware, has immediately (and especially with support) the possibility of being identified as well as the one who chooses. The experience of "I" or "self" is the identification with content-less awareness and will. It is both transcendent: more than, above and beyond content and story; and immanent: embedded in the exact here and now (Firman & Gila, 2002).

Subpersonality Theory

Psychological theories abound for why adult human beings experience themselves in a split fashion. Instead of **not this/not that**, the inner world of adults (in Western culture, to be sure) is of **this and that** and the other thing. And this consciousness moves ever so easily into polarities that impact both internally and externally. Good and bad, light and dark, this and that, and most poignantly and dangerously, **us and them**, leave the client with numerous identifications which are termed **subpersonalities** in psychosynthesis.

Subpersonalities, a concept quite commonly known in the field at this time, is most colloquially noted in language like **inner child, victim, critic.** Rowan (1990), in his book, *Subpersonalities* mentions the role of psychosynthesis, noting that "one of the first people to have started really making use of subpersonalities for therapy and personal growth was Roberto Assagioli" (p.72). Subpersonalities, in psychosynthesis theory, have been defined as "structured constellations or agglomerates of attitudes, drives, habit patterns," (Crampton, p.712) and "learned responses to our legitimate needs: survival needs, needs for love and acceptance, and needs for self-actualization and transcendence" (Brown, 2004, p.41). They are, most simply stated, the **parts** of every individual, that may or may not be in service of the whole. They are the parts that often take over, leaving the owner of these parts at their mercy. Identification, as noted earlier, is the process of accessing and recognizing the subpersonalities as the limited ways one knows oneself. Recognition of a subpersonality, (**Oh, there's that wounded part of me!**) immediately accesses the knower as outside of the content or story line of the subpersonality.

Work with subpersonalities is a key element in psychosynthesis coaching. Allowing for the extreme complexity of much coaching work and making it clear that subpersonalities are not to be mistaken for any of the dissociative disorders, the process can be immediately relevant to the coach and accessible as a technique. Recognition of a subpersonality, allows for the possibility of acceptance of that part. Rather than the typical strategy of rejecting un-liked parts, leading to denial, projection, and more: this recognition and disidentification into Self, creates an opening for acceptance. From that moment, the possibility of integrating that subpersonality—in a healthy way—exists. **There's that wounded part of me,** moves to **How can I heal and integrate that part into my life?** A simple stage process is noted in psychosynthesis: recognition, acceptance, coordination, integration and synthesis (Vargiu, 1975). The last three stages mark the movement from negotiating the needs, actions and healing of various subpersonalities, through the more seamless stage of having access to, but not being controlled by various subpersonalities, to the ideal end point as a unified, non-dualistic human being. Note that this process points, **like a finger pointing to the moon**, as the saying goes, simply, but profoundly towards the movement that anchors a client into Self-knowledge and choice. And that identification with Self is larger and more inclusive than any identification with the subpersonality, feeling or role that has become a limitation.

The Self (self)

The Self that each person is can be the internal unifying center that guides a lifetime, in the face of trauma and wounding, cultural and familial norms and the inner chaos that is so often brought into the coach's office. Reflecting back to the concept of Self, the key, defining characteristic is that Self is content-less (without content). As Self, one has access to all content, but knows itself otherwise. When Assagioli was interviewed by an American interviewer, she asked him how old he was. His answer, "My body has 85 years." (Besmer, 1974). Thinking his English was limited and thus the odd answer, the interviewer was surprised to find that in fact his English was perfect and that Assagioli's lived experience was of a Self that is not a body, an age, a race, a religion, a sex or a story-line. **I have a body and I am not my body.** (Likewise, thoughts and feelings, as well as identification with subpersonalities, roles, nationality, and more.)

What then? Saving myself from the impossible task of answering this question in an ultimate fashion, a note from Assagioli (2000) helps to define the large arena of psychosynthesis practice **and** its limitations. "Psychosynthesis does not aim nor attempt to give a metaphysical or a theological explanation of the great Mystery—it leads to the door, but stops there" (p.5). The gift of not answering this question with a specific definition is that, of course, any definition would be limited and might or might not fit for any individual experiencing themselves as Self. But, in fairness to the spirit and practice of psychosynthesis, a practical definition is that Self is the center of awareness and will. It is the **I am**, that is both transcendent and immanent. Awareness and will, like the in-breath and out-breath are the very lifeblood of this work. In claiming and living in the experience of Self, awareness is wide and choice is available.

Self and self, as they have been paired throughout this brief exploration, might be used interchangeably as they sometimes are. The capital S self has been referred to as **Self** looking through the lens of the transpersonal or spiritual dimension while the small **s self** or I looks out at the world through the lens of the personal. Both are **I am**: one at the kitchen sink, one on the mountaintop.

A metaphoric description that has often been used is that **self** is the conductor of the orchestra, **Self** the composer of the piece, and of course, the orchestra is the many parts, playing a powerful and unique piece of music, in harmony, under direction of self, in service of the inspiration of the Self. This, of course, is on a good day. The orchestra may sound like a group of contentious, angry, confused adolescents given loud musical instruments. And so, the need for coaching arises. And the need for exploration and vitalizing of the second function of the S(s)elf: Will.

The Will

Psychosynthesis brought the concept of will to the front line, particularly with Assagioli's book *The Act of Will* (1973). The field had, until that time, relied heavily on the awareness side of the coin or the more external aspect of the will, behavior. Awareness and will go hand in hand in psychosynthesis and thus the orchestra is brought into harmony. With the initial stages of coaching; gaining a thorough knowledge of the personality, the work of being a **willer** is birthed. **I have this part and I am more than this part**, immediately invites the reality of choice. The concept of will; the stages of will (purpose, deliberation, choice, affirmation, plan, action); the elements of will (strength, skill and goodness); the stages of knowing Self as will, (will exists, I have will, I am will) and the many other aspects of the theory of will are too elaborate for the purposes of this chapter. However, it is important to note that, theory abounding, will is an easy concept to get and an easy one to bring to life in the office. In-breath and out-breath, awareness and will. When a client (or the coach for that matter) has an awareness, an *ah ha*, or even a curiosity born of awareness, that awareness needs to move into action, whether that is a simple question asked by a coach—an intervention based on the coach's awareness—or a life plan of change, internal and behavioral, put in place by the client. Clients are the change agents; coaches, the allies.

The work of opening to the experience of will, work that spotlights the reality of on-going choice points, is some of the most powerful and immediately accessible work that can be accomplished. As a client comes to know the pulls of the inner world; the subpersonalities that have drives of their own; the feelings that come from a younger place; the impulses manifest by the conditioning of past experience, the anchor into Self is also an anchor into choice. The coach's job, stated simply, is to help stretch that moment when choice is available. It is the **count to ten** of psychosynthesis. Pulled towards a subpersonality reaction, a client who has just a moment's glimpse (awareness) of that experience as it prepares to take over, has the possibility of stopping the sequence. Conductor redirects the tuba player, to give voice to the flute. This simple concept of **choice point** is an important element in the conversational and practical domain of the client and coach. It is not enough to be aware. It is not enough, even, to know why (historically, causally). It is enough to have choice and to continue to fine tune Self as **willer** until the life lived is one that is resonant with the deepest purpose, meaning and values of the client, in that individual's most centered, internally unified Self. Working with the client as **willer** is working to free the client from being simply the outcome of their histories and into being the authors of their future.

That said, it would be naïve to assume that this is an easy task. The aware and conscientious coach will know what is important, in present time, that originates in the client's past. They will also know the real, external, historical and present limitations that each client faces. These may be biological, circumstantial, or commonplace. They may be economic, social, cultural and political. They may be limiting in minor and inconvenient ways. They may be life threatening. The invitation is to help each person who enters the field of the coach's influence to be as fully human and realized as they can be, as fully aware and as fully willing as they can be.

The Qualitative Reality

The forty-year-old client who wants to be twenty again, cannot be twenty, no matter how good the coach is, nor how well the client accesses Self. Nor can the client of color live in a world free of racism. This list of realities that can't be changed goes on… and on. Being a **willer**, knowing oneself as Self, does not change many of the cold, hard facts that define each individual's life. However, two powerful and life changing outcomes are available from this movement towards Self. The first is a profound increase in the experience of acceptance and compassion towards oneself and towards the world. The second is an increased ability to access the qualities needed for fullness and richness and then to live in relationship to those qualities (sometimes referred to as transpersonal qualities).

In a spiritual orientation, finding the deep, abiding peace that comes from acceptance of what is (and the willingness to change what can be changed), is an implicit goal. That inevitably forty-year-old client may discover the call to new aspects of themselves that are somehow represented in the image of being twenty. Playfulness, care-freeness, joy, creativity, release from the burden of being over-responsible, delight in the present, etc. These emerging qualities may, in fact, be the call of the Self to express itself. The client's passing wish to be younger is the Self's call to be whole. The soul in search of realization is not betrayed by the physical facts of reality, but only opened to the possibility of ever expanding qualities of being and expression.

Self is content-less, but is not empty or flat. It is the composer of this song of life. And Self has access to the transpersonal qualities that exist and that move through each unique individual, as the breath of life. Working with clients to help them identify and live through intrinsically experienced qualities is another key element of psychosynthesis work. In a positive orientation, such as this, the obstacles, pain and suffering are seen side by side with the gifts, qualities and essential nature of the client. Self has the life's story and the meaning that can be made in a given life. The path is being carved by wounding; the circumstances of life; and the flow of qualities, by past, present and the call of the future. From this wholeness comes the gift of meaning and purpose. And Self moves, by nature of the functions of awareness and will, through a variety of ways of internalizing the world and expressing itself back into the world. In psychosynthesis, these ways of knowing are referred to as psychological functions.

Psychological Functions

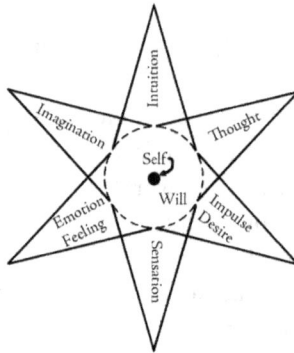

Each person accesses knowing and takes action through a variety of functions. Intuition, imagination, thinking, feeling, sensation, and impulse/desire are the functions that Assagioli (1973) elaborated as ways of knowing and ways of expressing. What this map speaks to is nothing new, but something profoundly important in the coach's office. Each person is unique. Each knows the experience of Self through different vehicles. For one, access to Self will be found in the clear path of thinking, for another through sensation, another through feeling. Likewise, each client comes with wounding and distortion in one or another (or many) of their psychological functions. One of the tasks in psychosynthesis coaching is to know (and help the client know) the functions they have that serve them well: their strengths, if you will. At the same time, healing the wounds that have accrued over a lifetime may specifically involve healing a psychological function that has been denied or distorted.

Accessing and supporting the psychological functions that most resonate for an individual, helps that person know themselves and their world beyond survival needs and cultural norms. The work of psychosynthesis invites the possibility of moving into the richness of a life fully led. Disidentifying from limiting subpersonalities; anchoring into the experience of Self; living with both awareness and will; accessing transpersonal qualities; and living through all psychological functions creates the realization that one is on a path. This path, for each person is the path of meaning, purpose and values.

Path

Carving out a path in life is done through the exquisite balance of awareness and will, the work of Self -identification, the willingness to know oneself, and the continual orientation towards the unique purpose, meaning and values that define an individual more deeply and fully than history and circumstances (Assagioli, 1991).

To know oneself, on a path, is to experience the meaning of one's life and the uniqueness of one's Self. In being supported to find Self, the client is being supported in finding a sense of path or purpose that can contain all aspects of that person's lived experience. It doesn't take long to see the famous examples of those who have taken the suffering in their life, along with their own unique gifts (or qualities) and created, from these resources, a path of meaning. Whether it is a Ghandi or the many unknown individuals, each person has the potential to carve out the path that will define them. Finding the path of one's life is not finding the right job or mate or any external thing. It is settling into an attitude and way of being that is resonant with Self, as Self. And it is not a job that is finished. Like all aspects of psychosynthesis theory, the assumption is that this life is a life's work. There is no end point to accessing the Self, no end to work with subpersonalities, no final destination. The path is the process and the work to be on our own path, is the work of psychosynthesis.

The Psychosynthesis Coach

Like any psychological orientation, psychosynthesis has, not only its own theories, techniques and strategies, but also its own orientation for the practitioner. And yet, in the end, the psychosynthesis coach will be, like any good, caring and present helper, a guide, in the best sense of the word. The belief in the essential nature of client as Self, requires that same work and realization in the coach. Coaches are not technicians. Like the client, a soul in search of realization, the coach travels the same path. That is, the coach travels the path that is uniquely theirs and in so doing, finds that this work of healing, of witnessing, of caring for another in a skilled and impersonal (or transpersonal) way, is a path that is resonant. When the coach is on their own purposeful path, there is revealed, in that professional role, an underpinning of Self that truly allows for an I-thou relationship. Few would disagree that, in fact, the relationship between coach and client, beyond theory and technique, can, in itself be healing. The Self is a given and it is to this Self that the psychosynthesis coach speaks, whenever possible. The alliance that is created, when it can be, is one between the Self in the client and the Self in the coach, each in a different role, both moving from authenticity.

Conclusion

All coaches, trained however they may have been trained, may welcome in themselves, if the inclination is there, an opening to the transpersonal dimension, both by their own personal inquiry into the dimensions of purpose, meaning, values and spirituality and by the simple exploration of these same things with their clients.

There are simple, yet profound, practices and orientations in psychosynthesis to support this process. Disidentification; work with subpersonalities, and the essential end point of that work, accessing the experience of Self; the realization of the many paths on which each human travels towards their own Self-realization; and the revitalizing of Will as a means of manifesting purpose, meaning and values will be the touchstones for moving towards a transpersonal orientation in the coach's office.

The work of coaching is often difficult, and even grasping an image of desired outcomes may be hard. A technique core to psychosynthesis work is the **Ideal Model**. It simply assumes that imagining, thinking about, acting in relationship to one's ideal, will help build that possibility. "Images...tend to produce the physical conditions and the external acts that correspond to them." (Assagioli, 1973, p. 51) As an ideal model of the desired outcome for all human beings, it is likely that psychosynthesis coaches the world around would agree with the sentiment of their colleague, Thomas Yeomans, in his monograph, *The Embodied Soul: Spirituality in the Twenty-first Century*.

In essence, this experience of the spiritual dimension is one of connection to all Life, a powerful sense of participating in the Universe as oneself, a unique being, and of having a place and part in the whole of the living world. From this core experience flow many attributes, such as, courage, wisdom, power, creativity, perspective, joy, and the ability to live fully one's chosen life with vitality and grace. And this is an experience, not an idea— it is the experience of being fully alive as oneself on earth, This very human experience highlights simultaneously the universality and particularity of our existence and the paradoxical fact of our differences from, and union with, all other life forms. It joins us to all others, while at the same time affirming our unique being. Everyone is capable of this connection, though it may be impeded in any number of ways, and it is the birthright we share as human beings. (Yeomans, 2004, pp. 4-5)

It is in service of this birthright that psychosynthesis exists as a healing modality.

References

Assagioli, R. (1969). Symbols of transpersonal experiences. *Journal of transpersonal psychology*, v.1, 1133-45.

Assagioli, R. (1965). *Psychosynthesis*. New York, NY: Hobbs, Dorman & Co.

Assagioli, R. (1967). *Jung and psychosynthesis*. New York, NY: Psychosynthesis Research Foundation (v.19)

Assagioli, R. (1991) *Transpersonal development*. London, England, Harper Collins Publishers.

Assagioli, R. (2000). *Psychosynthesis*. Amherst, MA: Synthesis Center Press. (12th printing).

Assagioli, R. (2010). *The act of will*. Amherst, MA: Synthesis Center Press.

Battista, J. (1996). Abraham Maslow and Roberto Assagioli: Pioneers of transpersonal psychology. In B.Scotten, A. Chinnen, , & J.Battista, (eds.), *Textbook of transpersonal psychiatry and psychology* (pp.52-61). New York, NY: Basic Books.

Besmer, B. (1974). Psychosynthesis: Height psychology–Discovering the self and the Self. *Interpersonal Development*. 4:215-225. Basel, Switzerland: S. Karger.

Boorstein, S. (Ed.).(1996). *Transpersonal Psychology* (2nd ed.). Albany, NY: SUNY Press.

Brown, M.Y. (2004). *The unfolding self: The practice of psychosynthesis*.

New York, NY: Helios Press.

Crampton, M. (1981). Psychosynthesis. In Corsini,R. (ed.) *Handbook of innovative psychotherapies*. (pp.709-723). New York, NY: J. Wiley and Sons.

Firman, J. & Gila, A. (2002). *Psychosynthesis: A psychology of the spirit*. Albany: NY: SUNY Press.

Goleman, D. (1977). *The varieties of the meditative experience*. New York, NY: E.P. Dutton.

Hardy, J. (1987). *A Psychology with a soul: Psychosynthesis in evolutionary context*. New York, NY:Rutledge & Kegan Paul Ltd.

Jung, C.G. (1938). *The basic writings of C.G. Jung*. New Haven, Ct: Yale University Press.

Rowan, J. (1990). *Subpersonalities: The people inside us*. New York, NY: Routledge.

Sliker, G. (1992). *Multiple mind: Healing the split in psyche and world*. Boston, MA: Shambhala Publications.

Sutich, A. (1969). Some considerations regarding transpersonal psychology. *Journal of transpersonal psychology*, v.1, 11-20.

Vargiu, J. (1974). Subpersonalities. *Synthesis: The realization of the Self*. V.1, pp.51-90.

Vaughan, F. (1980). Transpersonal psychotherapy: Context, content and process. In Walsh, R. & Vaughan, F. *Beyond Ego: Transpersonal dimensions in psychology* (pp182-189). Los Angeles: J.P.Tarcher, Inc.

Walsh, R. & Vaughan, F. (eds.). (1993). *Paths beyond ego*. New York, NY: Penguin /Putnam, Inc.

Whitmore, D. (2004) *Psychosynthesis coaching in action*. Thousand Oaks, CA: Sage Publications.

Wilber, K. (1982). *The Atman project: A transpersonal view of human development*. Wheaton, IL: The Theosophical Publishing House.

Wilber, K. (1983). *Eye to eye: The quest for a new paradigm*. Garden City, NY: Anchor Press/Doubleday.

Yeomans, T. (2004). *The embodied soul: Spirituality in the twenty-first century*. Association for the Advancement of Psychosynthesis.

Questions for a Traveler

There is a plain, wooden door,

a name carved deeply into it.

The name is yours

but it is not what you call yourself.

It is a curious language,

familiar to tongue but not to mind.

Did you find it as you hiked a forest trail,

life greening in early summer?

Was there a song in the back of your throat

as you climbed up the hillside,

a flush of sunlight washing through your eyes,

the entry in front of you?

Would you simply open it,

or knock first, standing

in the middle of everything, of nothing,

wind whispering high in the leaves?

Open. Your breath will catch

in a light you never imagined,

like walking inside the daytime sky,

stars scattered inside you.

—Paula Sayword

Chapter 8

Seeing Through Separation & Embracing Unity: Harnessing Contentless Awareness for Change in Coaching Dialogues

by Barbara Veale Smith

Introduction

Can you imagine what it would have been like if you were raised during the time when people believed the earth was flat, and then discovered that it was round? It wasn't that circular shapes were trending and it was time to change, as when a new style arrives. It just wasn't true that the earth was flat. Everyone knows that now. It's so simple to see.

In this chapter, I write of another simple truth. We are not separate from one another and we are not separate from the earth and all of the created order. There is an inherent oneness that surrounds, holds and lives as, and in its essence is, this world in its manifest form. Our times invite us to see and embrace this truth, so we may live with one another in a new way. By awakening to the universal oneness that is already and always present, we can participate in ushering in the next movement in the planet and humanity's unfolding development.

Psychosynthesis founder Roberto Assagioli (2000) describes the fundamental challenge of humanity in this way: "Feeling intuitively that he is 'one,' and yet finding that he is 'divided unto himself,' he is bewildered and fails to understand either himself or others" (p. 18)[1]. Mapping the constituent components of the human psyche as he understood them (known in psychosynthesis

---

[1] I recognize that Assagioli did not use gender-inclusive language, in his writing more than 50 years ago. However, I chose to keep his original wording intact, when quoting him and trust the reader understands that Assagioli was speaking of the whole of humankind.

as the egg or oval diagram), Assagioli notes that his framework "points the way to liberation" (2000, p. 18). Assagioli observed in 1965 that the human person, in a "blind passionate search for liberty and satisfaction, rebels violently at times, and at times tries to still his inner torment by throwing himself headlong into a life of feverish activity, constant excitement, tempestuous emotion and reckless adventure" (2000, p. 18). Given how much more magnified those tendencies are today, with a whopping 32,846 Federal Trade Commission licensed television and radio broadcast stations in the US (2017); a 24/7 news and entertainment cycle; ubiquitous internet and smart phone use; and a materialistic, celebrity, sexuality saturated, polarized and violent culture; one can only imagine what Assagioli would say on this point today, in the 21st century.

The good news, both as Assagioli clearly knew then, and as we can see now, is that we can come into new relationships with ourselves, one another and creation: ending discrimination, racism, homophobia, misogyny, and war. We can alleviate poverty and halt ecological degradation. As Assagioli wrote, "Let us feel and obey the urge aroused by the great need of healing the serious ills which at present are affecting humanity. Let us realize the contribution we can make to the creation of a new civilization characterized by an harmonious integration and cooperation, pervaded by the spirit of synthesis" (2000, p. 8).

Assagioli envisioned psychosynthesis as a method people could employ to free themselves from psychological and spiritual bonds that prevented them from living lives of joy. His theory and practices had three main aims: to foster "an harmonious inner integration, true Self-realization, and right relationships with others" (2000, p. 18). The subject of this chapter is the fundamental role that contentless awareness plays in these processes: in catalyzing Self-realization and unity consciousness; in helping coaches deepen their presence while in the coaching role; and in supporting the changes for which clients engage a coach.

By way of organization, I am using the five steps of the subpersonality process as a framework for organizing the chapter, in order to underscore the truth that, like a subpersonality, the Self can feel like an independent, autonomous reality, when in truth, Self is transpersonal and universal. As Assagioli indicated, "there are not really two selves, two independent and separate entities. The Self is one; it manifests in different degrees of awareness and self-realization. The reflection appears to be self-existent but has, in reality, no autonomous substantiality. It is, in other words, not a new and different light but a projection of its luminous source." (2000, p. 17) The five step process for working with subpersonalities involves: recognition, acceptance, coordination, integration, and synthesis.

Contentless awareness may be experienced as stillness or silence, unconditional acceptance, and universality; the function of will may be associated with the qualities of movement, expression, and individuality or one's unique humanness. Psychosynthesis as a theory and practice posits I/Self as **both** contentless awareness, **and** the function of will. When aligned with an individual's purpose, psychosynthesis coaching clients can be supported in experiencing "joy, serenity, inner security, a sense of calm power, clear understanding and radiant love" (Assagioli, 2000, p. 48)—not because those are the only qualities that make up the transpersonal or Higher/True Self. Rather, those qualities may be released as a result of direct contact with contentless awareness.[2]

Difficult emotions, repressed memories, and other unconscious negative material, however, may also arise, when one opens to contentless awareness. It as if the pure light of consciousness draws disharmonized energies to Itself, in order to be seen and harmonized. Spiritual teacher Adyashanti speaks of that movement as: Love coming back for all of Itself. (2006, pp. 79-80). In describing what psychosynthesists often refer to as the Higher Self, I am asserting that the transpersonal (as both I/Self, Higher Self and True Self) does not consist only of positive, beautiful qualities and characteristics.

Contentless awareness or the **being dimension**, as the term suggests, just is. It be! It is without judgement and therefore completely and totally accepting in its inherent nature, and is the context and source of all experience, emotion and expression. When our **being** nature is *consciously* brought to bear on human life experiences that are difficult or even tragic, a sense of spacious acceptance may be felt in the wake of that potent meeting. As Martha Crampton noted, however, "It takes time to trust that presence alone is sufficient to profoundly illuminate and heal what needs to evolve" (2009, p. 3).

Recognition
Human Being: Inherent Synthesis Revealed

Clients seeking psychosynthesis coaching services often arrive at the office (or on a phone or video call) with a psychosynthesis coach because something calls them to further life development. A dawning awareness of the need for change arises, either suddenly or over time, which becomes known to the client through an impulse or desire, a thought, feeling, intuitive understanding, sensation, or image. Assagioli (2010) called those the six psychological functions of a person. I refer to that realm of the individual's life as the **human dimension**, which includes all the particular contents of one's life, including the sense of one's **self** or me.

---

[2]On retreats that he leads, spiritual teacher Adyashanti often refers to such positive qualities as the "byproducts" of Self Realization.

Paying **attention** to that impulse to change, the movement arises to contact a coach. **Attention and awareness comprise the being dimension.** This aspect of a human is contentless and conscious, and thus akin to Assagioli's term, "essential Being." (2000, p. 48). It is simply and always aware and accepting, without judgement. Attention is the flash light form of that which is conscious and awareness can be likened to the flood light form of consciousness.

Implications of a False Split: The Problem with Polarizing Human and Being

Many people experience themselves as autonomous human individuals, completely separate from one another, and if they believe in or have a sense of the divine it is often as a distinct reality outside of themselves, that is observing and evaluating. A line from the 1991 Grammy song of the year "From A Distance" typifies this sensibility: 'God is watching us, from a distance.' That sense of separation does hold one's uniqueness (i.e., the **human dimension**), yet also showcases a fundamental mis-identification, in that it generally leaves one feeling lacking or not quite whole, split off from "luminous source" (Assagioli, 2000, p. 17). I am suggesting that this fundamental split is our original primal wounding, and leads to the ongoing experience of emotional, psychological and spiritual suffering.

Split off from a felt sense of one's divine or being nature results in suffering and concomitant attempts to drown, bury, anesthetize, meet or solve the problem of lack. I am not enough as I am, therefore I need more. I am not enough as I am, therefore I need to be better than others. I am not enough as I am, therefore I need something or someone in my life that I don't currently have. Notice that being (i.e., "I am") precedes the feeling of not enough in each sentence. I am missing being-ness. There is not enough being. There is no felt sense of the fullness of being.

Unable to understand that what is felt as missing is actually already and always here, humans try to satisfy the longing to feel whole in a myriad of ways, depending on conditioning. I will use the phrase **ego identification**, not to point to an object called ego, rather to describe the movement that an individual will employ to fill a sense of inner lack, emptiness or division that is at the heart of human suffering. Feeling deficient in some way, the movement of egoic identification may take the form of fixation with work, achievement or physical appearance. Overconsumption of food, drink and excesses in material accumulation; and extremes in the pursuit of a soul mate, perfect partner or in the realm of sexual experience are also ways people may attempt to fill the sense of emptiness. Competition and violence often follow from such mis-identifications.

The sense of lack or inner division may feel temporarily diminished through distraction. Television, internet surfing, drugs, alcohol, sports, recreation and even spiritual practice can be utilized for that purpose. **It is possible, however, to discover that the apparent disconnection from original Source creates an inner longing that cannot be satisfied by anything other than the recognition that the disconnection has never actually taken place.** This discovery is not a coming together of two parts, rather a clear seeing of the synthesis that has already and always been. I/Self is revealed to be none other than Source Itself, expressing in an infinite number of unique, individual ways.

It's as if Beingness has decided that every day is Halloween and Beingness is simultaneously dressing up as all of humanity and the entire created order. Egoic identification is the mask of separation that an individual unknowingly wears, until the inherent unity of our Being is revealed.

The human dimension and the being dimension are already synthesized. They co-exist simultaneously. However, because our being nature is subtle and invisible to the eye, it can easily go unnoticed. The contents of consciousness are more like the fireworks in an evening sky, and as such can absorb all of one's attention. Sometimes there is beauty, sparkling light, and delight; other times the fireworks can be incredibly loud, even frightening, or simply just a "dud." Invited to attend to attention or awareness itself, that unseen reality can become known, felt as a palpable sense of infinite possibility. With recognition of contentless awareness, now the canvas of the evening sky is in view, too: life is open, available and completely unlimited.

Acceptance in the Coaching Framework

Properly screened coaching clients may likely be on a path of spiritual awakening or in need of what Assagioli called "spiritual psychosynthesis" in that their development is unfolding along a "progressive" (2000, p. 48) framework. Perhaps a juncture has been reached such that one's job is no longer satisfying, or perhaps a realization stirs that one's work has never satisfied. Maybe one's relationships, typical enjoyments and hobbies are stagnant and a movement to discover what is underneath the lack of vital energy arises.

Those movements are in contrast to individuals that might need psychotherapy services. Assagioli writes, "the psychological symptoms of ordinary patients have generally a regressive character. These patients have not been able to accomplish some of the necessary inner and outer adjustments that constitute the normal development of the personality" (2000, p. 48). He goes on to say, "the contrasting, partly undeveloped, uncoordinated conscious and unconscious trends and functions have to be harmonized and integrated in a personal

85

psychosynthesis" (2000, p. 49).

In my coaching practice, after screening and initial intake, our conversation begins with exchanging greetings and the kind of chat that might be expected in a professional engagement. And then I offer a short bit of guidance. I invite clients (and I invite you, the reader, to follow along as well, if you are so inclined) to take some deep breaths, and feel the body supported by the chair or whatever it is one is sitting upon.

I continue, "Notice the space around you in whatever room or setting you're in. Notice the space in your lungs, as you breath. Become aware of whatever sensations are present in your body, whatever thoughts or feelings are arising and falling away in this moment." I pause. Then continue, "Now notice That aspect of you, that is aware of all that you experience. Notice that your awareness is simply aware and accepting. It's a spacious, alive, open capacity to perceive everything. It does not have content, itself. Yet it is not empty. Rather, it is full: of all possibility, full of every potential action, feeling, impulse, thought and image. Notice that all that is arising within and around you right now is intimately, nonjudgmentally appearing to your awareness. We'll rest in That together now. When you're moved to, feel free to share what it is that you'd like to bring forward in today's session." We drop in. Together. Into the space of silent, contentless awareness.

We rest into the space where no division exists. Before one word is spoken, before any dream or ideal is uttered, before any experience of inner or outer difficulty, challenge or suffering is recounted, before that which wants to be changed is described, we rest in and as the changeless, as wholeness, as contentment. The potency of resting together in presence in this way is extraordinary. If you have done this exercise while reading along, just notice this in yourself.

Through the functional capacity of I/Self known as will, we return to the felt sense of contentless awareness many times during the coaching conversation, doing so in an engaged, yet gentle manner. The tenor of the coaching conversation is not one of inviting the client to go out and search, as on a scuba diving mission or archeological excavation. Rather, questions such as "What wants to be made known to you?" or "What wants to be revealed?" are employed.

What is the value of such an approach? What is the value of employing the function of I/Self that is will to rest into That—which is aware of all content, but which itself is contentless?

Discovering that there is an aspect of yourself that holds and intimately witnesses, accepts and welcomes all that is present within and around you is nothing short of revolutionary. Becoming aware on a moment to moment basis that an unconditionally accepting reality is meeting and holding you, as you know yourself through the contents of your life—especially all that is challenging, disconcerting or calling for change—is to participate in an ongoing revolution that births, supports and celebrates Life in all its myriad forms and disguises.

Beginning and continuing in this way, therefore, the client shows up as present as possible, having been invited to attend to what is present (content) and to attend to presence itself (contentless awareness). And in so doing, I invite myself to settle, to trust, and to know that the coaching session is held in something greater than my professional skill set and personality. And it invites and honors all that will unfold through my particular professional skill set and personality. Both/And. Presence deepens.

Contentless awareness is not separate from all arising content, nor does it have opinions or judgements about content. Contentless awareness pushes nothing away, nor draws anything to Itself. It is Unconditional. It simply Is. And when considered, noticed, felt, or sensed as Itself, the experience of a something that is almost nothing—a no thing—becomes palpable, available, ever present. Sometimes suddenly, and sometimes over time, this subtle **being dimension** awakens as vibrant, alive and accessible. The more deeply a coach accesses and inhabits the presence of being so too, the greater the facility for transmitting and inviting forward the felt experience of spacious, nonjudgmental presence in the client and in the coach/client relationship.

The Practice of Identification/Disidentification/Self Identification

The psychosynthesis practice of Identification, Disidentification and Self Identification warrants particular attention within this coaching framework. The psychosynthesis coach assists the client to identify the nature of the content that has arisen, to disidentify from that content and Self Identify by helping the client to become conscious of contentless awareness and of the nonjudgmental, accepting relationship of contentless awareness to all content. The practice depends on one's ability to recognize that a contracted or conditioned aspect of oneself has come forward and been identified with, in a sense "hijacking" the free and aware "I" that clients gradually come to know as their adult or true Self. The practice also depends on one's ability to access something outside of the contracted, conditioned pre-personal or lower unconscious material, subpersonality or experience of wounding that has temporarily (and/or in an ongoing manner) arisen.

Keith Hackwood, in his address at the 2016 International Psychosynthesis conference in Taormina, Italy, noted his appreciation of A. H. Almaas' understanding of disidentification. "Many people think that disidentification is an activity: 'I see my identification, and I do something to it—I disidentify. In the same way that I identify, I can disidentify.' **But this is not the case. Identification is an activity, and true disidentification is the absence of that activity"** (2016). In other words, realization of contentless awareness, as the very ground of one's nature, roots one in the lived experience of That which is always present as Presence Itself. It is the continual coming home to That which is contentless, ever present and welcoming of all of the human condition. In the Taoist conception, this incredibly subtle and profound shift is spoken of as wu-wei, or non-doing. It is why, so often, awakening is spoken of as a remembering, a coming home, a resting into, rather than as an accomplishment of one's separate, individuated egoic function.

Coordination
Case Study: Angela

A mother of four children, caring for her aging parents and working full time as an educator, came for coaching so that she could "increase her capacity." Her nervous system was on overload and she was not sleeping well. She had studied mindfulness and knew a variety of wellness practices that she incorporated on an ongoing basis, however, she didn't feel she was able to deal with her very full life in a way that was satisfactory. She wanted more. Angela wished to show up for herself, her family members, coworkers and her students as more available and present. Together we accessed spacious, contentless awareness throughout our coaching sessions, while discussing other specifics of her work and family life. The client found the practice of resourcing herself in the **being dimension** to be extremely valuable and chose several touchstones to remind and root herself in contentless awareness, when in the midst of her busy days at her job and at home.

At her job, Angela worked with elementary aged students in specialized reading groups and one on one situations, and was also responsible for a great deal of record keeping, post student interactions. The work with the students was fulfilling, however, the volume of charting and administrative tasks required to track the students' growth often left her weary. In order to access the peace-filled, accepting nature of contentless awareness while she was involved in her student write ups and administrative work, the client chose to pause while beginning each student's paperwork. She would first call to mind the unique child and his or her progress and remaining challenges. As she wrote her notes, if she became stressed and time pressured, she would pause and notice the space between the words she was writing, and the space between each sentence.

The white space on the page became a tangible reminder of the nature of contentless, being based awareness. She would draw strength from this aspect of herself, that in our coaching sessions she had come to experience as always present, and allow it to fortify her for the remainder of her work in that period of time. If she became overwhelmed during the day, she would open her attention to the space in the classroom, the space between herself and a student, the space between her hand and the door handle as she moved in and out of the class or school building. The practice of attending to space itself, as a touchstone to access contentless awareness, felt nurturing and supportive.

In a similar way, I invited Angela to choose a place in her home where she could practice grounding herself in being. She said that on the window sill in front of the kitchen sink, she had a number of items that were special to her: a photo of a beloved relative, a symbol from her religious tradition and usually an object of beauty (such as some flowers or a special stone she had picked up on a walk in nature). When she was with her family, Angela often found herself in front of the kitchen sink. She began to utilize meal preparation or clean up time to rejuvenate herself, by remembering the dimension of being which we accessed together in our coaching conversations and which she came to see surrounded and permeated her. The objects on the kitchen sink began to serve as ongoing reminders of what Angela most deeply valued.

Over time, as she more frequently connected that spot in her home to the felt sense of unconditionally accepting, contentless awareness, she learned to rest more deeply into that. She was not always successful in remembering to access the being dimension, however, she came to see that even those apparent failures and her frustrations were held in being, even when she was not conscious of it.

The ability to nurture herself by resting in being **in the midst of her busy work and family life** allowed Angela to experience the space of unconditional acceptance and peace, more and more frequently. Prior to our coaching engagement, she had associated unconditional acceptance with quiet moments in church or in nature, or from time to time in particular relationships. Her sense of peace most often arose when she had accomplished her professional or family tasks well and completely enough, to feel like she could relax. Recognizing and immersing into a space that Angela came to know as always present, became a kind of 'non-doing' or recognition of this subtle, ever present unseen realm that allowed her to feel she had "more capacity" for her life on an ongoing basis, as was her stated intention for the coaching work.

Integration

Deepening Your Coaching Presence: Fertilizing the Being Dimension

The ever present presence of contentless awareness—which is completely outside of time and can only be experienced now, and which in its essential nature is effortlessness itself—paradoxically can take time and effort to recognize as your authentic nature, I/Self or "True Self" (Assagioli, 2000). When recognized, it can be fertilized. You cannot will its growth within, however, steps can be taken to invite it more prominently into consciousness, through your unique human expression. Try the following exercise as an example of such practice:

+ Sit quietly, with your eyes open or closed, and notice what is happening within and around you. Perhaps there are noises arising: birds chirping, the sound of the wind, the hum of a fan. Maybe a particular aroma is in the air: the scent of roses opening in a nearby vase or the laundry detergent from the basket of clothing you just took out of the washer. Perhaps you feel a sensation like warmth or discomfort, or feelings such as joy, sadness or delight. You may notice thoughts moving quickly through your 'mind's eye'. As you notice all that is happening within and around you, you are invited to look from the perspective of the contentless awareness itself. That—that is clear, awake to, aware of—all the phenomena that are present, including you in all your uniqueness. You may notice all manner of phenomena. More importantly, notice the space, the presence, the awareness that is contentless and that simply notices. Note that thoughts simply arise out of, and fall back into, that aware space. Notice feelings, sensations and images that arise, as you sit. Notice if the content falls away or remains. Notice if the noticing is ever present.

+ The part of you that is noticing is the aware, contentless space. Rest in and as That.

+ Can you sense the complete openness, and the complete absence of any judgment, opinion, or belief within That? As you sit and notice, can you sense the inherent peace or contentment that is the actual nature of contentless awareness, even if the contents that are appearing within the space of contentless awareness are difficult or turbulent?

What would it be like to inhabit the space of contentless awareness more and more fully, while you were in your coaching role? What might be the quality of your coaching conversations, if you could see that an aspect of yourself never experiences judgement about how the session is going, nor does it worry about what question or direction to choose next—even if your mind gets caught up in all manner of content?

+ Practice resting in this way when you are not functioning as a coach. The more familiar and comfortable it becomes to drop into the space of contentless awareness, the more easy it will become to do so when you are in your coaching role.

As you continue to rest as and within contentless awareness, you may notice a dialogue taking place, between one aspect of your mind and other arising thoughts, or even perhaps between several different parts of yourself. In psychosynthesis, the parts of you that show up on an ongoing basis having particular characteristics, are referred to as subpersonalities—meaning they are aspects of our larger personality that may express autonomously (if not made conscious).

For example, a person may recognize and at times, completely identify with, a critical aspect of themselves that could be called "the judge." Another common subpersonality is a youthful aspect, that could be called one's "inner child." That childlike part of a person could take on characteristics that were of value in the family of origin such as being "the responsible one" or "the good girl" or "good boy." People may derive their sense of identity from such autonomous subpersonalities or more generally, the 'voices' that they hear 'thinking out loud' in their heads. Those identities can vary, depending on what thoughts are more prominent at any given time. For example, you may feel like you're a really great coach because you are serving your clients well at one moment, and feel deficient and unworthy at other moments.

In addition, some thoughts may seem truer to you than others. The stronger you feel their truth, the more you are likely to strongly assert those thoughts when relating to other people. If the coaching methods you were taught, for example, seem better to you than other coaching modalities, you may feel some sense of inflation or a "better than" attitude within you when you are spending time with other coaches that have different training.

If you look closely, you may see that your thoughts seem true because of the way you were taught by someone whose opinion, training and expertise you valued. If you had been exposed to other coaching modalities and techniques, you might have a different set of thoughts arise within you. In that sense, we can say that there is some "conditioning" within each person, that is dependent on the family, culture or religion in which they were raised; the education they've received; or the neighborhood, state, and the country in which they were born. If we liken this conditioning to a computer, it's like everyone has their own unique "operating system" that is perpetually running, sometimes in the foreground (consciously), and sometimes in the background (subconsciously). Many people take their "operating system" to be true and when they do so, judgment, resistance, and anger can arise between human beings who operate from different systems. Is it any wonder that negative states—magnified as poverty, war, and ecological degradation—are present in the measure that they are on the planet as a whole?

You may be wondering, what's the alternative? Here are some pointers to help you engage and deepen your connection to contentless awareness (each a brief excursion into the **being dimension**) which can be traversed in a sequence, as follows.

1.) Sit quietly now for a few minutes, with your eyes open or closed. As before, rest as the wholeness that is contentless awareness.

2.) Can you sense how within you (and can you imagine that within everyone) there is an actual reality, a something that's like a nothing: within which every mistake, wrong doing and reprehensible or even evil action that you believe you or others have ever committed or witnessed disappears? Although contentless awareness notes all the stories and interpretations that occur to your mind or that arise in the world of phenomena, in contentless awareness itself, there is no story or interpretation about anything. When you perceive the world through and as contentless awareness, judgement falls away and at the absolute level, there is no wrong or right. There is only what is. The great poet Rumi, said it this way:

Out beyond ideas of wrongdoing
and rightdoing there is a field.
I'll meet you there.
When the soul lies down in that grass.
The world is too full to talk about.
Ideas, language, even the phrase each other
doesn't make any sense (translation by Coleman Barks, 2003).

3.) The memory of difficult events that occurred may remain within your unique human expression. Contentless awareness is witness to memories. It also witnesses any images, dreams or fantasies you have about what might happen later today, tomorrow or years from now in the future.

4.) Yet contentless awareness itself can't be experienced in the past or future. It lives now. It is now. It is always present. It is not beginning or ending, coming or going. It is eternal: outside of and inclusive of time.

5.) Can you imagine the potency of inhabiting contentless awareness as your everyday and ongoing identity, while serving as a coach and in every other aspect of your life? Can you feel that all your ideas of yourself , as a great coach, as one who made mistakes in the past, as one who is not enough, simply fall away in the space of pure contentless awareness?

6.) What possibilities live for you in your role of coach, from that ever present, accepting reality?

7.) With a partner, look at one another. Allow yourself to feel the font of unconditionally accepting energy, emanating from both your eyes and the other person's eyes. As you continue to gaze into each other's eyes, try putting a hand out and sensing where the contentless awareness that you experience ends, and where the contentless awareness that is present in the other person begins. Is there any boundary?

8.) Open your attention and feel the space of contentless awareness all around you. Notice that you can feel awareness to the left and right side of you, to the back and front of you, on top of and below you, and inside and outside of you. Consider this question. Is contentless awareness inside of you? Or are you inside of it? Is it both/and? Why does it matter?

9.) What is it like to feel the truth that the aware, awake contentless space has no boundary, and therefore is a place of unity in and out of which every human person and all of the created order exist? Is that not a form of universal peace, an ultimate reality or "Supreme Synthesis" (Assagioli, 2000, p. 27) that already and always simply exists?

10.) What can you imagine might be possible if you rested in that space of presence, if you were having a disagreement with another person?

11.) Can you feel that within you (and imagine that within all others) there is an experiential reality, an alive presence, that is completely at peace and in harmony with the totality of all existence, as it is right now? What would it be like to be moved to action—on behalf of the great injustices and issues of our day that call for change—as and from that place of aliveness?

Synthesis & Conclusion:

It is necessary to clarify that "essential Being" (Assagioli, 2000, p. 48) is not an object nor a state of consciousness that can be obtained. **An individual cannot will its knowing.** Nor can It be possessed. It is the ultimate Subject: consciousness Itself, to which and within which all objects of consciousness are registered. It can reveal Itself more and more fully, however, and with dedication, devotion and practice—or **willingness**—it can be embodied. Two essential movements that encourage realization are: resting in and as one's being nature, both on a moment to moment basis in the context of one's unique life situation and in the context of silent sitting practice (often referred to as meditation) and inquiry using a phrase such as 'Who or what is aware?' Such a question can elicit the felt, palpable experience of unitive consciousness in which one can come to know oneself as both an individual expression of life and as the One Life Itself.

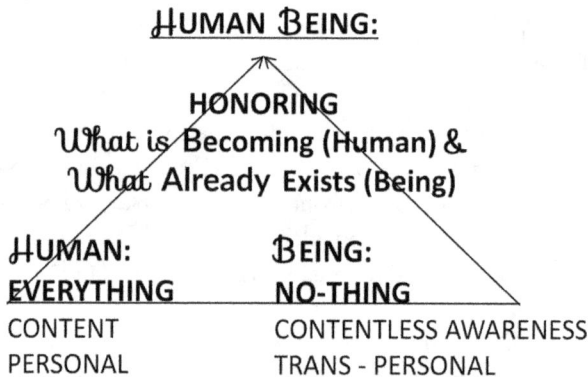

HUMAN BEING:

HONORING
What is Becoming (Human) &
What Already Exists (Being)

HUMAN:	BEING:
EVERYTHING	NO-THING
CONTENT	CONTENTLESS AWARENESS
PERSONAL	TRANS - PERSONAL

As these practices are employed, the realization may unfold that there is only awake, contentless awareness—which is Itself across all of the unique forms of life (i.e., it is transpersonal and universal) and It takes the forms of all of the unique aspects of the created order, including the experience of personal will, as it is sensed within a human being. **In other words, the personal and** the transpersonal are One, expressing simultaneously as each unique aspect of life Itself.

Assagioli affirms this underlying unbounded, reality: "The Transpersonal Self of each is in intimate union with the Transpersonal Self of all other individuals, however unconscious they may be of this. All Transpersonal Selves can be considered as 'points' within the Universal Self." (2010, p. 192). The 'points' or dots of our unique and varied expressions of humanity and creation are connected through and as contentless awareness. It is the universal common denominator linking all expressions of humanity and creation through and as the One.

By virtue of their training, interests and experience, psychosynthesis coaches are uniquely poised to make significant contributions in support of humanity's awakening to unity consciousness. Zen master Thich Nhat Hahn writes: "If we transform our individual consciousness, we begin the process of changing the collective consciousness. Transforming the world's consciousness is not possible without personal change. The collective is made of the individual, and the individual is made of the collective, and each and every individual has a direct effect on the collective consciousness" (2003, p. 56).

Psychosynthesis coaches and all others drawn to this vital work are invited to deeply know the ultimate, already existing "Supreme Synthesis" (Assagioli, 2000, p. 27), and to participate in the co-creation of that synthesis in the manifest realm, "uniting all beings with each other... through links of love." (Assagioli, 2000, p. 27). The moment to begin, or to begin anew, is now.

References

Adyashanti. (2006). *Emptiness dancing* (second edition). Boulder, CO: Sounds True.

Adyashanti. (2012). *The way of liberation.* Retrieved from:
https://d1c742hwzmv7ke.cloudfront.net/library/The_Way_of_Liberation_Ebook.pdf.

Assagioli, R. (2000). *Psychosynthesis: A collection of basic writings.* Amherst, MA: Synthesis Center Inc.

Assagioli, R. (2010). *The act of will.* Amherst, MA: Synthesis Center Press.

Barks, C. (2003). *Rumi: The book of love: Poems of ecstasy and longing.* New York: HarperCollins.

Crampton, M. (2009). *The synchronicity practice.* Retrieved from: https://www.synthesiscenter.org/articles/synchronicity practice.pdf.

Federal Trade Commission. (2017). *News.* Retrieved from: https://apps.fcc.gov/edocs_public/attachmatch/DOC-344256A1.pdf.

Hackwood, K. (2016). *The moisture of compassion – psychosynthesis, mindfulness & the luminosity of mind.* Retrieved from: http://www.keithhackwood.com/articles/psychosynthesis-for-the-future-international-congress-taormina-atahotel-giardini-naxos-saturday-4th-june-2016.

Hahn, T. (2003). *Creating true peace: Ending violence in yourself, your family, your community and the world.* New York: Atria Paperback, A Division of Simon & Schuster.

Kelly, L. (2015). *Shift into freedom.* [Audio CD] Boulder, CO: Sounds True.

Chapter 9

Practicing the Call of Self-Acceptance: Acting Out Your Lovers and Demons

by James Rogers

I was driving from my home in the Hudson Valley, New York to what is known as the north country near the Canadian border. I had left particularly early to start a work assignment by 10:00 am. These are the golden hours for me. I love to start driving in the darkness, to watch the sun streak the night sky. The unfolding of the earth is a time of peace and centeredness for me. But I was tight that morning. Confronting a recurring, painful habit filled me with dread and anxiety. Although, "confronting" may not even be the right word. Co-existing with dread and anxiety was a regular enough occurrence that it seemed fated or infused with truth—"the way things were."

The phone rang. I was expecting the call. My teacher, mentor and dear friend had been persistent enough with texts and e-mails and phone calls that I was able to quiet the voice of the Isolationist subpersonality long enough to agree to a phone call. (That's been a powerful "action" sub for me—one of the voices that keeps me away from people regardless of how many times I learn the truth of my Self: connection soothes and heals and centers).

"How ya doing?"
"Ugh"
"No really. Speak. Use your words." She said playfully. "How are you doing"?
"Not good. I cannot believe I am in the same place I always am and no matter how much I think I have changed, I haven't"

For the last 3 months I had not put a single word to the page or read a single background article as I was preparing to teach a workshop of my own design and original thought. The deadline (workshop day) was fast approaching.

97

Yes, the pattern was repeating. I was gripped by procrastination again. It was awful. I explained this all in a torrent.

> "I cannot seem to manifest anything. I have had a lifetime of great ideas, great interests and great passions but nothing ever gets produced. No ideas ever come into being. Nothing ever gets born!!"

> "What if you accepted that's the way you are? What if you accepted this is how you work? What if you always wait to the last minute and that's the way things get done for you?"

And just like that, the grip loosened and I was free, for the time being. Procrastination has not changed and I will—even as I write this—continue to look for strategies to make my processes more fluid. That is just what is. My relationship to the procrastination however, this was the question now before me. The voices my procrastinating behavior invited to the forefront of my everyday life were the things pulling me under. How the critical voices and subpersonalities came to answer the challenges of my life is of constant interest to me. But developing a practice to invite other loving and compassionate "me-s" to answer those challenges first and with greater visibility, was something I needed to cultivate. How then to invite or invoke the great voice of self acceptance, of self-love and compassion?

A friend who watched my self-punishment routine one time said, "Don't fire the second arrow." Then I read about the Buddha's words, and I am paraphrasing, "When you are wounded, don't fire the second arrow into your own heart." That made so much sense. It was before I studied a word of psychosynthesis (referred to at times herein as "PS") but I knew that in response to difficulty, there emerged a harsh critic who caused a much deeper wound than the "problem" at hand. This voice, the thing I would come to know as a powerful subpersonality, was insidious for so many reasons. The first was that I had shared space with it in my head for so long it seemed like "me". The second was that the voice, however nefarious, had shown up to help, to kick me in the ass and produce "results". In fact, he or it produced a level of misery that served to further entrench the practical problem of procrastination. If I took on a project or assignment, I would be assailed by the critic. So why bother starting?

Who is Doing the Talking?

In the first hour of the first day of any psychosynthesis education, the question of who is talking becomes the one to answer. And for me, I did not even know it was a question that existed in the universe. Such a simple question, yet so completely full of everything I would ever come to learn about psychosynthesis practice. It was the morning session of my first PS training and about one hour in I had asked a question of our teacher that was a powerful combination of multiple subpersonalities including, "The Guy that Wants to Sound Smart" + "The Guy That Wants to be Self Deprecating to Invite Sympathy" + "The Guy That Wants the Attention but Really Doesn't but Really Does". My question sounded exactly like this: "blah, blah, blah, blah blah and blah." Our teacher said, "I will answer that but first I want to know who is doing the talking right now?"' In the bright, beautiful light of her query, I was left both exposed and grounded. I was vulnerable but free of whatever subpersonality had taken all my time and attention and emotional band width. In the (temporary) absence of powerful subpersonalities, I was truly present. It was that easy.

Here then began the practice of identifying subpersonalities. After the subpersonality was named and seen, disidentification was mostly a natural outcome. Sometimes the disidentification process needed some help. It might be that a guide could help me try on another voice that was the polar opposite of what I was hearing in my head. Or maybe a guide could direct me to a place in my body, to let my sensations have a say. I could be invited by a guide to drop the thinking altogether and do something creative. It all ends up in the same place. The very process of accessing new ways of being, of calling on different parts of our human experience, demonstrated and demonstrates that there is "One Who Calls". The **call of Self** indeed may resonate mostly as **the** transpersonal phenomenon, and the greatest of blessings. But the everyday, even pedestrian calling of the Self, is where I want to practice now. Maybe I could hit upon a word or a mantra or physical act or Bat Signal to invite in other powerful subpersonalities, voices of love and acceptance. Its an invocation of content. I want a voice to say something even as I subscribe to the theory that there is a larger goal of content-less awareness. That may be the brass ring, but in the meantime I want softer sounds and kinder touches. There are endless ways to get there and each one will dissolve in time and give rise to others as needs change and the constant process of evolving, continues to... well, evolve.

Sketching Subpersonalities in Exaggerated Relief: Writing Your Own B-Movie.

To really be able to see the critic that was causing so much distress in the context of my procrastinating behaviors, I wanted to give "him" a life. I wanted to animate the voice by calling him out, by asking him to speak out loud. If I could become him or a terribly exaggerated version of him, I could, through a process of play, see him in a way that would distinguish his words from the truth of the I. And if that was possible, then other characters—loving angels, unconditionally loving parents, super wise gurus, gods and goddesses—could also be conjured. With a cast of characters, I could generate more choice points. I could ask for a hug before the arrow was removed from its quiver. What a thing! I had given hugs to my children, to my wife, to my siblings. I had never asked me to give one to me.

Certain non-classical acting techniques ask performers to fully inhabit their characters. I think Robert Deniro deliberately gained 60 pounds for his role in *Raging Bull*. Even though I have not done much acting in my life, I was always drawn to it. I chose a career, first as a trial attorney, that required some pitch perfect acting. I also worked for politicians and engaged the political process as a high-ranking government official, which at its core, required highly scripted engagements designed to over-simplify talking points that most resonated with voters. In those super-serious realms (where politicians like to make one believe the stakes are life and death), there is not much fun or playfulness to the process. But writing a script for a villain in a B-Movie or putting the words in the hero's mouth? Now we are talking.

B movies are the low budget, pulp or cult classics that are short on complexity, detail and nuance. To move the story along, the characters, particularly the villains, are one dimensional exaggerations, assigned awful lines and unbelievable behaviors. For me, this is a pretty close description of the most notorious of my inner critics. There is no budget in the B Movie or talent in the production team to draw characters that resemble actual people with their layers and complications and shades of gray. Likewise, my critic has a single job to do. No time for nuance and definitely no time for understanding. In the case of procrastination, one of my characters has some very unkind things to say.

So let's write the script and act out the parts. In this exercise, we will create a villain and a hero, a devil and an angel. Let's draw them almost one dimensionally. Let's call on our creative Imagination psychological function and have fun. There is no need for accuracy or truth. These are your characters and they are only for today. Or for as long as they are useful to you. When the scripts are finished, let's act them out. This can be done alone, but it might be more fun in groups. Up to you.

Take out some paper and think of an obstacle, a recent event, something you have been trying to accomplish or a difficult time. Anything really where you might have been or currently are struggling. It does not have to be deep. It does not have to be current or tremendously troubling. We just want to (gently) let the bad genie out of the bottle. Got it? Ok. Now let's write his or her or its script and its background and character development.

When I did this for myself, I needed to know:

What he looked like
How he dressed
How he moved
Where he was from

Next thing I wanted to do was amp it up. Give it some character, maybe some teeth and wild hair and some kind of a weapon. Lastly, I wrote down his words: the words that would come from his mouth up on the big screen.

After I listened to the voice first, the things he was telling me, the character began to take shape. For a lot of people, it is someone they know. For many it could be a parent. But the point of this exercise is to go beyond what you know. Develop a bad character. When you're finished, it's time to share. You might not want to act it out. Maybe your sense of reserve is geared that way or maybe it is too much to try. I encourage you to act out even a little bit of the script. Take it out of your head. Show it to other people. Play with it.

Here is a portion of the script of my critic, the villain I drew in this particular exercise. He is a middle-aged street thug from Bensonhurst, Brooklyn. He wears a graying T-shirt, a cheap gold chain and has a cigarette dangling from his lips. He takes a long drag and punctuates his statements by pointing the smoldering cigarette. His name is Mr. Fugghetaboutit and here, in part is what he said to me:

Jimmy, Jimmy. You sit there whining like a little baby. Like a **stunad**. All you say is "I can't do it. I can't do nothing." Cry, cry, cry all day long. That's not the weird part Jimmy. The weird part is that you thought you could do it in the first place when everybody KNOWS you would never do it. The whole neighborhood knows. Of course you wouldn't. Who were you fooling? You always was this way and you always will be. So just face facts.

It was great to bring Mr. Fugghetaboutit out into the open. It was great to act him out in front of some workshop participants. His shallow cruelty was a site to behold. And like any other B Movie character, I had to laugh when I was done. What a relief to see him in the light of day. Out of my head, onto the page and onto the makeshift stage.

Enter the Heroes and the Angels

The same thought exercises can give us a view into the shapes and sounds of our most loving and compassionate voices, the ones who accept us for who we are, like my teacher did for me on that early morning drive. I responded to her invitation to accept myself. But there was more than just an invitation. Her suggestion to me was also grounded in the reality that she already accepted me, she already loved me.

This realization made me reflect on what grows in the light of presence. PS students learn something that they can master right away. They learn to be present or to try to invite in presence or set an intention of being present. This was taught to me as step one in creating a holding environment. Here is where the magic happens. Here is where the **collective transpersonal** flows to a time and place of the guide's choosing. Once the "incantation" of presence is uttered, the holding environment is set. And for everyone who has had this experience, who has tuned their hearts and minds to the desire to be truly present for anyone you may coach or guide, you know that the holding that is created is beyond the sphere of thought or anything that we have come to know as existing exclusively in the realm of the personal.

It is true that my Teacher loved me as a dear student and friend she had come to know. It is also true that she had set an intention to be present. She invited the magic of presence into our conversation and in so doing the transpersonal switch had been flipped. As we draw, then cultivate, then learn to invoke our loving protectors, we do so in the light of presence. The love that will be carried forth is true love based both on the loving kindness these caretakers have for us and the love that is invited forth from the transpersonal place it always dwells.

One of the thought exercises I would do to get some perspective on the vast difference in the compassion I can demonstrate for others as compared to the compassion I bring to myself was to picture myself sitting on a couch next to a friend who had come to me with a problem. I doubt I would berate him. I doubt I would snicker or judge or look down on him. I have been in that position, so I know that I would offer kind words, a gentle touch, perhaps an embrace. I would make sure that I said and did the kind of things that would make him feel good. What are friends for?

Each of us has our own understanding as to why we are harder on ourselves than we are with other people. Exploring that understanding is its own journey and it may be a lifelong project. What I wanted to know for myself was not the why but the look and smell, feel and sound of either my most loving self, most compassionate me or other unifying center that could bring the most love in a challenging time. As we conjure a loving voice now, it may be that we are calling upon the best version of ourselves (that understanding friend on the couch) or the image and voice of a kind parent or the special embrace of a mythical character. I asked myself a question. Who is the most loving version of **me**? That is the outline of who I wanted to call forth.

In a recent workshop, the most loving characters came from so many different places. While, each participant had a different approach, each had a ready answer. It didn't require much thought. Powers beyond thinking were at play. One woman instantly thought of her father and was visibly moved when that clarity dawned on her. Another participant mentioned a composite character she had brought to her imagination a long time before, a loving auntie that she regularly asked for help. She told the group that she saw a painting in an antique shop one day and stopped dead in her tracks: "That's my auntie", she said and there she was, just as she always pictured her. Still others discussed the most at-peace versions of themselves, images and feelings drawn just from the personal realm with no need to look further.

Again, it's worthwhile here to get out some paper and describe this loving voice, this powerful and positive presence. We can give it a name. We can give it a shape, and appearance. What's most important now, once you have identified this presence in your life, is to give it words. Let's write the script. In contrast to the critical voices we wrote for in the last part of the exercise, this script is no laughing matter. These are words worth seeing on paper and brought to life on a makeshift stage not so they can be distinguished or disidentified from, but so that they can be animated and ready to come when called. Take a moment now to imagine it is you entering the living room, sitting on the couch and asking for help. We write now for the One who responds. How does she act? How does she move? What does she say?

When I wrote out my answer to this exercise, I drew from the dead center of the PS egg. I drew on the personal. I asked myself, "When am I my most loving?" And the answer was clear. My loving voice is called Summer's Dad. I have a two-and-a-half-year-old daughter, Summer. She has curly strawberry blond hair, a bellyful of joy, a sweet spirit and a very adventurous nature. She runs all the time as fast as she can, every time. No matter how many times she falls and gets hurt, the next time she runs, she still runs with abandon. She bangs her head and skins her knees and busts her lip. She runs over grass and gravel and ice and asphalt all at the same speed. When she falls I kneel down and open my arms. I fold her up tight in my arms. I squeeze and encourage her to cry and cry louder so she can shake off the lingering energy. I dry her tears and she is on her way.

Who would I be if I could be Summer's Dad to myself? What if I could fold myself into a deep embrace, if I could ask myself to cry louder, if I could release myself into the care of unconditional love? I cannot say who I would be. This is a new practice for me. I do not have answers. All I know is that by animating this voice and bringing it forth, I will have more choice points. Because now there are at least two options, two voices from which to choose and I just don't think Mr. Fugghedaboutit can withstand the clear, crisp stance and steady hand of Summer's Dad. I invite you to write out these precious words and then act them out for yourself or your group.

Calling Forth, Inviting and Invoking: Incantations of the Loving Arms

Having identified a voice or a presence I wanted in my life, I wanted it to be at the ready. I needed a shorthand or a ritual that captured my current understanding and called upon not just the loving voice but the experience of learning that I could give life to such a voice. The issue of how to recognize when to call on a better angel is something else all together. To exercise a choice point, you have to realize that the voice in your head is acting unkindly. Sometimes I can hardly distinguish the moments of sharp elbows from the moments of greater peace. Patterns on top of patterns in my life can obfuscate the flow of expansion and contraction. One thing I have come to realize is that my body never lies. If I feel physically bad I can be pretty sure there is some unkind tape loop on the reel to reel.

The Latin root of the word invoke means "to call". That is pretty much what I wanted to do. I wanted to develop a shorthand "calling forth", an invocation that had a sense of ritual. Since I was in a transpersonal mood, I also wanted something more mystical. Incantation has, at its root, another Latin phrase meaning to enchant. Within that Latin root is the word **cantare** which could be a chant but can also mean praise and sing. How beautiful! A song that calls forth a strong embrace, a loving word and a kind touch. That is what I was after.

The contours of what you can create as a ritual or shorthand or signal to invoke this love is entirely the product of a personal creative journey. The things I thought of during this exercise as fun categories were: a word or mantra and a movement or action. Again I played in the realm of the personal. What would Summer say to have me show up fully present for her after she fell down? She might just say "help". What physical action would she take to have me step forward? Well, she would probably come right up to me and lift her arms up to be picked up. With this in mind, I forged an incantation. A slight gesture of my arms upward and a soft voice (to myself or out loud) that said "help." If I do this, Summer's Dad will show up for **me**. I am going to get that bear hug and that soothing voice.

It was interesting that as I went through this exercise, it resulted in a mantra of "help". If there was ever a place I wanted major changes in my behavior it was in asking for help. I never did it, yet I was always grateful when I did. I stayed isolated but was always cured by connection. I didn't set out in this exercise to deepen my understanding of connection or to tackle the challenges of isolation. I was out to learn how to choose loving voices. But the journey took me right to the center of what I wanted most which was connection and what I needed to say to get it: "help". This then is the power of psychosynthesis. Things come together. They synthesize. They synthesize in ways you can know and ways you just have to trust are beyond the egg's dotted lines.

I understand I cannot eliminate challenges. I have struggles and obstacles just like everybody else. But I can be curious about the challenges without trying to obliterate them in the white heat of a critical subpersonality. I can choose something else. I can cast a spell, devise an incantation and call forth angels on my shoulder even while the devil is in my ear. My hope is that the playful methods outlined here, to see some of these forces in action, help you a bit in creating more space for more choices and more self-love to be chosen.

So yes, I was free of the critic when I was invited to accept myself during the early morning car ride, but its 4:00 am, and I am still writing and this chapter is already a week overdue. Some things never change but your love is always expanding.

Much Love,
Jim Rogers

Chapter 10

Spiritual Psychosynthesis in Times of Global Crisis

by Alejandro Negrete

Only through an awakening of our deepest souls, only when the sovereignty of the Spirit is recognized and made a reality, will the human race be able to achieve that true power, that secure peace and that divine freedom that is the unconscious goal to which it aspires.
— *Roberto Assagioli*

For me, this direct statement made by Roberto Assagioli gives us a very important perspective that allows us as coaches, not only to better understand Assagioli himself, but also to view psychosynthesis against the backdrop of a deeper spiritual framework. We could say that the final goal of psychosynthesis is to lead us to the gates of the authentic spiritual journey that will allow us to consciously return to the fold of the divine and merge with our Higher Self. As we shall see further on, this may be the ultimate solution to the problem of the global crisis we face as a humanity. In his illuminating book *Transpersonal Development*, Assagioli states that the story of the prodigal son could be used as a metaphor to represent psychosynthesis. In referring to it, he says:

> The personal 'I' comes down from the star, or from the spiritual 'I', in the form of a reflection... The personal 'I' is the prodigal son who has descended to the level of the material world and forgotten his origin, to the point where of his own free will he resorts to all the foolishness he is capable of... and only then feels a longing for his father's house, sets out in search of it and eventually finds it. (Assagioli, 2007, p. 78)

With a view to attenuating the subliminal messages latent within the distortions of our patriarchal language and in an effort to return to a vision of equality between the feminine and the masculine, as I proceed in exploring the symbolism of this story, I will from this point forward, refer to 'the Father' as 'the Parent' and 'the Son' as 'the Child'. If we relate this story to Assagioli's Egg Diagram, 'the Parent' represents the True Self and the child's descent into the 'material world', the process whereby the 'I', or individual consciousness, through identification with the subjective world of the psyche, is separated from the Self. In this process, as the child forgets its origin in the Self, an inner disconnection from the source of happiness, love, and wisdom gradually overtakes it. Eventually, the child's awareness is reduced to the limited field of consciousness described by Assagioli within which the vast majority of the three levels of the unconscious become veiled from its awareness, thereby leaving it in a fragmented and unconscious psychological state.

This wonderful story that symbolically represents both our individual and collective descent into a state of spiritual amnesia, in which we are governed by unconsciousness, is ultimately a powerfully hopeful vision of the possibility of returning to the Self and thereby to a state of wholeness. The story of the prodigal child allegorically describes the spiritual history of humanity; our divine origin, our descent into forgetfulness and our potential awakening once more to who we truly are. Let us therefore explore the stages of this process in the context of the global crisis we are currently facing.

The Collective Crisis and the Sickness of Materialism

Spiritual Psychology and the Perennial Philosophy teach us that what a person manifests outwardly is a reflection of the contents of the psyche. If we apply this principle to the current global crisis, we realize that humanity, as a whole, is currently enacting the tragedy of the prodigal child's inner state of desolation and confusion as it wanders through the foreign lands of fragmentation, mesmerized by countless illusions. It is this inner state of psychological hypnosis, caused by a blind identification with the contents of awareness, that prevents us from realizing our true nature as emanations of the Self.

One of the strongest signatures of our time is the collective sickness of materialism that so much of humanity has fallen into, in practically all spheres of life. Through the modern adaptation of contextualizing science within the framework of validating only what can be observed with the five senses, we have undergone a radical severance from the spiritual domain and the more subtle sciences that transcend the material world. In the process, we have been led inadvertently into an egocentric and pleasure-seeking culture that can all too easily consume us. Through being profoundly absorbed by these materialistic trends, we have forgotten many of the great universal principles that, when lived by, enable us to cultivate a state of integral wellbeing and true happiness, be a force for the good, and thus support the overall health of the collective. We are rapidly becoming a global culture that gives free license to the many base desires and impulses of our lower nature and this fundamentally selfish pursuit of pleasure leads us to perform increasingly destructive acts that do damage to ourselves, to others, and to the earth we live upon.

The prevailing materialistic philosophy of our times has also influenced many spheres of knowledge and has actually been a key factor underlying the development of modern psychology in the west. This has been clearly demonstrated and explored in Sotillos' collection of essays by many of the world's leading Perennialists, *Psychology and the Perennial Philosophy* (2013). In summary, what one discovers is that the very foundation of modern psychology rests on a materialistic point of view. It shows us that the paradigm upon which modern psychology has developed is flawed, in and of itself, because these principles are heavily biased, incomplete, and inevitably produce an imbalanced and psycho-spiritually sick society.

That the fourth force of Transpersonal Psychology (Sutich, 1969) has evolved within modern psychology as a whole is an inspiring testament to the enlightening vision of the pioneers within this field. Yet, there is much within Transpersonal Psychology that is still conditioned by the initial materialistic paradigm, which inevitably limits its capacity to meet humanity's deepest needs. I believe it is therefore necessary to seek out an integral spiritual psychology as free as possible from flawed theories and methods that can provide us with a holistic and objective 'science of the soul.' In my opinion, Assagioli is the one who most clearly lays the foundation for a universal psychology upon which we, as aspirants to reintegration with the Self, can most readily rely. Assagioli studied many of the principles and truths from a variety of spiritual traditions and mystical teachings, distilling the universal essentials within them and integrating them into the framework of Psychosynthesis. Psychosynthesis, then, can be considered a manifestation of the Perennial Wisdom, stripped of any specific religious orientation and presented in a neutral light.

The Path of Danger or the Path of Opportunity

The Chinese character for crisis has a double meaning, firstly, **danger**, and secondly, **opportunity**. If we apply this double meaning to our current collective crisis, from the perspective of the Perennial Wisdom, it means on the one hand, that there is the danger of continuing in our hypnosis of separation and unconsciousness and therefore precipitating our self-destruction. On the other hand, if we seize the opportunity inherent in the crisis, we can use it to awaken from our spiritual amnesia and thereby restore order first to our own psyches, and as a natural consequence, become instruments for wise action in the world, thereby serving to uplift the whole.

In the context of the mythical motif of the prodigal child's separation from its true home that we are inadvertently enmeshed in, many of us are now 'seeking to return to our Parents' home.' In relation to Assagioli's exposition of *The Act of Will* (2010), this return to the source represents the path of opportunity and is a deep manifestation of the Transpersonal Will. I believe we are, in essence, all faced with the choice so succinctly expressed by Hamlet: *"to be or not to be, that is the question."* If we apply this axiom at a spiritual level to the situation we collectively face, we can understand that through the current global crisis, we are being invited to either choose the ascending road of opportunity represented by traversing the path of Self-realization back to our spiritual home, or of allowing ourselves to be swept up by the trends of the culture, give in to our lower nature, and become consumed in psycho-spiritual darkness.

The great mystical traditions of the world tell us that true happiness and fulfillment are our innate birthright because at the spiritual level, we are inseparable from the ultimate reality. The enlightened spiritual teachers of humanity have pointed to the truth that the divine imbues all of creation with its presence and is the all-pervading reality underneath the countless forms it assumes. As applied to human beings, we are reminded that within us is the Higher Self, which is the storehouse of all transpersonal qualities and which in potential, through the profound process of spiritual psychosynthesis, can come to be expressed through us in a unique and individualized way.

Unfortunately, however, although we often do not realize it, we are governed predominantly by the many forces within our middle and lower unconscious, and so live in a state of spiritual blindness, identified with our bodies and the material world as well as the ever-changing thoughts, fantasies, emotions and impulses within us. We are therefore not able to perceive the ever-present reality of the Transpersonal Self with its attendant peace, beauty, and wisdom. Yet, if it is true that all sentient beings wish to be happy and free of suffering, as is emphasized by the Perennial Philosophy, then undertaking the process of Self-realization is innate to our deepest nature. The spiritual longing for wholeness, the universal call of the Self, which has always been present, is now being heard increasingly clearly by many in the face of the current global crisis. For those of us who are fortunate enough to hear the inner call to return to the Self, there is a knowing deep down that this is not only the ultimate medicine our souls need to be healed, but also the true remedy for our collective woes. If our individual and collective suffering can only ultimately be transcended through undergoing the process of spiritual psychosynthesis, our next natural step, both personally and as psychosynthesis coaches, is to ask ourselves how we can accomplish this great task in practical terms.

Many of us who are earnestly seeking wholeness occasionally glimpse the Self within us through transpersonal experiences. These experiences serve the important function of beginning to awaken our consciousness and stimulate our aspiration for reunion with the Self. Yet without a clear map and guidelines to support us on our journey, we can lose our way. Self-realization is fundamentally a process of making fully conscious the three levels of the unconscious as mapped out by Assagioli, transcending our lower nature through a process of purification, and gradually merging with the Higher Self. It is in relation to this process that we will explore the **Act of Will**, seeing this as a clear map that gives us the essential guidelines we need to successfully lay the foundation in order to undertake the process of spiritual psychosynthesis. The multiple ways to self-realization described by Assagioli, and which Piero Ferrucci explores in some detail in his book *Inevitable Grace* (1990), can be enhanced greatly by deepening our understanding and application of the **Act of Will**. Whether we are pursuing the path of the inspired artist, the inquisitive scientist, the social hero, the prayerful devotee, or the contemplative hermit, the knowledge and practice of the **Act of Will** is an extraordinary and even necessary support to the unfolding of our psycho-spiritual development. This highlights its importance for us as psychosynthesis coaches, since we will be working with many people who, in one way or another, are spiritual seekers.

The Act of Will: A Foundational Map of Self-Realization

All of the aspects of the Will—the Strong, Skillful, Good, Transpersonal, and Universal Will—are intimately interconnected with one another. The final goal of will-development is to achieve a harmonious synthesis of all of the aspects of the will. As we progress along these lines, we find that each aspect of the will synergizes with the others in such a way that they eventually function as one integral and united whole, seamlessly blending with one another in order to create the inner reality of the fully conscious and liberated individual. In other words, through developing all aspects of the will to their highest levels of expression, we can eventually fulfill our greatest potential and become Self-realized beings.

The Transpersonal Will or Spiritual Aspiration

I begin this exploration of the Act of Will with an analysis of the Transpersonal Will, because it is this aspect of will that both sparks and sustains our search for truth so magnificently represented by the archetype of the philosopher. Transpersonal Will is essentially the will to meaning and ultimately the aspiration to achieve Self-realization. It is perhaps one of the clearest manifestations of the True Self that encourages us to embark on the epic journey toward wholeness. Interestingly, the etymology of the word philosopher has two roots, which are phílos, "loving" and sophía, "wisdom". A philosopher then, is one who loves wisdom, one whose priority in life is the quest for truth. It is the process of 'falling in love with wisdom' that allows us to heed the spiritual call of Self which both enables us to move beyond the mirages of the multiplicity within and also begin to embrace our universal life purpose: that of achieving union with the Self. When this aspiration for liberation from the bonds that keep our consciousness imprisoned becomes strong enough, we are able to develop the single-pointed devotion that allows every aspect of our life to serve as a vehicle for the achievement of this purpose. All along the way, we learn to actively honor, nurture, and develop the Transpersonal Will within ourselves.

As I mentioned earlier, learning how to access transpersonal experiences is fundamental for stimulating and developing this aspect of the will, which, in most people who have not experienced the transpersonal dimension, lays dormant. Here however, we come up against the issue of learning how to correctly navigate, interpret, and integrate these experiences. It is in relation to this that the other aspects of the will must be developed and implemented, as well as in acquiring an understanding of the many potential pitfalls and illusions that can hypnotize our consciousness within transpersonal experiences. An integral part of our training as psychosynthesists is to learn precisely to navigate, interpret, and integrate our own experiences of the transpersonal dimension. As we gradually develop our capacity for discernment and the exercise of wisdom in action, we will acquire the necessary experience to naturally help our clients adequately metabolize their own transpersonal experiences. Let us now move on to an exploration of the Good Will.

The Good Will or the Exercise of Virtue

At the center of the concept of Good Will is an understanding of the inner and outer process of cause and effect. Applied to human life, this universal spiritual principle reminds us that every action produces an effect, whether for good or ill, which inevitably shapes us and our destiny. Taking responsibility for our actions in the context of this truth is essential to our spiritual development. Understanding life from the perspective that who we are is determined by our own past and present actions, leads us away from a psychology of victimization and blame and empowers us to take full responsibility for ourselves and for how we choose to respond to the vicissitudes of life. It then becomes apparent that we can achieve ultimate freedom only by performing truly good actions and abstaining from bad ones, not in a mechanical way, but guided by the voice of our own conscience, which bestows penetrating understanding and discernment on us. In this process, we recognize that our conscience, when not overshadowed by subpersonalities, is in fact the 'voice of the Self' that enables us to understand the effects of our actions and thereby choose the path of conscious virtue. In relation to this, Assagioli says the following:

> …Anyone advancing along the path of the spirit must not only observe the great ethical principles of humanity, but must actually have a purer, stricter and more conscious concept of morality than the ordinary person… For instance, when they learn that thoughts, feelings, and the intent of the will are not abstractions, but living forces, powerful realities operating at subtle levels, and that they are real creations for which we are responsible, they become more conscious of the use of those forces than a person with no knowledge of them. For them, wrong thoughts and unworthy intentions now become faults as serious as those committed in reality. (Assagioli, 2007, pp. 154-155)

In this context, 'actions' refer not only to those we carry out in the physical world, but also to the more subtle 'inner actions' such as our thoughts, imaginings, emotions, motivations, and desires. In coming to know the contents of our own psyche we learn to take responsibility for both the 'light' and the 'dark' forces that operate within us. As Assagioli suggests, by observing "*the great ethical principles of humanity,*" we lay the foundation for a luminous future. This commitment to live by a conscious morality implies an inevitable process of wrestling with the elements of our lower nature; the subversive inner forces that seek to hypnotize and enslave our consciousness. This does not entail repression, rejection, or 'spiritual bypass' (which, without proper understanding and training, we can fall into), but rather is based on an objective process of coming to regulate and eventually master the forces within our psyche. This is so that we, as the conscious 'I' guided by the Self, can create order and harmony within rather than falling into the inevitable psychological fragmentation that ensues when subpersonalities or the shadow possess our consciousness.

Among the multifaceted symptoms of the current age we are living in, is the degeneration of language. In his book *The Hidden Messages in Water*

(2004), author and researcher, Masaru Emoto, clearly demonstrates the power of words to influence matter by photographing frozen water particles that had certain words attached to them. Words that were of a positive nature such as "love", "gratitude", and "peace", had the effect of producing geometrically harmonious patterns within the frozen water particle, while words of a negative nature such as "I hate you" produced incoherent and chaotic patterns. These scientific experiments reveal what we intuitively already know about the power of words, and therefore thoughts, to influence our emotions and physiology. Each word or thought has a specific vibratory frequency that can be either life affirming and aligned with the truly good or be life denying and destructive. Thus, if we seek psycho-spiritual wholeness, we must be committed to consciously directing our words. How easy it is to harm others through judgmental gossip and words of sarcasm, disdain, or criticism. On the other hand, when we seek our highest welfare and that of others, and use supportive, sincere, and truthful words, we experience the power that words have to strengthen and uplift. To walk a path guided by the Self, we would do well not only to integrate this truth in our coaching work with clients, but we must also seek to embody it in our personal lives and intimate relationships through a commitment to cultivating conscious non-violent communication.

The Skillful Will or Wisdom in Action

The development of **Skillful Will** is very much related to the cultivation of conscious awareness or mindfulness, which, when practiced through direct observation, gives us an understanding of how the psyche functions. Because we are habituated to externalizing our awareness onto the material world, in order to develop a Skillful Will, we must once more learn to shine the light of awareness on the contents of our inner experience as it processes through our multiple functions from moment to moment. It is by doing this that we come to an experiential integration of Assagioli's (2010) "Psychological Laws" (see page 417) and actually see them at work in ourselves and others. It is through this practice that we gradually learn to navigate our inner experience more skillfully by using the knowledge of the Psychological Laws to our advantage. Through the development of the Skillful Will, we learn to intelligently utilize all aspects of the will in order to harmonize the psyche and keep ourselves aligned with the Self, thereby connecting us, to varying degrees, with the Universal Will. The concept of serene self-observation or conscious awareness denotes the moment-to-moment practice of disidentification from the contents of awareness, which creates the **psychological distance** that allows us to experience life from our true identity as the conscious 'I', as impartial witnesses. In relation to this,

Assagioli points out:

> Let us remember that the conscious 'I' is a 'reflection' of the Self and is thus essentially of the same nature, however much it is weakened and 'colored' by the contents of the middle level of the personality. When one manages to eliminate those contents by means of certain exercises (particularly that of disidentification), the conscious 'I' tends to return upwards towards its origin. (Assagioli, 2007, p. 40)

So, we see that cultivating this conscious awareness is an indispensable practice that can help us as the 'I', still conditioned by the contents of the psyche, to return to our origin in the Self. Conscious awareness is then the necessary state of being to cultivate in order to have direct access to the influence of the Self. It enables us to 'see life like a dream', that is, to create the necessary psychological distance from both inner and outer experience to be able to respond serenely and intelligently. Through this practice, we are able to shed light on the contents of awareness and thus make conscious the territory of the unconscious. As we do this, we gradually acquire the capacity to discern between the inner forces that are aligned with our true nature and those that are not. Through this direct understanding of the mechanics of our psyche we learn to identify, comprehend, and finally abandon unwholesome psychological states of being and simultaneously develop those that are genuinely wholesome, which enables us to become embodiments of the **Good Will**.

In his writings, Assagioli (2007) makes a clear distinction between the Analytical Mind as an inferior function and the Synthetic Mind as a source of true penetrating understanding. Normally, we do not have access to the Synthetic Mind because it is a higher form of intelligence that emanates from the Self. When we operate solely from the Analytical Mind, we are not able to see reality as it is. The Synthetic Mind is developed through the practice of conscious awareness and is gradually perfected through undergoing a process of inner purification. In referring to the Synthetic Mind, Assagioli says that it:

> ...gives a correct and clear view of whatever it focuses its attention on. In addition to its capacity for true perception, it has the function of recognizing and correctly interpreting intuitions when they present themselves to the conscious mind. This is the true meaning and function of discrimination. But before it can perform this task, this area of consciousness needs to be purified... (pp. 159-160)

This process of purification implies a subtle, yet continual inner effort of the will. Cultivating conscious awareness is an active practice in which we learn to live from the content-less awareness of the 'I' and come to know ourselves deeply from this perspective. When this process is executed in a healthy way, we gradually learn to establish ourselves in the equanimity and love of the Self, which allows us to know that we are ultimately **not** the unwholesome content we see within, but that it only constitutes our subjective psychological conditioning. Adopting this perspective to our psycho-spiritual inner work is essential so as not to fall prey to either self-destructive subpersonalities that seek to feed our guilt, fear or self-judgment when we discover 'the unwholesome' within ourselves, or the self-exalting subpersonalities that do not allow us to see ourselves as we actually are because we are identified with a false idealized self-image.

In order to develop conscious awareness, we must gradually establish ourselves within the calm attention and inner tranquility, which is the nature of the detached witness or 'I'. Apart from Assagiloi's (2007) disidentification exercise, (which seems to me especially useful in the initial stages of this process) one of the simplest yet most powerful techniques I have found for developing this inner skill is the mindfulness meditation known as **Anapanasati** taught by the Buddha in which we learn to concentrate awareness on the breath and thereby detach it from the contents of the mind and external impressions. As we progress daily in this practice, eventually our entire life can become one uninterrupted meditation in which we are conscious from moment to moment of the dynamics of our inner world as it interacts with the outer world, thus affording us the possibility of gradually achieving self-mastery.

In our work as coaches, perhaps one of the greatest gifts we can offer our clients is the discovery, experience, and development of the 'I' or content-less awareness that brings us naturally into contact with the nature of the Self. Through helping our clients to learn to disidentify from the contents of awareness, we can guide them towards the path back to true freedom so that they can once more learn to navigate their life skillfully and eventually become the directors of their inner worlds. It is the development of the power of disidentification, grounded in learning to live from a space of conscious awareness, that then becomes the foundation for the entire process of both personal and spiritual psychosynthesis. It is for this reason that I believe this skill should be continually cultivated within ourselves and actively encouraged in our clients.

In addition, by learning to connect to the stillness and conscious awareness of the 'I' within our coaching work, we are able to access the wisdom and compassion of the Self. Through 'listening' to its guidance by being attentive to its signs and signals as they manifest through the functions, we can then learn to allow for the higher intelligence of the Self to guide the process. The more we learn to consciously connect to the Self and correctly interpret its guidance through the power of discrimination, the more the Self can act as a guide within our coaching work, helping us support the highest possible good both for ourselves and our client. In this way, we can also cultivate the bi-focal vision that allows us to acknowledge our client first and foremost as a 'Thou', a reflection, however dimly, of the Self, a person full of potential, thirsting for healing and wholeness. If we can serenely and lovingly witness their personal 'story', their wounds, and conditioning from this space of connection to the Self, our clients will receive great benefit simply through our presence and a relationship of deep appreciation, respect, and trust can naturally develop. Undertaking our work as guides from this space also implies understanding the great responsibility that we are assuming and a deep desire to be an instrument for the Self to work through, in order to serve the highest good of the client and thereby support the overall healing of humanity, one person at a time.

The Skillful Transformation of Impressions

Practicing conscious awareness also helps us to develop another necessary life skill: that of transforming impressions. Our life experience is constituted by a continual stream of impressions from the outside world that come into our awareness through the senses. As we meet the impressions of each passing moment, they leave their imprint on the psyche. Impressions are like 'psychological foods' that are usually received by us unconsciously. They can be of a wholesome or unwholesome nature. When we are on the path of spiritual psychosynthesis we seek to metabolize these impressions consciously and this can only happen if we cultivate conscious awareness, as well as a deep commitment to preserving our psycho-spiritual wellbeing. By doing so, we are able to see the impact that impressions have on our psyches and so navigate them more wisely. Some common examples of these 'psychological foods' are the type of literature we choose to read, what we watch on the Internet or on TV, the music we listen to, and the advertisements and images we see. Ultimately, every experience is a 'psychological food' that can be metabolized consciously or unconsciously.

In our current age, we are bombarded by countless negative impressions that stimulate an inferior form of imagination within us. There are so many examples of this, both impressions that come into our psychological space unbidden, and those that we choose, unaware of the potential consequences. If we live unconsciously, these "collective poisons," as Assagioli (2007) calls them, that we are exposed to daily, can dehumanize us in powerful ways. As we tread the path back to the Self, it is of great help to be aware of this psychological contamination so we can avoid, to the greatest degree possible, feeding the lower aspects of our nature. One way of doing this is by being selective about the psychological foods to which we expose ourselves. Whenever possible, we would benefit by 'feeding' our psyche with all types of music, literature, films, and experiences on the basis of whether they nourish our higher nature and support our process of awakening or not. At the same time, through cultivating conscious awareness, the negative impressions we cannot avoid, as we interact with our modern world, can be transmuted so they cease to have a negative impact on us. Another practice that also helps us become more conscious in our daily life and one that enables us to transform the impressions of the day is the "Daily Review" exercise. In this exercise, we retrospectively bring to mind the events of the day in order to review them and adequately metabolize them through a process of analysis and integration.

The Strong Will or Power to Act

In order to truly exercise the impetus to carry out the process of both personal and spiritual psychosynthesis, the development of the **Strong Will** is indispensable. It becomes the motor that gives us the power, discipline, and determination to actually develop the other aspects of the will and thereby master ourselves. The Strong Will is fortified every time we make a conscious decision and follow through with it. In relation to the inner work of recognizing, accepting, coordinating, integrating, and synthesizing the many subpersonalities and energies within ourselves, the Strong Will in combination with the Skillful, Good, and Transpersonal Will enables us eventually to reach the stage of becoming the conscious director of our inner worlds. In combination with the other aspects of the will, it provides us with the capacity to be consciously self-regulating beings, to metabolize adequately both our inner and outer life in such a way that we are able to remain in our center of consciousness and will. In our coaching work, it is also fundamental to help our clients develop this much-needed quality in order to support them in achieving a life well lived through applying it to their process of transformation. We have many wonderful psychosynthesis techniques to support us and to assist our clients to gradually forge a strong will.

The Universal Will

When our personal 'I' finally merges with the Transpersonal Self, we reach the heights of our spiritual development in which there is no longer separation from the divine reality and we thereby become instruments of the **Universal Will**, partaking of its illuminated and transcendent reality. Yet, long before we reach these heights of illumination and even as we begin our spiritual journey, guidance from the Universal Will as revealed by the Self is made available to us, and this increases as we progress. As we develop a conscious relationship to the Self, we learn to follow its guidance and inspiration and apply it to all aspects of our life.

The Synthesis of the Will: Embodying the Archetype of the Spiritual Warrior

In the context of the process of Self-realization, the synthesis of all of the aspects of the will can be symbolically represented by the archetype of the spiritual warrior or hero. The spiritual warrior is then an embodiment of the transpersonal qualities associated with every aspect of the will. As we become spiritual warriors ourselves, the Strong Will enables us 'to act,' to put into practice the process of self-realization and to make consistent progress in this direction, eventually, in every moment. The Skillful Will enables us to remember and to dwell in our true identity as the 'I' in the process of returning to the Self and to wisely and consciously navigate each stage. The Good Will allows us to cultivate the commitment to the highest good in all circumstances, to become impeccable both within as well as without. The Transpersonal Will propels us forward on our path of Self-realization, enables us to access increasingly higher levels of awareness within the super-conscious dimension, and strengthens our relationship to the Self, who guides us on the profound journey of making conscious the three levels of the unconscious. The Universal Will, as accessed through learning to 'listen' to the Self, guides our steps throughout the entire process, eventually leading us to the achievement of incarnating the Self and becoming crystalline vehicles for its expression.

Becoming Pillars of Light: Our Role as Guides in Dark Times

As the global situation becomes more critical, I believe we must prepare ourselves inwardly for the difficult times ahead. When we harness the courage to face the many manifestations of the current world crisis, many of our deepest fears and insecurities will inevitably arise, which, if not consciously counteracted, can lead us away from contact with the Self and its much-needed transpersonal qualities. As we know, we are not influenced only by the mechanisms of our inner and outer world, but also by the subtler manifestations of the Collective Unconscious, and some of these manifestations include the unconscious reactions of collective fear, depression, anger, hatred, violence, selfishness, and despair. In order not to allow these destructive forces to possess our consciousness, we must develop the necessary skills and qualities to navigate them with equanimity and deep understanding, which will allow us to

119

respond intelligently and effectively. Through becoming spiritual warriors and undertaking the inner work of mastering these collective forces and their inner counterparts, the challenges we face in every situation, no matter how difficult or painful, can be transmuted into valuable experiences that help us to forge the necessary spiritual qualities to prevent us from being consumed by our Shadow or the collective darkness. In order to achieve this, we benefit greatly by learning to deeply disidentify both from the material world and from the subjective processes of our psyche.

When we learn to disidentify from the material and psychological dimensions of existence and cultivate ever more contact with the forces and truths of the spiritual dimension, we can access that which is permanent and dependable within us, namely the Self. By becoming aware of who we are, as a soul and even more importantly as consciousness itself, we can learn to overcome our multiple fears and to respond intelligently to the critical situation rather than mechanically and unskillfully. If we integrate the truth, that in reality we are an extension of the mysterious undying Self, we can preserve our strength and inner peace even in the face of the greatest challenges because we know deeply that we cannot really die. In order to fully realize this truth, we must metaphorically become like deep rivers that can sustain life in abundance rather than shallow rivers that have little life within them. To do this, our process of Self-realization must be continually cultivated so that we can eventually come to undertake the process with enthusiasm and devotion. Through deepening our relationship with the Transpersonal Will, we come to learn that the fundamental purpose of our lives is to achieve Self-realization. Sincerely treading the path back to the source mysteriously opens us to receive the unlimited abundance of the Self, which brings us the conditions and support we need in order to carry out our process of awakening.

Tending Ourselves and Tending to Others

Now that we have looked briefly at the **Act of Will** in the context of spiritual psychosynthesis, let us explore our role as guides and coaches in the context of our present times. As we develop all aspects of the will within ourselves and gradually move toward becoming embodiments of the spiritual warrior, we gain the necessary foundational skills and knowledge to learn simultaneously how to support our clients in developing and transforming themselves. Through integrating and implementing the broad range of exercises and practices, as well as the knowledge and maps that psychosynthesis gives us, we can become effective in assisting others in their process of psycho-spiritual transformation.

Perhaps the most important factor to keep in mind as we embrace our path as coaches is that our priority should be, first and foremost, to develop ourselves psycho-spiritually so as to 'keep our inner light shining brightly' and as a result be able to assist others more skillfully in their own processes. Often, in our desire to help others, we make the mistake of neglecting our own development. Assagioli addresses this point:

> Too often we forget that it is not the amount of work that counts, but the quality of that action, and that even where others are concerned, and for their good, our first and most urgent duty is to improve ourselves. (Assagioli, 2007, p. 232)

We are reminded of the truth that our capacity to serve another is dependent on the **quality** of the service given. That quality is determined by our level of development, depth of understanding, and direct experience of our own process of both personal and spiritual psychosynthesis. We cannot guide anyone into territory that we ourselves have not experienced and it would be a mistake to try to do so, because we would inevitably misguide and potentially, inadvertently harm them. That is why, if we wish to become vehicles in service of others, our priority must be our own inner development. As we undertake this process, we would benefit by learning to strike a balance between our inner and outer work. Assagioli suggests that we should seek to simplify our outer life as much as possible in order to create the necessary room for the unfolding of our inner life and to avoid being engulfed by the chaos of the outer world. In relation to this, Assagioli says the following:

> The calm inner silence, conscious reflection, meditation, prayer and contemplation—in short, all those essential elements of a work deep within—are not only the necessary preparation for external action, they continue to be indispensable for inspiration and renewal… (Assagioli, 2007, p. 234)

By engaging in this *"work deep within"* through engaging in a daily spiritual practice, we access the spiritual nourishment our soul needs to continue evolving as well as receiving guidance and inspiration from the Self to guide us in supporting others on their journeys toward wholeness.

In concluding this consideration of spiritual psychosynthesis in the light of the present world condition, to support our intention of being beacons of light for others, I would like to close with the following prayer:

May I be a guard for those who need protection,
A guide for those on the path,
A boat, a raft, a bridge for those who wish to cross the flood.
May I be a lamp in the darkness,
A resting place for the weary,
A healing medicine for all who are sick,
A vase of plenty, a tree of miracles,
And for the boundless multitudes of living beings,
May I bring sustenance and awakening,
Enduring like the earth and sky
Until all beings are freed from sorrow
And all are awakened.
—*Shantideva, (Indian Buddhist Sage, 700 AD)*

References

Assagioli, R., (2007). *Transpersonal development: The dimension beyond psychosynthesis.* Findhorn, Forres, Scottland: Smiling Wisdom.

Assagioli, R., (2010). *The act of will.* Amherst, MA: The Synthesis Center Press.

Benedeck Sotillos, S., (2013). *Psychology and the perennial philosophy: Studies in comparative religion.* Bloomington, IN: World Wisdom.

Emoto, M. (2004). *The hidden messages in water.* Hillsboro, OR: Beyond Words Publishing.

Ferrucci, P. (1990). *Inevitable grace.* Los Angeles: Jeremy P. Tarcher, Inc.

Sutich, A. (1969). Some considerations regarding transpersonal psychology. *Journal of Transpersonal Psychology,* v.1, 11-20.

Part 3

Inviting Transformation: The Deep Work of Psychosynthesis Coaching

The transformation of energies is a natural process going on at all times, both 'horizontally,' within each level—physical, biological, and psychological—and 'vertically', between all levels...
                                                        —Roberto Assagioli

When the unifying center has been found or created, we are in a position to build around it a new personality—coherent, organized and unified. This is the actual psychosynthesis...
                                                        —Roberto Assagioli

Editor's Note:
The field of coaching has expanded, since its inception, to cover a wide range of viable "content" that is appropriate for coaching work. While all coaching is clearly differentiated from psychotherapy and counseling, psychosynthesis coaching offers deep and transformative work. Beyond simply reaching a goal, there lies the invitation to change, in ways that not only meet the stated objective, but in profound, life enhancing ways. Both client and coach are opened to the emergence of next steps in the unfolding of Self. As a transformational practice, psychosynthesis works in alliance with many themes, many practices, and many issues: all designed to enhance and revitalize the quality of life. Thus, the alchemy, if you will, of coaching is born and manifest in this work.

What do we Know about Psychosynthesis Coaching?

In 2013, at a Psychosynthesis Conference, 10 certified Psychosynthesis Life Coaches, came together to introduce this field and its powerful potential. Together we created the "short form" of what this work is. We defined ten core statements to help understand psychosynthesis coaching.

1. In psychosynthesis coaching we work from the foundation of an adult to adult, I-Thou relationship, lessening the power differential, without the weight of transference and countertransference. We are allies.

2. Clients come with an embedded capacity for disidentification from their story, holding and honoring primal wounding, but living with it as history. They've been there and done that work or it is work that is not being called forth in this engagement with their coach.

3. The Call of Self, as it asks clients to be true to themselves, truer and truer over time, is the guiding wisdom. We learn to hear it as they do and we stay committed to each client's deep connection to that Call.

4. Purpose, meaning and values, come forth as goals and intentions, which we help clients to define, then make manifest. Goals may be inner or outer, wide and global, or precise and articulate. All become goals that the client can monitor as they progress. Goals are actionable.

5. Our job is to support the Act of Will and the client as Willer, both empowering purpose, and inviting, even requiring deliberation, to check the clarity of purpose, giving space to note subpersonality agendas, but not let them lead. We coach the client towards certainty that the voice who speaks and chooses, is speaking from the guidance of Self.

6. In service of Soulful goals, be they helping to create world peace or cleaning the bathroom, we nourish our clients in accessing, strengthening and living through all psychological functions; thinking, feeling, bodily experience, deep desiring, imagination and intuition.

7. We show up fully present, willing and able to access our most receptive and our most assertive selves, balancing the yin and yang of presence. We are aiming for transformation. We know it is emerging for each person with whom we work.

8. We ask our clients to show up fully, but not laden with old stories and limiting beliefs as their only foundation. "Leave the basement and come into the house you are building" we say. "It is a beautiful house and only you can build it."

9. They are the architects and we the consultants. They the travelers, knowing just where they need to go. We are the guides. In service of their ideal models, we consult, we ask important questions, we listen deeply, we enliven their act of will from purpose and deliberation into affirmation, choice, planning and realization.

10. We are psychosynthesists. All of psychosynthesis is brought to bear. We are helping professionals. We are coaches. We are caring, perfectly imperfect adults, committed to the growth of individuals and the planet. We are psychosynthesis coaches.

Contributers to this statement include: Patricia Breen, Didi Firman, Konnie Fox, Jean Gran, Marjorie Hope Gross, Yonti Kelly, Meredith Maislen, Audrey McMorrow, Carlyn Saltman & Jon Schottland.

Chapter 11

Body (Soma) Wisdom

by Sara Vatore

*Psychosynthesis ought really to be called "biopsychosynthesis,"
thereby including the body in a complete synthesis of the
human personality. The continuous reciprocal interrelation
between the body and the psyche is already generally
accepted...A healthy human body is an admirable example of
psychosynthesis: a harmonious synthesis of many different and
opposing functions. Thus, the way a body is functioning can
reciprocally illustrate how the mind is functioning. The dual
influence of the body on the mind obviously indicates that the
human being operates from both these spheres and that we
ought to work on both sides.* —Roberto Assagioli

As coaches, we support our client's growth and development towards
Self-realization and hold a safe space for their "on-going process of integrating
all the parts, aspects, and energies of the individual into a harmonious powerful
whole" (Brown, 2004, p 1). In order to be most effective, we must have a clear
understanding of how all these different parts, aspects, and energies work together and separately, as well as how they affect the psyche. A challenge for us,
as coaches, is to learn how our body and psyche are affected by our autonomic
nervous system and how this system comes online and has an impact for both
the coach and client during a session.

Through our social conditioning, we develop habituated ways of thinking, being in our body and responses to social and environmental stimuli.
Our mind is intricately connected to our body and this is critically important because, as mammals, we are continuously governed by our biology. This
means that if we are confronted by danger, be it physical or emotional, we will

reflexively respond physiologically, in an attempt to protect ourselves from this "danger." Our heart rate and breathing will speed up, our muscles will tighten and we will prepare to meet the perceived danger. Developing an awareness of this "felt sense" response is critical to being effective as coaches. This "felt sense" response or sensation is the language of the nervous system and how we recognize certain needs and desires that we have. By cultivating a strong and nuanced body awareness, through development of our sensation psychological function, we can begin to understand and use this biological lens with both ourselves and our clients, to improve the effectiveness of our work.

A heightened awareness of how our nervous system response and our sensation psychological function operate will also provide the coach with additional tools and strategies during a session. This chapter will explore the roles that our nervous system and habituated embodied responses play in coaching. In addition, it will discuss how to work with the sensation psychological function and the body as well as how to protect clients from getting too overwhelmed during a session. Similarly, it will help us, as coaches, stay embodied during the process, so we don't get overwhelmed ourselves. In this way, we will be able to access our most effective, intuitive coach self.

We are Mammals: So What?

As mammals, our bodies are hard-wired for one sole purpose: survival! Peter Levine, the pioneer of Somatic Experiencing®, researched and tracked mammals and their responses to threat and danger:

[Given] obvious patterns in anatomy, physiology, behavior and emotions, and since we share the same survival parts of the brain with other mammals, it only makes sense that we share their reactions to threat. Hence, there would be great benefit gained from learning how animals...respond to threat, and then observing how they rebound, settle and return to equilibrium after the threat has passed. Many of us humans, unfortunately, have become alienated from this innate capacity for resilience and self-healing. (2010, p. 27)

The body is designed to take us through the same response pattern to danger as any animal in the wild. The nervous system is responsible for a series of automatic functions in the brain and body in order to keep the organism safe. It is this "wiring" in the body, almost like a grid system connecting and communicating with the other major centers in the body, including the brain, the gut, and the heart, that is the core mechanism of our survival.

Why We Need A Regulated Nervous System

When we are regulated, we continually flow through cycles of activation and deactivation throughout the day. In the same way, all of life reflects this organic ebb and flow. We wake up in the morning (activation) and then go to sleep at night (deactivation). Someone cuts us off in traffic and we get angry (activation), and then, as we keep driving, we eventually calm down (deactivation). We get excited about a new coaching client (activation) and then we settle down (deactivation). We get nervous about a presentation (activation), and then when we complete the presentation, we calm down (deactivation). A healthy nervous system will always flow with this natural, wave-like up and down movement.

When our nervous system senses a threat to our safety, it automatically responds in a self-protective manner. Back in the days when we lived in caves as hunter-gatherers, danger was relegated to our physical survival. Every day we were on alert to make sure we did not end up as another, larger animal's lunch. Now, because of our highly developed thinking brain, we are on top of the food chain, however, we live in a culture that regularly generates a significant amount of stress emotionally, environmentally and socially. As a consequence, our nervous system is continually on high alert and often activated for extended periods of time without deactivating. Lack of sleep, excessive stressful work hours, emotional turmoil and the inherent anxiety from environmental disasters and the uncertainty of the world's future, are just a few examples that leave our nervous system in a continual state of high activation and danger.

As a coach and helping professional, our personal history, culture of origin and past emotional and physical wounds also affect the activation and "danger" that we experience. For example, being embarrassed, humiliated, failing or needing to set a boundary can activate our nervous system. Even though those experiences are not life-threatening, our nervous system still automatically responds as if the danger is physical. To our nervous system, danger is danger. When this danger or fear is first perceived, our nervous system revs up, adrenaline and cortisol are released and there is an increase in our heart, pulse, and breathing rates. Our mind speeds up and our nervous system automatically instructs the body to either fight or flee. If neither of these options is possible, and we feel trapped in that danger state, then our body, by default, goes into a freeze or shutdown mode.

This self-protective response is the same whether the danger is real or perceived. Unlike other mammals, whose nervous systems are able to completely deactivate once the danger has passed, humans, because of their advanced neocortex and thinking abilities, have managed to keep the danger state present in their mind and body, long after the threat has passed. One reason for this is that we have a tendency to memorize 'trauma' and hold it in our nervous system and body, out of awareness, for months and even years after the event. When we are, in any way, reminded of these past upsets, components from the original 'trauma' are activated, bubble up into awareness, and leave us feeling unsafe. This feeling of "danger" then triggers our self-protective motor programs to come online.

Another reason that these past upsetting events stay alive for us is because, at the time that they occurred, we were unable to complete our self-protective motor programs. When an animal is in danger and flees for its life, flight is engaged. If it is able to escape successfully, the animal's nervous system gets the clear message that the danger has passed and it is then able to fully discharge this high energy state of flight, deactivate, and then completely settle. When our self-protective motor programs cannot be completed, our nervous system never gets the message that things are safe. As a result, our nervous system continues to try to protect us from the "danger" by attempting to complete these old self-protective motor programs. Because of this, our nervous system frequently gets confused between what is real and what things felt like from the past. This is what happens with those suffering from Post-Traumatic Stress Disorder (PTSD). The soldier, recently home from war, hears a car backfiring and instinctively drops to the ground as if under attack. The nervous system and body respond to the loud bang as if it is gunfire coming from a present-day enemy. This is why that danger state can be easily triggered in our interactions with our clients and others.

We can think about the nervous system (composed of our body, all of our senses and our mammalian biology), like a subpersonality. In her book, *The Unfolding Self* (2004), Brown describes a subpersonality as "a constellation of behaviors, feelings and thought that is left over from a time when we needed it for survival, to meet lower-level needs" (p. 27). Subpersonalities develop over time, based on our environment, our life experiences, needs, wounding, and more. They emerge to protect us in some manner and usually show up when they are triggered and their needs are not being met. Similarly, our nervous system functions, reacts, and responds out of this same self-protective place. There is a way to get to know our nervous system as we would a subpersonality, so when it shows up in the body, we can quickly identify what it needs. When we know what our body feels like and does when it goes into a fight, flight, or freeze state, we can then learn what to do when those sensations are triggered. These nervous system responses are going to show up continually in our life and in our career as a coach.

When we are in a session, as the coach, we can have these fear-based, felt-sense responses activated by a triggering story, our subs, our related worries, etc. Simultaneously, our clients can have their own fear-based, felt-sense responses arise in a session with us, especially as they are working with any "charged" content. When we learn our felt-sense experience of our own regulated nervous system and how to sense and be aware of our stress response cycle, we are then more able to engage with our activation and triggers differently. Noticing our activation and disidentifying from it by inviting in the Observer self, just as we do with subpersonality work, brings in:

> [awareness] of its attributes, its worldview, its style of behavior and its emotional pattern, so that it can be recognized from within…In this way, the energies…can be freed and made available for integration. We can begin to exercise choice over inner and outer reactions and behaviors. (Brown, 2004, p. 46)

Trauma—What You Need to Know

Our own range of responses and our clients' responses are dependent upon our past experiences and 'traumas.' What is registered as trauma can vary greatly depending upon the individual's perceptions of the event. It is important to note that trauma is NOT the event itself, but our nervous system's response to the event. Trauma is always in the eyes of the beholder. It can range from "Big T" traumas, such as car accidents, war, environmental disasters or abuse, to "Little t" traumas, such as surgery, witnessing others being hurt, negative medical experiences, shame/embarrassment, or other upsetting events. Accumulated stress is another form of trauma that keeps our nervous system in a highly activated danger state for prolonged periods of time.

We want to cultivate our own nervous system awareness as coaches, so we can prevent reflexive nervous system responses within ourselves that might not be in the client's best interests. Ultimately our goal is to foster our own healthy nervous system's process of self-regulation. If we are aware of this natural process of "the constant changes in our inner and outer environment, we can mobilize and manage them" (van der Kolk, 2015, p. 98). We will be able to notice when we are activated or triggered in a session, because there will be an increase in activity from our psychological functions. Thinking intensifies and soon turns negative; images rise into consciousness; emotions become dominant; our body changes physiologically, (heart rate increases, breathing speeds up and becomes shallower, muscles tighten, etc.).

When most people are triggered emotionally, they instinctively follow their thoughts, images, and/or emotions in an attempt to get rid of them.

Instead, we want to learn to disidentify from those psychological functions, invite in our Observer self, and move towards neutrally observing the potentially scary physical sensations in the body. When coaches are unaware of their own increasing activation, they will be more vulnerable to having their trained "performance skills" kicked offline and replaced by a self-protective, instinctive response. When this happens, our effectiveness as a coach greatly diminishes.

Our Inner Compass: The Sensation Psychological Function

The first step in getting to know our own unique nervous system is to build an awareness of sensation, because it is the language of the nervous system. When we start to invite in an exploration of sensation, it is important to examine what we notice with a "beginner's mind." That is, to be open to whatever comes up with an attitude of curiosity. There is no "right" way to start to tune into the body. Some people are easily able to identify and differentiate a variety of sensations, while others aren't. This is an important framework we need to hold with our clients as well. We want to cultivate an environment of patience and safety for our clients and ourselves as we explore the world of sensation. "If you have a comfortable connection with your inner sensations—if you can trust them to give you accurate information—you will feel in charge of your body, your feelings, and your self" (van der Kolk, 2015, p. 98).

Building Awareness of Sensation

As you sit and read this, I invite you to become aware of your body's contact with the environment. Take a moment to notice the surface that you are sitting on. Notice your feet and sense the connection with the floor or ground. What does the book feel like in your hands? Can you sense the texture of the cover? Take a moment and rub both of your hands together. Pause. What do you notice? Now, I invite you to turn inside and notice your breath. Can you feel the rise and fall of your rib cage, the expansion and contraction of your belly, the air coming out of your nostrils on your upper lip, or something different?

The first step to working with your sensation psychological function is simply building an awareness of the existence of sensation. We are often so closely identified with other functions that we forget about the vast inner landscape within the body and all the ways it can sense. For the purpose of this chapter, we are going to explore two aspects of our felt-sense experience: First, through sensing our self/body/system in connection to the physical outside world; Second, through our perception and sense of our internal environment, (interoception). As we build our awareness of both of these aspects of sensation, we begin to gain additional insight into the nervous system's experience and what it is communicating to us. This supports and assists our role as coaches, along with providing insights into our own felt-sense experiences during sessions.

As we start to develop this skill of noticing sensation, we want to work on receiving the sensations as opposed to "thinking" them. We want to let the body experience the sensations and let our Observer self, non-judgmentally watch. When we take a moment to notice what our feet feel like as they make contact with the ground or that our back rests into the chair, we invite in the awareness of our body connecting to the physical environment around us. Noticing the texture of our clothes, air on our skin, or touch of our own hands, we expand our awareness. What happens when you turn your awareness to receiving the sounds in your immediate environment? What do you notice? Can you sense the vibrations of sound, or something different?

To practice cultivating this awareness of our connection to the environment, take time to pause throughout the day, disidentifying from thoughts or feelings, and simply inviting the Observer to notice and sense your surroundings. When you are standing at the kitchen counter washing dishes, what do you notice? Can you sense the bubbles of the soap, the texture of the sponge, the weight of the plates, or the warmth of the water? What about when you are lying in bed? What do you notice? Can you feel the softness of the blanket, the pressure of you head resting into the pillow, the texture of the sheets? Take time to practice these types of observations in the different settings and environments that are available in every moment.

Likewise, we always have access to noticing our internal physical sensations. When we take the time to notice all the different parts of the breath, we are building our interoception awareness. Other sensations we can notice are our pulse, heart rate, breathing rate and depth, vibrations/tremblings, tight muscles, pain, impulses to move, etc. Have you ever experienced an eye twitch? Take a moment and bring your attention to the inside of your mouth. What do you notice? Can you sense 'wet' or 'smooth'? Rub your tongue on your teeth and what are you aware of? When you are lying in bed, take a moment to notice your breath as you settle into the bed. Observe what you sense. Do you notice the weight in your limbs or heavy eyelids? Does your mouth twitch? Take some time to explore your internal physical landscape of interoception in different situations.

"Cultivate Interoception" Exercise:

Stand up (or stay seated) and take a moment to sense your feet underneath you. Without trying to change anything, bring your awareness to your breath, and observe the organic inhale and exhale. Take a brief moment to observe your heart rate, temperature, pulse and anything else you may notice. Next, spend a minute jumping (or moving in your chair) consistently in place or around your space as rigorously as is tolerable. When the minute is up, stop jumping and stay in place. Take a moment to observe what you can sense in your body. What do you notice about your heart rate? Breathing? Pulse? What about your hands? Do you notice any tingling, temperature change, or something different? As you notice, invite in your Observer to simply watch the sensations. Let yourself notice if the sensations increase, decrease, stay the same, or do something different over time. After doing the exercise over time, our observation and awareness expands to noticing both overt and nuanced sensations in the body.

Tracking Sensation

Jumping is a form of activation of the nervous system. When we jump, our heart rate increases, pulse quickens, and breathing becomes more shallow, etc. When we stop jumping and observe what happens with the sensations in the body, we will notice that they start to decrease in intensity and slow down. Eventually, if the system is given enough time, the sensations will settle and the body will return to a resting state. This activation-deactivation cycle is a pattern that was described at the beginning of the chapter and governs our lives.

When we observe this cycle or wave, we are tracking sensations in our body. As our awareness of these sensations and patterns of activation/deactivation increase, we can start to recognize its natural flow and be more attuned to a disruption in the regulatory state. Van der Kolk (2014) states that having "agency" or being in charge of our lives starts with "interoception, our awareness of our subtle sensory, body-based feelings: the greater that awareness, the greater our potential to control our lives. Knowing what we feel is the first step to knowing why we feel that way" (pp. 97-98).

When we begin to track sensations in our body, there are a few steps to follow. First, identify the sensation in the body. Second, disidentify from any thoughts or subpersonalities who have come into play. Third, invite the Observer self to become curious about the sensations. Fourth, give the sensations plenty of time to unfold. Fifth, use the Observer self to notice if the sensations increase, decrease, stay the same or change in anyway and continue to watch what happens next.

When we are just beginning to work with sensation, there can be a desire to "do something." Other times, tuning into our internal physical sensations can be overwhelming. There are specific ways to guide and work with sensation, and there is a lot to be said on how to go about that process, which is beyond the scope of this chapter. The first step is to simply invite in this awareness of our natural nervous system rhythm and begin to notice the nuances of sensation as the waves of activation and deactivation move through us. We want our body to implicitly get the message that what goes up, always comes down. When our nervous system is regulated and attuned to the natural regulation, it expands our capacity to process events, memories, situations, anxieties, etc., and handle stress. This makes us much more effective in our work as coaches. Cultivating awareness of our own interoception and noticing activation-deactivation cycles informs our understanding of our unfolding self in any moment. This is a skill that can take some time to develop. We start by observing our healthy nervous system patterns. What does it feel like when I am in a naturally regulated state of ebb and flow, activation/deactivation? What is my felt sense experience of this?

The Regulated Coach: Coming Back to Embodied Presence

As we expand our awareness of our sensation psychological function, as coaches, we can utilize its wisdom to help us develop an embodied sense of self, a way of being present with the client. When we do this, we are connected and rooted in self through sensation, open to receiving messages from the client and tuned into our inner coaching wisdom. When we are embodied and present, we are in the here and now. When we work with sensation and become more fluent in utilizing this psychological function, we expand our capacity for presence. When I am sitting with a client and fully present, I can feel a connection deep within my belly, with my pelvis, which grounds my being into the floor. I have an awareness of the pressure of my feet resting purposefully on the floor and can sense the contact between the surfaces. While strong, my belly is relaxed and soft. My shoulders are down and back, with a gentle opening at my heart chakra and upper torso. The back of my throat is soft, and my tongue rests down into my lower palate. I sense connection throughout my being.

In getting to know what our felt-sense experience of presence is, and spending time in that space of embodiment, we create new neural pathways, which make it easier for us to find this embodied state of presence. "Full presence rests upon physical and energetic presence, a willingness to touch and be touched, and a readiness to experience our own physical responses and to learn

135

from them" (Brown, 2004, p. 58). When you are present with a client, rooted fully in the moment, connected to your self and your body, what do you sense in your body? How do you notice your physical connection to your environment? What tells you that you are present?

Triggered During a Session? What to do

During a session, we want a safe, familiar place to rest back into if we become triggered, notice ourselves drifting to negative thoughts, or find ourselves being seduced by a self-doubting sub. As coaches, we want to be as present as possible with our clients, but there are different situations that can come up that may challenge our ability to stay in the moment. When this happens, we want to simply recognize that our nervous system is being activated. Pause and notice if any subs have come to voice their opinions. Are we getting emotional? Can we feel our heart rate or breathing speed up, or notice any other physical changes?

I sometimes have a sub that comes out to tell me that my adult client looks bored. She also shows up if I am working with a child and she "helpfully" lets me know that my client looks confused. When I hear those kinds of thoughts, I often get a sinking feeling in my stomach. I could make the choice to engage with that sub and have some more dialogue about how I am not worth the money I am charging, or not helping my client as much as I should be, but that would further distract me from being present in the session. There are moments to engage with our subs, and it is never when we are facilitating a coaching session! Instead, I notice that negative thought as it arises into consciousness and I disidentify from it. I do this by bringing my awareness to the support of the chair underneath me and to the feeling of the soles of my feet pressing into the ground. I reorient my focus externally to look at the client. I physically sense my presence in the room. I am centered and refocused. I may have to repeat this process multiple times in a session, depending on the day!

When we become activated, we always have a choice to disidentify from the thoughts. It takes an act of will, but it is possible. We can choose to follow our thoughts, the accompanying images, or our emotions. However, if we do so, it's like throwing logs on the fire of activation. Our activation level will only intensify, increasing our thoughts, images and the strength of our emotions and this will ultimately make us ineffectual as a coach. However, if we instead disidentify from the thinking and follow the physical sensations of the activation with curiosity and without trying to direct anything, we will notice a surprising development: our activation level will go up, reach a peak, and eventually come back down all by itself. This is because our nervous system is designed to deal with the high-energy state of a crisis and then deactivate. By focusing on our felt-sense internal physical sensations and simply observing them with curiosity, within two minutes or so, our nervous system will deactivate all by itself.

When we are triggered/activated in a session, we want to notice this as a choice point that will help us return to an embodied sense of being present. Staying connected to our felt-sense experience while we are present allows us to stay connected to this moment. We use this connection when we find ourselves pulled by time traveling to the future or past, distracted by our self-doubts or ruminating about some difficulty we might have had before the session. This embodied presence is how we access our wisest center, a deep intuitive knowing and sensing. This is the space we want to embody when we are with our clients and it is always accessed through understanding our felt-sense experiences. "By contacting the body deeply and fully we can comprehend the saying 'the body never lies', where the body experience verifies, in its inclusion, the congruence of our deeper truth in a true alignment of the various levels of the journey of consciousness" (Rosselli, 2006, p. 3).

When we practice this choice of returning to the felt-sense experience of presence after being distracted by our thoughts, we become more receptive to connecting with our inner coaching wisdom. If we become too activated and our system gets overwhelmed, our trained coaching skills go offline and we don't have access to them. The more we can observe when we drift to our thoughts/images/emotions and use this awareness to return to actively embodying and sensing a state of presence, the easier it becomes to stay present and be effective as a coach. As we build this awareness and felt-sense experience of embodied presence, we may start to notice our nervous system becoming activated by our clients' own activation.

> We can also use our physical responses to learn more about the other individual in the same way we use emotional responses. Areas of tension and holding in someone's body will often generate a sympathetic tension in our own bodies. We can literally sense where that person is in pain or is energized. On the other hand, we can model relaxation and openness in the way we sit and move. (Brown, 2004, p. 58)

Let's think about how this manifests in a coaching relationship by looking at an Equestrian's relationship with the horse. Equestrians I work with will often report the same theme occurring when they are more stressed out about a competition. When they are in this activated state and riding, their horse (another mammal) will start to become more agitated and difficult to control. This, in turn, feeds the rider's own activation, creating a negative feedback loop between the two nervous systems that ends up with both rider and horse becoming over-activated. This leads to the rider going into freeze and shutting down. However, the more settled the rider's nervous system becomes, the calmer the horse will become.

Similarly, when we are in a session with a client, if our nervous system becomes over activated, our client's system is going to immediately and sensitively pick up on that. This same exchange happens when an upset or activated client emotionally triggers us. However, if your client is upset, and your nervous system remains calm, your client's system will respond to that and begin to settle!

In his research, Van der Kolk outlines how connected and attuned our body's systems are as human beings. He discusses our body-brain connection:

> Our mirror neurons register their inner experience, and our own bodies make internal adjustments to whatever we notice. Just so, the muscles of our own faces give others clues about how calm or excited we feel, whether our heart is racing or quiet, and whether we're ready to pounce on them or run away. When the message we receive from another person is "You're safe with me," we relax. (2015, p. 80)

Protecting Clients from Overwhelm

Just as we do not want to become too activated during a session, it is our job to make sure that we are protecting our clients from getting overwhelmed during a session. As our clients bring in content from their lives, it is likely that past and present emotions, felt-sense experiences, difficult thoughts, and images may enter a session. As we learned above, this often happens outside of conscious awareness. It is our responsibility, as the person holding space for the client's growth and development, to cultivate an environment of safety. Having education around the function of the nervous system and stress response cycle is key in protecting our clients from not getting stuck in a particular emotion, or becoming too overwhelmed.

It is our job as coaches to hold a "safe space" for our clients. As we begin to recognize the manifestation of activation in our clients, we will have more information to inform the direction we take in our sessions. Some who teach Somatic Experiencing® refer to this critical role, as the "Guardians of Overwhelm." In coaching, we ARE the Guardians of Overwhelm. We hold a space for our clients to safely dip into various prepersonal (lower unconscious), personal, and transpersonal experiences, utilizing all of the psychological functions, activating the will and the "I", identifying and disidentifying, and supporting the unfolding Self. In working with awareness of our basic nervous system and how it manifests, we help our clients build their own capacity and expand their resiliency.

As you read this, I am curious if you can remember a time when a client got too overwhelmed or you were emotionally triggered in a session. Maybe you are making images in your mind's eye about that time right now, or maybe you are noticing an emotion emerging. Take a moment to observe what you are aware of in your body. Can you sense your heart rate or breathing? Do you have any tightness in your stomach, or something different? Take a moment and notice what you sense. I invite you to look around the environment in which you are sitting. Let your eyes land on an object and neutrally describe it to yourself in vivid detail. When you finish, let your head and neck turn until your eyes catch another object and describe that to yourself in detail. Repeat turning your head and neck a third time and describe another object. Now, check back inside and see if sensation-wise, there is any small change or shift in what you noticed before.

How to Help Overwhelmed Clients

If we are feeling triggered in a session or our clients are overwhelmed, we have the ability to help them "orient". Orientation is a skill to help settle the nervous system and can help both you and your client return to the present moment. Just as you did above, you would ask your clients to look around the space and describe three things in detail that catch their eye in the environment. Animals observe their surroundings in the wild to evaluate whether they are safe. By looking around and neutrally describing objects, we are able to sense safety, which then settles our nervous system. Levine discusses how:

> ...these instinctive responses are as primitive as the reptilian brain that organizes them. They allow an animal to respond fluidly to an ever changing environment...Orienting responses are the primary means through which the animal tunes into its environment. These responses are constantly merging into one another and adapting to allow for a range of reactions and choices. The process of determining where it is, what it is, and whether it is dangerous or desirable happens first in the subconscious. (1997, pp. 93-94)

Additionally, while we have a client looking around and orienting, we also want to invite our clients to sense their feet on the floor, their seat in the chair, and any other connections they are making to their environment. We want to pull them back to the present moment and help them to return to their embodied, regulated, sense of self.

Grounding and Ending a Session

Not only does this information about the nervous system and working with the sensation psychological function inform how we protect our clients, it also truly helps ground our clients at the end of a session. It is important, that after we work with a client and have them utilize different psychological functions, or work with subpersonalities, the transpersonal, and/or other psychosynthesis processes, that our clients return to "I" before they leave the session. How do they identify that they are centered in their "I" space? What does it feel like in their body when they are most connected to self? The more embodied experiences our clients have of self, the easier it is to return to that centered, connected place when a subpersonality comes online or they get triggered. It is our job as the guide to highlight these moments of connection and invite in an awareness for the client to expand and ground themselves in their current experience.

Having an awareness of these activation-deactivation cycles of the nervous system will provide us with a new lens to view the client's system in front of us. This will allow us to have a much better sense of where our client is physically and emotionally as the session is ending. If we are running out of session time and we are at the deactivation stage of the nervous system, we are right where we want to be. We want to end the session noticing that our client's nervous system has returned to a regulated state. We want clients to return to their world, embodied, centered, and running their own show!

It is important to note that we must also use this information about the nervous system and its response to trauma to help us identify which clients may be outside our scope of practice. By having a greater understanding of the stress response cycle, we will be in a better position to know what issues we can work with and which need to be referred out to another type of professional.

Soma Wisdom

From a very young age, we learned to ignore or override our gut responses to our social environment in order to stay safe. Often our authentic voice got ignored or silenced in our development and as a result, we lost connection to our body wisdom and true self. We learned to become overly dependent upon our thinking psychological function. However, when we are able to return to our biological roots as mammals, we become more deeply connected to our regulated nervous system and our body and recapture our authenticity and sense of "I."

As coaches, learning to stay aware of our nervous system and its response to "danger" will allow us to more effectively help our clients move through their stuck places. Having a somatic awareness of our own felt sense response to activation will provide us with an invaluable lens to view and understand the coach-client interaction and how to more effectively resolve client issues. More than that, our felt sense awareness serves as a highly effective tool to support ourselves and our clients during the work.

When we learn to work with our own nervous system and are aware of and follow the natural waves of activation and deactivation, we help our own coaching and performance skills stay online, so we can be the present and engaged coach that we want to be, even if we get triggered or pulled off track by our subs during a session. This will lead us to more ease and confidence in our work and increase our effectiveness as coaches. Best of all, we will be able to model and teach this regulated nervous system approach to our clients, who will then be able to successfully adapt this "Soma Wisdom" to all aspects of their lives.

References

Assagioli, R. (2000). *Psychosynthesis: A collection of basic writings.* Amherst, MA: The Synthesis Center, Inc.

Brown, M.Y. (2004). *The unfolding self: The practice of psychosynthesis.* New York: Helios Press.

Levine, P. (1997). *Waking the tiger: Healing trauma.* Berkeley, CA: North Atlantic Books.

Levine, P. (2010). *In an unspoken voice: How the body releases trauma and restores goodness.* Berkeley, CA: North Atlantic Books.

Rosselli, M. (2006). The Body in the Process of Psychosynthesis. *Psychosynthesis and the Body: Conversations in Psychosynthesis* (pp. 1-15). Cheshire, MA: Association for the Advancement of Psychosynthesis.

Van der Kolk, B. (2015). *The body keeps the score: Brain, mind, and body in the healing of trauma.* New York: Penguin Books.

Chapter 12

Coaching Through Trauma

by Richard Lamb

Introduction—Unblocking the River Within

Since following the Call of Self back in 2011, involving a journey of self-discovery that brought me to psychosynthesis coaching and hypnotherapy, I've worked with a growing number of people who, at some point in their lives, sustained trauma of varying degrees. You'll find that trauma (and PTSD, its "complex" variant) is a pretty common experience in the 21st century, and can come about at any age, in any demographic. We have only to refer to recent experiences of combat veterans returning from the conflicts in Iraq and Afghanistan as a relatively well-known example of the terrible short and longer term consequences of living with trauma in our societies (US Department of Veteran Affairs, 2016; Van der Kolk, 2014).

Yet sometimes content from the past, in the form of trauma, can block working with the context of our coaching with clients. A couple of examples might help to illuminate this. The first is a client, the second myself. On working through the details of a performance-related target shooting goal, the space between the client and I seemed heavy with an embodied, physical energy, radiating from the client, as he described his most recent attempt at resolving an emotional block when he was mid-flow in a tournament. His voice began trailing off, and I noticed a youthful turn to his speech, a little too vulnerable for a man I knew to be very matter of fact about his emotions. It seemed to me that he'd been transported to a time in his childhood, where his father paid him scant attention for any success he had. The flow of his embodied vitality was blocked, like the blocking of a river, preventing life further downstream from receiving the much-needed nutrients of the past.

Being fully present with him, I listened intently. The simple act of acknowledging his psychological pain invoked by the traumatic flashback opened a door to accessing deep inner resources of emotional resilience and perseverance he didn't believe he possessed. For a brief time the client didn't believe such long-term indifference to his hopes and dreams could have affected him so deeply, and yet, over the course of the work, he came to recognize, accept, and transcend those inner limitations. By supporting his own inner growth through inspecting those childhood memories (which included both neglect and physical abuse), and by reconnecting his experience somatically through the body, he was able to move forward. And he did so boldly and with renewed self-confidence and clarity.

This kind of scene isn't likely to be unfamiliar to many coaches whose clients have experienced trauma. By entering his "basement" briefly—which included excursions into his 'loft' of the Higher Unconscious, where split off potential resided—those locked away resources were made accessible through the body. It is encouraging to note that a number of coaching authors have engaged the challenge of coaching through the body, such as Strozzi-Heckler's *The Art of Somatic Coaching: Embodying Skillful Action, Wisdom, and Compassion* (2014) and Aquilina's *Embodying Authenticity: A Somatic Path to Transforming Self, Team & Organisation* (2016).

So sometimes we may, out of necessity for the client's intention to realize their goals, be required to enter the basement of the Lower Unconscious in order for them to acknowledge the potential wholeness of their experience (and so explore their inherent, unique greatness). For them to fully, 100% be present with us and their own process, going into the dark of the Lower Unconscious is part of what we do as Guides. By doing so, the client potentially has access to a greater range of experience, and along with that a deeper, higher, and wider access to their inner resources. However, it needs to be made clear that some material is better suited for psychotherapy and that the Lower Unconscious work, that is, "working in the basement," is perfectly appropriate in coaching, when it is not the only identification, and when the client has access to a disidentified self.

My own journey really began in late February 2001 on the icy slopes of Ben Nevis in Scotland, when I survived a winter mountaineering fall from a beautiful, exposed 600 meter long route called Tower Ridge, killing my climbing partner and leaving me to freeze overnight with significantly disabling, and lifelong, injuries. The physical injuries were, over time, recognized for what they are. Decisions were made on how to move forward, based on an awareness of my limitations and capabilities, together with application of strong, skillful, and good will (in hindsight) in re-forging a new life from the wreckage of the old.

However, the psychological injuries, the "wounds to the soul," were more often than not quietly side-lined. I sustained episodes ranging from extreme anger and outrage to despondency and the blackest despair. It was during such later episodes that the "I" that is me began recognizing and accepting the presence of a very quiet, yet insistent voice within. I acted on those inner messages and embodied intuitions, and embarked on a concerted program of hypnotherapy, counselling and stress reduction. I reflected on my own waking inner processes and dreams through journaling, voraciously studied psychology and its application to recovery from trauma and, in 2004, I followed the Call of Self in planning to return and re-climb Tower Ridge. I had been climbing this beautiful granite ridgeline when that 650 foot fall changed my life forever. As a result of this fall and overnight stay in temperatures exceeding −21 degrees Celsius, 75% of my fingers were removed due to frostbite, while the injuries to my legs required a below knee amputation of the right leg, and resetting of the dislocated and broken left ankle. I spent 13 days in ICU, with only a 50% chance of survival. Three and one-half months later, in mid-June, I walked out of the hospital, and onto a new path. Learning how to walk, to use my hands again, learning how to write (and use chopsticks) again, were many of the humbling, testing, and illuminating goals. The psychological journey was no less challenging, as I learned, that by exploring the basement of the Lower Unconscious, I was helped to understand, move through and beyond the fears and memories that day in February, 2001 represented.

So I set myself a 'fulfilment goal' of reaching the summit cairn, where I imagined myself beside the cairn of stones, in good order and in good company, surrounded by supportive friends, clutching a victory cigar in one hand and a small dram of Scottish whiskey in the other to celebrate! Without realizing I had done so, I set 'balance' and 'process' goals supporting this fulfilment goal, and in June 2004, I found myself standing at the foot of the first section of the climb up the ridge, a little edgy though grounded and fully present with my experience. It was not until I reached the start of the narrow stone bridge-like formation out to Tower Gap, no more than 30 metres from the summit, that I was fully confronted by the "wounds to the soul" I had sustained that bitterly cold night three years earlier.

My body shook almost uncontrollably in that warm June air, as I shuffled across the natural bridge to Tower Gap, on all fours, where I had to set up a belay for my climbing partner—and local mountain rescue team member, Mike—to follow me across the gap. I remained with these difficult experiences, focusing my awareness on each body area in turn, being present with those sensations, while acknowledging the beauty of my environment, my slowing thoughts, my steadying emotions, my natural desire to be anywhere else but where I was, until I was able, in my own time, to continue with the rest of the climb.

The feeling of working through how my body responded, of the "fight or flight" sensations I felt, led me to the summit cairn, to my goal; and to a realization. Having read *Waking the Tiger: Healing Trauma,* (1997) during the months of preparation for the climb, I understood first-hand how our deepest, instinctual, primeval responses to threat were anchored in our bodies. I knew how we process our physical sensations, and the links to the other 5 psychosynthesis psychological functions, seemed to be a key. The physical shaking I experienced in re-climbing Tower Ridge was a closing of a primeval survival loop that had been running, almost without end, from March 2001 to the day of the climb in June 2004. The unblocking of that inner river released, in me, as it does for others, much needed nutrients of Soul.

Speaking now as a psychosynthesis coach and hypnotherapist, it is my view that psychosynthesis trained coaches are in an almost unique position to work with self-actualizing people who present trauma as part of their life's journey. I intend to share my experiences of working with people's trauma, and how we might move forward as a community in serving our fellow human being's highest potentials. It is this facet of the 'Work within the work' that I feel drawn to, as part of answering the Call of Self.

What is Trauma?

Before we look to how we can apply our psychosynthesis 'Maps of Soul' to understanding and working with trauma as transpersonal coaches, I want to make a brief excursion into previous work on trauma that can inform our way forward. I am not going to waste precious time with an extensive review of the literature, as I am going to focus on tried and tested "maps" that can complement psychosynthesis maps.

One key point to recognize is that we assume that, as coaches, the people who come to us are sufficiently integrated functionally to recognize and work through Lower and Higher Unconscious blocks to their potential. We are not dealing with pathological manifestations of trauma, though there may be instances where that occurs. We need to do our due diligence, through training and through referring such clients to trauma specialists. So, with that said, let's take a closer look at the existing landscape of trauma work.

There is a strong possibility that as transpersonal coaches, we are likely to encounter more than one client "who has experienced significant trauma or suffers from a mental health problem" (Campone, 2014, p. 3). So, odds on, when we first contact a new client, it's most probable, and more and more likely in the current age of civilization we find ourselves in, that they have experienced a mental health problem. Charles Tart (2012) refers to the "consensus state" or socialized trance of the emerging global civilization as a veritable wellspring for inducing trauma. Based on my current experience, the majority of coaching clients I work with present trauma of varying degrees.

Our survival as a species has, and continues to, rely on effective responses to external threats. In evolutionary terms, as mammals, we are no different physiologically from our ancestors who migrated out of the East African plains over 100,000 years ago. We can classify those instinctive "fight, flight, freeze" responses of old, which are still evoked today, whether in a stressful corporate office or out on the street late on a Saturday night. So, our embodied, sensation-based (and therefore largely unconscious) responses are with us pretty much every moment of the day. As Levine (2008) and Van der Kolk (2014) compellingly state, as arguably the most avoided, misunderstood, and untreated form of human suffering, trauma does not have to be based on a single, major event. We needn't expose ourselves to the horrors of war to experience the life limiting effects of trauma. It can occur from a sequence of apparently minor events, and when such events are experienced in childhood in particular, the effects are compounded and follow on into adulthood. What might we consider as common triggers for trauma? Here's a short list to get started with:

- Manual labor accidents, e.g. construction sites
- Automobile accidents of varying degrees of intensity
- Sports injuries
- Loss of those close to us (including pets)
- Personal betrayal
- Social isolation
- Natural disasters
- Loss of faith in a belief system or "worldview"
- Various hurts as a child, while feeling unsupported by parents

The list is far from exhaustive, and yet we respond **physiologically** much in the same ways our ancestors would have as hunter/gatherers. When exposed to the shock of trauma for extended periods, complex trauma (or CPTSD) develops, resulting in a range of responses (Bal, n.d.).

From what we have so far, how might we define trauma? From a "small" self-perspective (referring to the Egg map for a moment, in Figure 1), trauma can manifest when any perceived threat in the environment overwhelms our ability, through our inner resources, to respond from the choice point, from a (relatively) integrated space of Awareness and Will. When the capabilities and resources of the conscious, unfolding "I" are overwhelmed, through however major or minor an event, a "survival personality", a term created by Firman and Gila in their seminal work on trauma, *The Primal Wound* (1997), takes form within the personality and dominates the "I" space, limiting the person's range of responses. A negative internal unifying center forms, often as an internal punitive image/figure. From the physiological perspective, the freeze/immobility response kicks in, locking away the energy and resources in the body. The energy of trauma is an experience codified in the body. To release that energy, we work with the body's sensations.

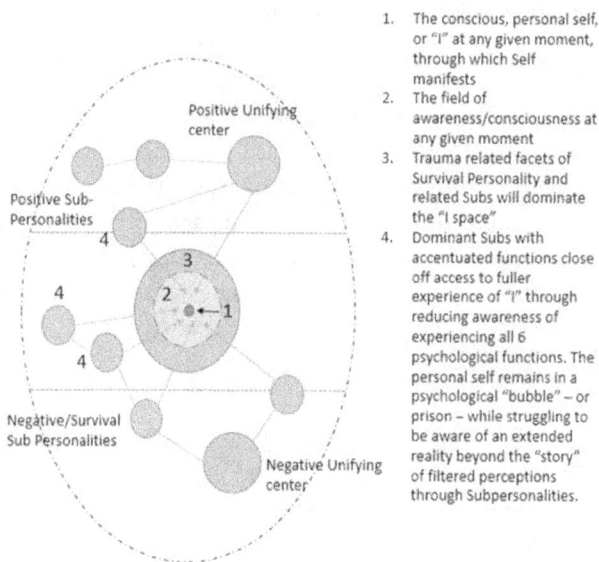

1. The conscious, personal self, or "I" at any given moment, through which Self manifests
2. The field of awareness/consciousness at any given moment
3. Trauma related facets of Survival Personality and related Subs will dominate the "I space"
4. Dominant Subs with accentuated functions close off access to fuller experience of "I" through reducing awareness of experiencing all 6 psychological functions. The personal self remains in a psychological "bubble" – or prison – while struggling to be aware of an extended reality beyond the "story" of filtered perceptions through Subpersonalities.

Figure 1. Energy normally available to the personality is locked away through trauma, triggered by external and internal stimuli and acted out through the Survival Personality.

As far as our psychosynthesis maps are concerned, we can also make use of Firman and Gila's work in *The Primal Wound* (1997) to guide us. In Figure 2 we have an image of the developmental layers of the personal, socialized, "conditioned" self. A trauma inducing event pierces the person's being to their core essence, the 'spark' of "I" that unfolds as life evolves.

If the primal response cycle options for responding are not able to effectively complete, the personality can no longer maintain itself as a whole, and a split occurs to protect the "I". While the "freeze" response manifests, the traumatized person is, in fact, in a state of hyperarousal, an altered state of awareness that narrows and focuses the person's capacity to operate across all six functions. It is at this point, where a facet of survival personality may be created, such as an anxious, ever vigilant subpersonality. The shock reaction to the event(s) is stored somatically, and re-invoked by an unconscious pattern match in the immediate environment (e.g. a windy day results in a traumatized tornado survivor running for shelter). The traumatic experience is driven into the Lower Unconscious, where it lies ready to be triggered in response to an unfortunately close pattern match. Our highest values and potentials likewise can be split off into the Higher Unconscious, if such natural, emergent qualities are denied by external unifying centers in positions of authority (for example, parents, teachers, experts).

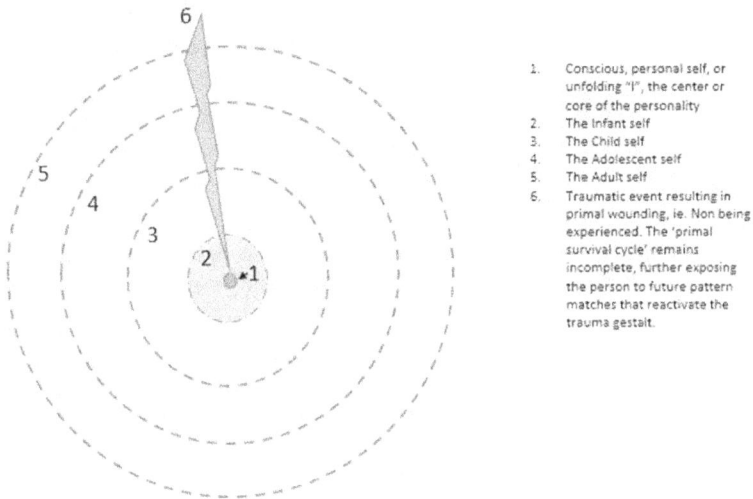

1. Conscious, personal self, or unfolding "I", the center or core of the personality
2. The Infant self
3. The Child self
4. The Adolescent self
5. The Adult self
6. Traumatic event resulting in primal wounding, ie. Non being experienced. The 'primal survival cycle' remains incomplete, further exposing the person to future pattern matches that reactivate the trauma gestalt.

Figure 2. Developmental layers of the personal self, and their relationship to trauma.

The trauma of nonbeing is created, a disruption and disconnection from authentic personality, our deepest wellspring of internal resources and gateway to Self. It is, in effect, an altered state of consciousness, or hypnotic state; what Tart (2012) refers to as an identity state, which we can map to dominant subpersonalities and the prevalence of dominant psychological functions that disconnects "I" space from a fuller, richer experience of the present moment.

As the "trauma trance" locks an individual into avoidance/denial of feelings, repressive, recursive thoughts, and avoidance of circumstances requiring an openness to life, awareness of choice becomes more and more constricted.

149

Loss of freedom to choose and act as a 'Willer' (a useful identification, though for many in the grip of trauma, unattainable) results in a departure of emotional and physical vitality, and a narrowing, a blinkering, to perceiving and acting on life's possibilities. This resonates well with Levine's work (2008, p.9), where he summarizes trauma as "...a loss of connection to ourselves, to our bodies, to our families, and to the world around us." This is as close to the psychosynthesis definition as I can come across; a dissociation and overwhelming identification, an overriding of the "I" space at the center of the Egg, where facets of a survival personality, however resourceful though limited, drive the personal self into a trancelike state. There are surely spiritual/transpersonal facets of trauma, such as a connection with Oneness through dissociation. Such experiences may be explored in future work.

As mentioned earlier, Tart (2012) presents a compelling and complementary view on trauma. A "trauma trance" is induced, what Tart refers to as an identity state. As psychosynthesis coaches, we might label such identity states as altered states of awareness/consciousness (akin to a hypnotic trance) that tend to correlate well with subpersonalities aligned with a survival personality, and its respective survival/negative unifying center (see Fig. 1). Perceptions of experience become filtered and narrowed. This process of identification with a given identity state (a constricted, distorted process of experiencing the present) leads to limited adaptations through survival oriented, instinctual responses; we dissociate from our environment, and enter an altered state that is controlled by one or more subpersonalities, with their own limited perspective and functional bias.

Grof's work (2012) echoes that of Levine's, where the "I" of a traumatized individual decides to 'check out' and split off a part of themselves, whether to the realms of the Lower or Higher Unconscious, in order to cope and remain present in a "less than" way. The split off facet of authentic personality that did not have the resources to deal with the traumatic event is removed from conscious awareness, and yet the energy of that viscerally, emotionally charged experience and its related impulses have not been processed and resolved through the completion of the primal response cycle.

The original "identity state" (that is, the splitting of primal wounding) is activated through pattern matching, where unconscious responses map similar, though unrelated, events "out there" to the original event. The survival unifying center is evoked in the Lower Unconscious, drawing on whatever resources the traumatized individual possesses, regardless of the circumstances and consequences.

Let's now extend our psychosynthesis frame. Although trauma operates emotionally and cognitively in our daily experience, that is, as a stream of potentially overwhelming experiences passing into and across the field of awareness (Figure 3), at the root of this stream of experiences is the body; physical sensations and their related impulses/desires lie at the heart of trauma. In Figure 3 we have a normal, non-trauma related experience passing into the field of awareness.

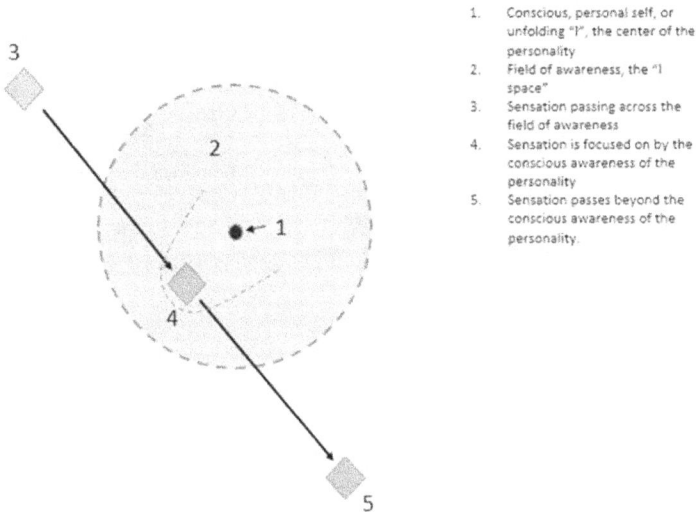

1. Conscious, personal self, or unfolding "I", the center of the personality
2. Field of awareness, the "I space"
3. Sensation passing across the field of awareness
4. Sensation is focused on by the conscious awareness of the personality
5. Sensation passes beyond the conscious awareness of the personality.

Figure 3. The field of awareness containing a sensate experience, that the "I"'s attention is drawn to.

Here we have a healthy passage of an experience across the "I" space, where "I" can choose to hold the content in awareness in order to choose to act through will, or not. In Figure 4 we have another layered approach, another map. If we hold the "I" as the font through which the source of being, transcendent immanent Self, emerges, then we can model this healthy experience as coaches. An unimpeded unfolding of "I" brings forth physical sensations, through which impulses/desires to act emerge. Emotions inform those thoughts, which enable "I" to evaluate the impulse to act (that is, to fight, flee, freeze, please). This might be framed at this point as transition from Strong Will to Skilful Will. If the desire to act is aligned with thoughts, feelings, and sensations, then action can be taken "out there" in the external environment.

Note that I have focused on the 'Four Pillars of Experience': of sensation, impulse/desire, feelings, and thoughts. This distinction is pivotal when we encounter trauma with our coaching clients, so creating a safe, non-judgemental holding environment is crucial. In the case of a traumatic event that results in a splitting—where the primal response cycle is unable to complete, Figure 4 illustrates the 'cleaving through' of the natural defense systems of the individual. The capability to act consciously (#6) is truncated by the state of physical overwhelm in the body (#2).

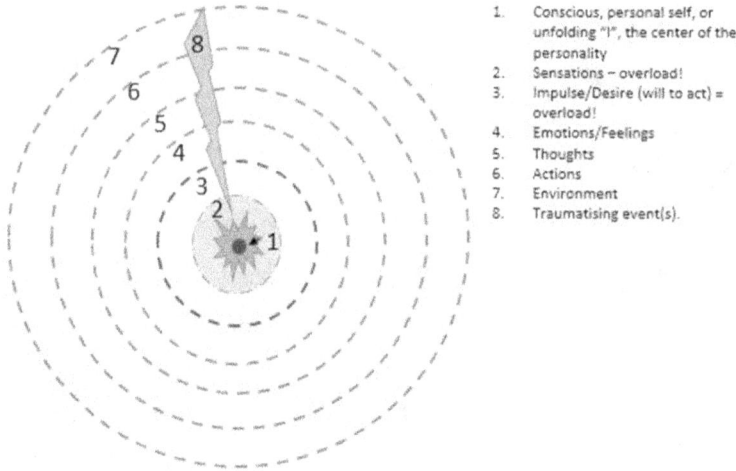

1. Conscious, personal self, or unfolding "I", the center of the personality
2. Sensations – overload!
3. Impulse/Desire (will to act) = overload!
4. Emotions/Feelings
5. Thoughts
6. Actions
7. Environment
8. Traumatising event(s).

Figure 4. The psychological functions as layers of experience encapsulating "I," pierced to the sensate ground of being that encodes, stores, and replays the traumatic content.

The instinctive, natural defense responses to 'fight, run like hell, stay still and hope you don't get eaten immediately' are not able to play out to their conclusion, and so an overwhelmingly identified trauma trance is induced (Fig. 5). Please note that this is a somatic, instinctual process, and as such cannot be directly accessed. It is through presence of and in the "I" space that a synthesis can be established.

The short and long-term effects on the person's life (irrespective of the trauma patterns they happen to embody), and their capacity to operate effectively from the choice point of awareness and will, are fundamentally inhibited.

While drawing on the work of Levine (2008) and Tart (2012), and having some maps to work with, which expand on Firman and Gila's work (1997), we are now in a much better position as psychosynthesis coaches to look deeper and yet more expansively on and into our maps, thereby assisting our clients in following their inner compass. As we guide our client's process through facilitating the body connection, we are returning full circle to Dr. Assagioli's (2007) original vision, a **biopsychosynthesis**. It is through our bodies that we reconnect to our wholeness.

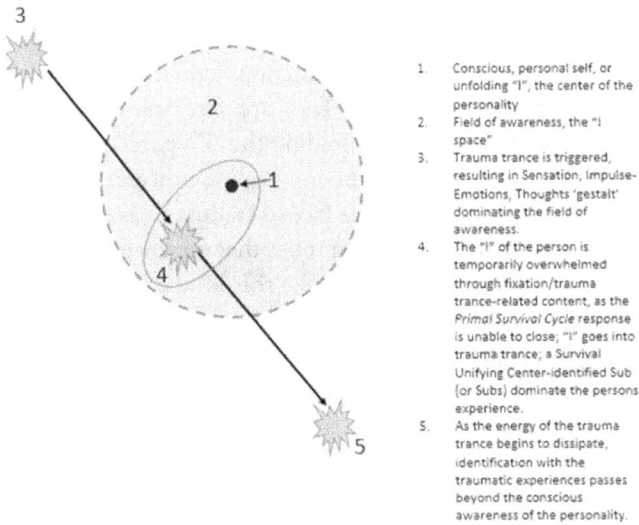

1. Conscious, personal self, or unfolding "I", the center of the personality
2. Field of awareness, the "I space"
3. Trauma trance is triggered, resulting in Sensation, Impulse-Emotions, Thoughts 'gestalt' dominating the field of awareness.
4. The "I" of the person is temporarily overwhelmed through fixation/trauma trance-related content, as the *Primal Survival Cycle* response is unable to close; "I" goes into trauma trance; a Survival Unifying Center-identified Sub (or Subs) dominate the persons experience.
5. As the energy of the trauma trance begins to dissipate, identification with the traumatic experiences passes beyond the conscious awareness of the personality.

Figure 5. Inducing of overwhelming identification as traumatic experience.

Is Psychosynthesis Coaching a Good Fit for working with Trauma?

On the face of it, working with trauma and PTSD might not seem to be a good fit for life coaching, and yet if we return to one of the fundamental maps, that is, the Egg, the following statement starts to make sense. That is: Coaching Clients come with an embedded capacity for disidentification from their story, for holding their wounding/trauma but living with that trauma as if it's in the past, as history (Firman, 2016 p.8). So, the past becomes a place to visit, draw lessons from, and exit, not to stay in.

As psychosynthesists we can draw from our deep understanding and experience with the act of identification and disidentification. If a client is able to disidentify from a potentially overwhelming experience, even a trauma induced "identity state" that is embedded in a subpersonality, then we are in a position to work with that person. Tapping into the client's Strong Will to assist in moving them 'skillfully' into a more resourceful identity/Sub is essential. Provided the client is sufficiently 'whole' and present with us, that is, they are not presenting signs of serious dissociation and pathology, we can move forwards with the engagement.

Now I've emphasized the first paragraph for good reason. We are coaches, not trauma-focused psychotherapists. However, as psychosynthesis coaches,

153

we are in a powerful and well-trained position when it comes to working with content emerging from the Lower and Higher Unconscious. The maps we work with, such as the Six Psychological Functions and Subpersonalities, provide us with the perspective and tools[1]. They are, after all, founded on a counseling and psychotherapeutic frame. Holding the "I" space as a compassionate external unifying center is a given in any healing process. Developing our own endurance, our own integrity in the face of trauma so as to be wholly present ourselves with a traumatized client, implies that our own work within the work has progressed sufficiently to undertake this kind of challenge. I do however have one caveat; as coaches, we need to have a plan b (and maybe even a plan c) so that we keep our clients safe and resourceful, whatever they bring into the consultant space. With that in mind, ensuring we have a trauma and PTSD trained psychotherapist or counselor to refer a client to is a must have.

Psychosynthesis Maps and Methods: Waypoints to Negotiating Trauma

This quote is from a fellow psychosynthesis coach, Alan Haras, a yoga teacher, who shared some pearls of wisdom on the fit between psychosynthesis and yoga, and which informs part of my work with coaching clients who present trauma. "The more awareness we have, the more choice is possible".

Just as the shaman reconnects the fractured experience of a tribal member whose soul is split, so must we, as coaches, create and facilitate a secure and safe environment, a holding space to begin that work within the work. This very first step involves a gentle dance with the content of trauma, yet we maintain the context towards the client's goals— we keep them out of the story. The external unifying center (EUC) is the holding environment, with the Coach at its center, providing the security and compassion through which clients can negotiate the story of trauma. As the states of overwhelm are negotiated, the client begins to access more and more of their split-off resources in the moment. This expansion and strengthening of the "I" space accompanies the flowering of authentic personality as the layers of the survival personality (and their respective trauma energies) are recognized, accepted, integrated and moved beyond (Figure 6).

By reconnecting to the totality of our experience through the body, we are tapping into the core, the source of life energy that fuels us all. As psychosynthesists, we have the tools, and the maps of Soul, to guide our clients to their most resourceful, authentic selves.

---

[1] Which includes the necessity of confronting and working through our own Primal Wounding. Being aware of the potential for clients to "light up" our own wounds has to be considered through the transference-countertransference relationship.

1. The conscious, personal self, or unfolding "I" at any given moment
2. The field of awareness/consciousness at any given moment
3. Authentic Unifying center emerges and expands, as awareness grows of "I Self" connection through the External Unifying Center of the Coach
4. Through relationship with the Coach, the Client's I Self connection evolves; the Authentic Personality, via an unfolding, evolving Authentic Unifying Center (what we might refer to as the 'inner Sun'), embodies more and more of "Self" as a unique expression of the person's purpose, meaning and identity. As the "heat and light" of Self (consciousness) expands into the prepersonal and transpersonal realms, the Traveller establishes and transforms relationships with Positive and Negative facets of the psyche.

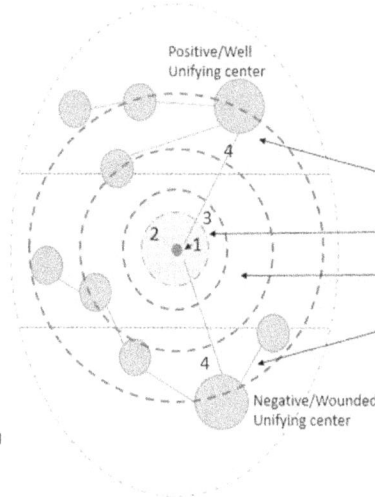

Positive/Well Unifying center

Negative/Wounded Unifying center

Authentic Unifying center expands, as the I Thou relationship with the Client is re-established, bringing them into contact with deeper (LU), elevated (HU) ranges of experiences, without the "overwhelm" of the I space/consciousness through trauma.

As the I Self re-connection brightens through Presence, Authentic Unifying Center continues unfolding (eg. pre-wounding, unconditioned personal self) into conscious awareness, supporting the on-going dialogue between split-off facets of the personality in the Lower (LU) and Higher Unconscious (HU). This may be facilitated further through inner images, such as the Wise Old One.

Figure 6: A bird's eye perspective on the gradual unfolding of Authentic Personality, in response to integrating traumatic experience.

Sensations and Impulse, Returning the Mind to the Body:

As part of our work as psychosynthesis coaches, our intention is to facilitate a respectable distance between a client's content and the context of their experiences. By keeping their (and our) eyes on the prize, that is, the goal we are working towards, we avoid unnecessary excursions into a client's traumatic content (more often than not residing in the Lower Unconscious). We acknowledge it is there, for sure, yet we maintain that the content of the past should be circumnavigated through identification/disidentification.

Our physical form is the wellspring of our vitality, energy, and creativity, and so returning to the body to reintegrate split-off parts of experience has been demonstrated by a number of authors, such as Levine (2008) and Strozzi-Heckler (2014). It is this holding of the individual, unique **Being** in the body, that we are intending with the client. Going through a purpose driven, embodied process enables the client to access more of who they are, to enact life-affirming action from awareness and will.

Reconnecting the client's awareness, their "I", with truncated parts of their experience in the Lower and Higher Unconscious results in their core regulatory system resetting, restoring inner balance, emotional equilibrium, physical poise, and relaxed alertness. The energy locked away in the body through the freeze/immobility response is released and made available. As the embodied experience is related to, we facilitate the process of expanding beyond the physical, sensate experiences to include emotions, thoughts, and impulses/desires. I call this the "Four Pillars of Experience". Once the grip of coping mechanisms, acted out by Subs associated with trauma, are loosened, new process and balance goals can be explored and agreed on, which may include alterations to lifestyle, a change of environment, and addressing ongoing social support measures. Once again, if required, seek out the wisdom of trauma-focused mental health practitioners with the client's permission.

What Needs to Come First - Creating the Crucible for Change

Our intention as coaches is to provide a secure environment that is physically safe, comforting, and emotionally supportive. During this time, we are laying out agreements with the client to facilitate their ongoing physical safety, emotional grounding, and resilience. Resilience is emphasized, as the past cannot be changed, only the context in which we perceive the meaning of the content. Initial work focuses on identifying the story relating to the trauma, and taking note of any physical sensations and where they are located in the body. Developing a routine in each session to relax the client, can help to clear the space for negotiating trauma content.

This process requires our being wholly present with the client. It is gradual, slow at times, and cyclical in nature. As part of establishing this safe and supportive environment, we first ensure that we are present with our own experience immediately before we start each session. Developing a routine or "ritual" for clearing my own inner space for evoking presence (that is, invite Self to "I") before meeting the client has been immeasurably helpful. So, evoking presence is absolutely vital, and by this word I mean two things. One is our ability, through awareness of our own functional processes and the will to choose in each moment through self- witnessing (that is, the Observer), while the other is bifocal vision. The latter comes from self-witnessing our own "I" and that of the client's: to hold the "I" space with the client while keeping an eye on the purpose and meaning provided by the client.

Guidelines for Navigating Trauma in the Coaching Space

What follows are the steps that I have adopted during coaching sessions. I have found these effective at facilitating a client's journey of recognizing, accepting and circumnavigating trauma related content.

1. Create a here and now experience of relative calm presence, aware-ness, will, and grounding. In this state, the client is taught how to visit positive body sensations, as well as tentatively visiting difficult, trauma-based sensations. Their development of an understanding of the role that the fight-flight-freeze process plays, and their aware-ness of it, is part of the process of coming to terms with trauma content, as their relationship to that content is changed.

2. Once the client is comfortably seated and engaged, we first 'check in' together, which necessitates our being fully present with our own experiences by function, and of what we perceive of the client's. This requires practice of the coach's bifocal awareness; of perceiving the inherent wholeness of the client while recognizing the challenges the client faces in relation to trauma content. We come to awareness of our bodily sensations together, such as pressure, temperature, and the subtle movements of muscles taking place. As our sensations are inextricably linked to our desires, thinking, feeling, intuiting, and inner images, the 'check in' facilitates opening the 'portal of experi-ence' through the body. The intent is to come fully into the present moment; we are evoking Presence. We are collaboratively creating the container that allows the client to be with this highly charged somatic energy that, once released, can become available for real-izing their goals.

3. Discuss and agree on any process goals; this enables the client to establish purpose and intention for the work within the work. We're after "good enough" for each session, where the client is safe and re-laxed; we are not aiming for perfection. From this purpose, we can work with the client in crafting a statement of Good Will which frames the experience for the client and for ourselves as external unifying center.

4. As the client focuses their awareness internally on physical sensa-tions, prompt them first to focus on remembering positive sensa-tions as a resource anchor. By doing so, we keep the client present with their experience, yet embodying a positive reference that we can return to if the client is uncomfortable and wishes to withdraw to this "safe place". The key here is actively choosing to identify with these positive sensations, so it is developing Skillful Will, that re-assesses Strong Will, through the Good Will statement of intent at Step #3. Levine (2008) refers to this as sensate tracking, where the client is aware of the embodied energies. The following kinds of

questions (or words to this effect), can prove useful in guiding the client:

- What sensations are you experiencing right now in your body? NB: pay close attention here, as subtle shifts in the client's physiology may manifest themselves/appear, such as a gentle trembling of muscles, a slight turning of the head as an orientation response to a remembered threat, or other clear physiological signal.
- Where are those sensations in your body? NB: Consider asking the client to place their hand on that part of the body, to connect with the sensation from a place of awareness.
- Do you notice your posture (or shape) as you say that? What might that be saying to you?
- What would you like to do next with the way your body is positioned (that is, moving from a hunched over posture to an upright posture with a straight spine)? And how would you like to move?
- Can you breathe into that place—what is that like?
- Could it help to take a deep breath?—maybe take a few, slow deep breaths (and breathe with them— we are intending to pace and lead the client)
- What words are coming to awareness right now, and who is speaking them? NB: This helps us to identify any subpersonalities that are associated with the trauma content.

5. Now to identify the embodied sensation that is anchored to the traumatic experience. Pay attention to any inner images and words that the client reports. These are likely to be subpersonality related, as an opening to the truncated experiences of the trauma. The intention is to hold the space for somatic awareness here, with as little discomfort as possible, while coming to awareness of those subpersonalities. This might be an awareness of numbing, or an ache/pain that was not present before, or perhaps of dissociation from sensation. Some questions to consider asking:

- As you become more aware of that space, what do you want to say?
- As you step out of that space, what do you notice or become aware of?

6. Notice any involuntary bodily movements that accompany these sensations. For example, subtle muscular twitches, flushed skin and

increased breathing rate are indicative of the primal survival cycle running, as the trapped energy is accessed and released. This can also include a relaxing tingling sensation. As the client's awareness is drawn to this, it will reinforce and expand the belief that the survival cycle is closing naturally. Query the client on any spontaneous imagery associated with these movements and sensations to assist in easing any anxiety and vulnerability. Acknowledge any positive emotions that arise during the process, and in particular note any references to transpersonal values—Assagioli's (2010) evocative words. These can act as reference points for further synthesis work once the trauma energies are released.

7. If the client's posture seems to be closing, they may be identifying with trauma content through a dominant Sub. Keep the client present with their experience through a suggestion of moving the body, for example, straightening of the spine, drawing back of the shoulders, ask them to stand up and move around the room. Remember that we are attempting to facilitate embodied awareness through self-witnessing, and that requires encouraging the client's awareness of choice. Take note of any internal images the client may share (do not be afraid to prompt them for this), as these may relate to sub-personalities that require working with, either in the present session or in subsequent sessions. Accessing and engaging Subs with a dominant sensate function expands the client's awareness of any split off functions; for example, emotions that are associated with the trauma.

8. Notice any opening of the body during this process. Bring their attention to this movement, anchoring the opening by prompting them to place their hands on that body area. If they instinctively feel like standing up and moving around, encourage them to embody this energetic shift. Positive engagement is key here, as the trauma trapped energy releases slowly. Move the client between positive, easy bodily sensations and difficult bodily sensations iteratively. We're aiming to activate the body's biological response to releasing that trapped energy, allowing the client a greater capacity for experiencing any shaking/discharge without any feelings of overwhelm/shutdown.

9. As the client begins to settle, close the session work by accessing the transpersonal in one form or another, while moving into grounding. I have found this helps in facilitating the synthesis of the work done in the session (Howard, 2017).

Through this process of moving back and forth between the positive and negative sensations (what Levine (2008) refers to as "pendulating" between resilient and overwhelming states), the client gains an increasing flexibility in identifying with, and then disidentifying from elements of the trauma content/ memories, strengthening their capacity to self-witness and maintain presence. Through the course of a number of sessions, I have witnessed clients' trauma-anchored Subs, that once elicited, evolve and transform, which includes name changes, form of image changes, together with the embodied feelings associated with those Subs. Figure 9 provides a summary of the steps, as a recursive process.

Wrapping Up – The Story Beyond Trauma

The experience of trauma, as a guide for others on that road, and as traveller on that road myself, raises a question that I encounter each time I work with people. That question is about the stories we habitually tell ourselves, about ourselves. Without those stories, even the ones founded on traumatic experiences, who are we, each and all, beyond these stories?

We come into this world as unique Souls, each with an innate sense of self-worth, of implicit capabilities and purpose that somehow goes beyond the "clean slate" perspective of which the kneejerk, reductivist, paradigm of these times tries to convince us. As we grow over the years, that light of Self—of Soul—becomes covered, its light dimmed. We are conditioned through our parents and culture to accept beliefs about who we are, what we are to be and do, and so on. Some of these layers are painful, some overwhelmingly so. These layers of experience act like the stories in the chapters of a book, and yet, did we author these stories with the outcome that arose in mind? Of course not. Yet, what is the story of Self/Soul, that is paradoxically unstoried, unwritten?

It is my earnest belief, based on my own journey through trauma and in assisting others to circumnavigate and rewrite their own stories, that we can unveil our Soulful authenticity, beneath the conditioned responses of having lived our lives. As we navigate the pain of our pasts, those stories of trauma act as identifications that persuade us to act as if we are our stories. If we are layers of stories, then what story, as seed, lies at our uniquely Soulful, authentic center? Paradoxically, we are the author and conductor along with the unstoried Self, the author, and, at times, conductor of our lives. We have the capacity to act from awareness to re-author our lives.

As psychosynthesis coaches, we are presented with opportunities to assist our clients in unveiling their own uniquely Soulful potentials, and part of that Soulful work requires us to acknowledge and hold, in compassion, the pains of the past, the joys of liberation from the past in the present, and the flowering of that paradoxical seed in the future.

References

Aquilina, E. (2016). *Embodying authenticity: A somatic path to transforming self, team & organisation.* London: Live IT Publishing.

Assagioli, R. (2007) *Transpersonal development.* Scotland: Inner Way Publications.

Assagioli, R. (2010). *The act of will.* Amherst, MA: The Synthesis Center Press.

Bal, R. (n.d.). Why complex trauma is called complex trauma. Available at https: //rolandbal.com/why-complex-trauma-is-called-complex-trauma/.

Campone, F. (2014) At the border: Coaching a client with dissociative identity disorder. *International Journal of Evidence Based Coaching and Mentoring,* 12 (1), pp. 1-13. Available at: https://radar.brookes.ac.uk/radar/file/f0eb1fe8-6d5a-4afd-8c6d-2182e2c52b6d/1/vol12issue1-paper-01.pdf.

Firman, D. (2016). *Supporting the future of Psychosynthesis: Coaching as a path to self-realization.* Taormina, Italy: International Psychosynthesis Conference.

Firman, J., & Gila, A. (1997). *The primal wound: A transpersonal view of trauma, addiction and growth.* Albany, NY: State University of New York Press.

Levine, P. (1997). *Waking the tiger: Healing trauma - The innate capacity to transform overwhelming experiences.* Berkeley, CA: North Atlantic Books.

Levine, P. (2008). *Healing trauma: A pioneering program for restoring the wisdom of your body.* Boulder, CO: Sounds True.

Grof, S. (2012). *Healing our deepest wounds: The holotropic paradigm shift.* Newcastle, WA: Stream of Experience Productions.

Howard, A. (2017, April 1). The somatic path of coaching. [Web log post]. Linked-In. Available at https://www.linkedin.com/pulse/somatic-path-coaching-aubyn-howard/.

Strozzi-Heckler, R. (2014). *The art of somatic coaching: Embodying skillful action, wisdom, and compassion.* Berkeley, CA: North Atlantic Books.

Tart, C. (2012). *Waking up: Overcoming the obstacles to human potential.* Napa, CA: Fearless Books.

Van der Kolk, B. (2014). *The body keeps the score: Mind, brain and body in the transformation of trauma.* New York: Penguin.

Chapter 13

The Path of Self-Realization: Yoga, Psychosynthesis, and the Goodness of Fit

by Alan C. Haras

"In the right view both of life and of Yoga all life is either consciously or subconsciously a Yoga."—Sri Aurobindo,

In October of 2016, my wife and I were in Florence making plans to visit the home of Roberto Assagioli. While sitting in our hotel room one evening, I begin searching through the online archive of Assagioli's writings. Combing through this treasure trove, I stumbled upon a hand-written note that read "Psicosintesi = Yoga." As soon as I read this, a deep, true voice within me exclaimed, "I knew it!" I felt as though something within me simultaneously settled and flowered. That night I had a dream where a voice told me that I would discover in Florence a "symbol," a mandala, in which all the pieces of my life would fit. I woke up incredibly happy, and immediately understood that the "symbol" was psychosynthesis—a center around which the various dimensions of my work as a yoga teacher and guide would find their proper place.

My training in psychosynthesis coaching has been like a Rosetta stone that has helped me understand the inner meaning of the yogic teachings, and a key that has helped me unlock the purpose of my work as a yoga teacher. Over the last 12 years, I have contemplated what it means to live out this unique vocation in the modern world. I have taken much inspiration from the yoga tradition, but also recognize, as a white man raised and living in suburban Michigan, the severe limitations of attempting to adopt and replicate the rich and ancient Indian perspective on the formation of teachers and students. With great reverence for the ancient tradition, I have questioned what the role of the modern (and in my case, Western) yoga teacher is in the world. What does it mean to teach yoga, and what does it mean to be a yoga teacher? What skills are needed? What are the pitfalls to be avoided? For me, psychosynthesis coaching has given me the context, form, and training not to approach only these questions, but it has also empowered me to live out my vocation as a yoga teacher with greater integrity, sincerity, and effectiveness.

From my own experience and observations, I see yoga teachers playing various roles within their communities. I think a yoga teacher is someone who primarily practices yoga. By "practicing yoga," I do not mean simply the physical postures, but that one is consciously engaged in one's own process of integration, synthesis and wholeness. As a "teacher," I see the yoga teacher as an "educator"—someone who designs classes with the aim of "drawing out" the hidden potential of his or her students (Assagioli, 1968). As leaders, they model and support students in expressing the values of Yoga in their daily lives. As guides, they have the privilege of companioning students as they discern and unfold their unique dharma, or Call of Self. However, as someone who has taken five different yoga teacher trainings, I have become aware that the current system aimed at forming yoga teachers does not offer adequate training for developing these various roles, which are essential if the yoga teacher is going to create opportunities for individuals to experience yoga.

The word "yoga" is often translated as union, wholeness, integration, or synthesis. Much like psychosynthesis, yoga can refer to both the method practiced and the goal to be experienced. Derived from the Sanskrit root yuj, meaning, "to yoke," the two things that yoga seeks to yoke together are the personal self and the Higher Self. In the yoking of two animals together, the yoke is always custom-fit, crafted with the individual animal in mind, as to not create discomfort or irritation. When yoked together properly, the two animals are able to grow together, and work together toward the accomplishment of some task or goal. As the animals grow, the yoke also must be re-shaped and refashioned.

The practice of Yoga is exactly the same. Yoga is a method by which we "coordinate and integrate all our inner resources, so that they are working in a unified way and in line with our aims" (Firman & Vargiu, 1977, p. 5). Texts like the Yoga Sutras of Patanjali were meant to be a kind of framework for teachers to fill out and elaborate upon for the sake of their students (Desikachar, 2003). The transmission of yogic knowledge was always "custom-fit" to the individual student, affirming Assagioli's approach to working with clients: "For one person, one thing: for another, quite the opposite" (Assagioli, as cited in, Yeomans, 2010, p. 2). There has never been a one-size fits all yoga, in the same way that there is not one "right" way to do psychosynthesis. These vast traditions allow for, and celebrate, the diversity of the individual, while at the same time being in service of individual, social, and global harmony.

According to a 2014 research study conducted by the Yoga Alliance and Yoga Journal, 36 million Americans now consider themselves yogis (Macy, 2016). Another study notes that 62% of yoga students and 85% of yoga teachers originally were drawn to yoga for exercise and stress relief, but later noted that spirituality was the primary reason they maintained their practice (Park, Riley, Bedesin, & Stewart, 2014). Modern yoga teachers are not only leading groups of individuals through a contemplative practice, but they are also acting as guides to individuals seeking wholeness, authenticity, and purpose.

While completing my Master's degree, I did a research project where I surveyed about 100 yoga students and found about two-thirds of those students asked their yoga teachers' advice about topics unrelated to the physical practice—about spirituality, relationship issues, and decision-making (Haras, 2015). When asked why they approached their yoga teachers, many of the students surveyed said they found their yoga teachers to be safe, non-judgmental, and people they could trust. In that same research project, the term that arose repeatedly about how yoga students see their teachers, and how yoga teachers see themselves, was "guide."

> *The quality of the helping relationship, based on unconditional love and close attunement, is the indispensable context without which techniques are mere gimmicks which lack true healing power. The level of the guide's personal integration is a crucial element which determines the amount of clarity and love he or she is able to bring to the traveler on the path.*
> —Martha Crampton (as cited in, Brown, 2004, p. 63)

As Yoga continues to grow and evolve, the skills and training of a modern yoga teacher must also evolve to reflect those roles accurately. I have found that training in psychosynthesis provides incredibly useful maps for guiding individuals and classes, as well as an invaluable opportunity to consciously engage in the process of integration. As a contemplative psychology and educational framework, psychosynthesis has helped me better understand the various practices and techniques that support the natural process of growth and transformation, as well as the pitfalls, distortions, and obstacles of which I need to be aware. When I teach, I now see my yoga classes as 75-minute group psychosynthesis sessions, where the yoga class itself becomes a holding environment that invites students to travel upon the path of Self-Realization.

Because my classes emphasize the spiritual dimension of yoga, it is not uncommon for students to visit me in my office either before or after class to talk about their journeys. As a fellow pilgrim on the path, I did the exact same thing with my yoga teachers. This kind of interaction can be traced all the way back to the *Upanishads*, the ancient books that form the very roots of Yoga. These texts contain discussions and stories regarding the great questions of life: Who am I? What is the nature of Ultimate Reality? What is the nature of the world, and what is my role in it? The word "Upanishad" means "to sit down near" or "sitting near devotedly" (Prabhavananda & Manchester, 1957, p. ix). One meaning is that the student sits down near a guru in order to receive the transmission of sacred knowledge, while another meaning is to "sit down near" the inner guru to hear "the still, small voice" of the Higher Self whisper its wisdom to the personal self.

One story from the *Chandogya Upanishad* involves a seeker who approaches a sage asking to be taught the knowledge of Self. Before instructing him, the sage asks the seeker to "Say what you know; I will say what you do not" (Yeats, 1965, p.96). The man then gives an exhaustive list of arts and sciences that he has mastered, to which the sage replies, "It appears that you have learned all there is to know!" The man then responds by saying, "But, I have gained no peace of mind. I have studied all this, but the Self I do not know" (Prabhavananda & Manchester, 1957, p. 71). The sage then agrees to teach this man, saying that he has known all of these things in "name" only, and now he was going to guide him in understanding their "meaning."

In many ways, this has been my quest. Having read numerous books on yoga, I have been seeking the inner meaning of these beautiful teachings, as well as a way of sharing them in an authentic way with my students. I have been afforded every privilege and advantage in this quest, training with some of the greatest yoga teachers of our time, studying Sanskrit at my local Hindu temple, spending two-months on pilgrimage in India, and experiencing the beauty and nuance of Indian culture through my relationships with my Indian in-laws. However, to be honest, until recently, I have felt much like the man in the Upanishads—that all my knowledge about yoga was "but the knowledge of names" (Yeats, 1965, p. 97).

That is, until I discovered psychosynthesis. In the summer of 2015, when I came across a collection of online interviews given by a number of psychosynthesis practitioners, I had the immediate experience of an internal knowing being validated. At the time, that felt like a completely unique experience. For all those years while I was reading books on yoga, I was hoping to experience what those authors described. But when I began reading books on psychosynthesis, I found that they perfectly articulated what I already intuitively knew. Strangely enough, this immediately made all of my yogic studies make sense in both a fresh and familiar way.

"A guru lies within all of us. That guru is known as the inner guru, or satguru. And, ultimately, there is no guru other than the one who lives within each and every one of us."
—*Swami Satyananda Saraswati (1976, p. 163)*

One of the distinct features of the Upanishads, which I think predisposed me to psychosynthesis coaching, is its unique pedagogy. The sages, rather than giving prescribed answers, often employ a series of questions to elicit or evoke the innate wisdom of the student. These artful conversations inevitably culminate in Self-Realization, a moment of Self-recognition that transforms the disciple's life. These days, forest hermitages are in short supply and genuine gurus seem hard to find. However, today we have an abundance of yoga teachers and dedicated yoga practitioners. What is not in short supply, and what can never be diminished no matter how much it is overlooked, is the presence and guidance of the Higher Self.

By training yoga teachers as psychosynthesis coaches, this archetypal teacher-student relationship can be reimagined in a way that honors the ancient Upanishadic tradition while adapting it to the modern world. Psychosynthesis coaching offers both yoga teachers and yoga students a clear understanding of roles, appropriate boundaries and expectations, and frees both from the baggage of misguided ideas surrounding gurus and disciples. By shifting from a guru model to a coaching model, the relationship shifts from a hierarchical "social dynamic of disempowerment" (Whitwell, 2015), to a strengths-based, peer-to-peer relationship where the coach is in service of the student's Higher Self. By honoring the personality as well as the Self, psychosynthesis coaching circumvents the view that says the purpose of yoga is to annihilate the ego (Sovik, 2016). The coaching dynamic, rather than tearing down the self, builds up and empowers the 'I', while simultaneously placing it within the larger, empathic context of Self. It fuses the best of transpersonal psychology with the best of spirituality. By supporting the view of "both/and," psychosynthesis is a medicine to an industry that can easily polarize the quest for enlightenment with the responsibilities of house/car/job/family.

Dimensions of Growth

In our own times, increasing numbers of people involved in spiritual life are realizing the need to develop well-integrated, capable personalities in

167

order to make their spiritual values work. And more and more people who have been successfully expressing themselves in practical ways are reaching for the transpersonal to find deeper meaning, more certain direction, and greater effectiveness.
　　　　—John Firman and James Vargiu (1977, p. 2)

One of the most useful psychosynthesis "maps" for yoga teachers and students is Assagioli's Path of Self-Realization, which harmonizes the two dimensions of growth.

This middle way puts into context two different, classical definitions of yoga. One definition comes from the *Bhagavad Gita*, which says "yoga is skill in action" (Nikhilananda, 1987, p. 28). This horizontal dimension of yoga is often forgotten in the modern yoga culture. It corresponds to Assagioli's personal psychosynthesis, which promotes, fosters, and supports the development of a well-integrated personality, and the engagement of the will to accomplish meaningful goals.

The second, better known, definition of yoga comes from the *Yoga Sutra of Patanjali*, which says "Yoga is the settling of the mind into silence" (Shearer, 1982, p. 90). This definition of yoga emphasizes the vertical dimension of growth through meditation and contemplation, as well as the essential nature of the self as contentless awareness and will. This dimension of growth, what Assagioli calls spiritual psychosynthesis, allows practitioners to see themselves from a higher, more inclusive perspective. According to Patanjali, when one disidentifies from the contents of one's consciousness, the result is that one abides in one's essential nature (Satyananda, 1976, p. 42). Through dedicated yoga and meditation practice, we learn the art of first becoming aware of various limiting identifications, then the ability to disidentify from them, and finally to identify with Self.

These two dimensions of growth are often held in a polarity, but in the opening chapters of the *Bhagavad Gita*, Sri Krishna (who represents the Higher Self) encourages his friend Arjuna (who represents the personal self), to practice both simultaneously. He invites him to connect to his essential nature and to live out his truth in the concrete realities of life. As Firman and Vargiu (1977) write, any time we over-emphasize a particular dimension of our growth to the exclusion of the other, we experience a kind of "crisis of reorientation." That is exactly where we find Arjuna in the first chapter of the Gita: despondent, confused, and recognizing that the way he has always done things is no longer adequate to the task he now faces. At different times in our lives, and for different reasons, the Self asks us to grow along one of these two dimensions, or in terms of yoga practice, to consciously engage in skillful action or deep meditation. Assagioli synthesizes these two dimensions of growth, recognizing that it is only in holding both dimensions that we can develop and express our full potential as human persons.

Kriya Yoga—The Path of Self-Realization

The goal of yoga is Self-realization: to find out who you are, why you're here...
—*Sri Dharma Mittra (2013, Interview by A. Dubrovsky)*

Psychosynthesis refers to the harmony of these two dimensions of growth as the Path of Self-realization. As we navigate this middle path, there are three stages that we will repeatedly pass through:
removing the obstacles of the personality, orienting toward the Higher Self, and expressing the energies of the Higher Self through the personality into the world (Firman & Vargiu, 1977, p. 22).

To me, these stages beautifully express the goal of the three components of a spiritual practice that Patanjali refers to collectively as kriya yoga. The word kriya comes from the root word kr, meaning "to do" or "to make." Swami Satyananda Sarasvati (1976) writes, "Kriya yoga means practical yoga, yoga with practical techniques. It involves acts of self-purification, self-observation and evolving self-awareness. These three acts constitute kriya yoga" (p. 141). Kriya yoga is those actions, skills, and exercises which, when practiced, lead toward yoga. These practices are essential because they "purify the body and nervous system so as to allow a seeker to endure the energy of higher states of consciousness" (Grimes, 1996, p. 168). When seen through the lens of psychosynthesis, these three yogic practices—tapas, svadhyaya and ishvara pranidhana—give yoga teachers a simple set of guidelines that can aide in facilitating their students' journey, as well as a framework for psychosynthesis coaches to guide dedicated yoga practitioners.

Tapas – Removing Obstacles of the Personality

The first action that leads toward Yoga is tapas, which translates as austerity, discipline, asceticism, or purification. According to Swami Satyananda (1976), tapas is "a process which completely illuminates the imperfections, the dross of the inner personality" (p. 139). The word tap means to heat, to burn, or to boil. Tapas is the heat generated from the daily discipline of our practice that burns away the dross of physical, mental, or emotional impurities. As a form of asceticism, tapas is the way we govern our appetites in order to live in alignment with our values.

One of the yoga postures that corresponds to tapas is mayurasana—the peacock pose. It is said that the digestive fire of the peacock is so strong that it is capable of eating poisonous snakes and poisonous insects without adverse effects (Muktibodhananda, Satyananda, & Svātmārāma, 2004). Furthermore, the poison that the peacock digests transforms into the beautiful colors and iridescence of its tail. This ability is a metaphor for the yogi, whose inner fire, strengthened through dedicated practice, is capable of digesting not only food, but also his or her own life experience. From the standpoint of Yoga's sister school, Ayurveda, whatever is left undigested can build up, and if left unattended within our system, can potentially become a kind of "poison" that obstructs our growth.

This is where Assagioli's insights into "subpersonalities" can be such a boon to yogis. Subpersonality work allows yogis to integrate parts of themselves that may have created a state of indigestion in the personality. Once recognized, accepted, and integrated, these parts of our personality, rather than being an obstacle, can contribute to the beauty of Self-expression. This piece of psychosynthesis theory has been incredibly healing to my yoga students and coaching clients. A great amount of self-compassion and inner freedom comes from simply hearing that these parts of themselves are trying to help them, albeit in a somewhat limited way. They no longer see these parts of themselves as something to be eliminated. Through cultivating this inner stance of maitri, or friendliness, toward all parts of oneself, the yoga practitioner utilizes one of the main techniques that Patanjali recommends for overcoming obstacles to a "serene and pure" mind (Iyengar, 1993).

Svadhyaya—Orienting Toward the Higher Self

The way that I often think about my yoga center is that it is a tree in the center of my community where individuals can come, build a nest made out of their intention to grow, and have a safe place within which to hatch a larger version of themselves. Many times, I have seen students come, practice very intensely and consistently for a period of time, right before they make a big jump in their life. One man in particular, who has an affinity for Shiva—the embodiment of transformation—practiced almost daily for 6 or 8 months, when unexpectedly he was offered a new position at work, and became his boss's boss. The two dimensions of growth map have offered me quite a bit of insight on this. We journey along the horizontal path for a period of time, until we either intuit or are forced to confront that the image we have for ourselves may be too small for us to move into the next phase of our life. It is then that we are invited to traverse the vertical path of orienting toward the Higher Self, in order to discover a larger context, a larger vision of who we are and who we might become.

This radical re-orientation is represented in a yoga class by the practice of inversions such as shoulder stand, headstand, and handstand. Considered the most powerful of the asanas because of the numerous health benefits they offer, inversions symbolize our ability to see our life and ourselves in a completely new and unexpected way. For example, the name for handstand in Sanskrit is adho mukha vrkshasana—the "downward-facing tree." In inverted postures, we metaphorically discover our hidden roots "above," tapping into the transpersonal dimension in order to access the energies of Self.

Having harmonized the personal self, the practitioner orients toward the Higher Self, of which the personal self is an expression. Patanjali refers to this as the practice of svadhyaya, literally meaning "Self-study." Sometimes it is translated as "to examine" or "to draw close to" the Self. There are myriad ways that psychosynthesis techniques can enrich and illumine a yoga practitioner's experience of svadhyaya, such as guided imagery, inner dialogue with a Wise Being, the evening review, and evocative word cards, to name a few. Although the methods are various, the aim is the same: aligning the personality with the Higher Self.

One of the main practices of svadhyaya is the study of sacred texts. What makes reading a spiritual practice, is the consciousness we bring to it. For example, reading the *Bhagavad Gita* in order to gather interesting ideas is what Assagioli called "informative education" (Assagioli, 1968). However, reading the *Bhagavad Gita* as a way of encountering one's own Self transforms the act into an experience of formative education. This type of study touches the heart, reaches the core of the person, and allows one an opportunity to discover the personal relevance and lived reality of the text. This kind of contemplative education knits the person together in a special way, creating the conditions "to 'draw out' the latent possibilities from the unconscious, to activate the energies dormant in it, particularly in its higher sphere, the superconscious" (Assagioli, 2010, p. 42).

Ishvara Pranidhana—Expressing the Energies of the Higher Self through the Personality into the World

One of the things that I often emphasize in my yoga classes is that the asanas (the poses) are designed to elicit an inner mood or experience, what is called bhavana. This corresponds to Assagioli's psychological laws, where he says "Attitudes, movements, and actions tend to evoke corresponding images and ideas; these, in turn evoke or intensify corresponding emotions and feelings" (Assagioli, 2010, p. 39). The shape or alignment of the pose can potentially draw forth an inner experience of a particular archetype or transpersonal quality. Just as study without a contemplative orientation is relatively flat, an asana class without awareness of bhavana loses some of its transformative power.

The practice of yoga includes and celebrates embodied existence, using the body and breath as a door to access deeper levels of our existence, including the transcendent. Each pose is connected to a set of qualities that, if meditated upon throughout the class, can link us to the transpersonal. The tree pose can invite practitioners to embody what for them is the archetypal tree. One might consider what a tree has to teach them about Yoga, or what qualities of a tree they most need to develop. For example, meditating on the steadiness of a tree can influence the body's ability to balance on one leg, but it also opens the door to meditating on the transpersonal quality of "steadiness." The tree pose becomes a doorway through which yoga practitioners express the quality of steadiness—in their body, in their mind, and in the world.

Here, the personality, rather than being eliminated, comes into service of Self. This is what Patanjali refers to as ishvara pranidhana. Pranidhana means to "set down before." It sometimes is translated as "surrender," however this translation seems to convey a feeling of defeat and diminishment, rather than collaboration and right relationship. The personality recognizes itself as not merely a "me" but a part of a "we". This alignment of I and Self is not a goal to be achieved, but rather a relationship in which to be engaged. In *Psychosynthesis: a Psychology of Spirit*, Firman and Gila (2002) write that a person might make a choice that alienates one from Self one moment, and in the next moment make a choice that brings one back into alignment. Having made efforts to remove blockages within the personality and oriented toward Self, the Self has an opportunity to express itself with greater ease and effectiveness through the personality, for the betterment of others.

A Cordial Appeal

The first practical aim of a yogi is to understand one's own personality, which includes the body, mind, emotions and intellect. The second practical aim is to awaken one's inner powers. ... The third practical aim of a yogi is to serve society. After attaining some ability through yoga, one should contribute to the development and maintenance of society.
—*Swami Niranjanananda Sarasvati (2012, p. 14)*

In his book *Psychosynthesis*, Assagioli (1965) makes a "cordial appeal to all therapists, psychologists, and educators to actively engage in the needed work of research, experimentation and application" (p. 9). I feel that yoga teachers are in a unique position to contribute to this experimentation, applying the principles and techniques of psychosynthesis in their classes and in their relationships with students. With yoga centers now covering the globe, the introduction of psychosynthesis into these communities can support the good work already being done, as well as further encourage "the creation of a new civilization characterized by harmonious integration and cooperation, pervaded by the spirit of synthesis" (Assagioli, 1965, p. 9). As I continue to go through the Archivio Assagioli, I get the impression that Assagioli somehow anticipated this growth of modern yoga. As someone who supported many of his students starting institutes and training programs, I think he would be over-joyed at the idea of yoga teacher training programs including a psychosynthetic curriculum. Furthermore, I think he would be ecstatic to see yoga teachers trained as psychosynthesis coaches in order to serve their students in hearing and responding to their own unique Call of Self.

> *The stunning paradox of human spiritual maturity is that, as we become one with all Life, we also at the same time become completely and uniquely ourselves.*
> —*Thomas Yeomans (2010, p. 7)*

Not everyone is called to become a yoga teacher, and yet, because it is so popular, becoming certified as a yoga teacher has become almost a kind of default dharma. However, what if, rather than trying to fit all seekers into the same mold of "yoga teacher", yoga centers became places where practitioners could identify and live out the "blueprint that is implicit" within their own psyche (Whitmore, 2004)? Piero Ferrucci writes:

> According to the Eastern doctrine of dharma, we are called upon to achieve a particular life-pattern. And while all patterns have equal dignity, each one of us should avail himself or herself of the possibility that is uniquely one's own and not someone else's. Each of us should try to discover the pattern and cooperate with its realization. (Ferrucci, as cited in, Brown, 2004, p. 157)

While psychosynthesis coaching helps those called to be yoga teachers unfold their unique dharma, it also trains them effectively to guide others in unfolding their own. It supports both teachers and students in deepening their self-knowledge, accessing and integrating the potential hidden in the higher unconscious, and serving society by supporting individuals as they grow in wholeness. Rather than creating followers, psychosynthesis coaching allows yoga teachers to support their students' autonomy and unique unfoldment more consciously. In this way, the modern yoga teacher expresses some of the great beauty of the Upanishadic tradition, creating not only a safe environment for community members to grow spiritually, but also acting as a skilled guide who understands the terrain of the path of Self-realization, and is available to individuals seeking to engage in the process of transformation.

Like the Upanishadic sages of old, today's yoga teachers equipped with psychosynthesis training, can serve the people who come to them by helping them unlock their own dharma, and discover the Self who has been their true guru all long.

References

Assagioli, R. (1965). *Psychosynthesis: A manual of principles and techniques.* New York: Hobbs, Dorman.

Assagioli, R. (1968). Notes on education. Retrieved from http://synthesiscenter.org/articles/0321.pdf

Assagioli, R. (2010). *The act of will.* New York: Association for the Advancement of Psychosynthesis.

Aurobindo, S. (1996). *Synthesis of Yoga.* Twin Lakes, WI: Lotus Press.

Brown, M. Y. (2004). *Unfolding self: The practice of Psychosynthesis.* New York: Allworth Press.

Crampton, M. (1977). *Psychosynthesis: Some key aspects of theory and practice.* Montreal: Canadian Institute of Psychosynthesis.

Desikachar, T. K. (2003). *Reflections on Yogasutra-s of Patanjali. Chennai,* India: Krishnamacharya Yoga Mandiram.

Firman, J., & Gila, A. (2002). *Psychosynthesis: A psychology of the spirit.* Albany, NY: SUNY Press.

Firman, J., & Gila, A. (2007). Assagioli's seven core concepts for training. Retrieved from http://synthesiscenter.org/PDF/Seven%20Concepts.pdf

Firman, J., & Vargiu, J. (1977). Dimensions of growth. *Synthesis 3-4,* 59-120.

Gheraṇda, S., & Niranjanananda, S. (2012). *Gheranda Samhita: Commentary on the yoga teachings of Maharishi Gheranda. Munger, Bihar,* India: Yoga Publications Trust.

Grimes, J. A. (1996). A concise dictionary of Indian philosophy: Sanskrit terms defined in English. Albany, NY: SUNY Press.

Iyengar, B. K. (1993). *Light on the Yoga Sūtras of Patañjali.* London: Thorsons.

Macy, D. (2016). Yoga in America study, *Yoga Journal.* Retrieved from http://www.yogajournal.com/yogainamericastudy/

Mittra, D. (2013, June 10). *Dharma Mittra: No yama, no yoga.* (A. Dubrovsky, Interviewer). Yoga International. Retrieved from https://yogainternational.com/article/view/dharma-mittra-no-yama-no-yoga

Muktibodhananda, S., Satyananda, S., & Svātmārāma, S. (2004). *Hatha yoga pradipika: Light on hatha yoga: including the original Sanskrit text of the Hatha yoga pradipika with translation in English.* Munger, Bihar: Yoga Publications Trust.

Nikhilananda, S. (1987). *The Bhagavad Gita.* New York: Ramakrishna-Vivekananda Center.

Park, C. L., Riley, K. E., Bedesin, E., & Stewart, V. M. (2014). Why practice yoga? Practitioners motivations for adopting and maintaining yoga practice. *Journal of Health Psychology, 21*(6), 887-896. doi:10.1177/1359105314541314

Prabhavananda, & Manchester, F. (1957). *The Upanishads, breath of the eternal: The principle texts selected and translated from the original Sanskrit.* New York: New American Library.

Purohit, S., & Yeats, W. B. (1965). *The ten principal Upanishads.* New York: Collier.

Satyananda, S. (1976). *Four chapters on freedom: Commentary on yoga sutras of Sage Patanjali.* Munger, Bihar, India: Yoga Publications Trust.

Satyasangananda, S. (1984). *Light on the guru and disciple relationship.* Munger, Bihar, India: Yoga Publications Trust.

Shearer, A. (1982). *Yoga sutras of Patanjali.* New York: Bell Tower.

Sovik, R. (2016, April 1). *Yoga and the Ego.* Yoga International. Retrieved from https://yogainternational.com/article/view/yoga-and-the-ego

Whitmore, D. (2004). *Psychosynthesis counselling in action.* London: Sage Publications Ltd.

Whitwell, M. (2015). *The relationship between yoga teachers & students* [Video file]. Retrieved from https://www.youtube.com/watch?v=OIKv-FDkibw

Yeomans, T. (2010). *Occasional note #10 descent of the higher self.* Retrieved from https://www.synthesiscenter.org/PDF/Tom's%20pdfs/OCN10-Descent-of-the-Higher-Self.pdf

Chapter 14

Psychosynthesis in Dreams: Engaging Dream Imagery in Psychosynthesis Coaching

by Wilka M. Roig Rivera

To the memory of teacher and mentor Jeremy Taylor, DMin.

Imagery is a flow of thoughts you can see, hear, feel, smell, or taste.
An image is an inner representation of your experience or your fantasies
—a way your mind codes, stores, and expresses information.

Imagery is the currency of dreams and daydreams;
memories and reminiscence; plans, projections, and possibilities.
It is the language of the arts, the emotions, and most important, of the
deeper self.

—Martin L. Rossman, M.D.

Introduction

In its endeavor to support waking life, dreaming is highly creative and transformative. History shows that the evolution of civilizations was greatly influenced by the promptings from dreams. In the external collective, it has been observed that many of the greatest discoveries, inventions, and creative contributions throughout history were sparked by images, activities, and events first witnessed and experienced in dreams. In the internal collective and the personal, humans have the same potential for evolution from what takes place in dreams and how they engage them.

Some theories of human evolution support the role of dreaming as essential in personal and collective learning and growth. Some say the biological evolutionary purpose of dreaming is that of testing and practicing physical and mental skills for survival while asleep. Dreams help simulate possible, more complex waking life experiences so that humans are primed to face them. Dreaming is one way of working with and processing past, present, and potential challenges in life. Because dreams often represent old ideas, experiences, attitudes, and beliefs in new and unfamiliar ways, dreams help to: (a) consolidate, enhance, and transform memory; (b) deal with emotions and regulate reactions to experiences; and (c) conceive innovative approaches to transform old behaviors and integrate new ways of being. Individually and collectively, dreaming is the laboratory of self-reflection, psychological maturation, and clarification of purpose.

Several conditions are required for psychosynthesis to occur in dreams: (a) developing waking skills in reflective awareness, self-monitoring, and self-regulation; (b) setting a waking intention for cognitive-behavioral change; (c) being willing to change old frames of reference, cognition, and behavior; and (d) working with dreams (Kahan, 2011).

Dreamwork—engaging dream imagery in conscious self-exploration— is a psychosynthetic process that includes: (a) self-awareness, (b) observation and disidentification, (c) psychological change and psychic transformation, (d) engagement with the unconscious raw material for new identity patterns, (e) recognition and development of new characteristics of personality, (f) overcoming factors that block personality development, (g) emergence of new states of being, (h) discovery of nascent aspects of individuality, and (i) actualization into new behaviors (Rossi, 1971). The significant role the conscious lived experience of dreams plays in the psychosynthesis process is the phenomenological adventure of going through the dream drama, stimulating the modification and synthesis of neuronal protein structures at the basis of psychological development (Rossi, 1973). These protein structures are the neurological bedrock of the emerging Self.

Psychosynthesis in Dreams

Through observation and experience in the practice of dreamwork, it is evident that psychosynthesis takes place in our dreams. Remembered dreams contribute to and broadcast the progress of our personality integration. Dreamwork offers an extensive and multifaceted approach to working with the **unconscious**—everything of which we are unaware, yet is part of us—through our **psychological functions**: (a) imagination, (b) senses and sensation, (c) emotion, (d) thought, (e) impulse and desire, and (f) intuition.

Psychosynthesis models easily support dreamwork, and dreamwork significantly assists the dreamer's process of psychosynthesis. The **diagram of the psyche**, or egg diagram (figure 1), helps to illustrate how dreamwork supports communication among all levels of the unconscious, the personal self, and transpersonal self. This map also aids in the understanding of the dream ego, that aspect of the dream's imagery with which we most identify and recognize as "myself." The **dream ego**, in turn, reveals our limiting **selves**, those unconsciously assumed idealized standards of who we should be or were led to believe we needed to be in order to survive, be accepted, and loved, yet which keep us from being our most authentic self. Other dream elements reflect our **subpersonalities**, the many aspects of our personality, each containing specific patterns of behavior developed in response to our experiences, each having a survival motivation of its own.

We can further tackle dreamwork through the **star diagram** (see p. 9), which details our relationship with our authentic self through the psychological functions. The star diagram serves both to identify imbalances by means of the various dream selves that the unconscious presents for our consideration, and to measure our levels of familiarity and comfort with, and our trust in, the various ways we experience, express, and know.

In the process, we develop our unique way of tapping into our truth through embodiment—our **felt sense**—and intuition, and of anchoring the work while exercising our Will—good, strong, skillful, and attuned to our life's purpose. Ultimately, we can come to value dreamwork as a practice of **disidentification**, ceasing to identify with aspects of our personality, assuming the role of empathic observer, and discovering that we are more than any one aspect of our personality.

Dreamwork

Far from being an exercise of dream interpretation, which forms thoughts and opinions about imagery, dreamwork is an exploration of the unconscious and an engagement with the images generated by the psyche. Rather than trying to analyze or decode the content of dreams by looking to specific, established prescriptive definitions, dreamwork, as a way of working with imagery, revisits and delves into that which comes through dreams: (a) sensory stimuli, (b) characters, (c) elements, (d) environments, (e) events, (f) actions, (g) feelings, (h) attitudes, (i) beliefs, (j) reactions, and (k) ideas. Dreamwork is practiced individually, guided by another, or in a group. It is practiced in order to dive into the unconscious and discover what information, insight, and instruction is available beyond what is already conscious.

179

Those of us who work with dreams go by the premise that dreams contain important data and messages from the unconscious that can guide us to support our client's health and wholeness. We regard nightmares as overdue messages calling attention to something that requires careful tending, which our client has been ignoring. Dreams "do not come to serve or flatter the ego" (Taylor, 2001, p. 198) but rather to reveal the secrets kept from conscious awareness, including fears, vulnerabilities, shortcomings, personal narratives, and insecurities.

Dreamwork facilitates an inner perception and comprehension beyond the conscious waking mind's capacity. It offers valuable insights into the whole person and daily progress updates. Together, coach and client come upon a very rich and often difficult-to-articulate domain full of innovative prompts to spark clarity, creativity, inspiration, and new ways to attend to the existing circumstances. As clients become cognizant of that which was until now unknown to them, they are able to shift and expand their outlook about themselves, those around them, and their present situation. With this new information, they are able to appreciate their range of choices and make decisions that improve their current life conditions and their chances for a better future.

As a process of personal growth, self-awareness, and meaning-making, dreamwork contributes to integration and the full realization of Self. **Self-realization** is the engaged relationship to life's purpose. Self, also known as Higher Self or Transpersonal Self, is the "deeper source of wisdom and guidance...that operates beyond the control of the conscious personality" (Firman & Gila, 2002, p. 38). In dreamwork, as in psychosynthesis, we approach Self-realization as the ebb and flow of alignment with that which gives meaning to life.

Dreamwork is especially useful for assisting clients to become aware of and shift how they may be getting in their own way, what may be limiting, resisting, sabotaging, preventing their progress, development, and the fulfillment of their life's calling. Dreamwork both asks the questions and symbolically answers them: "'who am I, now, in this moment, how did I get to be this way, and who am I becoming as I grow and mature?'" (Taylor, 2009, p. 37).

This investigation into dreams allows for less striving and more intention on the part of our clients dealing with their apparent obstacles. Pursuing the unconscious through dreamwork can prove more effective than consciously maneuvering their emerging issues and conflicts. Rather than spending weeks, months, or years talking about issues and conflicts and often failing to achieve depth or clarity, clients have easy access to them when working with dream imagery. Little effort is required when employing dreams to assimilate the outcomes of unconscious travails into consciousness; working with dream imagery bypasses direct resistance and defenses while indirectly confronting them. Consequently, dreamwork is a powerful way to support and expedite the processes of synthesis.

The Unconscious

The dread and resistance which every natural human being experiences when it comes to delving too deeply into himself, is at bottom, the fear of the journey to Hades.
—*Carl Gustav Jung*

Harboring the unknown and the as yet unseen, the unconscious is the place of our most hidden creative resources. The unconscious is "a psychological cosmos" (Hillman, 1979, p. 46), an underworld to descend into and know in order to claim our psychic and psychological being, and the Self's existential and phenomenological manifesto is inherent in the imagery from the unconscious. It is a "psychic matrix" (von Franz, 1992, p. 11), the fount of our dreams and of the inexplicable, the unexpected, the magical in waking life. Abiding in the unconscious allows that which is beyond conscious awareness to influence and affect conscious experience.

Through sleep and waking dreams, the unconscious speaks a language that is specific and broad enough to trigger resonance, associations, insights, and revelations. The language of dreams does not reiterate what we already know, but rather what we humans fail to see or are in denial of. Those who think they know what a dream means are often projecting what is familiar and comfortable, often while missing the point. In order to understand the language of the unconscious, we must genuinely renounce our preconceived notions and assumptions about current life conditions, and be open to the language it speaks. This language is cross-cultural and parallel to the language of symbol, metaphor, and archetype present in mythological and religious stories around the world, with inherent multi-layered meaning and implication (Taylor, 2009).

The Diagram of the Psyche

To better understand the unconscious in dreamwork, the diagram of the psyche (Figure 1) is especially useful. This map illustrates the source of dreams as the various permeable parts that comprise wholeness: (a) lower unconscious;

(b) middle unconscious; (c) higher unconscious; (d) "I," direct reflection of Self, functioning through awareness and will; (e) field of consciousness; (f) Transpersonal Self, pervading all parts of the whole and beyond; and (g) collective unconscious, encompassing everything outside the egg.

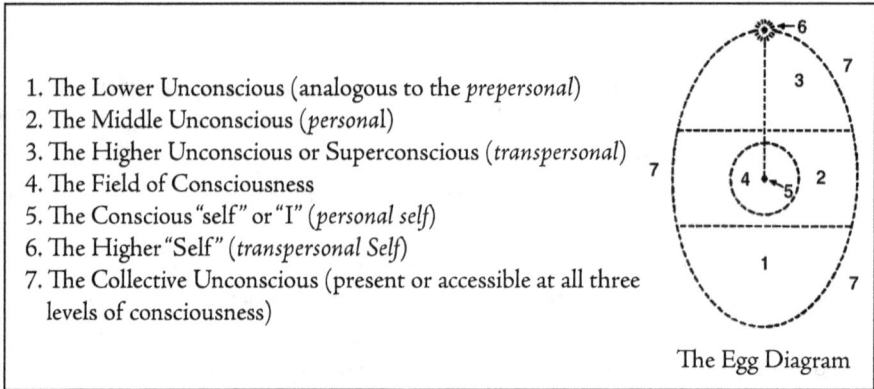

1. The Lower Unconscious (analogous to the *prepersonal*)
2. The Middle Unconscious (*personal*)
3. The Higher Unconscious or Superconscious (*transpersonal*)
4. The Field of Consciousness
5. The Conscious "self" or "I" (*personal self*)
6. The Higher "Self" (*transpersonal Self*)
7. The Collective Unconscious (present or accessible at all three levels of consciousness)

The Egg Diagram

Figure 1. Diagram of the psyche, or egg diagram.

The collective unconscious contains common tendencies and archetypal experiences shared across cultures and generations. The lower and higher unconscious hold everything we have forgone from waking awareness through denial, splitting, or repression for being "bad" or "too good." The middle unconscious organizes and contains patterns and representations of our everyday life that we access automatically without having to consciously remember. The middle unconscious is where we assimilate and "integrate the experiences, learnings, gifts, and skills—guided by the patterns from the collective unconscious and in relationship to our particular environment—which serve to form the foundation of our conscious personality" (Firman & Gila, 2007, p. 25). It is also where imposed or assumed models and identities have been incorporated, as revealed by our dream ego, which behaves and reacts as the waking self does, and this points to the detrimental or counteractive attitudes by which the dreamer acts in waking life.

Most notably, the middle unconscious expands as it incorporates that which was once denied, split, or repressed into the lower or higher unconscious, such that wholeness and integration are realized there. The egg diagram reminds us that negating or pushing back the shunned aspects, also negates and pushes back that which will help us actualize our potential. The Transpersonal Self is the dream maker, administering, from any and all parts of the whole, information ready for conscious awareness, so we may reincorporate the shunned parts, striving always toward greater wholeness. Through dreams, Self's investment is in turning all aspects into allies—our personality aspects and our personal self—such that they collaborate toward transformation. These are "still-unconscious and as-yet unmanifested potentialities of full humanity" (Taylor, 2009, p. 39) that long to be made conscious, fully present, and further developed. It is only the most self-aware and authentic being, rather than identification with personality, that can recognize and appreciate the potential of becoming, and it is up to us to bring its efforts and successes to conscious awareness through imaginal processes.

The Imaginal

The world is full of the rational mind...mostly it seems to be used to support the ego's defence system. Process bypasses the defensive ego and brings out the real self.
—*Strephon Kaplan-Williams*

Inherently, dreams first reveal attitudes and motives of the dream ego, then release dreamers from their conscious identification with personality, because dreams' resource is in the pre-personal, personal, higher, and collective unconscious, as guided by the Transpersonal Self. Working with dreams requires that dreamers intentionally disengage the rational, waking mind in order to objectively observe the dream ego and return to the source of dreams, which "simply ignores even the most passionate and sincere opinions of the waking mind when they are rooted in self-deception and denial" (Taylor, 2001, p. 198).

Imagery, as a glimpse into the inner condition, is "a means of transformation and liberation from distortions in this realm that may unconsciously direct...life and shape...health" (Rossman, 2000, p. 13). Engaging the imagination with intention, as exercise and direction of the Will, is the most productive way to inquire into and reap benefits from the unconscious. One of the advantages of entering the imaginal is how it connects right and left brain, unconscious and conscious, intuitive and rational, furthering integration, health, and wholeness.

For this purpose, dream maker (Higher Self) provides a number of unfiltered imaginal anecdotes—remembered dreams—from the unconscious every night, prompted by inner and outer experience in waking life. Through dreamwork, we incite clients to consciously enroll the imagery of their nighttime dreams in the coaching process, rather than having to induce images through guided visualization while awake in order to extract meaning and receive guidance from the unconscious. Because dream imagery is already there for clients to engage with at will, there is no danger of accidentally suppressing imagery by becoming anxious about getting it right, trying too hard, forcing images, or fearing coming up with nothing. Within the imaginal dream experience we guide clients to find not only the material to work with but also the specific focus and direction that their inner work requires in the moment.

Substance

The substance of dreams reflects in symbolic and sometimes literal form whatever our clients are facing and engaging with in their inner life and while awake. Dreams also communicate what has already transpired psychically and physically. Often transformations have already occurred unconsciously, and it takes time for conscious awareness to catch up and begin to implement the transformation in waking life. The content of clients' dreams offers information, guidance, and generous suggestions for the development of their qualities and attitudes, making direct commentary on whatever they are dealing with. Eagerly aligning with the inner processes of personal growth in which clients' invest, dreams reveal the direction to take to arrive at life's purpose. Exploring dreams discloses developmental aspects and new psychological potentialities as they express themselves through dream dramas.

> [Dreams] have a superior intelligence in them: a wisdom and guiding cleverness which leads us. They show us where we are wrong; they show us where we are unadapted; they warn us about danger; they predict some future events; they hint at the deeper meaning of our life, and they convey to us illuminating insight. (von Franz, 1992, p. 11)

Dreams will present recurring themes—obviously, subtly, or confoundedly—echoing the inner process of psychosynthesis. "Our dreams appear 'confused' and 'pointless'…because they regularly address possibilities of evolutionary growth and development that we are not yet sufficiently conscious of and sophisticated enough to recognize and appreciate" (Taylor, 2009, p. 38). Thus, we encourage clients to ask for clarification if dream messages are not clear. We invite them to detach from the issues they are exploring in order to allow for the answers to emerge. The **aha** of recognition and the felt sense of symbolic resonance help recognize what rings true with our clients' authentic self in response to their inquiries. There is no point in trying to fit into and apply something that is not in alignment with their authentic self. The **aha** is the moment when, "you **remember**, consciously for the first time, what you already knew unconsciously" (Taylor, 2009, p. 5).

The experience of this moment of creative realization is, "an involuntary gasp, the 'double take,' a freezing of the musculature, a sudden quietness, a certain stare or widening of the eyes and dilatation of the pupils...interest, curiosity, puzzlement, wonderment, awe, fascination, and joy" (Rossi, 1973, p. 36). Sometimes the aha of recognition is not pleasant; sometimes clients feel a knot in the stomach, a gagging response, or some other disagreeable sensation. Opposition, repulsion, disconnection, or lack of response are but a few indicators of our clients' resistance to and defense against that which is emerging from the unconscious. It will be up to us to recognize and urge our clients to own their aha moments with discrimination and with detachment from expected outcome.

Preparing Our Clients for Dreamwork

Dreams have multiple layers of meaning, such that a dream speaks to every aspect of our client's life and being, individually and collectively. In dreamwork we, together with our clients, reenter dreams—as we do with guided imagery—with intention through our imagination in order to witness and experience our thinking, feeling, sensing, and impulse from a more intuitive place and thus begin to uncover some of these layers. Facilitating dreamwork for our clients accesses more of these layers than when they work dreams on their own.

Dreamwork is grounded on the assertion that there is more to a dream than whatever our clients think they know; if they believe they know what a dream is about, they are not going deep enough. While our role as coaches is that of facilitating and guiding, when we work with dreams, we too must go deeper with our clients' dreams. We know we have gone deep when our clients are surprised by what emerges. To practice dreamwork we must prepare clients to be willing and ready to purposely go into and navigate the unknown, the unfamiliar, the uncomfortable, using the dream's imagery and our shared experience of it in order to discover something new.

Going into the unknown requires that clients relinquish filters from previous experiences, and that they step out of conscious waking mind and its identification with personality. It requires that they surrender their need to already know and to control, and that they reenter dreams with curiosity and openness. As coaches, we model and foster a focused but relaxed and receptive posture. The goal in dreamwork will depend on our client's current pressing issues, and the intention derived from previous inner work.

To achieve an expectant attitude, we facilitate ways to quiet the mind, relax the body, and neutralize the emotions. We guide clients through visualization toward an empty mind that lets go of assumptions and expectations—a beginner's mind. In order to return clients to a beginner's mind, we first help them disengage mind and emotions by becoming present in the body. This can be done by inviting clients to (a) close their eyes, (b) bring their attention to and follow the breath as it expands the belly, and (c) allow for long, slow exhales. We then invite them to involve their imagination function to reenter the dream and, in the greatest detail possible, envision and describe the dream experience through all psychological functions. We invite clients to mindfully tell the dream as if it were happening in the present moment. We give instruction and also participate, going through the dream in our imagination. Both coach and client pay attention to: (a) what we see; (b) how we feel, respond, and react; (c) what we think; (d) what we sense; and (e) what we want or refuse. Reliving any dream through the imagination, from an embodied place of presence and not-knowing that allows for intuition to arise, we begin to uncover the richness and depth of wisdom from the unconscious that is ready to be brought to conscious awareness.

The Process

As we regularly undertake dreamwork, we notice that dreams tell and retell perceptions of experience from unfamiliar, unusual, even unlikely, points of view. Dreams choose different storylines and evolving images to help us recognize and understand the myths clients have been living by, greatly exaggerating how they have been misleading themselves, and offering new possible attitudes, roles, and perspectives so that they may shift their story to become more true to who they really are. Hidden in every dream story are potential **transpersonal qualities**, those higher values and ways of being that are cultivated through the growing relationship with Self and purpose.

The transformative potential of dreams is in the conscious engagement with unconscious self-images and the integration of the layers of meaning present in dreams. While the transformation takes place in the dream itself, self-reflection through dreamwork allows for the conscious synthesis of new patterns already assimilated in the unconscious.

Case Study

The following case study illustrates how dreams contribute information and new images to work with when becoming involved in the process of self-reflection as it happened in the case of a 41-year-old woman, here referred to as Grace. Grace was struggling with anxiety after choosing to take a trip to pursue her own interests rather than buying tickets for her mother's biannual visit. In making this decision, she acted in alignment with what she understood to be her life's calling.

As anxiety and irrational fears crept up as a result of her decision, Grace focused on the sensation of these feelings in her body without trying to label them, and observed what happened. She described a sensation of pressure in her chest, and heaviness over her shoulders. The pressure in the chest moved into her belly and became an unbearable dark void sensation. Holding that sensation, an image came:

> There is an island on a small planet, like the planets in the story of The Little Prince. The island is the home base—safety, security, protection— and there is a small boat tied to a thick, heavy chain that allows the boat to wander off into the dark, unknown, and scary space of the ocean. Everything is dark, except the island. If I dare get on that boat, I cannot lose sight of the island, or I will be lost. Meandering in the dark is danger- ous and I am risking my life.

Grace acknowledged that while she had never concretely thought of or imagined this image, it was very familiar to her as far back as childhood. She explored the various aspects of this image with her eyes closed, making gestures that represented the island, movement away from the island, and feeling jerked back toward the island. In exploring the image further, she sensed something very wrong with this image, but could not identify what. Grace thought the island was her mother, and the chain represented all the fears her mother in- stilled in her around leaving her mother as she was growing up. She remem- bered when she was very young her favorite song was "She's Leaving Home," and her mother would insist it was not so. She then observed that perhaps she should be the island, but that did not feel right either. Grace recognized she needed a new image.

In continuing to work with sensations and the imagination, the follow- ing week Grace tried to allow transformation of the island image, and in the process of contemplating whether she could become the whole planet, the im- age from a dream of a "second Earth" came. Three days earlier she had had a dream, which she titled, "The Second Earth is Coming Into Orbit:"

> We are walking out of somewhere, at night, through a dark, narrow pas- sageway with an arched gateway exit. Something is happening in the sky; an energetic natural disaster. My mother is there and says, "it's the Second Earth coming into orbit, and as it aligns, it disrupts things energetically." I think for a moment it will be great to have a Second Earth to move to, but I also fear if it fails to align, it will collide with and destroy Earth as we know it. We must go home for safety in this transition. It is starting to

hail. My mother walks ahead with a few other women. Over the gateway, live electrical wires are hanging, as if cut or pulled apart. I am worried I will get electrocuted and call out to my mother, who continues walking ahead. I attempt to get through the gateway and because everything is wet, the live wires connect to me and I am electrocuted. I call out to my mother again, and figure I can walk slowly away from the cables to disconnect from them. I manage to disconnect, and I am very angry that my mother never looks back to see if I am OK.

The image offered by the dream—that of a second Earth coming into alignment—along with sensations arising from the feelings of hope and fear, gave Grace more material to work with in the process of transforming the island image. She voiced an impulse to become the second Earth, acknowledging her reservations and resistance. The image brought a sense of expansion, and Grace understood her fear of losing everything familiar to her as different from being lost herself. She explored a sense of urgency around needing safety, as discovered through the dream, and allowed her feeling of shock in coming out on her own. Grace noticed her independence from her mother and her survival despite her mother, and was then able to feel anger and frustration toward her mother for fostering dependence on a rejecting and neglectful caregiver. Grace acknowledged she had a hard time feeling anger or resentment toward her mother, and she remembered the exact moment when she, at age five, decided to forgive her mother for neglecting, forgetting, abandoning her, and leaving her behind. Coming back to the image of the second Earth, Grace felt unable to fully identify with it, puzzled by how it could serve a different experience and perception in challenging the introjection, or unconscious adoption, of her mother's precedence despite her mother's obvious and repeated failings.

Five days after this development, Grace had a series of dreams in one night, all to do with a period in her adolescent life she had long forgotten, when her mother definitively left home and left her to fend for herself without tools or guidance. Subsequently, Grace, in her attempts to move ahead into her own life—to "get on the boat and leave the island"—failed with catastrophic results, returning to depend on her absent mother as all she could hope for and apparently deserved. This series of dreams illuminated what was left to understand about the island image before she would be able to transition to a new image.

Three days after this part of the process, Grace had a dream she called "New Earth":

I am at the mall with my mother. She looks for the beauty salon; her focus is on the high quality of stylists who work there. I look for sandals, but her agenda has me following her and I do not have time to find what I need. My mother asks for directions, and we go down to the floor below to find the salon. In the hallway outside the salon is a rack with pure white linen items on sale at 81% discount. I see skirts, and then a very simple and pretty dress that could be a bridal gown. I like it and secretly want to buy it, but immediately remember I am sad and I do not know what to do about my projection problems in relationships. I look at myself, and I'm wearing an off-white wedding dress, battered, soiled, like I've worn it for a long time. I look for the pure white linen dress's price tag; it's $41. The label says "New Earth" and I look around for the store. In front of me is an immense store with glass windows, expansive and bright. It is a house wares and home décor store. Everything in it is sustainable, organic, responsible. I look up and see the sign that spells New Earth.

The evolution of the image and sensation of a second earth threatening to collide with home-as-we-know-it into a pure white linen dress to replace the battered one indicates a softening of Grace's original issue around choosing herself over continuing to invest in a one-sided relationship with her mother. The new image announces the advancement in her process of accepting the discomfort that comes from challenging her introjected mother's precedence—it will have cost her 41 years—and uncovers the false belief that her only two options were remaining trapped on an island of abandonment and neglect or risking her safety and security by trying to get away. The image of the new earth as an organic, sustainable, and responsible source of everything Grace could need and want to furnish her own sense of home reassures safety and security in her budding commitment to herself.

In revisiting the original image of the island with its chain extended out into the unknown on the boat, Grace no longer identified herself in it. Instead, she saw herself preparing for a rite of passage, an initiation in partnering with herself to move forward into her own life, and she reported a progression of her anxiety into excitement and anticipation as well as more clarity about and confidence in taking her next steps.

Whole-Brained through Dreamwork

Using imagery while engaging the whole self has a positive influence on the efficacy of human body systems and brain functions. As witnessed in the above example, dreamwork utilizes left-brain, sequential, linear, logical processing, and right-brain, simultaneous, random, holistic processing. In its course, we observe how dreamwork has positive effects on our clients' physical, mental, emotional, and spiritual health. The right brain's capacity to appreciate the

189

far-reaching context of experience allows clients to consider elements otherwise overlooked and to create and revise social, relational, and emotional images of themselves from the broadest perspective. In a left-brain favored culture, integrating right-brain functions, not to become specifically right– or left-brained, but rather "whole-brained" (Rossman, 2000), is called for.

> Most of us understand and use left-brain language and logic every day. We are relatively familiar with our conscious needs and desires. Imagery gives the silent right brain a chance to bring its needs to light and to contribute its special qualities to the healing process…Imagery allows you to communicate with your own silent mind in its native tongue. Imagery is a rich, symbolic, and highly personal language, and the more time you spend observing and interacting with your own image-making brain, the more quickly and effectively you will use it to improve your health. (p. 23)

Two brain processes are essential in explaining the transformative nature of dreams: (a) the promoter of development and organization of neural connections in the brain due to life experience, and (b) the expediter of the brain's improved coding efficiency due to increased neural firing and its capacity to influence and shift our perceptions. Studies (Kahan, 2011) that focus on the adjustments in framework and function of the brain when intentionally applying mental focus, a left-brain activity, and the imagination, a right-brain activity, show that this approach has the same transformative effect as waking lived experiences involuntarily have on the brain, manifesting in the person as new ways of being and perceiving.

The balancing of right and left hemispheres of the brain has positive effects on our health and wellbeing. This **bilateral integration** is achieved through: (a) focusing our attention, (b) working with sensations, (c) working with imagery, and (d) exposing ourselves to new ideas and experiences. When our brain fires neurons and produces new proteins, old connections between synapses are strengthened while new ones are formed. As a result, our brains have the capacity to physically change and cultivate different or improved mental skills, and this capacity is not limited to early development stages, but rather extends throughout our lifetime (Seigel, 2010). In dreamwork we expose ourselves to new ideas and experiences as we focus our attention through the reliving of the dream drama in our imagination while engaging body sensations; this amounts to a valuable exercise of bilateral integration.

Embodiment and Meaning

It is imperative to become familiar with and exercise our clients' facility to involve the body and the senses in dreamwork. Transpersonal guiding principles are channeled in dreams through imagery and clients assume these principles through embodiment, transforming concepts into functions and actions. Embodiment is the awakening of the human ability to act from exploring dream imagery, "trying out and living the potential which the image seems to symbolize" (Kaplan-Williams, 1991, p. 26).

Clients find meaning in aspects of their dream imagery, and, in turn, the dream further unveils its various layers of meaning and significance applicable to their waking life. Dreamwork has the ability to reveal and develop values and transpersonal qualities through the meaning found therein, as dreams exemplify and act out new and innovative ways to manifest and express them. Our active exploration and embodiment of meaning from dreams directly results in the discovery and deepening of life purpose.

Synthesis, Disidentification, Grounding

As clients acknowledge and accept that which surprises them in their dreamwork's unfolding, they consciously enter the process of both disidentification and synthesis. Experiencing themselves as the characters and elements of their dreams allows clients to observe with empathy that they represent unacknowledged or disowned aspects and tendencies of their personality that can now be integrated. Achieving inner harmony and healing may simply require "better communication and cooperation" (Firman & Gila, 2007, p. 21) among the various aspects of personality, without the need to integrate them all. This implies altering our perspective of wholeness from integration and unity into empathic acknowledgement, understanding, acceptance, and connection. It is a process of recognition of ourselves as "loving, empathic, transcendent-immanent…more disidentified and more embodied at the same time" (Friman & Gila, 2007, p. 11).

Since in the midst of dreamwork clients may discover they have been identifying with an ideal model, false self, or subpersonality, it is important to step into a neutral position to fairly observe each element in the dream. Discernment and objectivity are recommended because even if clients catch themselves identifying with one of these aspects of personality, it will serve deeper understanding of motives and behaviors driven by them. We can guide clients to work with an inner compassionate witness with a vested interest in their most optimal life, especially when they uncover conflicting elements in their dream imagery that make them uneasy. The compassionate witness will find unbiased direction and insight that will drive them toward conflict resolution and acceptance.

The more accustomed clients become to the dreamwork process and the more consistently they step into the role of the observer, the more they are able to do so in waking life. The observer shifts through and among the many "patterns of feeling, thought, and behavior" (Firman & Gila, 2007, p. 5) that constitute personality, able to recognize them as parts of the whole and to relate empathically with them.

Once our clients arrive at this place in both their dreamwork and in waking life, it is important to ground the work and honor what they have received through their imaginal experiences. We must help them prepare to bring these new experiences consciously into their everyday life in order to engage the momentum built by the dreamwork and promote their growth and transformation.

We instruct our clients to honor the work by committing to a gesture they will make or action they will take in waking life that directly refers to something they harvested from their dreams. Sometimes clients are unclear as to what happened, because as we have seen, the results of the dreamwork process may touch upon possibilities that the conscious mind is simply yet unable to grasp. In all cases, we encourage clients to trust that the work has been done, and that the change has already occurred. Since in dreamwork we are dipping into the intangible unconscious, a physical act makes the results of our clients' inner work more immediately tangible. This is a symbolic, transpersonal act that affirms they have, in fact, reaped the benefits of working with the imagery from their dreams and that they are materializing them in waking life.

Ways to honor and ground dreamwork include but are not limited to: (a) making a statement or affirmation of what has been learned; (b) further exploring the feelings and sensations brought up by the dreamwork; (c) expressing and exploring dreams through movement or sound; (d) making a resolution based on realizations; (e) using creative expression to represent elements of the dream or the synthesis of the work; (f) imbuing an object with meaning derived from the dream; (g) making direct contact with an aspect of the dream that exists in waking life, whether an object, animal, person, or place.

In the end, we want clients to walk away from dreamwork feeling in some way improved. To conclude the work with imagery through dream dramas, we guide clients to synthesize the learnings from their process, extracting the essence of the dream stories and noting how it illuminates aspects of their inner work and waking life. The constructive, positive ending to the imaginal process is very important; clients recognize and embody their capacity to engage and enforce their Will, overcome obstacles, and fulfill their goals.

References

Firman, John & Gila, Ann. (2007). *Assagioli's seven core concepts for psychosynthesis training*. [Monograph]. Retrieved from http://psychosynthesis-paloalto.com/

Firman, John & Gila, Ann. (2002). *Psychosynthesis: A psychology of the spirit*. Albany, NY: SUNY.

Hillman, James. (1979). *The dream and the underworld*. New York, NY: Harper & Row.

Jung, Carl Gustav. (1961). *Memories, Dreams, Reflections*. New York: VintageBooks.

Kahan, Tracey L. (2011). Possible worlds, possible selves: Dreaming and the liberation of consciousness. In Sudhir Kakkar (Ed.), *On dreams and dreaming: boundaries of consciousness* (pp. 109-126). New York, NY: Viking.

Kaplan-Williams, Strephon. (1991). *The elements of dreamwork*. Rockport, MA: Element.

Rossi, Earnest Laurence. (1971). Growth, change and transformation in dreams. *Journal of Humanistic Psychology*, 11:147.

Rossi, Earnest Laurence. (1973). Psychosynthesis and the new biology of dreams and psychotherapy. *The American Journal of Psychotherapy*, 27, 34-41.

Rossman, Martin L. (2000). *Guided imagery for self-healing: An essential resource for anyone seeking wellness*. Tiburon, CA: HJ Kramer Inc.

Taylor, Jeremy. (2001). Group work with dreams: The "royal road" to meaning. In Bulkeley, Kelly (Ed.), *Dreams: A reader on the religious, cultural, and psychological dimensions of dreaming* (pp. 195-207). New York, NY: Palgrave.

Taylor, Jeremy. (2009). *The wisdom of your dreams: Using dreams to tap into your unconscious and transform your life*. [Kindle Edition]. New York, NY: Tarcher/Penguin.

von Franz, Marie-Louise & Boa, Fraser. (1992). *The way of the dream: Conversations on Jungian dream interpretation with Marie-Louise von Franz*. Boston, MA: Shambhala.

Additional Resources

Aizenstat, Stephen. (2009). *Dream tending*. New Orleans, LA: Spring Journal, Inc.

Bosnak, Robert. (1986). *A little course in dreams*. Boston, MA: Shambhala Publications.

Gendlin, Eugene T. (1986). *Let your body interpret your dreams*. Wilmette, IL: Chiron Publications.

Johnson, Robert A. (1986). *Inner work: Using dreams and active imagination for personal growth*. New York, NY: HarperCollins Publisher.

Mellick, Jill. (1996). *The art of dreaming*. Berkeley, CA: Conari Press.

Moss, Robert. (2001). *Active dreaming: Journeying beyond self-limitation to a life of wild freedom*. Novato, CA: New World Library.

Pinkola Estés, Clarissa. (2003). *The beginner's guide to dream interpretation* [Audiobook]. Louisville, CO: Sounds True.

Signell, Karen A. (1990). *Wisdom of the heart: Working with women's dreams*. New York, NY: Bantam Books.

Woodman, Marion. (2004). *Dreams: Language of the soul* [Audiobook]. Louisville, CO: Sounds True.

Chapter 15

The Alchemy of Coaching

by Aubyn Howard

As above, so below:
As within, so without.
—*Hermes Trismegistus*

Introduction

Alchemy is making a comeback. Cast into the shadows by the enlightenment and modern science, the notion of alchemy, albeit in a metaphorical sense in relationship to human consciousness and will, is seemingly becoming relevant again.

---

alchemy

noun: alchemy
    the medieval forerunner of chemistry, based on the supposed transformation of matter. It was concerned particularly with attempts to convert base metals into gold or to find a universal elixir.
    synonyms: chemistry; magic, sorcery, witchcraft
    a seemingly magical process of transformation, creation, or combination.

From: English Oxford Living Dictionary: https://en.oxforddictionaries.com/definition/us/alchemy

---

Paulo Coelho's allegorical novel, *The Alchemist*, written in 1988 and 150 million copies sold, with its central message that "when a person really desires something, all the universe conspires to help that person to realize their dream" (Coelho, 1988, p.22), helped bring the theme of alchemy back into modern consciousness. More recently, David Rooke and Bill Torbert in their 2005

Harvard Business Review article on *Seven Leadership Transformations,* use alchemist to describe their highest stage of leadership development, with the description that alchemy "generates social transformations. Integrates material, spiritual, and societal transformation" (p 3).

I find alchemy a useful metaphor for thinking about psychosynthesis coaching in a number of ways, which I explore in this chapter. Before I go there, I want to retrace my steps to sketch out the wider picture of how alchemy has been used as a metaphor by Roberto Assagioli and others within a psychospiritual context.

Alchemy and Psychosynthesis

When I first posted an article on LinkedIn on this topic (Howard, 2017), I was largely unaware of the extent to which alchemy is part of the psychospiritual tradition and can be seen woven into the life and work of Assagioli. I must thank friends and colleagues for their comments that started new threads of inquiry.

From among the many supportive comments I got, I heard that: *"just this very morning I was reading about philosophical gold and its base elements of salt (the body), sulphur (the soul) and mercury (the spirit)."* Another post describes alchemy as powerful metaphor in coaching: *"I call this an Alchemical Process, as we work on all the aspects of ourselves."* Another colleague alerted me to Carl Jung's *Psychology and Alchemy* (1944), as the major psychological work in this field, in which he realizes *"that the original alchemists, who were trying to turn base metals into gold, were actually projecting their own psychology onto their endeavours. This is what we do in life, try to turn the stuff of our life into gold. We are all trying to get there, whether we realize it or not, so we are all alchemists!"* (With thanks to Anne Donald, Anne Welsh and Paul Emmet)

I must admit, I didn't make great progress with Jung's massive tome (although I recommend it for the illustrations and symbols alone!), so I went in search of others who had already followed this path. Mijares' (2006), *On the Alchemy of Psychospiritual Transformation* explains how deep mystical and alchemical traditions informed both Assagioli and Jung, who *"studied the records of these ancient Sufi and Jewish mystics—alchemists. They recognized the alchemical ideal concerning the transformation of base metals into gold was an allegory regarding the conversion of the limited human personality into its higher Self"* (para. 23).

In his *Introduction to Psychosynthesis,* Parfitt (2011) takes this a step further:

Like Carl Jung, another pioneer who took his inquiry into psyche far beyond the confines of analysis, Assagioli was very interested in alchemy, not as a method for literally changing lead to gold, but as a metaphor for deepening our understanding of the development of the human being from childhood to maturity. In fact, 'analysis' and 'synthesis' are the main twin components or activities of alchemy. (para. 20)

Assagioli can be found speaking more directly about this himself, for example in *Transpersonal Development* (1988): "The mind is brought into harmony with the spirit and includes the body, achieving an organic, harmonious unity of all aspects of the person's being, what we might call 'bio-psychosynthesis'. This is true spiritual alchemy" (p. 92).

Another example is in response to a question by Keen (1974) on the nature of the transpersonal Self in "The Golden Mean of Roberto Assagioli", in *Psychology Today*. Assagioli's response includes:

…language is always inadequate to speak about transpersonal or spiritual experiences. Every expression is highly symbolic, and a large variety of symbols have been used: enlightenment, descent into the underworld of the psyche, awakening, purification, transmutation, psychospiritual alchemy, rebirth and liberation. (p 8)

At some point in my research, I came across Ramsay's wonderful book, *Alchemy: The Art of Transformation* (1997), which I recommend to anyone wanting to immerse themselves more fully in this topic. Ramsay asserts alchemy's uniqueness in the western tradition "for the way in which it brings spirit and matter together rather than separating them", and explains how "Alchemists were in fact pioneers of the unconscious," naming alchemy as a "path to the soul" because it "speaks to our dreaming mind, to our unconscious, where we see with the eyes of the soul" (p.5). Ramsay traces the history of alchemy and tells the story of how Jung revived alchemy by bringing it into the psychological realm culminating in his study *Psychology and Alchemy* (1944).

In his introduction, Ramsay draws out the essence of Alchemy:

Above all, alchemy is about wholeness—about the whole of who we are, which includes looking at the what we haven't lived, at the shadow of who we think we are, or who we have so far been. And this is where the potency of alchemy lies because in that recognition is a place where we can no longer escape ourselves, a place of confrontation where the Work, and the process it entails, begins. (1997, p.7)

In psychosynthesis coaching terms, this takes us into the gap, the space between the reality of where we are now and the potential of the Self, which leads us to engage with our Great Work or Magnus Opus (or Will Project?).

Ramsay describes the two phases of this as the 'lesser work' and the 'greater work,' which correspond, in many ways, to Assagioli's personal and spiritual psychosynthesis.

It is clear that, at the very least, Assagioli's vision and formulation of psychosynthesis was informed and infused by wisdom and insights of alchemy (and as we know, by many other mystical traditions and sources that we don't have space to acknowledge and explore here). Both alchemy and psychosynthesis embrace wholeness, bringing together spirit, mind, and body rather than separating them; both involve processes that include at least two essential phases of work on ourselves to achieve wholeness, for example personal and transpersonal; both bring us to the doors of the mystery, allowing it to work its magic beyond the comprehension of our rational minds.

Alchemy in Coaching

I now want to shift focus to the more specific context of coaching and how alchemy, metaphorically or otherwise, can inform and enhance our understanding and practice as psychosynthesis coaches. In this context, I am using **alchemy** in a similar way here to the terms synthesis or transformation. The practice of alchemy, to my mind, involves at least four essential parts: (1) a **crucible**, container or context and (2) a combination of **elements** that come together within the crucible (3) through an essentially mysterious **process**, as guided or initiated by (4) the **alchemist**, guide or wise person.

The coaching session

How is coaching like alchemy? Firstly, the coaching session can sometimes be experienced as alchemy, both by the coach and the coachee. Clearly, the coach here is the alchemist or guide, but what is the **crucible**? Within psychosynthesis coaching, this is created by the coach containing or holding the being of the other and the space that opens up between the coach and client in right relationship. We sometimes call this "the space between", and other approaches might describe this in terms of active presence or authentic engagement.

The **elements** are represented by the contents or substance of the coaching conversation, which can be viewed through different dimensions, for example; the inner and outer agendas the coachee brings, awareness raising, exploring options and finding available will. In terms of inner exploration, these elements might then include: different parts of our personality (we call these subpersonalities); aspects or levels of consciousness; our thoughts, feeling and bodily experience; the somatic, the systemic and the superconscious.

The mysterious **process** is what happens beyond the conscious mind to bring these elements into creative tension or synthesis, to initiate transformation or emergence, giving rise to something more than the sum of the parts. When this happens successfully, both parties experience heightened awareness or engagement, in gestalt terms contact or resolution. If we are fortunate, a sense of grace might descend, a moment of timelessness and shared experience, although this is seldom explicitly acknowledged. Good coaches draw upon the energy released to guide the client towards choices, actions, and future testing by the end of the session rather than simply basking in the experience. Of course, most coaching does not flow so perfectly as this and there are bumps, deviations, and challenges along the way. However, it may be useful for the coach to hold this template of the alchemical process in their awareness, not in the same way as conventional coaching processes such as the GROW (Goal, Reality, Options, Will) model (Whitmore, 2017), but as a way of staying open to what is between and beyond.

Dimensions, levels or elements at play within the coaching space include:
+ Levels of engagement—what level are you working at as a coach? Who is your client?
  * Individual—team—system

+ Coaching agendas—Which agendas is your client bringing, both explicitly and implicitly?
  * Inner: change, development, purpose; personal, being, self-reflection, inquiry
  * Outer: change, behavior, performance; practical, planning, action, review

+ Coaching horizon—When in time is the client's energy blocked or in need of attention? What is their temporal orientation?
  * Past—Present—Future (near to far)

+ Levels of consciousness—Which levels of consciousness are engaged? Where are the unconscious blocks?
  * Prepersonal—personal—transpersonal

+ Body–Feelings–Mind—What parts of their experience does the client access easily? Which aspects are suppressed?

- Somatic awareness—emotional intelligence—mindsets and thought patterns

+ Leadership and personal development—What are the priorities for the client's development? For example: skills, intelligences, worldviews, self-esteem, confidence, awareness, will? What are the key inter-dependencies?
  - Horizontal—vertical—inner
  - Focus on awareness and will – For example, self-awareness; awareness of others; systemic awareness; availability of free will; humility, and openness to help

As psychosynthesis coaches, we might touch upon any of these elements as we engage in the coaching process and support the awareness and responsibility of the client. We open up a transformative space between the client's inner and outer worlds, where we are working with Self and Will across different domains according to the client's purpose, needs, and goals. The coaching space thus becomes the crucible within which the mystery can enter and the alchemical process takes place. As the alchemist, the coach needs to hold this all very lightly or the rational mind may crush the crucible.

We might characterize the work we do as alchemy in many other ways. You might already have thought of some. I will touch upon just three more.

Inner development

Coachees (clients) can also be viewed in terms of alchemy. The **crucible** is the client's sense of purpose and values, their pull towards meaning and growth, which create a context for personal development, whether conscious and articulated or not. This is the place of confrontation between the life we have so far lived and the potential of the Self and Will that we referred to earlier. The **elements** include the interplay of awareness and will, and the harnessing of the psychological functions (for example thinking, feeling, sensing, intuition, imagination) and other resources by the will, as well as the challenges and opportunities the coachee is faced with, the contents and landscape of their journey. The mysterious **process** of development itself can be described in terms of the personal journey towards self-actualization and self-realization or in terms of lines and levels of development, for example, see Wilber's *Integral Model* (2000) or Laloux's *Leadership Paradigms* (2014). Who is the alchemist or conductor of all this? In psychosynthesis terms, we view the higher Self as an inner guide. Part of the coach's role is to nurture the client's sense of I-self and connection with the higher Self, to facilitate the process of inner development. Every client has an inner alchemist, which we are seeking to awaken through the coaching engagement.

Coach development

Coach development can be described in terms of this alchemical process. In psychosynthesis coaching, we use the holistic and integrative psychology of psychosynthesis as our *crucible*, with Assagioli's egg diagram providing a perfect container for bringing various elements into synthesis as part of our individual learning journey. For example, there is a creative synthesis of the elements of experiential learning, skills practice and theoretical ideas. In our courses in London, we seek to create a tension between these elements that opens up a transformative space within the learner. In this respect, our approach flies in the face of conventional wisdom that advocates keeping learning simple, straightforward, and linear. Meanwhile, each participant engages in a continuous reflective dialogue between workshop learning and professional practice. This whole process of synthesis takes place differently and unpredictably for all of us and in different learning environments, depending upon the participants and the unique individual experience and perspectives they bring. Thus, we are always learning and evolving something new. Much the same process happens for the coach in ongoing practice, moving between the coaching work, self-reflection and supervision or peer community, where, likewise, synthesis is in play, developing coaches who continue to evolve over a lifetime of work.

Psychosynthesis in evolution

This book is about psychosynthesis coaching, and by implication, how psychosynthesis is being adapted today as a psychospiritual psychology to support the modalities of life coaching and business/leadership coaching. At the same time, psychosynthesis itself must evolve and develop in response to emergent challenges and other developments taking place in the world. Assagioli always envisaged and encouraged this, and I am concerned that this process has slowed as a consequence of psychosynthesis becoming over-identified with the relative backwater of the psychotherapy profession and the pluralistic paradigm that characterizes it. My hope is that coaching, closer to the evolutionary *zeitgeist* and learning edge within the organizational and personal world, might help infuse psychosynthesis with new elements in its own alchemical process.

Some of the elements we bring into the mix in teaching psychosynthesis coaching include *developmental* psychology (for example, Laloux, 2014), *somatic* coaching (for example, Strozzi-Heckler, 2014), *systemic* coaching and constellations (for example, Whittington, 2016), mindfulness, and neuro-psychology. These are amongst the most interesting developments and innovative approaches in coaching today, which on their own, can equip coaches to better support clients to respond to emergent challenges of growth and development, in an increasingly complex and high-pressure world. At the same time, we bring these elements into the crucible of the integrative psychology of psychosynthesis, thus working alchemically to create a new synthesis.

The Coach as Alchemist

What does it feel like to consider yourself as an alchemist when working as a coach? How does this shift your attitude, perspective, or mindset towards coaching? What space might this open up for you in relationship to the coachee? Maybe you will find less need for conscious control and more trust of the unconscious process. The alchemist needs to be able to hold paradox, to work with the interplay of opposites, and containing seeming contradictions. I return to the description of the alchemist from Rooke and Torbert's stages of leadership development, which include: "the interplay of awareness, thought, action and effect. Transforming self and others", and "anchoring in inclusive present, seeing the light and dark in situations; works with order and chaos". (2018, p. 1) This seems an apt description of how the psychosynthesis coach might be seeking to work.

At the same time, I remind myself of the need to stay grounded and avoid the traps of grandiosity or inflation. One of the reasons I like this alchemy metaphor is that despite the aura of mystery, the original purpose was to create gold from base metal, something very practical and material. Our challenge, as coaches, is to stay open to mystery (or that which is beyond the control of our conscious minds) at the same time as staying grounded in the practical and pragmatic, and to help our clients do the same. To continuously hold the creative tension, for ourselves and for our clients. To quote Roberto Assagioli (handwritten note) "What is synthesis? It could be defined as a dynamic, creative balance of tensions".

References

Assagioli, R. (1974). *The act of will.* Baltimore: Penguin Books.

Assagioli, R. (1991). *Transpersonal development: The dimension beyond Psychosynthesis.* London: Crucible.

Coelho, P. (1988). *The alchemist.* New York: HarperTorch.

Howard, A. (2017). Alchemy as coaching, article posted on LinkedIn, Retrieved from https://www.linkedin.com/pulse/alchemy-coaching-aubyn-howard.

Jung, C. G. (1944). *Psychology and alchemy.* (2nd ed.) 1968 Collected Works Vol. 12 ISBN 0-691-01831-6). London: Routledge.

Keen S. (1974, December) The golden mean of Roberto Assagioli. *Psychology Today*, 97–107. (http://synthesiscenter.org/articles/0303.pdf)

Laloux, F. (2014) *Reinventing organisations: A guide to creating organisations inspired by the next generation of human consciousness.* Belgium: Nelson Parker.

Mijares, S. G. (2006). On the alchemy of psychospiritual transformation. *Voices: The Art and Science of Psychotherapy*, 42 (1), 59-67. Available at http://www.psychospiritual.org/publications-papers/psychospiritual/1-alchemy-of-psychospiritual-transformation.

Parfitt, W. (Winter, 2011). Psychosynthesis: An introduction. *Thresholds*, 14-16. http://www.willparfitt.com/wp-content/uploads/2015/04/psintro.pdf.

Ramsay, J. (1997). *Alchemy: The art of transformation: The path of the soul.* London: Thorsons.

Rooke, D., & Torbert, W.R. (April, 2005). Seven transformations of leadership. *Harvard Business Review* 83(4), 66–76.

Strozzi-Heckler, R. (2014). *The art of somatic coaching: Embodying skillful action, wisdom, and compassion.* Berkeley, CA: North Atlantic Books.

Whitmore, J. (2017). *Coaching for performance: Growing people, performance and purpose* (5th ed.). Boston: Nicholas Brealey Publishing.

Whittington, J. (2016) *Systemic coaching and constellations: The principles, practices and application for individuals, teams and groups.* (2nd ed.) London: Kogan Page.

Wilber, K. (2000). *A theory of everything: An integral vision for business, politics, science and spirituality.* Boston: Shambhala Publications.

Acknowledgements
Anne Welsh (Owner, Synthesis-in-the-City)
Anne Donald (Owner, Oxford Meta Ltd)
Diana Howard (Healer, Teacher, Coach)
Paul Emmet (Editor at Let's Do it! World)

Part 4

People with People: Working in Systems

Finally, all human individuals and groups of all kinds should be regarded as elements, cells or organs (that is, living parts) of a greater organism which includes the whole of mankind. Thus the principle of, and the trend to, synthesis carries us from group to group in ever wider circles to humanity as an integral whole. The essential unity of origin, of nature and of aims, and the unbreakable interdependence and solidarity between all human beings and groups are a spiritual, psychological and practical reality.

—Roberto Assagioli

Editor's Note:
We live in systems, small and large and the work of becoming whole, is work that requires not only a clear assessment and alignment of will towards inner change, but an awareness of how each of us lives and is impacted by and within systems. And systems run the gamut from "inner" systems that are often as tightly bound as outer ones, to smaller systems, like families, through to the largest systems we exist within: our world. And what psychosynthesis coaches know, is that every change in a small or large system will move all the puzzle pieces. This is larger intention of all good work: Creating healthier individuals and changing the world we live in, so that every human being has the possibility of safety, peace and well-being.

Chapter 16

A Systems Perspective and Psychosynthesis Coaching

by Mark Horowitz

Indeed, an isolated individual is a nonexistent abstraction. In reality each individual is interwoven into an intricate network of vital, psychological and spiritual relations, involving mutual exchange and interactions with many other individuals. Each is included in, and forms a constituent part of, various human groups and groups of groups, in the same way in which a cell is a tiny part of an organ within a living organism.
—Roberto Assagioli

(Due to the length of the footnotes and the fact that two appear on this page, they are collected at the end of the chapter–Ed.)

When Roberto Assagioli states that an isolated individual does not exist, even though I might experience myself (and others) as such, he is reminding us of a crucial reality: Our individual psychodynamics are inextricably tied to the individual and collective psychodynamics in which we participate. He is stating that in our work on ourselves and with others, whether it be in psychotherapy or coaching, it is necessary to focus not only on the individual internal dynamics, but also on the external forces that might be affecting our health and vitality. In other words, Assagioli is calling us to incorporate a systems perspective into our work[1].

What is a System?[2]

When people come together in groups, these groups over time, form a whole that is greater than and different from the sum of its constituent parts. The system has a boundary which defines who is in and who is outside of the group. The group becomes an entity with an "identity": we are Americans; we are Catholics; **we** are the Boston Red Sox. This entity that emerges out of the multiplicity of relationships in the system also develops what might be called a "personality," a way of being in the world that has qualities that may be different than the individuals that comprise it. We've all known families that are "fun-loving" or "adventurous" or "intellectual" or "rigid." The personality or culture of Apple Computer is very different than the culture of Bank of America. You can sense that difference from the moment you walk into each of their headquarters, just as you can feel the personality of families when you are with them.

When this larger whole begins to unconsciously emerge with its own identity and personality, it begins to behave in ways similar to an individual human being, with its own drive to survive and its own purpose and values. This entity (or system) then becomes an energy field in which the parts live and to which the parts contribute. This energy field of the system exerts pressure on its parts to maintain the system's integrity and identity, its personality, its purpose, its values and its conscious and unconscious rules.

System Forces

As psychosynthesis coaches, it is important for us to be mindful of this energy field or these system pressures and how they might be affecting our clients and the growth steps they are trying to make. In the same way that a client's unconscious fears might be blocking a step forward, the unconscious rules of the system that he or she is a part of might be a block to development. Let me give you a personal example of how these unconscious rules create very palpable pressures on us to behave in certain ways when we are not aware of them.

As I was growing up, each member of my family sat in the same seat every night around the dinner table. These seats were not assigned, didn't have our names on them, and the arrangement was never discussed. I came home from college once and happened to sit in my father's chair at the dinner table. When the others came to the table, they just stood there. No one knew where to sit because I had unintentionally broken one of the unspoken family rules. We all laughed because everyone was so uncomfortable. It felt as if there was an actual force keeping the others from sitting down while at the same time pushing me to get up. It was only after I had moved to "my seat" that everyone else was able to sit down.

The children's story, *The Emperor's New Clothes* by Hans Christian Anderson (1978), is an excellent example of the power of system forces and of unspoken rules, beliefs, and myths that hypnotize or enthrall a group of people, including the leader of the system. In case you don't remember the story, the Emperor was very fond of clothes and spent large sums of money on them.

Two swindlers heard about the Emperor's passion and came to town claiming to be weavers who could make very elegant cloth with special powers. They claimed that their magnificent cloth was *"invisible to everyone who was stupid or not fit for his post."* This was the real magic—planting the seed of a kingdom-wide belief in how things work—what I am calling a 'rule.' This un-discussed rule then affected the behavior of everyone, including the king, who didn't want to be seen as unfit for his post.

These rules cause people to behave in ways that are often different than they would have if the system were not in place, and while the leader may be contributing to the creation of the system forces, he or she is being influenced by them as well. Many of us would like to be able to point to the leaders—our parents, our politicians, our bosses—of the various systems to which we belong and hold them responsible for the faults of the system, thus absolving ourselves from any consequences of our own behavior. This way of seeing often leads to finger pointing, blame, and polarization among the very people who need to be working together to solve the systemic problem. It also leads to paralysis and gridlock as we wait for those "other" people who are causing our problems, to change. Yet they rarely do. So we change husbands and wives, or the director of manufacturing, or our friends, or the president of the United States, but nothing really changes.

As coaches, this means that part of our task is to help our clients stop taking everything personally or making everything personal to another; in other words, to stop blaming ourselves or others for our condition, and try to understand how the system forces are affecting us all. Blaming leads to fracturing and separation of what is in fact whole. When our clients are participating in this blaming behavior, it is useful to ask them to step back and look at how they are contributing to the situation they are upset about. But it is also important to ask them to disidentify enough to look at the **whole system** and how it is influencing **everyone's** behavior. The reality, from a systems perspective, is that **no one of us is to blame**, but each of us is responsible for the systems in which we participate.

For our coachees, the first step in becoming effectively responsible for the systems of which they are a part is to become aware of these conscious or unconscious forces. As coaches, we can then help them step back from the system pressures, and rather than **unconsciously react** to them, make choices about how they **choose** to respond.[3]

Disidentification and Self

> *"Disidentification means…the cessation of taking something to be you, or to belong to you, or to define you."* —A. H. Almaas (1990, p. 172), *author, spiritual teacher, founder of the Diamond Approach*

> *"We are dominated by everything with which our self becomes identified. We can dominate and control everything from which we disidentify ourselves."*—Roberto Assagioli, M.D. (1971, p.22)

Part of our work as coaches is to help clients disidentify, or step back from internal dynamics such as the fears, desires, or pressures of subpersonalities, and become more aware of themselves as self with consciousness and will. But our role as coaches is also to help clients become aware of the external system dynamics that may be making them forget who they are, what they truly value, and that they do, in fact, have power (will) and awareness that is available for them to use within the systems of which they are a part.

The difficulty however is this: how does one know the difference between when one is acting on her own volition and when she is merely succumbing to system pressures of which she is unaware? "Peer group pressure" is a fundamental example of this. Sometimes the group or system of which I am a part is behaving in a way that makes me uncomfortable. Being conscious of this discomfort reminds me that I am separate from the group (I have disidentified from it to some extent) and that I have a choice about whether to participate in this group behavior or not. But at other times, I may be so caught up in the group (identified with it) that I lose myself and my ability to act on my own volition. I am swept along in the group dynamics without any awareness of this fact. It could be as innocuous as when a family teases one of its members about his girlfriend at the dinner table, or as serious as those who were caught up in the Abu Ghraib prison humiliations.

Until a person is aware of the system forces moving him, there is little freedom in how to be, see, or act. This is why individual and group mindfulness is so important within family, organizational, or corporate systems. Awareness is the important first ingredient of "stepping back," or disidentifying from system forces in order to re-establish one's freedom to act. But the internal and external system pressures can be very powerful, so an individual also needs to liberate his power—call it initiative or will—and muster the courage to use it. When he does, he will be in the system, but not of the system, that is, he will not be controlled by it.

One of my coaching clients, Samuel, was a corporate employee who was aware that the unspoken system rules were pressuring him to act in questionable ways, and he didn't know what to do. He realized that he was afraid that if he didn't go along with the system forces he might lose his job. He felt trapped in a system he couldn't control. He felt like a victim with no choice and no awareness of options for action. I asked him to try a creative visualization exercise and to imagine standing outside the company and seeing himself in the system with others around him. I invited him to explore the degrees of freedom he **did** have, individually and collectively with others. I requested that he "look from the outside at Samuel in this system. Yes, in most ways Samuel and others have no control and few options, but what if that is not the whole picture nor all of who he is? He believes he has absolutely no choices. Looking from the outside, are there **any** choices that you see he **does** have in this situation that he just isn't aware of? If he got creative, what options might he and others come up with that he/they might act on?" This disidentification visualization allowed him to step back far enough to see the whole system, the ways he was participating and contributing to the system forces, and some possible alternatives for action.

In summary, when people are identified with a system:

+ They are unaware of just how much of their behavior is being controlled by the pressures from the system and therefore, how little agency they have in their own lives.
+ They don't realize that their perspective of the world is being dictated by the system. Their sense of self is constricted or gets lost completely.
+ As we help our clients begin to disidentify from a system of which they are a part, and become in the system, but not of it:
+ They become aware of system pressures and begin to have some choice in relation to those pressures. They liberate their will.
+ Their sense of self broadens or fills out. For example, they might have the experience that "I am a member of my family, but I am also more than just a family member."
+ Their perspective or worldview widens. They can see other possible viewpoints and more possibilities for action.

Healthy and Dysfunctional Systems

Systems are not inherently good or bad; they just are. Natural life seems to be organized in larger and larger systems or wholes that are nested inside of each other.[4] Each larger whole possesses capabilities that exceed that of the parts that comprise it. Atoms comprise molecules that, in turn, make up cells that come together to create organic entities. Human systems tend to mimic this nested hierarchical structure: individuals, families, communities, cities, nations, etc. In healthy human created systems, as in healthy natural systems, there is a mutually beneficial, co-dependent relationship between the larger whole and its component parts. The parts work together to assure the survival, health, and growth of the larger system, while the larger whole provides for the needs, health, survival, and growth of its parts. In a healthy human system there is a mutual recognition and honoring of this co-dependent relationship. These healthy systems are Life-affirming in that there is a natural flow of energy in the form of feedback and information that allows for and encourages the growth and development of both the whole and the people in it at all levels.

Problems arise in human systems when this mutually beneficial relationship breaks down. One type of breakdown comes when the parts become more concerned with their own short-term survival or growth and ignore or neglect the life of the larger whole. There were many examples of this in the financial crash of 2008 where a number of investment firms were so focused on their own greed they destroyed their own companies and nearly destroyed the global economy. It is also visible in our non-sustainable use of the earth's resources that contributes to global warming and its threat to our species.

Another type of breakdown comes when the system's natural process of taking on a life of its own becomes rigid and the system focuses more on its own survival than on the survival of its parts. In this type of dysfunction, the system pressures the parts to behave in ways that become Life-deadening for the parts, and ultimately for the whole itself. We see this in abusive or alcoholic families where there is often strong unconscious systemic pressure to keep silent in order to preserve the family.

These dysfunctional, Life-deadening human systems disempower and control individuals and groups of people in four key ways:

+ They treat people as objects and in doing so, cause individuals to sacrifice their humanity by treating themselves as objects, seeing and treating others as if they were merely resources to fulfill the system's purpose.
+ They separate people from each other and groups from other groups, thereby ignoring or rejecting the fact that the system is one interconnected, interdependent whole.
+ They kill creativity by dampening members' aliveness (first two

bullets) and by stifling the flow of energy and information within the system. Information sharing is the life-blood of a healthy system.

♦ They demand allegiance to the values of the system over individual or more inclusive values. This cuts members off from their own personal highest values. It also cuts the larger system off from the even larger systems of which it is a part, and ultimately from the largest Whole, which is Life itself.

As we will see below, the antidotes to these dysfunctional system pressures are the forces of **power** and **love**. One of the frameworks that I use to help my clients develop the qualities that they need to counter the dysfunctional systems they're in, is the idea of balancing the forces of love and power in themselves and within their systems. But first it will be useful to understand what I mean by "power" and "love."

Balancing Love and Power in our Coachees

Since our culture has multiple understandings and misconceptions about love and power, I usually need to define what I mean when I use these terms. I also help my clients gain deeper understanding of love and power by guiding them to experience these inner forces in their own lives.

By "power" I mean **becoming subject in one's own life**—being able to stand at the center of your being with the recognition that you have volition and agency. But I also mean more than the awareness that you have will. I mean that you are power and purpose because you are a human being channeling the energy of Life. Assagioli speaks of this when he speaks about the three stages of disidentification:

The first [stage] is the recognition that the will [power] exists; the second concerns the realization of having a will. The third phase…is that of being a will (this is different from having a will). He perceives that he is a 'living subject' endowed with the power to choose, to relate, to bring about changes in his own personality, in others, in circumstances. (1973, p.7)

I refer to this type of power as the **power of one's being** which is embodied in one's presence in the moment—to one's self, to another, and to the environment or system of which one is a part. I distinguish this **power of being** from **power over others** or the **power to** make things happen in the world. The power of one's being means standing in who you are and manifesting your purpose, your note in the symphony of Life, in whatever you are doing in the moment.

Martha Graham, the dancer and choreographer, beautifully describes this force of Life—this power—flowing through us:

There is a vitality, a life force, an energy, a quickening that is translated through you into action, and because there is only one of you in all of time, this expression is unique. And if you block it, it will never exist through any other medium and it will be lost. The world will not have it. It is not your business to determine how good it is nor how valuable nor how it compares with other expressions. It is your business to keep it yours clearly and directly, to keep the channel open. (deMille, 1991)

By "love," I mean that force which bridges the distance between our self and another. Love reminds us that we are already interconnected and interdependent with others and moves us to act on that fact. Love knows that you are a being of power who has value and deserves respect simply because you are an expression of Life, while simultaneously knowing and acting on the fact that this is true of every other being you meet. Love bridges separation by moving us to attempt to really see another and to be curious about their note in the symphony of Life and by doing so, helping to draw that note out of them into the world.

Bill O'Brien, former president of Hanover Insurance Company expressed it this way:

By "love," I mean a predisposition toward helping another person to become complete: to develop to their full potential. Love is an act of will . . . you do not have to like someone to love him or her. Love is an intentional disposition toward another person. (Kahane, 2010, p.26)

As individuals, whether by nature or nurture or both, we have a tendency to be attracted to and better suited to use either love or power. And therein lies the problem. As Assagioli says,

Love and will are generally present in individuals in inverse proportion. That is to say, those in whom love is predominate tend to possess less will and are little inclined to use what they have, while those endowed with a strong will often lack love or even exhibit its contrary. (2010, p.96)

Both Martin Luther King and Assagioli go further to describe the cost that comes from the lack of understanding of, and balance between love and power in our systems:

The danger of untempered will is that it lacks heart...on the other hand, love without will can make an individual weak, sentimental, overemotional, and ineffectual...One of the principal causes of today's disorders

is the lack of love on the part of those who have will and the lack of will in those who are good and loving. This points unmistakably to the urgent need for the integration, the unification, of love and will.
—Roberto Assagioli, M.D. (1980, p.91)

One of the greatest problems of history is that the concepts of love and power are usually contrasted as polar opposites. Love is identified with a resignation of power and power with a denial of love. What is needed is a realization that power without love is reckless and abusive, and that love without power is sentimental and anemic. Power at its best is love implementing the demands of justice. Justice at its best is power correcting everything that stands against love.
—Dr. Martin Luther King (1967, August 16)

Bringing More Life and Spirit Into Human Systems

The balancing of love and power is fundamental to individuals being able to work effectively with and within their systems. Once my coachees start seeing systemically, it often re-orients their goals for the coaching sessions. Their focus often shifts from "how do I change myself?" or "how do I change my wife?" or "how do I get rid of these problem-members of my team?" to "how can I/we become aware of and not be so controlled by these dysfunctional system forces?" This usually leads to work on balancing love and power in their own life and bringing that balance to the systems of which they are a part in the following ways.

If dysfunctional systems objectify us and cause us to objectify others, then the work becomes helping our coachees reclaim their humanity and **stop treating others and themselves as objects.** In Psychosynthesis terms, this means helping our clients remember that they are **self,** a being with consciousness and will, **subject** in their own lives and a vehicle for the expression of something larger—Life. I refer to this as true **power.** In addition, this means helping our coachees to remember that this is also true for every human being that they are interacting with, including the ones that they are most polarized with. Seeing this expression of Life in others is the essence of **love.**

If the pressures in dysfunctional systems separate our clients from others, then the work becomes learning how to move toward those with whom they are in conflict in order to **lessen the distance between themselves and others.** We can help our coachees learn the skills of curiosity and deep questioning in order to truly understand other human beings with whom they are in interdependent relationships. This form of inquiry for true understanding is an expression of respect and love.

215

Since dysfunctional systems kill creativity and control information, I help my coachees look for ways to **increase the flow of meaningful information** by strategies such as including all relevant voices in conversations and promoting recognition of the benefits of diversity and creativity. This means helping them remember that, as self, an expression of Life, their own piece of input is important to the larger system, which might mean learning to speak their truth in a way that can be heard (power). It also means teaching them how to be aware of and draw out others' truths and how to include those truths with respect in the system (love).

If they are in a system that demands loyalty to the system's values over their own values, I help my coachees to **remember that they and the system are parts of a much larger Whole.** The work then becomes to reconnect with their more inclusive or "higher" values in their individual and group decisions and actions and to ask, "What does this decision or action, say about what I or we are valuing in this moment?" Again, in Psychosynthesis terms, this means remembering that all of our individual selves, and the systems that we create, are expressions of something greater: **Self**, Spirit, God, Oneness, or Life.[5]

Humility

Family, social, economic, political and other systems are powerful forces in our lives and we need to have a little humility about just how hard they are to change. If we do not help our coachees bring to consciousness how dominant these systems are and how they are being influenced or controlled by them, they will continue to unconsciously react and blame themselves or others for their current circumstances. However, once they begin to disidentify from the systems they are a part of, our clients begin to liberate their power and love from the clutches of the system dynamics. As they begin to free up their will, one of the first things our clients often set out to do is to change the systems they are in. This is good and should not be discouraged; but as they do, it is important for them to have some recognition of how powerful the systems are and some humility about how much one person can accomplish.

Hopefully we can help our clients learn how to stand in their power and love in kinship with other powerful and loving people. It is this change of relationship—to themselves and with others—that will begin to change the systems they comprise. And, if it does not fully change the system, it will most certainly change their experience of the system and of their fellow beings within it.

Footnotes

[1]For a comprehensive explanation of psychosynthesis and systems theory see: Evans, J. (2014). Systems, synthesis and group dynamics. In S. Simpson & J. Evans (Eds.), *Essays on the theory and practice of a psychospiritual psychology*, Vol. 2, (pp. 3-21). London: Institute of Psychosynthesis. For another perspective on psychosynthesis coaching, see: Evans, R. & Elliott, P. (2013). An introduction to psychosynthesis coaching. In S. Simpson, J. Evans, & R. Evans (Eds.), *Essays on the theory and practice of a psychospiritual psychology*, Vol. 1, (pp. 190-208). London: Institute of Psychosynthesis.

[2]There are many schools of systems theory. I'm writing particularly about human systems. See my book: Horowitz, M. (2014). *The dance of we: The mindful use of love and power in human systems*. Amherst, MA: Synthesis Center Press, for a more thorough explanation

[3]For another perspective on system forces and for an extremely useful model for organizational coaching, see Barry Oshry's two books: Oshry, B. (1995). *Seeing systems: Unlocking the mysteries of organizational life*. San Francisco: Berrett-Koehler, and Oshry, B. (1999). *Leading systems: Lessons from the power lab*. San Francisco: Berrett-Koehler

[4]For a more detailed discussion of nested hierarchies or holarchies, see Wilber, K. (2000). *A theory of everything*. Boston, MA: Shambhala, p. 40 (and many of Wilber's other writings).

[5]In my work with clients, I try to use as little Psychosynthesis jargon as possible. For that reason, I usually use "Life" to describe that larger whole or Self that we (and our systems) are expressing.

References

Almaas, A. H. (1990). *Being and the meaning of life*. Berkeley, CA: Diamond.

Anderson, H. C. (1978). *The emperor's new clothes*. New York: Random House.

Assagioli, R. (1965). *Psychosynthesis: Individual and social*. New York: Penguin.

Assagioli, R. (1971). *Psychosynthesis: A manual of principles and techniques*. New York: Viking.

Assagioli, R. (1980). *The act of will*. London: Wildwood House Ltd.

de Mille, A. (1991). *Martha: The life and work of Martha Graham*. New York: Random House.

Kahane, A. (2010). *Power and love: A theory and practice of social change*. San Francisco: Berrett-Koehler.

King, M.L. (1967, August 16). *Where do we go from here?* Speech given at 11th Annual SCLC Convention in Atlanta, Georgia.

Chapter 17

Transforming Family Life Through Psychosynthesis Coaching

by Ilene Val-Essen

There is no other relationship that has the same combination of intimacy and trust. No relationship makes us feel quite so at ease and none other will challenge us as much.
>—*Peggy O'Mara*
>Publisher, editor, and owner of *Mothering* magazine

When introduced to psychosynthesis in 1975, I knew I had found my theoretical "home." Inspired by these ideas, I began to live a more loving, inclusive, and meaningful life. This was exactly what I wanted for my future clients: a theory and practice that seemed boundless in its capacity to support personal and spiritual growth.

During my advanced psychosynthesis training, I enrolled in a class with a most unappealing title, **Emotional Maturity Instruction** (EMI). Many of the psychologically sophisticated ideas examined in this course were translations of ancient wisdom originating in the East. It was in this class that I sensed the depth of the concept of the **higher self**: the wise teacher within who guides our growth and embodies the potential for our highest and best. Seeds were planted that continue to grow today.

Parenting

Before I discovered my passion for psychosynthesis and transpersonal psychology, I had lived my passion for parenting, teaching classes since my son was a toddler. Throughout this period, parents shared stories of change that made our hearts sing. As helpful as these classes were in offering parents effective communication skills, I knew so much more was available.

During these years of teaching parents, I earned a doctoral degree in education, established a private practice as a Marriage and Family Therapist, deepened my knowledge of transpersonal psychology, and raised my son. I wanted to integrate what I had learned in these studies into a parenting program of my own.

When I thought about what to include in the program, I placed a wide array of cherished books and articles on my king-size bed. Leaning against my headboard, I looked at these treasures. They contained the ideas that helped me make sense of the world and navigate when I found myself in troubled waters. They inspired me to come closer to the parent and the person I wanted to be. Surrounded by my muses, I attempted to create structure.

The Birth of Quality Parenting

In time, I created a basic and an advanced **Quality Parenting** program, with a Leader's Guide and Parent's Guide for each. I also authored two self-help books, which support the programs. *Bring Out the Best in Your Child and Your Self: Creating a Family Based on Mutual Respect* expands upon the teachings in the basic class. *Parenting with Wisdom and Compassion: Bring Out the Best in Your Family* develops the ideas in the advanced program. Both books are written as independent resources for parents of toddlers through late teens.

Although the **Quality Parenting** programs have been designed to strengthen family life, the principles, attitudes, and skills within these materials are equally as relevant in other relationships: couples, teachers and students, and at the workplace.

The Purpose of This Chapter

"Transforming Family Life Through Psychosynthesis Coaching" highlights the key components of the **Quality Parenting** programs and the books I've written. This summary is intended to serve as a guide for coaches to help parents bring out the best in their children—and discover the best within themselves. As parents gain mastery, the whole family benefits.

Quality Parenting Principles

Have you ever heard yourself say to a mentee, "If there is only one idea you take away from our experience, I hope it would be this…?" That's how I feel about the **Quality Parenting** principles. They have the power to change the quality of the parent-child relationship. No matter what experiences parents face with their children, these principles remind them of who their children are, and what they need from them. When parents internalize these ideas, wise and loving actions follow.

The basic and advanced programs each introduce a unique set of principles. Those below serve the basic class:

Principle One

Children have an innate drive to express their best selves—to develop their highest potential.

The key word is **innate**. Principle one suggests that we all have an inner drive, a yearning to find and express our best selves, to become all that we can be. It's human nature. We all fall short and that's human nature as well. As coaches, we want to help parents remain aware, to remember their children's innate longing, no matter what behavior they display.

Principle Two

Children depend on us to help them.

Children need and want adult help. They are immature—works in progress—still learning how to handle their feelings, develop strength of will, and expand their minds. They can't do it alone. As coaches, we want to help parents remain calm and steadfast so that they can create an environment based on mutual respect, to help their children and teens mature and become the capable people they yearn to be.

How Can We Help Parents?

We help parents as we would help any individual or group we work with: we support them to expand their awareness and strengthen their will. Psychosynthesis' levels of self provide a powerful vehicle to facilitate both.

Levels of Self

You're likely familiar with these three distinct levels:

+ lower self
+ centered self
+ higher self

And you're also aware that since these levels emerge from different areas of the brain, each expresses a different level of maturity and growth, affecting the quality of relationships.

You may want to share the chart below with parents. It provides examples of children's and parents' behavior at each level. It also reveals how parents describe their children's behavior and how children experience their parents at each state of consciousness.

Three Levels of Self
We all shift back and forth

Lower Self

Children whine or ignore us completely, criticize, or become sarcastic. They hit, curse, yell, or act as if they cannot see or hear. Parents yell, threaten, criticize, over-supervise, or otherwise express aggressive attitudes. Or they withdraw, give up and give in, and become passive, letting the children take charge.

Parents describe children's behavior as out of control, irritating, demanding, hurtful, unpleasant, frustrating, frightening, and overwhelming. Children experience us as angry, mean, controlling, weak, unkind, or unfair.

Centered Self

Children are reasonable, responsible, cooperative, independent, considerate, and loving. They do their homework without being told, get ready for school on time, do their chores, talk kindly to their siblings, enjoy entertaining themselves, share openly with us, and feel good about themselves. Parents acting from the centered self are patient, express their needs clearly, listen with interest, and show care and concern. They are relaxed, clear-minded, assertive, flexible, realistic, and capable in their own lives.

Parents describe children's behavior as cooperative, thoughtful, responsible, competent, open, and independent. Children experience us as available, reasonable, loving, safe, engaging, and respectful.

Higher Self

Children are generous, sensitive, humorous, giving, courageous, persistent, loyal, ethical, conscientious, and highly creative. Parents are compassionate and trust in the possibility of growth; they act wisely and love without conditions. They readily express their finest qualities.

Parents describe children's behavior with humility: "These qualities seem to come from deep within the child; we are enriched by their gifts." Children experience us as wise, compassionate, joyful, "special."

As coaches, we acknowledge that we all express these three levels, and all of us have the desire and capacity to change levels. In this light, we can invite parents to view lower-self behavior as a **cry for help**, a yearning to come back to center, a longing to express their highest and best. Children depend on their parents and caregivers to help them be all they can be. But parents must count on themselves. As we work with parents, we prepare them to support their children to become centered as well.

A Process for Change

To help parents make these shifts I developed a Six-Step Process. When I presented this original design, parents made it clear that trying to take all six steps in one course was too tall an order. They needed time to feel confident in their ability to shift from the lower self to the centered self before making a quantum leap to the higher self. Trusting their assessment, I divided the course material into two separate **Quality Parenting** programs: the basic and advanced.

The basic **Quality Parenting** program is structured around a **Three-Step Process:**

Step One: *Recognize the lower self*
Step Two: *Cross the bridge to the centered self*
Step Three: *Express the centered self*

The advanced **Quality Parenting** program completes the **Six-Step Process:**

Step Four: *Cross the bridge to the higher self*
Step Five: *Identify with the higher self*
Step Six: *Express the higher self*

We'll examine the material in the basic class; then briefly introduce the final steps of the advanced class. Since the initial steps meet the essential needs of the families you'll serve and dramatically improve the quality of family life, they'll be addressed in more depth.

The Three-Step Process

How do we help parents climb the "consciousness ladder"? How do we help them shift from the knee-jerk reactions of the lower self and enter into the calm, caring, and respectful consciousness of the centered self? The Three-Step Process offers a practical, systematic approach you can use with the parents you coach.

Step One: Recognize the Lower Self

Inviting parents to practice the exercise "Draw Your Subpersonality" plays a key role in helping them gain awareness. As you know, without recognition of the lower self, change is not possible.

Draw Your Subpersonality

To begin, ask yourself:

- *Who or what is that part of me that most interferes with a positive relationship with my child?*
- *Who is my subpersonality?*

Draw a picture of the image that comes to mind, whether a character or an object. The quality of artwork is irrelevant; stick figures are fine. Drawings are often humorous exaggerations.

If you feel stuck, simply allow yourself to reach out to the different colors in front of you and choose a few. Then begin to draw. Give yourself permission to accept whatever unfolds. I have never found a drawing that wasn't valuable.

After you've completed the picture, write down answers to the following questions:

- *How does it look and act?*
- *How does it feel?*
- *How does it think?*
- *What does it need?*

When you finish drawing, give this character a name. It's fun and often helpful to use alliteration; for example, one of my subpersonalities is called *Frenzied Franny.*

Parents in all parts of the world discover that their subpersonality drawings either reflect an aggressive attitude, **Mighty Parent**, or a nonassertive attitude, **mini parent.**

MIGHTY PARENT

mini parent

Parents often comment that they flip back and forth between these two, though they have a tendency to act out one of these extremes. Clearly these characters appear and behave quite differently, yet they actually spring from the same emotion: fear. Parents either worry that their children will get out of control, so they cope by becoming aggressive. Or they dread confrontation and avoid it by becoming passive.

Step Two: Cross the Bridge to the Centered Self
Since stress triggers lower-self behavior, this first exercise on page 226 combines well-proven techniques to help parents relax: focusing on the breath and visualization.

After completing the relaxation exercise, parents generally feel calmer and more positive. The bridge exercise on page 227 then follows.

Relaxation Exercise

Preparation:

Find a comfortable sitting position: legs crossed or placed evenly on the floor. Spine erect, eyes closed.

Step 1: *Inhale slowly as you raise tension up an imaginary elevator, located behind your body, parallel with your spinal cord.*

As you breathe in, visualize lifting tension from your solar plexus (an area just below the navel). Raise this energy so that it can be transformed by your loving heart—and then by your wise head.

Step 2: *Hold your breath as the energies of love and wisdom blend.*

Imagine the energies from your heart and head fusing, filling your brain with the blended energy of loving wisdom.

Step 3: *Exhale the relaxed energy into the room.*

Allow the energy of loving wisdom to radiate out through the space between your eyebrows, filling your aura and the room with calm and tranquility.

Step 4: *Affirm that you changed tension into the relaxed energy of loving wisdom, creating peace and calm.*

Affirm what you did: you raised tension-filled energy from the solar plexus, lifting it in an imaginary elevator—first to your loving heart and then into your wise head. Through this action you created the relaxed energy of loving wisdom. You then radiated that energy from the area between your eyebrows, filling your aura and the room with peace and calm.

The exercise is complete when it is repeated three times.

Time Required:

28 seconds per cycle x 3 cycles = 84 seconds total

Bridge Exercise

Purpose: To recognize that you are more than the lower self—and that you have the choice to identify with the centered self.

Preparation: Relaxation Exercise.

Directions: Remain in a comfortable sitting position with legs crossed or evenly placed on the floor. Be sure your spine is upright, eyes closed. Recall the drawing of your subpersonality and your description of it. Use that information to practice this exercise silently.

Step 1: **Describe the physical appearance and actions of your subpersonality.**

Affirm to yourself:

I am more than the appearance and actions of my subpersonality.
I am the centered self.
I choose how I act.

Step 2: **Describe the feelings of the subpersonality.**

Affirm to yourself:

I am more than the feelings of my subpersonality.
I am the centered self.
I choose how I feel.

Step 3: **Describe the thoughts of the subpersonality.**

Affirm to yourself:

I am more than the thoughts of my subpersonality.
I am the centered self.
I choose how I think.

Step 4: **Describe who you are and the choices you have.**

Affirm to yourself:

I am the centered self.
I choose how I act, feel, and think.

The *Bridge* is an adaptation of the "Disidentification Exercise" found in Roberto Assagioli's book *Psychosynthesis*.

Parents love these simple, yet powerful exercises. Instructors consider them the "magical key" to respectful parenting and encourage parents to practice them as a part of their daily routine. With repetition, parents discover their ability to choose becomes more and more realized—and what a difference that makes.

Step Three: Express the Centered Self

When parents have learned how to give their subpersonalities less time on stage, they're able to spend more time feeling composed and in control. Instead of reacting impulsively, they've gained the ability to remain calm and think clearly. They've entered the domain of the centered self.

To strengthen this experience, I've identified **relationship** issues—specific areas where conflict may arise—and developed a cast of centered-self characters. Parents can learn to emulate them as models of respect.

Centered-Self Characters

ISSUE	CHARACTER
Authority *Who knows what's best?*	**LISTENER** *We respect each other's knowledge.*
Needs *Whose needs will be met?*	**HUMANIST** *We respect each other's needs.*
Perception *Whose point of view is right?*	**OBSERVER** *We respect each other's thoughts, feelings, and perceptions.*
Control *Who should decide?*	**PRAGMATIST** *We respect each other's desire for autonomy.*
Expectations *How do we deal with expectations?*	**REALIST** *We respect each other's expectations and create family agreements.*

The description below explains how each character thinks and acts:

Listener:
> Values what children know about themselves and their world.
> Listens deeply and acknowledges what children share.

Humanist:
> Recognizes the importance of meeting needs versus wants.
> Teaches children how to work cooperatively to help meet each family member's needs.

Observer:
> Acknowledges that family members perceive the world differently.
> Shows respect for all members' points of view no matter their age.

Pragmatist:
> Recognizes that children and adults want to have a voice in decisions that affect their lives.
> Creates an environment that supports independence and cooperation.

Realist:
> Accepts that family members have expectations of themselves and of each other.
> Develops family agreements that clarify expectations, increasing the likelihood that they'll be met.

As coaches, you have many skills you can offer families. You may want to consider teaching some of these skills described on the next page, which are designed specifically to help parents prevent and solve problems.

Skills Chart

Preventing Problems

Visualization:
We imagine an ideal version of how our family communicates and interacts. Holding a clear vision of our dream inspires us to make it real.

Assertion:
We communicate with respect, skillfully making assertive requests, providing assertive responses, setting limits, and actively expressing appreciation of our children.

Reflection:
We respectfully acknowledge our children's upset or discomfort. This helps them calm down and clears a path for effective communication.

Planning skills:
As we change the environment and prepare our children for new or difficult situations, we discover that effective planning prevents problems.

Family agreements:
We create and implement democratic agreements to avert a wide range of problems.

Natural consequences:
We allow our children to experience the consequences of their behavior, empowering them to learn essential life lessons.

Solving Problems

Express concerns:
When we describe our children's behavior without judgment, express our feelings respectfully, and explain to them how their behavior affects us, we create a safe environment for our children to take responsibility for their behavior. The skill of reflection helps the discussion remain cool.

Conscious listening:
When our children struggle with their own problems and we act as facilitators, we support them to find their own solutions.

As parents gain mastery with these skills, they gain confidence in their ability to model respect more often—and family life becomes so much easier. But to parents' great dismay, inevitably something sets them off and they lose their cool or become a doormat.

Oh, No, the Lower Self, Again!

Dealing with conflict can be bewildering and confusing. Slipping to the lower self is frustrating. Parents question: "What went wrong? Is there a better way to handle the situation?" Being able to name who comes on stage can be helpful.

In the chart below, parents become aware of five aggressive characters; one for each relationship issue. Parents often chuckle when they look at these archetypal characters and their attitudes. They recognize familiar facets of Mighty Parent, who essentially believes: "I am more deserving of respect than my child."

Aggressive Lower-Self Characters

	CHARACTER	ISSUE
	KNOW-IT-ALL	**Authority**
	The world's greatest expert possesses vast and superior knowledge. When facing the issue *Who knows what's best?* the answer comes with certainty: *I know. You don't.*	
	V.I.P.	**Needs**
	"I'm more important than you," claims the V.I.P. When the problem is *Whose needs will be met?* the message is clear: *My needs come first.*	
	GURU	**Perception**
	The wise and all-seeing one perceives reality with greater clarity than ordinary mortals. When the question arises *Whose point of view is right?* there is no hesitation: *I'm right. You're wrong.*	
	DICTATOR	**Control**
	The powerful one rules by decree. When we face the question *Who should decide?* the command is clear: *I decide. You follow.*	
	ROYAL HIGHNESS	**Expectations**
	How do we deal with expectations? From high atop a lofty throne comes the royal proclamation: *I show respect only if you meet my expectations.*	

The cast of nonassertive characters—the facets of mini parent found on the following page—adopt attitudes that reflect the opposite extreme, "My child is more deserving of respect than I am."

Nonassertive Lower-Self Characters

CHARACTER	ISSUE
KNOW-NOTHING	**Authority**

KNOW-NOTHING   **Authority**
Awed by the question *Who knows what's best?* this humble character bows low and says: *You know. I don't.*

MARTYR   **Needs**
Suffers quietly in the corner so as not to disturb anyone. When the question arises *Whose needs will be met?* this self-effacing character whimpers: *Your needs come first.*

MUTE   **Perception**
Anticipating defeat, this character refuses to stand up for its feelings, thoughts, or opinions. When there's disagreement about *Whose point of view is right?* the safe response is: *I'm wrong. You're right.*

SHEEP   **Control**
When the question arises *Who should decide?* this obedient follower mumbles: *You decide. I follow.*

PEOPLE PLEASER   **Expectations**
Hungry for approval, this character hides real feelings and puts on a happy, compliant face. When considering *How do we deal with expectations?* the answer is: *I do what you expect, even if I don't want to.*

Conflict: An Opportunity to Strengthen the Will

When parents see themselves slipping into old patterns, the Help Chart on page 233 provides direction. Parents look on the left side of the chart and find the aggressive or nonassertive lower-self character that most closely resembles the attitude they're holding. Then they look to the right and substitute a centered-self character. Sometimes parents are uncertain if they've chosen the most appropriate character or issue, but rest assured: they can't go wrong. If they're willing to identify with the centered-self, they'll model respect.

Help Chart

IS ONE OF THESE CHARACTERS ON STAGE?		SUBSTITUTE THIS ONE!
		LISTENER
KNOW-IT-ALL **KNOW-NOTHING**	*I know. You don't.* *You know. I don't.*	*We respect each other's knowledge.*
Authority—*Who knows what's best?*		
		HUMANIST
V.I.P. **MARTYR**	*My needs come first.* *Your needs come first.*	*We respect each other's needs.*
Needs—*Whose needs will be met?*		
		OBSERVER
GURU **MUTE**	*I'm right. You're wrong.* *You're right. I'm wrong.*	*We respect each other's thoughts, feelings, and perceptions.*
Perception—*Whose point of view is right?*		
		PRAGMATIST
DICTATOR **SHEEP**	*I decide. You follow.* *You decide. I follow.*	*We respect each other's desire for autonomy.*
Control—*Who should decide?*		
		REALIST
ROYAL HIGHNESS **PEOPLE PLEASER**	*I show respect only if you meet my expectations.* *I do what you expect even if I don't want to.*	*We respect each other's expectations and create family agreements.*
Expectations—*How do we deal with expectations?*		

Many parents view the Help Chart as a godsend: a reliable resource they can count on to guide them back to center.

You're now acquainted with the materials that comprise the basic

233

Quality Parenting program. With them, parents can visualize the family environment they want to create and have access to skills to realize their dreams.

The Centered Self Is Not Always Enough

Yet even with life-altering changes, parents discovered that the respectful attitudes and effective skills of the centered self don't always provide the psychological octane they need to deal with the toughest challenges they face. This is disappointing, but familiar to all of us. It's not always easy—more accurately, often it's quite difficult—to stay centered during the tense and often highly volatile situations that I call **extraordinary stress**.

Extraordinary Stress

It is during the unnerving experience of extraordinary stress that parents have their greatest opportunity to parent from the higher self. Unfortunately, when they're most vulnerable, parents are often most critical and ineffective. Rather than reaching toward the higher self, many find themselves slipping to the lower self. But even those parents who at first are able to stay identified with the centered self, frequently face a brick wall. Frustrated, they slip again!

Whatever unique set of circumstances may trigger each parent's personal hot spot, the root causes of extraordinary stress fall into two broad categories: unfinished business and frustrated dreams.

Unfinished Business

Unfinished business represents "baggage" from the past that parents bring with them into their adulthood and into their role as parent. This may be **psychological pain** that wasn't fully resolved when it occurred, and hasn't yet fully healed at present. Or it can be personal regrets: decisions parents made in the past that they realize in retrospect have negatively influenced their lives by either limiting their choices or having proved to be poor choices.

Frustrated Dreams

Frustrated dreams, **differences in values** and **unmet expectations**, can take a toll on all family members. Parents and children have strong feelings about their values and when they collide, the family often experiences agonizing conflict. Similarly, failure to meet expectations—our own or others—can undermine relationships and hurt to the core.

Parenting from the Higher Self

The advanced **Quality Parenting** program, supported by *Parenting with Wisdom and Compassion* and structured around the Six-Step Process, focuses on these toughest of times. Parents find to their great delight that the attitudes and skills they acquire to deal with extraordinary stress also enhance their relationships with their children when no stress exists. In the daily routines of ordinary life, when parents listen with deep understanding and engage with their children in loving-kindness, they face fewer problems and enjoy more smiles, laughter, hugs, sensitivity, and closeness—the rewards of family life!

This program begins by helping parents identify their unfinished business and frustrated dreams. As they gain awareness, parents discover that to help their families they must look within at their own reactions to their extreme stress and the stories they tell themselves that fuel them.

Quality Parenting Principles

As with the basic class, the advanced program is founded on a set of principles. The second set is built upon the first and further explains what motivates children. By shedding light on some of children's most baffling and infuriating behavior, these new principles help parents understand why, at times, the untrained eye may have difficulty recognizing their children's drive to express their best.

Principle Three

Children's primary motivation is to satisfy their own personal needs and goals.

Principle three suggests that children are self-interested: they are acting first and foremost to meet their own needs and goals. Contrary to our fears, children don't calculate their behavior to defy, hurt, or upset us. They are not out to make our lives miserable, nor are they our enemies.

As parents dig deeper into this principle, they learn that goals are often conflicting or unconscious. This discovery sheds light on the limits of parents' ability to accurately interpret their children's motivations. Considering the challenge they face, we can help parents to avoid familiar traps: taking their children's behavior personally or reacting from the lower self. We can also help them to stay alert: by focusing on the truism, "actions speak louder than words." When parents pay more attention to the behavior they see, rather than what they hear, they're better prepared to discover their children's most pressing goals.

Principle Four

Children act to satisfy their own needs and goals in the best way that is available to them in the moment.

Although this principle suggests that children are doing the best they can in the present moment, it doesn't deny parents' awareness that their children have responded more acceptably or skillfully in the past or that they may behave more capably in the near future. Principle four simply claims that at this time, and in this situation, children's current behavior represents their best.

The first set of principles invited parents to view their children's difficult behavior as a cry for help. Since challenging behavior may actually stem from a child's lack of skill, will, or awareness, the second set of principles invites parents to view their children's challenging behavior as a cry for **understanding**.

Step Four: Cross the Bridge to the Higher Self

To support parents to enter the consciousness of the higher self, you can offer them the second **bridge exercise**: a simple, yet powerful meditation that strengthens their connection with the higher self.

Parents first stabilize in the centered self. Then they identify with the higher self by visualizing the radiant sun pouring into their heads and filling their whole being with light and love. This exercise is found on the next page.

Bridge Exercise

Relax the body

Adjust your sitting position so that you're comfortable and upright. Focus your full attention on your breathing, as if nothing else is more important at this moment. Allow your rhythm to be as natural as possible. As you inhale, breathe into your belly. As you exhale, let your full breath leave your body. This type of breathing has a calming effect. Continue deep belly breathing for a few minutes. Notice and enjoy your more relaxed physical body.

Quiet the feelings

Imagine that in addition to the physical body, you also have a "feeling body." Envision the feeling body to be in the shape of an oval that extends about a foot or two beyond your physical body. Fill this oval with the color blue to evoke peace and calm. Take a few moments to enjoy the serenity of your feeling nature.

Clear the mind

Consider that you also have a "mind body." Envision this mind body to be in the shape of a sphere or circle that extends about a foot or two beyond your feeling body. Fill this sphere with the color yellow, inviting clarity and openness. Take a few moments to acknowledge your clear and receptive mind.

Identify with the higher self

Imagine a brilliant golden-white sun or star a foot or so above your head, symbolizing your higher self. Just like the Earth's sun, this sun shines on all parts of you. It gives each of us light, warmth, and love to support our life and growth.

With heightened awareness, imagine these rays of light reaching down and entering your body through your crown. This radiant light infuses your head, pours into your neck, chest, back and arms, then continues to fill your abdomen and lower torso, moving down your legs all the way into your toes, saturating your whole physical body with healing energy.

Let the light flow beyond the physical body into your feeling body, allowing you to experience greater love and compassion.

See the light flowing into and illuminating your mind body.

As a luminous, wise being, you are now identified with the higher self. Bathe in your radiance.

Higher-Self Characters

Having crossed the bridge, parents meet the higher-self characters and their attitudes of understanding.

Higher-Self Characters
Attitudes of Understanding

ISSUE	CHARACTER
Authority *Who knows what's best?*	**INTUITIVE** *The intuition is the source of our deepest knowing.*
Needs *Whose needs will be met?*	**PEACEMAKER** *In a conflict everyone's needs can be met.*
Perception *Whose point of view is right?*	**FAIR WITNESS** *Each person's point of view has value.*
Control *Who should decide?*	**FAITHFUL** *When we value relationship more than our upset, growth is possible for everyone involved.*
Expectations *How do we deal with expectations?*	**PURE LOVE** *Even if expectations are not met, we can always give love.*

When parents take **step five** and **step six**, they enter a new paradigm of parenting that profoundly improves the way they relate to their children. As doors open that were previously closed, they become free to parent with a wiser and more compassionate heart—even during extraordinary stress. They learn to:

Develop the intuition: To recognize the messages of wisdom hidden within the ordinary cues their children give them daily.

Strengthen family bonds through creative problem solving: Trust grows when parents commit to finding win-win solutions that meet everyone's needs.

Transform painful conflicts into opportunities for growth: When parents value relationship with their children more than their upset, they find unexpected possibilities for genuine understanding and healing.

Embrace the power of acceptance as a catalyst for change: Acceptance provides emotional safety, the ideal environment for children to flourish and mature.

Love unconditionally: As parents learn to practice forgiveness, they're able to give the ultimate form of love.

The Help Chart, on the final page of this chapter, guides parents to shift from the centered self's attitudes of respect to the more inclusive attitudes of understanding.

The higher-self material warrants an in-depth discussion, but that would not serve the scope of this chapter. Hopefully, this brief introduction provides a glimpse into the consciousness of the higher self and the gifts it offers family life.

Help Chart

PARENT FROM THE HIGHER SELF BY SHIFTING TO THE RIGHT

LISTENER
*We respect each
other's knowledge.*

INTUITIVE
*The intuition is the
source of our deepest
knowing.*

Authority—Who knows what's best?

HUMANIST
*We respect each
other's needs.*

PEACEMAKER
*In a conflict
everyone's needs
can be met.*

Needs—Whose needs are met?

OBSERVER
*We respect each other's
thoughts, feelings, and
perceptions.*

FAIR WITNESS
*Each person's point
of view has value.*

Perception—Whose point of view is right?

PRAGMATIST
*We respect each other's
desire for autonomy.*

FAITHFUL
*When we value
relationship more
than our upset,
growth is possible
for everyone involved.*

Control—Who should decide?

REALIST
*We respect each other's
expectations and create
family agreements.*

PURE LOVE
*Even if expectations
are not met, we can
always give love.*

Expectations—How do we deal with expectations?

Summary

As we help families spend less time in the lower self and more time in the centered self, respect becomes the hallmark of family life. With respect, parents create emotional safety: the ideal environment to support their children's natural yearning to express their best. Family life becomes so much easier.

When parents face extraordinary stress, respect may disappear. And even when they maintain respect, parents often face resistance. As they enter the paradigm of the higher self, they're able to parent with a wiser and more compassionate heart. Family life becomes deeply rewarding.

Chapter 18

Guiding Towards Purpose in Career Transition

by Susan Jewkes Allen

When work isn't working, whether due to external forces, inevitable developmental life changes, or an internal call of Self, an individual may enter into the experience of being in the in-between, "the neutral zone" of career transition (Bridges, 2004). This can herald a time filled with possibility and new beginnings. It can also bring confusion and stress as a person navigates between what has or is about to end, and the something new that has yet to begin. William Bridges describes transition, as a process comprised of an ending, a neutral zone, and a new beginning (2004). In career coaching the neutral zone is a place of opportunity and challenge as a client is guided through "the natural process of disorientation and re-orientation marking the turning points in the path of growth" (Bridges, 2004, p. 4).

Within the energetic tension between holding on and letting go, we can do some of the most important work as psychosynthesis coaches; guiding a client toward an expanded sense of self as we offer support in the exploration and discovery, planning, and manifestation of a purposeful new beginning in life and in work.

Being in career transition can feel chaotic and overwhelming. A client once described the experience as if he was "moving through an asteroid belt": unpredictable, risky, dangerous and difficult to navigate. Roberto Assagioli made reference to the "dynamic conception of life" and understood that growth and evolution occur through problems and crises (1973). The maps and methodology of psychosynthesis can offer a sense of order and direction for a person in career transition. The task of the coach during transition is to normalize and guide a process that will maximize the rich potential and value of this time.

When an individual enters into a career coaching relationship, it is not uncommon for many transitions to be concurrently unfolding. And, while a career change may be the presenting problem, the larger and more fundamental questions of purpose will emerge. Psychosynthesis coaching supports this time of exploration and discovery toward deeper self-awareness and growth. The coach guides the client's journey in getting to what really matters through the alignment of purpose, meaning and values with work that supports a vision for a fulfilled and authentic life.

Work and employment impact well-being, and are key determinants of health: physical, mental, social, emotional, economic and spiritual. Work can be a medium for a calling, an outlet for expression and accomplishment, for creativity and contribution. Work can also be transactional, just a job, demanding performance within a specific and sometimes narrow set of competencies to produce a paycheck. And in some circumstances, work can be soul draining and toxic. Over time, work can become a career, whether intentional or by default; a specialized and focused path, or a patchwork of diverse skills and experience. Work, whether a job, career, or calling, is a financial necessity for most and demands a significant amount of time, energy and commitment in adult life. It offers the form and material requirements for psychological integration, a vehicle for ambition and a medium for the human drive to perform and produce.

Work can also support the expression of spiritual needs; to live and work in calling, is to engage in a livelihood that is infused with values and purpose. Psychosynthesis coaching during career transition honors both the personal and psychological dimensions of work and the spiritual/transpersonal needs of the unfolding Self. Clients may enter career coaching having focused most of their attention and priorities on achieving personal and material rewards from work. And, this is likely to contribute to an existential crisis that Assagioli termed, "the crisis preceding the spiritual awakening" (1999, p. 110). Others, who may have engaged on a spiritually focused life path, rejecting materialism and the more practical aspects of sustaining a life may find themselves entering career transition in a "crisis of duality". John Whitmore describes this as the "...split between their idealistic vision and the harsh realities of mundane life. They are brought down to earth with a bump, and may find themselves compromising their values to get a proper job" (2009, p. 208).

For the person in career transition there is often a skew or distortion towards one of these dimensions over the other, what Assagioli described as the "two dimensions of growth" (1965). The work of coaching is to assist the client in transition to more fully integrate or synthesize the two dimensions so the client may proceed with greater alignment and clarity on their path of Self-realization.

In order to realize more and more of our essential humanness, we need to include both the personal and transpersonal dimensions...Therefore, self-realization, the realization of our Transpersonal Self, involves the progressive unification, at higher and higher levels, of the two dimensions of growth. (Firman & Vargiu, 1977, p.64)

Psychosynthesis coaching recognizes that the client in career transition will be experiencing this tension, or pull, to develop a more harmonious balance of the personal and transpersonal aspects of being. This is a movement toward wholeness, an organic process of synthesis. A psychosynthesis coach can describe and guide this process to support the client in the creation of a vision of the life they are called to live, and the ways that work can enhance, rather than diminish, their life's unfolding purpose.

Carving out a path or way in life is done through the exquisite balance of awareness and will, the work of Self-identification, the willingness to know oneself, in darkness and light, and the continual orientation towards the unique purpose, meaning and values that define an individual more deeply and fully than history and circumstances. (Firman, 2007, p. 20)

As we extend the invitation for our client to experience an expansion of self-awareness and engagement with the will, the coach must honor both the presenting, and sometimes immediate issue around work and career: **"What is the career for me?"** alongside the larger question of **"What is the life I am called to create?"** This is what Assagioli called, "bi-focal vision" the holding of both "immediate need and far-reaching vision".

Bifocal vision involves perceiving the client from a dual perspective; first, as a Self, a being with a purpose in life and with immense potential for love, intelligence and creativity; and, second, as a personality, an individual made up of a unique blend of physical, emotional and mental characteristics. (Whitmore, 2013, p.68)

With this holding, the purpose of the psychosynthetic coaching relationship is about much more than facilitating the process of 'finding a job'. The coach considers the full spectrum of an individual's life and work experience. There is an understanding that the challenges and uncertainty of transition can be an invitation to explore and discover what is emerging and help our client "make choices rather than merely mend brokenness" (Whitmore, 1996, p.127). This can be a time for a client to take the steps that support the journey of identification and manifestation of their unique purpose; to engage in a process Assagioli described as "the act of will" (1974).

When a client sets the intention to utilize their time of transition to silence the noise of the choir and hear their own true voice, they are responding to the call of self and igniting the experience of being a 'willer'. At the choice point of transition, stages in "the act of will" (purpose, deliberation, choice, affirmation, plan and action) are activated, as the coach guides the client in assessing, defining and taking concrete steps toward experiencing work as livelihood; identifying the ways for work to contribute to, rather than detract from, a fulfilled and authentic life.

Assagioli defined the will as, "a constructive force guiding intuition, impulse, emotion, and imagination toward a complete realization of the self." (1973, p.33). One of the first tasks in working with a client in career transition is to identify and affirm that they have the capacity for the fullness of choice in their life and work; that they have "a will". Recognition that the will exists and that one has a will are the first two phases of a client's awakening to the possibilities inherent in becoming whole. The activation of the will is what Piero Ferrucci (1982) calls, "the key to human freedom and personal power," the power to choose our own path, to live and work in alignment with our own unique definitions of meaning and values.

Assagioli created a questionnaire to assess and 'develop' the will (1974). These self-reflection questions are useful in enhancing self-knowledge and facilitating the coach's assessment of a client's will-alignment and areas for development. Some psychosynthesis theorists, including Ann Gila and John Firman, argue that the will is not so much developed, but emergent, and, as an individual works with identifications that limit the "I", the will is "uncovered and made manifest".

> Given the nature of "I," we posit that will is by nature good, strong, skillful, and attuned to the transpersonal will (the will of Self). When these aspects are not apparent, it is because "I" is identified with some part of the personality that does not allow the full expression of will. Just as "I" does not technically "develop," but rather emerges, so will does not technically "develop" but instead emerges." (Firman & Gila, 2007 p. 13)

Whether developed and/or emergent, the coach supports a client's "connection with the source of will within themselves…to help the person "ground" the insights achieved through active techniques and by applying these insights in the course of day-to-day living" (Crampton, 1977, p.2).

The will is the energy that directs and brings form to the expression of our unique purpose. This is activated through the harmonization of the major aspects of the will: the strong will, the skillful will, the good will. These aspects are the energy that ignites movement within the six phases of the act of will (Assagioli, 1974):

1. Identifying Purpose or a Goal
2. Deliberation
3. Choice
4. Affirmation
5. Planning
6. Action

Assagioli likened these phases or stages to the links of a chain, with "the act of willing…only as strong as its weakest link. So, the performance of an act of will is going to be more or less successful and effective according to how successfully and effectively each of the stages is carried out." (1974, p. 136).

Utilizing the stages of the act of will as a map, the coach's role is to assess, assist and hold safe space at each stage of the process, beginning and ending with clarification and affirmation of purpose. Applying skillful will through the selection of appropriate tools and techniques, the coach will help the client free their will and more fully connect with Self. The coach is also ready to identify and guide a client when they come to a 'weak link' in the chain, a stuck point, and to use this as an opportunity to help the client in building their capacity and experience of strong, skillful and good will.

If the process is handled with sensitivity, it can be just as valuable to reflect on goals not achieved as to actually accomplish the goals…A coach provides needed permission and support for people to dream big dreams and to follow through on them. (Crampton, 2000, p.2)

While the act of will is presented as a sequence of staged steps, it is often lived as a cyclical process of beginning, sometimes doubling back, deepening and expanding; always returning back to the 'I' of awareness and purpose. These stages of the act of will are both a linear sequence and a spiral of nonlinear, multi-dimensional progression that is inherently dynamic and complex. And much like the metaphor of the nautilus shell, each stage of growth offers a larger, more spacious 'chamber' for crafting a purposeful life of which work plays a meaningful role.

When a client begins career coaching, there may be a concrete and tactical presenting issue or goal: **I need to do my resume; I want a new job; I have to develop better interviewing skills.** Others may present with a more direct and attuned question of purpose: **How might I find more meaningful work? What is my calling? How can I make a living doing what I love?** As coaches, we attend to the "both/and" of what is immediate, while listening for and encouraging movement toward what is emerging around the larger questions and direction of a client's purpose. This bifocal vision allows us to hear and see what is present, while listening and watching for the call of self.

> Bifocal vision invites the practitioner to see the client through the lens of that client's presenting issues, diagnoses or problems, while at the same time seeing that person as a soul in search of realization. (Firman, 2007, p. 8)

As a client presents these initial questions and/or needs, it is useful to begin by collecting information about the major internal and external influences in their life and work, including family, community of origin, early memories from childhood and school, through to first experiences with work and money. The life-work autobiography, written and/or oral, gives coach and client the opportunity to identify patterns, crossroads, important life events and role models, challenges, successes and failures. It is not unusual for a client, in the telling of this life story, to become aware of skills, gifts, interests, even passions, that may have been put down in service of external demands, opportunities in life, schooling or work experiences.

Insights can emerge, through guided reflection, surrounding the ways early impressions about money and work are carried into adulthood. The autobiography can also be a vehicle for a coach to assist the client in engaging in a central concept and feature of psychosynthesis, identification and disidentification. Sometimes a client's story reveals content from the past that points to an identification in the present that may be an emotional, mental, or even physical block to their professional/personal growth. Disidentification offers the opportunity to separate from the limiting beliefs and energy that keeps an individual stuck in the content and stories from the past.

Joanna was a successful leader at a growing technology company who dreamed of becoming a founder of her own venture. As her life-work autobiography unfolded, she shared many examples from childhood of initiating and running creative, small business experiments. From a make-your-own lemonade stand at eight years old to a pop-up birthday party business in high school, Joanna was an "idea and implementation machine" who enjoyed coming up with small business ventures and making them happen.

She described herself in these years from childhood through high school as being highly self-managing and self-directed, and remembered this as a time filled with freedom, focus, and great fun. Upon entering a top-tier university, Joanna became absorbed with the social scene at school, joining clubs, enjoying parties and staying up late into the night with the diverse and interesting people she was meeting. Her schoolwork suffered and she was put on probation at the end of her freshman year. This was Joanna's first experience of "failure" and returning back after summer break she was single-minded in her determination to graduate at the top of her class and to never fail again.

Joanna succeeded in this by learning and applying a disciplined, structured program of schedules and study. When she entered the work world, she chose employment over her natural gifts for entrepreneurship, out of fear that she could not find continued success without external structure and accountability. Now, more than ten years later, she carried a sense of shame and guilt for disappointing herself and others in that first year of university. This identification with her 19-year-old self and her determination to never fail again was holding Joanna back from her inherent gifts and dreams. As Joanna began to step-back from this identification and to view her younger self from a distance, with compassion and forgiveness, she was able to connect with a greater sense of possibility and potential in exploring how she might seize her future as an entrepreneur.

Autobiography can also facilitate an invitation for the client to identify with a forgotten, neglected or dismissed aspect that may have been left behind or put down at a particular choice point in life. To gain greater clarity around purpose, it may be necessary to re-identify with a quality of self that was not fully mirrored or acknowledged in childhood or at some other significant choice point in life and work. Sometimes this essential part has not been re-embraced because of sadness, regret or hopelessness in losing this aspect of being. By disidentifying from the story of how this loss unfolded, the client can choose to reclaim an essential aspect of self and identify with a more expansive sense of possibility.

Robert, a successful accountant and businessman in his late 40s, came to career coaching with a goal to explore how to phase out of his day-to-day involvement in his role as founder and CEO of a mid-size accounting firm. He wanted to experience a more engaged and productive life, and potentially, a second act career. As a respected and admired member of the community, Robert sought greater connection to purpose, "I have it all, a lovely wife, healthy adult children and a thriving business that I built myself. Why does it feel like my life is incomplete?"

As we began an extended life-work review, Robert shared his growing up as a first generation child in an immigrant family of farmers. The oldest of five siblings, he was a good student and as a young child was assigned the role to be first in the family to attend and graduate from college. Excelling in math, teachers encouraged him to study accounting and he complied. After "paying his dues" in a Big Four accounting company, he struck out on his own and built his own highly successful business.

Recounting early memories, Robert would light up as he described life on the farm, the rhythms of the day and the seasons, the pleasure and satisfaction of working on the land. In a moment of identification with this love of the farm, he began to sob, "All I really wanted was to be a farmer." In the realization of what had long been set aside in order to walk a career path mapped by others, the quiet whisper of Self, long ignored, was given voice. Robert immediately became engaged in a community gardening organization and began to explore how he might start a hobby farm. He could now begin, at mid-life, to acknowledge and take steps to live in alignment with fuller experience of his rightful purpose.

The Ideal Model is another psychosynthesis technique that can support a client's discovery and connection to purpose. Guiding a client through the "evocation of potential" (Whitmore, 2005) can bring form to possibilities and connection to the higher unconscious.

> The ideal-model technique provides a positive thrust…and expands the context within which an exploration of the unconscious, the catharsis of repressed emotions and the treatment of symptoms takes place. It reframes counseling to include the client's exploration of life purpose, eliminating obstacles to it and facilitating its realization. (Whitmore, 2013, p.59)

Karen, in her late-thirties, worked at the director level for a large corporation. She came to coaching feeling stuck and unmotivated in her senior management role. Karen had been on a "fast track" career path, achieving rapid promotions in her first job after completing her MBA. Her accelerated career path, which included long hours and extensive travel, left little time for a social life. Naturally extroverted, Karen had spent her adult life "being busy", but had taken little time for "just being". She came to career coaching as a way to process and reflect upon the meaning and value of all she had experienced and to sort out how to have more life-work balance.

As Karen made her way through the stages of the Ideal Model she began to give form and order to the competing and sometimes conflicting ideas she had in her self-perception and how she was perceived by others. She described her drawing of an ideal model with less-than-perfect hair, a big smile on her face and arms open wide to life. She realized that she had become so absorbed in fulfilling an incomplete, limiting model of a successful career woman, that she had become disconnected from her joyful, less studied and more spontaneous way of being. She shared that her unattainable "secret, daydream model" (Yeomans, n.d., para. 122) was a perfectly poised professional, who 'never let them see you sweat (or cry)', who efficiently 'ticked off the boxes' while thriving on 6 hours or less of sleep, was immune to jet lag and lived her life outside of work effortlessly and with great charm. This was not, she declared, who she wanted to be. Karen set an intention that her purposeful next steps, would be to create a plan and take action on investing more time "zooming out and zooming in"; experiencing herself more fully, "really and realistically" in the blend of "doing and being". She would commit to creating a life that was more purpose driven and whole.

A client in career transition may be able to articulate a clear sense of purpose, and yet may be at a crossroads in determining how to live and work in a sustainable manner that honors their call of self. Sometimes this requires taking the time for deliberation and accessing their sources of knowing through their psychological functions: intuition, imagination, thinking, feeling, sensation, and impulse/desire. The coach assesses which are the preferred functions and strengths for the client, as well as those functions that are not fully utilized or expressed. In the work of bringing forward less utilized functions, as well as expanding the repertory of stronger functions, the client is more readily able to gain clarity of choice in manifestation of purpose.

Kevin, in his late fifties, expressed a desire to explore "a third act career", one that would offer more meaning than he was experiencing in his current work. He worked as a project manager for a tech company and was finding his day-to-day uninspired and routine. He had successfully navigated a "second act" career change in his late 30s after working for 15+ years as a musician and teacher. Kevin continued to engage in his music, which he considered his true "calling", on weekends and holidays, and yearned for more creative expression in his current career. He described his workplace, colleagues and manager as supportive and friendly, "...just not my people" and the work itself as "fine, just not very interesting or meaningful." When asked what worked most for him in his current role, Kevin said "the money" and began to describe the exponential increase in his earnings from his early work as a struggling violinist and schoolteacher. After training and a transition to project management he had bought a home, took yearly vacations to music retreats, events and workshops, and had built a small sound studio in his garage to pursue a variety of mediums and forms for his creative expression.

Kevin had formulated a key question around purpose: Should he invest the time and effort in exploring a different role or new career that would be in alignment with his artistic calling? Or should he stay the course in his current job and wait it out until retirement? He identified his strongest psychological functions as thinking, feeling and intuition, with sensation and impulse/desire being the least developed. Recognizing that his "thinker self" could use more data to analyze his options, he arranged to meet with a financial planner to explore the financial options and requirements for retirement. A series of meetings revealed that 4 – 5 more years in his current job would allow him to build his savings to the point of being able to maintain his lifestyle with only a modest annual supplement to his income. Kevin acknowledged that this made "a lot of sense", however he was not convinced that he was ready to stay in his current role "just for the money."

As he deliberated about his options to live and work more fully in purpose, Kevin agreed to utilize a variety of techniques to access information from his more developed functions of feeling and intuition, and his less developed functions of sensation and impulse/desire. He committed to an activity that would invite intuition to help him with his choice point question: to stay the course in his current job, or explore a new career path. Partnering intuition with sensation, his least developed function, Kevin scheduled a daily morning walk with the intention of opening to intuition and allowing his answer to emerge organically as he focused on the movement and action of his body.

After almost a month of regular walks, Kevin decided he would stay in his current job. He described walking in the park and watching the city workers maintaining the landscape. He said that it was their toil that supported all the beauty of the trees and flowers that gave him so much pleasure. And, that this was what his current job provided him, the financial capacity to fully enjoy the making and appreciation of music and creativity in his life. A few months following his decision, Kevin checked in for a follow up session and shared that he had just had his annual review. His manager had commented that his work, which was always excellent, was now accompanied by what seemed to be a happier and friendlier persona; he was awarded an unexpected and much welcomed bonus. Kevin smiled in the retelling and shared that while work was still essentially the same, it was now more meaningful: "I understand that it supports my purpose."

Purpose is a journey of making meaning. It is often put together one step at a time, and emerges through the work of introspection, living in integrity with personal values and attending to the Call of Self. Career coaching can guide a person at the crossroads of transition, supporting and focusing the client on attunement to the call. Facilitating structure, safety and affirmation for a client's self-exploration, the psychosynthesis coach provides a bridge to span the space between the ending and the new beginning. With unique discoveries to be found and choices to be made within the perennial questions of "who am I?" and "what really matters?" client and coach affirm and plan the steps that will lead to manifesting a livelihood that supports of life of fulfillment and joy.

References

Assagioli, R. (1965). *Psychosynthesis*. NY: Penguin Books.

Assagioli, R. (1973). *The act of will*. NY: The Viking Press.

Bridges, W. (2004). *Transitions making sense of life's changes*. Cambridge, MA; Da Capo Press.

Brown, M. Y. (2004). *Unfolding self: The practice of psychosynthesis*. New York, NY: Allworth Press.

Crampton, M. (2000) *Empowerment of the will through life coaching*. Retrieved from: https://www.synthesiscenter.org/articles/Empowerment%20 of%20the%20Will%20through%20Life%20Coaching.pdf

Crampton, M. (1977). *Psychosynthesis: Some key aspects of theory and practice*. Montreal: Canadian Institute of Psychosynthesis.

Ferruci, P. (1982). *What we may be*. NY. JP Tarcher.

Firman, D. (2007). *A Transpersonal orientation: Psychosynthesis in the counselor's office*. Retrieved from: https://www.psychologytoday.com/sites/default/files/attachments/42788/transpersonal-orientation-didi.pdf

Firman, J. & Gila, A. (2002). *Psychosynthesis: A psychology of the spirit*. NY: SUNY Press.

Firman, J., & Gila, A. (2007). *Assagioli's Seven Core Concepts for Training*. Retrieved from https://synthesiscenter.org/PDF/Seven%20Concepts.pdf

Firman, J., & Vargiu, J. (1977). "Dimensions of Growth". *Synthesis 3-4*, 59-120.

Whitmore, D. (1996). "Psychosynthesis A psychology with a soul" *Counselling: Journal of the British Association for Counselling*, vol.7, no.2, pp. 127-31 1996.

Whitmore, D. (2005) *Psychosynthesis counseling in action*. Thousand Oaks, CA: Sage Publications.

Whitmore, J. (2009) *Coaching for performance*. London, Nicholas Brealey Publishing.

Yeomans, T. Psychosynthesis practice volume I. *Psychosynthesis Exercises for Personal & Spiritual Growth*. Retrieved from http://synthesiscenter.org/articles/0011.pdf

Recommended Reading

Assagioli, R. (1991) *Transpersonal development*. London, England, HarperColllins Publishers.

Brown, M. Y. (1993) *Growing Whole: Self-realization on an endangered planet*. MN. Hazelden Educational Materials.

Ferruci, P. (1990). *Inevitable Grace*. NY: G.P. Putnam's Sons.

Figler, H. & Bolles, R. (2007). *The career counselor's handbook.* NY. Crown Publishing Group.

Firman, D. (2016) *Supporting the Future of Psychosynthesis: Coaching as a path to Self-Realization.* Retrieved from https://www.synthesiscenter.org/PDF/SupportingTheFuture.pdf.

Firman, J. & Gila, A. (1997). *The primal wound: A transpersonal approach to trauma, addiction and growth.* NY: SUNY Press.

Hardy, J. (1987). *A Psychology with a soul: Psychosynthesis in evolutionary context.* NY: Rutledge & Kegan Paul Ltd.

Chapter 19

Introducing 5 Dimensions of Leadership

by Roger Evans

Introducing 5DL

This chapter introduces a new way of thinking about leadership. It introduces you to a few discrete human dimensions that characterize all leaders we, at Creative Leadership Consultants (CLC), UK, have worked with over the past 20 years. What I and my colleagues have seen repeatedly over this time is that when a small number of underlying human dimensions are developed to a significant level and when they come together in an individual, then remarkable and great human leadership can take place. The critical part of this statement is when they come together. It is not the same when one or two are present. All five need to be present, to a reasonable extent, to ensure the transformation of the individual into a high quality leader.

These leaders are characterized by a vision of the future based upon sustainability and values. By sustainability I mean a much longer perspective to development and growth where appropriate, rather than the short term "wins" of today, one that includes the environment and their long-term impact upon that. They have a deep understanding of themselves and of the people around them. They have compassion and humility, are innately strong, and have the ability to repeatedly deliver and make things happen by bringing people with them. It sounds like an impossible dream. It isn't, it works. Radical yes, but then 5DL goes to the essence of fine leadership.

So, what do we mean by 5DL?

5DL is:

+ A state of mind
+ A way of being
+ A way of living
+ Intensely practical
+ A practice, and a discipline which needs practice

If a leader has all 5DLs plus good organizational knowledge and management skills, they will consistently:

+ Build organizations that are sustainable, responsible, honest, and transparent
+ Repeatedly deliver organization strategy and goals
+ Build confidence, and wake up tired organizations, divisions, teams, and individuals
+ Develop talent and build new leaders at all levels quickly and consistently deliver change appropriately

5DL is both simple, yet profound.

Will it be understood? I hope so. Will it be used? I hope so. Will it pull together so much of what has been trying to emerge in leadership for the past generation? I believe so. Will it work? Yes it already does because people who really have a passion and a vocation to lead and to make a difference will recognize and understand the power of these dimensions and make them part of their daily practice.

Is 5DL the future of leadership? No and yes.

No, because it is only a starting point, a point of departure.

Yes, because it provides a simple roadmap based upon empirical research.

Is it easy to follow? No, but I believe our lives and our children's future well-being depend upon us developing and practicing this starting point.

Uncovering the Five Dimensions of Leadership

So, how did we come to uncover these crucial leadership dimensions?

For the past 30 years, through our management consulting practice, we have worked with many different levels of leadership. We have done so within global and national organizations in Europe, United States, and Asia. Our focus has always been to advise and help develop competence and excellence in both individual senior leaders and in their leadership of teams as they grapple with complex organization dilemmas. We have been involved across a broad range of sectors, as consultants, educators, and trusted advisors in large scale global change projects, global Mergers and Acquisitions, strategic implementation projects, regional and global resizing, and global leadership education programs.

Within this context, we have worked directly, and in many cases deeply and personally, with many thousands of managers and leaders.

Our experience of leaders we have worked with has been both inspiring and frighteningly awful.

+ **Inspiring** – in terms of the extraordinary courage and tenacity of many of these established and emerging leaders as they face themselves in their strengths and significantly in their vulnerabilities, sometimes having to keep going and serve their people and their vision in the face of limited support and resistance from their Chairman or CEO.

+ **Frighteningly awful** – inasmuch as some leaders— including some senior leaders such as Chairmen, CEO's, divisional heads as well as new leaders—are very poor in this role, with awful consequences for their people and the organization as a whole. Frequently we have seen, as we gradually understood their history, that these men and women have usually had little or no development or support from their senior management during their journey to become a leader. Many of them face the nightmare of leading people who are often better able to do the job than they are. Unfortunately, many of these ineffective leaders believe that because they have been appointed to the leadership role they do not have to earn the respect of their people and can tell them what to do and believe that they will be followed. They frequently preside over disasters because of their incompetence, while failing to understand that these failures are their responsibility.

In the early 1990s, my closest colleagues and I began to realize that the huge investment in leadership development that our clients and many other large global corporations had been making did not really get to the "heart" of what was required to both evoke and develop very fine leaders. We defined "fine leaders" as those who demonstrated the following abilities:

+ Able to deliver repeatedly to deadlines
+ Very good human leadership that
    • aligned and brought their people with them
    • built empowering environments
    • faced conflicts head on, handled and resolved them
    • was team focused
+ Future oriented and able to set clear direction
    • Repeatedly delivered
+ Driven by deep human values
+ Thinks systemically and sees the part as well as the whole
+ Long term perspective and focused on sustainability

255

What we saw was that most leadership development was focused primarily upon measurable skills and competencies. These included strategic thinking, influencing and negotiating skills, team building skills, system thinking skills and latterly significant focus upon personal development skills including emotional intelligence.

In our attempt to get to the "heart of leadership," we systematically began our own empirical observations of the leaders with whom we were working. The overriding question we held was; What were the factors, the competencies, and the skills that truly differentiated the very best from the worst leaders? Was there an x-factor that set them apart? And could it be measured?

Although we didn't realize it, we had begun a journey that was to last approximately ten years. And, what we discovered over these years was very surprising, yet consistent and repetitive. We uncovered a small number of underlying personal dimensions that determine "outstanding leaders" and in our terms the "very best leaders." We also found that these "best leaders" consistently reflect these dimensions time and time again

Our process of discovery and uncovering these "underlying dimensions" was interesting. We did not suddenly uncover all 5 dimensions. They emerged one by one, as we observed and followed a specific trail. On reflection, this is probably why they have not been uncovered before. The discovery followed a sequence that became obvious once we had started to trust where these findings were leading us.

We uncovered the first three dimensions of leadership in the following order over the years 1997-2003.

1. The ability to Self-Reflect – Self-awareness
2. Awareness of one's impact on others and of how different people behave and interact together, and awareness of the power of group dynamics, and how to use them
3. The inner freedom to make clear choices and to deliver on these choices again and again, often in the face of considerable resistance "to be blown in the wind, to bend but to stand firm"

There was then a gap of about 2-3 years before the other two highly connected dimensions fully emerged.

1. The ability to ask for appropriate help and support—internally and externally to the organization
2. The ability to consistently "see and think" about the whole picture and its effect on individuals and teams. The art of thinking systemically and understanding "system forces"

To make the most effective use of these 5 Dimensions of Leadership (5DL) we decided to group them in a different sequence.

The first three are focused around awareness: Self-Awareness (1DL), awareness of the other (2DL), and awareness of the system (3DL) followed by the individual Will and freedom to choose and act (4DL), and finally the one that seems to us to harness the potential in the other 4 DLs and the one that makes good leaders, great leaders is the ability to ask for appropriate help and support (5DL).

Operationally we now use the following sequence
1DL – Ability to Self-Reflect—Self-awareness

2DL – Awareness of one's impact on others, understanding their differences and their group dynamics and different cultures

3DL – The ability to consistently see the whole picture and the dynamics between the "part and the whole." Deeply understanding culture in an organization and the art of "thinking systemically" and understanding system forces

4DL – Individual freedom (the Will) to both make clear decisions and then to drive delivery in the face of resistance

5DL – The ability to ask for appropriate help and support – internally and externally to the organization

So, this was our journey of discovery. It took a group of close colleagues approximately ten years to observe, research, rigorously test and retest the hypothesis of 5DL, in relation to hundreds of mangers and leaders. We think that there are maybe one or two more dimensions that are still to be discovered but, so far, we haven't been able to uncover them ourselves. I believe these 5 Dimensions of Leadership underpin fine and great human leadership.

The Unfolding of 5DL
Over the next few pages I will talk about how these five dimensions unfolded. On reflection, it seems obvious, in reality it wasn't. There is, I believe, an inescapable logic to the unfolding process.
1DL
Our starting point was clear. We had seen for many years that the best leaders and potential leaders that we worked with had—either as an innate

ability or had developed—a significant ability to, stop, self-reflect and challenge themselves deeply in terms of their capacity to deal with a situation, a person or a task. They did so either to prepare themselves or to review how things went. They were able to do so as though they were looking in on themselves and looking at their intellectual and emotional availability to deal with the situation. Interestingly many did so as a personal risk assessment and talked about their self-reflection in this way.

So the starting point was the hypothesis that: the finest leaders are highly self-aware, and that it is this inner radar that keeps them true to themselves and enables them to be authentic[1] and real. As we unpack each one of the 5DLs, I will discuss what phrases like being "authentic and real" mean in the leadership context and how their followers model this authenticity and see that its repetition builds confidence and trust.

So, we began to use the hypothesis that the finest leaders are highly self-aware in all our corporate work. In doing so, we observed the whole range of leadership effectiveness, from the most outstanding performance to the most ineffectual. In every situation, it was clear to us that where there was some degree of Self-Reflection and Self-Awareness there was the potential for quality leadership. Where it was missing, then the leader was in trouble and what we observed repeatedly over the years in these cases, was that they failed in the short and medium term by creating around themselves an environment of dysfunction.

Where this dimension is reasonably well developed, we saw that it confers significant perspective and provides a base for the leader to build upon. We began talking about this dimension amongst ourselves and in our team supervisions as:

1DL—The ability to self-reflect: Self-awareness or personal awareness

---

Our continuing research showed us quite clearly that this dimension is the foundation of all the other dimensions. Without developing self-awareness and the ability to reflect upon ourselves and our thoughts, feelings, and behaviors, we are almost completely focused outside ourselves. We tend to objectify everything outside ourselves. Thus, we are controlled by the environment around us, by other people and their thoughts and feelings, by the events of business, of family, and of society. In the extreme, without the ability to self-reflect we become, in effect, victims to the world around us. We react rather than being proactive and responsive and we are not aware that we are doing so!

---

[1]For more on this topic, read: George, B. (2003). *Authentic leadership: Rediscovering the secrets to creating lasting value.* San Francisco: Jossey-Bass.

Many new leaders find themselves—after a few months—caught in this way. They may start out with some sense of their own ground, and have some self-awareness. If this awareness is not strong enough, they soon become caught up in the demands and pressures on them from within their organization, by pressure to achieve their targets, the pressure from above, from their people, and externally (through compliance, regulators, shareholders, as well as competitors). Within a short time, they slowly become overwhelmed, tired, and less able to step back and self-reflect and, as a consequence, find themselves reacting and becoming caught in the vicious cycle of adaptation and reactivity.

Some strong and not necessarily good leaders may have significant self-awareness at home with their partner and family and can reflect on how they behave, think, and feel about themselves and those close to them. However, in their corporate leadership role, it is as though they become a different person. It is as if they don a corporate persona and organizational mindset and get completely taken over by this other way of behaving and thinking. In this way, they become identified with the role and thereby caught. They lose themselves, and are usually unable to see how caught they are.

We have found this condition common—particularly when these leaders have been part of a particular corporate culture for a long time and don't realize how this culture has seeped into them and how it has conditioned how they think, feel and behave as leaders at work. Their dilemma is that they don't realize how identified and how caught they have become.

The key to whether we get caught in this way and the degree to which we get caught will be the relative strength of your 1DL. To help us, and our clients measure the relative DL strength we use a scale of zero to five (0-5). In the case of 1DL, zero is no self-reflection and complete lack of self-awareness and a five is where the leader is consistently self-reflecting about whatever they are doing. This simple scale is very effective in helping leaders score themselves and get some perspective on where they are. In scoring yourself or being scored, if your self-reflectiveness and self-awareness is a score of 2 or less, you will struggle continuously. The difficulty of course with a low self-awareness score is that you will not consciously be aware of it and therefore unable to realistically score yourself.

Others including your direct reports and your colleagues however will know and see that and give you clear feedback about your 1DL score. This is where a good 360° degree test, a well-developed Performance Evaluation and good team and self-assessment tools can help you uncover where you are. It is often difficult initially because in a way it is a vicious circle where you can't become aware until you are aware.

I believe that the real value of psychometric tests such as these is essentially to hold a mirror to leaders, potential leaders, and managers to help them develop this ability to self-reflect. Unfortunately, for some people this comes too late. These tools should be used in schools—not as tests but as reflective mirrors—for the student then begins to self-reflect on themselves and their experience, thoughts, feelings, behaviors and their personal needs. Similarly, at university and college, I believe, there needs to be a much greater self-reflective dimension to all academic programs, so that students are encouraged to self-reflect, not just about their success or failure in test and papers, but much more importantly about themselves and their thoughts, feelings, and behaviors about themselves, and the implications for their learning process both in relation to themselves and others.

Integral to these mirrors is, I believe, the experience of being part of a group and being mirrored and asked to reflect on others. This is the core of building an ability to reflect on others and consequently what it means to build what we will call right relations.

What is both interesting and important for you to understand, is that as leaders your goal does **not** have to be perfect scores of 5/5 on each of the dimensions. Each DL serves the other and builds over time. That is why they are all interconnected and interdependent. However, we have found as an ongoing principle that you do need to know where you are and we recommend regular self-assessment.

As self-awareness builds and if a leader can genuinely score themselves mid-range say 3/5—that is to say that they are able to self-reflect around key issues they face, and don't necessarily do so all the time—they know they can look back at events and themselves and they can reflect upon what was happening for them in terms of the mindsets (Evans & Russell, 1989) they were holding and operating out of, as well as the feelings that were present, and increasingly the needs that they had, which were or were not being met. At this stage they may not have been able to do anything about the awareness or change the way they behaved, but looking back they can reflect on what is happening and most important, are willing to do so!

Once there is a level of willingness to self-reflect and to build self-awareness, the other 4DLs can be assessed and, similarly, be developed and begin to "kick in."

2DL

While 1DL got us started on our 5DL journey it soon became clear to us, as we observed this first dimension, that another distinct but very connected inner competence emerged. This second dimension is about the leader's aware-ness of others. That is to say the awareness of how they themselves impact oth-ers. Their ability to see how different other people are from themselves, the dy-namics that exist between individuals, and how these other individuals operate in groups together and, using this awareness, how to work with other people.

Initially we thought that this ability was an extension of 1DL. It soon became clear that it is not. It is a distinct dimension in its own right. 1DL is a prerequisite, however a strong 1DL does not automatically mean that a leader will demonstrate 2DL. This dimension describes a very different, although complementary, awareness to build a good awareness of others. Often we found that many leaders with a relatively strong 1DL tended to be preoc-cupied with themselves and how others perceived them and therefore found it difficult to really open up to the reality of "who is this other person." This means stepping outside the narcissistic limited self-construct of self-reflection to fully include and reach into another. This was a powerful insight for us as we observed many strong 1DL leaders who had little or no awareness of their impact on others and were often blind to the real differences of others and the dynamics that existed between them.

Significantly, the more we understood the distinctness of this dimen-sion, the more we were able to help self-aware leaders (1DL) build this 2DL dimension and learn to work with others' needs and differences and thus create what we call a field of right relations.

Over the next year we observed that leaders who were both able to self-reflect well and had a significant awareness of others and some awareness of the dynamics operating in groups or teams, were far more effective as a leader than those who did not. They were better able to understand, inspire, and motivate as well as understanding and identifying conflicts in a more authentic way.

This dimension builds significantly upon 1DL and gives the leader the wherewithal to understand and engage people they work with, either as peers, their direct reports or, as importantly, their own line manager. As this dimen-sion of awareness builds, they become better able to see the difference in other people by learning to put themselves in the shoes of the others, and learning how to respond to their needs and begin to understand how they tend to react and need to respond to them, a skill that is critical if the leader is to build a highly effective team. It also brings with it the willingness and ability to face conflict both with and between other people and provides the basis from which to handle and resolve conflicts, an area, which for many leaders has been their Achilles heel. So, we called this dimension:

> 2DL—Awareness of their impact on other people – aware-
> ness of others, their differences and the dynamics that differ-
> ent individuals bring to one another, to groups and to teams.

4DL

Having got to this stage and the identification of these two core dimensions an interesting dynamic began to shape our observations and analysis.
While we knew that we had uncovered some important core inner dimensions
of leadership, we also knew that we were not really breaking new ground given
the personal development culture that had already become effectively embedded within the leadership development community (Evans & Russell, 1989)
through the landmark work of people such as Senge (1990) and his powerful
personal mastery breakthrough.

We knew that although we had uncovered dimensions of leadership that
brought balance, some depth and a more human perspective to decision making, we had not really uncovered what it was in really good leaders that enabled
them to repeatedly make clear courageous decisions and focus on delivering
these decisions. We described this quality as the inner courage to see things
through and deliver, despite the reactions and resistance that they inevitably
encountered from their direct reports, colleagues and their own superiors.

As we looked more deeply at the best and the least effective leaders
among our clients it became very clear that the most effective leaders demonstrate significant levels of 1DL and 2DL plus an astonishing ability to hold
their ground—not in reaction, nor in opposition, nor through inertia— but
from a completely different modality. It was as though these leaders were free
enough and secure enough in themselves to stay with the choices they had
made and to keep going, sometimes in the face of extraordinary odds. To show
guts and perseverance in the face of great adversity and hostility. And if they
had this dimension well developed we saw that they tended not to get caught
and become reactive.

What we had uncovered, we saw, was a remarkable dimension which
when strong, characterized the very best leaders: That, of an individual leader
with truly free Will, one who is able to make and trust his or her choice to per-
sist and follow through "no matter what" (Assagioli, 1973). These leaders are
characterized by great individuality and autonomy—distinctly different from
being and acting independently.[2] We called this dimension:

We define 'independent' as a state whereby the individual is acting against or out of reaction to a situation or
most often another person. In effect, they are polarized and in that sense, they are still caught in reaction and
are not free in themselves. This is often seen in adolescence, where the young person is acting against parental
control/norms. An essential step along the road towards being able to free themselves enough to choose to
conform or not "to be able to wear my raincoat even though my mother told me to." (Evans J., 2001)

> 4DL—The inner freedom to make choices and to see them
> through so as to fully deliver, whatever the resistance and the
> odds stacked against them "The ability to 'listen to the Self',
> to be blown in the wind, to bend but not to be broken"

At this point we believed we had finished and had uncovered the three core dimensions at the root of great leadership. We hadn't!

Over the next two years we began to see that that these three dimensions did not fully answer everything we were observing in the best and in the poorest leaders. Even if the best demonstrated high quality self-awareness; awareness of others and their impact on them; and had the freedom and choice to drive delivery in spite of resistance and opposition, they also showed us something else that was significant.

5DL

These very best leaders consistently demonstrated a quality and the behavior of being able go beyond their own "ego and its defenses" (Freud, 1937) and their own narcissism (Freud, 1914). This quality was so unlike that of some of the worst leaders we worked with, who always had to be at the center of everything and believed that they had to be in control.

In the very best leaders there was a quality of humility and openness that did not just come from their own self-awareness (1DL) and being able to be in right relationship with others and work with them (2DL). This was clearly a very specific and dynamic dimension in its own right.

The more we saw this dimension working and began to reflect upon it, it became clear to us that it had to do with the ability of these leaders to consistently ask for help and support when appropriate and at the same time feeling ok about not having all the answers oneself. To us this was a sign of significant confidence and maturity and not being caught in the hubris of their own individual identity. It enabled these leaders to reach out to key talent, to create thoroughly empowered environments and in doing so, critically align and bring people with them. The ability to call on internal and external help as needed and using it properly is the mark of these leaders.

By comparison those leaders who were unable and not free enough to ask for help, even though they had both significant 1DL & 2DL, tended to over control and operate within severe personal limitations. They were frequently highly insecure, although this characteristic was often defended and hidden by an arrogant and aloof stance of not needing help. While they seemed to be powerful and effective, in the short term, they were usually unable to sustain this position over time and bring very bright people—who want their own autonomy—with them over the long term. We called this dimension:

263

> **5DL**—The ability to consistently ask for appropriate help and support at the right time and feeling ok about not having all the answers oneself

What is significant for me about 5DL is that its absence characterizes much of the lack of sustainability of today's corporate world. What it means to build trust and a powerhouse of coherent and aligned talent for the future.

3DL

As we uncovered 5DL, it also brought us to another interesting realization. We had observed that these leaders who had a significant degree of this dimension were not only able to consistently ask for help and support, they were also able to see the whole picture much more consistently than many other leaders.

They were able to see patterns in the organization complexity that they faced; they were better able to see how things "**fitted and hung together**" and thus were able to see their own part in the whole and that of others. They clearly understood and lived by a systemic view of their world and the organizational system within which they lived and worked. This is in part what Senge (1990) called the ability to "think systemically" in his work *The Fifth Discipline*. In addition, however, we observed that these leaders had great ability to see and work with what we call 'system forces'[3].

This is an awareness whereby these leaders accept that the system or organizational culture around them is always at work, albeit unconsciously, impacting what they do as individuals and what their teams do (Killmann, 1985).

We live in an interconnected world yet suffer from acute fragmentation.
—Killmann, 2011

As leaders develop this dimension they not only have an awareness of these forces but are free enough in themselves to choose to cooperate with them or to act differently. This dimension has important consequences for the way that these leaders make choices in relation to a corporate culture for themselves and their teams when innovation requires that they challenge the prevailing norms about the "way we do things around here" and the NIH (not invented here) syndromes.

We called this inner dimension of leadership:

---

[3]System Forces - we describe as the way the system, an organization, a family, a culture impacts the group the team, the individual

> 3DL—The ability to see the whole picture consistently. The art of "thinking systemically"—to see how things fit/hang together and, critically, awareness of the power of systems forces (their own part in the whole and that of others as well as the impact of whole on themselves and others)

So this was the journey that we made, as a small group of consultants over a ten year period. We were able to test and retest our hypotheses with the best, the poorest and the mediocre leaders we worked closely with in our client companies. These companies were located in very different sectors, from Financial Services, Life Science and Health Care, Heavy Engineering, Petrochemicals and in Government Agencies. Most were global, and what is significant is that across these very different national cultures, we observed and confirmed our hypotheses regarding these same five dimensions.

5DL underpins outstanding and great human leadership

From everything we have seen through our work and research with leaders over these past twenty years, I believe these 5 Dimensions of Leadership underpin fine and great human leadership. More importantly we believe that these dimensions will characterize the new leaders that we hope to see evolving in the corporate world. These leaders will have a deep sense of values and take responsibility for building sustainable organizations that are there to serve the society, environment and nature, nationally or globally and which are ethically governed.

It is in this sense that I believe 5DL takes us to "the heart of future leadership" and actually provides leadership with a powerful resolution to its existential crisis. Through their self-reflective nature these dimensions will automatically and naturally challenge and face leaders with questions about purpose and meaning and values.

I also see that we have uncovered a set of dimensions that can most certainly be developed and which should underpin all future leadership development. Without them leadership will continue to be characterized by the past, by the skills, competencies and outer tools and measurements tools that we know only too well. Not only can 5DL transform the quality and authenticity of individual leaders they will naturally inculcate new human values in organizational life. I think that with 5DL we go where Hamel (2012) and Starkey and Hall (2012) suggest that we need to go. To the "soul" and to the "spirit of leadership" and thus provide a context for these skills and competencies, rather than these competencies providing the context as they are currently doing.

I do hope that this introduction to 5DL has provided you with a new context for thinking about your own leadership and leadership development. I hope that in some small way it helps you to recognize and also affirm what you already know, that the reliance upon developing more skills and competencies, however well-honed and effective in themselves, will not ensure great human leadership.

I also hope that it serves to help create a future leadership that is steeped in honesty and transparency that consistently delivers while ensuring sustainability, corporate responsibility, as well as providing best practice in terms of ethical organizational governance (private and public).

For full details of the 5DL book, go to www.5DL.co.uk or www.clc.co.uk

References

Assagioli R. (1973). *The act of will*, New York: Viking Press.

Evans, R., & Russell, P. (1989). *The creative manager*. London: Allen & Unwin.

Freud, A. (1937). *The ego and the mechanisms of defence*. London: Hogarth Press and Institute of Psycho-Analysis.

Freud, S. (1914). On narcissism: An introduction. In J. Strachey et al. (Trans.), *The standard edition of the complete psychological works of Sigmund Freud*, Volume XIV. London: Hogarth Press.

Hamel, G. (2012). *What matters now: How to win in a world of relentless change, ferocious competition, and unstoppable innovation*. San Fransisco: Jossey-Bass.

Killmann, R. (1984). *Beyond the quick fix: Managing five tracks to organisational success*. San Francisco: Jossey-Bass.

Kilmann, R. (2011). *Quantum organizations: A new paradigm for achieving organizational success and personal meaning*. Newport Coast, CA: Kilmann Diagnostics.

Senge, P. (1990). *The fifth discipline: The art & practice of the learning organization*. London: Century Business.

Starkey, K., & Hall, C. (2012). The spirit of leadership: New directions in leadership education. In Scott Snook, Nitin Nohria, & Rakesh Khurana (Eds.), *The handbook for teaching leadership: Knowing, doing, and being* (pp 81-98). Los Angeles: Sage Publication.

Chapter 20

Executive Coaching: A Psychosynthesis Perspective

by Blake McHenry

Current Perspectives

In the world of executive coaching there is a dynamic struggle for definition and clarity which to this point is largely ambiguous and unattended to by the executive coaching industry. This struggle is far reaching, and it has exacerbated and contributed significantly to the inability of professional coaching to become a true mainstream and requisite resource for senior leaders around the world. In my view, this struggle speaks to significant identity challenges for the coaching industry and its coaches. This challenge is steeped in a lack of contextual understanding of what executive coaching is and what requisite coach skills are necessary and expected to effectively perpetuate partnership in the development and long-term satisfaction of the executive client relationship. Until this role identity confusion is made clear, coaching will continue struggling to be fully appreciated and utilized.

Additionally, there is an underlying lack of genuine empathic regard for the executive client that often enables stereotyping of the executive clients that coaches solicit and serve. Executive coaching will need a new resolve in these directions if the profession is to permeate the meaningful and impactful work that is in front of it. As coaches, we stand challenged to evolve our understanding of the complex dynamics of the work we have chosen while developing our capabilities to a higher level of competence. As stated, this evolution begins with a deeper and more empathic view of our clients who inevitably occupy roles of high responsibility and who contend with immense pressure daily around the culture and performance of the organization they lead.

In my own experience, as both a long term corporate executive (15 years) and a long-term executive coach with more than 12,000 hours of coaching, I have developed perspectives and suffered setbacks that have informed and led me to my current thoughts on executive coaching. I am passionate about the evolution of executive coaching, as I have seen firsthand the deep unmet needs of leaders that coaching is uniquely positioned to provide. As an executive, I have had the privilege of working with three exceptional coaches and I personally realized immense benefit from those relationships. The high functioning organization begins with the development of the high potential leaders of these organizations. High functioning leaders result in high functioning organizations. This reality speaks to a massive opportunity for leaders and to the potential impact of executive coaching on both leaders and the organizations they lead.

I share my perspectives here with passion and hope that, as coaches, we become more committed to doing better and more effective work with senior leaders. This commitment calls for a relentless and open-minded pursuit of new capability and understanding well beyond the current coaching industry standards. New paradigms driven by genuine desire to impact leaders and leadership positively will bring a level of impact that begins to meet the deep yearning and often unconscious needs of the leaders we serve. The evolution of these leaders will inevitably impact the lives of the many, many others both directly and indirectly within the domains of the leader. It is in this truth of great need and meaningful opportunity that my passion for the evolution of executive coaching lives.

I will elaborate further on the current break down in the identity of professional coaching work. It is, in my mind, for the same reason that one would not choose a dentist over a heart surgeon for open heart surgery, that the role of executive coach must be clarified. While both the dentist and the heart surgeon are sophisticated medical professionals, the difference in competencies are clearly very important. In other words, the skill sets are unique and relevant to entirely different pieces of professional work. Professional executive coaching is a very specialized and complex role which requires a significant level of specialized understanding and skill. Those who might label themselves as executive coaches and then embark on advising a CEO on company brand strategy or providing organizational consulting on company organizational charts are doing important and specialized work of their own, but are clearly not functioning as executive coaches. We can stipulate that while a very few individuals may have skill sets and the capability for dual or multiple roles in the work, the roles cannot effectively be integrated if the coaching work is to yield what is intended by and for the client. If well-meaning and often highly competent advisors continue to present themselves as coaches, when they are, in fact, functioning as consultants and strategic advisors, then the executive coaching profession will not progress. The solution for the coaching profession is to more clearly refine the specialized body of work that it is then uniquely equipped to do. Once this specialized capability is clear and realized then the consultants and advisors will present themselves as such and coaches will be left with clearer identity and a meaningful body of work that executive clients will rely on them for. The solution to this dilemma belongs with the coaches who are committed to doing the intended work of executive coaching: the work of collaborating and facilitating the development of more effective and satisfied leaders. This opportunity, when realized, will inevitably yield the development of greater coach presence, new personal narratives for clients, and the disidentification of old subpersonalities in the client.

This is not only specialized work but is a meaningful piece of the essence of executive coaching work. In conclusion, the importance of the coach recognizing the core responsibilities, skills and opportunities in the coaching role magnifies the opportunity to do work that catalyzes authentic and meaningful progress for clients and organizations. It is time to defer the business of strategic advisor and organizational consulting roles to those fully equipped for those roles and for executive coaches everywhere to identify as capable professionals in the business of developmental relationship and meaningful change agents for the long-term growth of executive leaders.

Thus, as a working definition, I would define the executive coach as one who attunes deeply and uniquely to the needs, demands, and opportunities of the executive client, an attunement that is more specific to the individual client potential and less toward the strategy and structure of the organization.

There are, then, in my experience three core understandings to be recognized between the coach and client as the coaching relationship begins to form. The first of these core understandings is the importance of the coach understanding the role of an executive coach and conveying this clearly to the client. Additionally, the coach will do well and should bring deep curiosity to understanding the roles, responsibilities and pressures of each executive client from the perspective of the client. Lastly, it is imperative that both the coach and the client understand the specific purpose of the work they will do together. In other words, is our client seeking a strategic advisor, an organizational consultant, a professional coach or none of the above? In my experience, this is a requisite clarity that is too often left to chance in the initial contracting and intake in the "coaching" relationship. When left unclarified or in the hands of those without specialized executive coach skill sets then the work misses the frameworks, tools and focuses required to obtain forward movement and desired results.

In the hands of a competent and caring executive coach, the coaching relationship will yield meaningful outcomes consistent with the initially stated client agenda and often much more.

Coaching from a Psychosynthesis Perspective

There is, in me, a personal bias that I will attempt to identify as I begin this section of my writing. Simply stated, my bias is that I believe, and have believed for years, that without a keen understanding of human behavior and human change processes, a coach is in a great sense handicapped and will have a difficult time being fully effective in the work of executive coaching. As coaches, we are responsible to facilitate and support the movement of desired changes as determined by our clients. We are also essential in the facilitation of those same determinations of desired change, if these determinations are to be appropriately rooted in the personal core values and authentic passions of the leader. Therefore, the requisite responsibility and competence of the coach cannot be overstated as clients determine and pursue new direction and work through old impediments. Change, as a process, is difficult for people and often with executive clients the context of change is riddled with complex competing priorities and pressures. The work of change, then, requires that the conflicts within our clients be sorted out in a highly effective manner. The ability of the coach to facilitate effective depth work that tethers the client more closely to core personal values, while bringing forward and dissipating old patterns (subpersonalities) which are no longer useful, is imperative in the work. The acquisition of these executive coach capabilities must be a core expectation of ourselves.

For me, it was not until I began working with psychosynthesis perspectives and tools that I became more fully aware of and capable of facilitating these complex and high stakes processes in the working through of change. I am yet at the early stages of my journey into what psychosynthesis brings to coaching and to the understanding of human behavior for coaches. It is then true that I write this piece from a place of an experienced executive coach, experienced former executive and an early stage beginner in the learning on psychosynthesis applications to executive coaching. I do know now, without hesitation, that in psychosynthesis I have found a complete and highly effective guidepost and framework for the work of executive coaching. I will continue to practice and pursue greater competence and personal development as coach for as long as I do this work. Psychosynthesis provides me the holistic and complete body of wisdom, tools and structure for my continued learning journey as a coach as well as for my own lifelong development as a person.

The Leader

The job of leading an organization in today's world brings much demand and strain even for the most capable leaders. The pressures for leaders to deliver results are daunting and these expectations often carry a threat to the leader's job and the jobs of those in their organizations. It is the opportunity to develop, "in leaders" a greater resilience for ambiguity, a greater willingness to compromise and more clarity of purposeful direction that executive coaching is intended to address. There is a great need in our executive leaders to feel fully understood, to be recognized for their good work, and to have a resource that brings a relationship of complete trust and genuine empathic regard. In simple words, it is in the nature of leadership roles that the individual leader will often be left with a deep sense of being alone due to the decisions and hierarchical nature of their role. My experience has also taught me that, contrary to current myths about leaders, there are in fact some fundamental needs that most executive clients bring to the work and that coaches need to understand.

Myth#1 – Executive clients seek coaches who will agree with them and validate them constantly. My experience is that most leaders are surrounded by individuals willing to tell them what they want to hear, and this is not useful or desirable to the developing high potential leader. Most leaders seek a trusted relationship that provides insight and candor. These are relationships that are virtually impossible to find within the power structure of an organizational system.

Truth #1 – Contrary to myth #1, executive clients need a relationship (coach) that drives candor, collaboration and accountability in the work. There are reasons why individuals ascend to leadership roles and many of these reasons are connected to demonstration of candor, collaboration and accountability. The opportunity for the coach is to show up in ways that engage the client as a peer relationship, as opposed to a subordinate relationship.

Myth #2 – Executive clients are self-absorbed individuals who are primarily motivated by power, money and a need for the spotlight. These kinds of stereotyped myths stand in the way of the evolution and integration of professional coaches and the executive client. I have not personally met an executive client who was unable or unwilling to access, communicate, or embrace their own authentic set of intrinsic personal values.

Truth #2 – Executive clients, like all human beings, are primarily motivated by intrinsic sense of responsibility and an innate drive to improve the situation of self and others. The inherent bias for action required in senior leadership roles should not be mistaken for a lack of depth or intrinsic motivation on the part of the leader. Upon reflection, most leaders demonstrate high integrity and strong personal values. There are often great extrinsic challenges to these personal values in the form of financial and political performance issues.

Myth #3 – Executive clients are shallow individuals who carry a resistance to reflection and depth work. These stereotypes often come from decisions which polarize popularity and lack of popularity within, as well as outside, of the organization.

Truth #3 – Executive clients need and prefer depth over surface and carry a keen ability for deep and reflective work when there is a safe and trusted partner (coach) tethered to an effective coaching process (stages of the Act of Will). The decisions that senior leaders are responsible for require critical thinking skills, contextual nuance and an ability to find the greater good. This decision-making process requires depth of thinking.

The Coaching Process – A Psychosynthesis Perspective

As I have delved deeper into my understanding and utilization of psychosynthesis executive coaching in recent years, I have a more clear and useful understanding of my role as a professional coach, as well as more competence to share with the client. The psychosynthesis theory and practice have provided me with three core insights that have become a significant piece of my toolkit and which I will elaborate on.

The first of these insights is that I now have a deeper understanding of the importance of "presence of the coach" in every session. This presence contributes to genuine empathic responding, trust building and forwarding of positive outcomes along each stage of the coaching process. The pathway to increased presence in the coach is a personal self-care practice, as well as having a personal coach and coach supervisor.

The second of these insights is that psychosynthesis has provided greater access to quality reflection and depth work with clients. The utilization of tools that bring forward subpersonalities in clients and that enable clients to do meaningful disidentification work contributes significantly to progress. This work removes staunch impediments from the past and makes room for a more authentic, preferred future for the client. As a core principle of psychosynthesis, the process of identification, disidentification, and self-identification supports the movement forward, freed of old obstacles and beliefs. In psychosynthesis it is said that we are dominated by everything which we become identified and we can, therefore, direct, and utilize everything from which we disidentify.

The third of these insights is that the personal stories that our clients tell will inevitably change the arc of their lifespan. In other words, if we change our stories we change our lives. As a mentor of mine, Didi Firman, once said to me, "You are not your story and you ARE so much more than your story". The depth work of identifying personal core values, disidentifying with subpersonalities which are old and limiting, ultimately results in the client formulating new and more useful stories. These new stories ultimately serve to illuminate and progress the manifestation of the client's plan.

I believe that psychosynthesis offers the most significant available opportunity for improving coach effectiveness and making the work of executive coaches more effective and clear. Recently I have begun using Assagioli's stages of the act of will as the guide to change process or coaching process with my clients. This implementation creates a framework for competent work as a coach. Each of the six stages plays an integral part in my work with clients. I now walk through those stages in my intake sessions with new coaching clients so that they recognize there is a framework that holds our work together. I have found that this framework is palatable and calming to executive clients. The stages include: purpose, deliberation, choice/decision, affirmation, planning, and manifestation. Revealing the stages also clarifies to the client that they are working with a coach who brings specialized processes, skills and attributes to the work. Again, once acquired, these coaching processes, skills and attributes become as clear and apparent as the distinct skills of the surgeon and the dentist. What follows is a further elaboration of the three core coaching insights derived from psychosynthesis.

Presence in the Coach

The full presence of the coach in each moment of a coaching session is an imperative component in maximizing quality outcomes with our clients. Coach self-care will contribute significantly to the presence of the coach. The identification and practice of conscious self-care will lend itself to a deeper more centered coaching presence. For each coach, the implementation of self-care practices will be a very personal and authentically designed set of practices. Some of the practices that have contributed meaningfully to the personal and spiritual growth of coaches and other helpers historically include journaling, meditation, yoga, disidentification exercises, and self-identification exercises.

I want to mention an additional component that will significantly further presence in professional coaches. For coaches to take care of themselves and bring more presence to their work, they will benefit greatly from having a coach of their own. It has always concerned me that many, many executive coaches do not seek out a coach for themselves. To invest in a coach for the coach is to invest in your business of coaching. To me, it seems unaligned for any professional coach to ever stop working on their own development and coaching is a highly effective way to do this work of development. The coach who does not continually work through their own subpersonalities, life patterns, limiting belief and current development edges will inevitably bring their own impediments into the work with clients. These impediments will likely stand in the way of client progress, as well as coach satisfaction with the work. Additionally, when coaches choose to engage as a client with an accomplished psychosynthesis coach, they receive the added benefit of a coach that is utilizing the toolkit that executive psychosynthesis coaches utilize. Whether in personal coaching or with work with an independent coach supervisor, there is great benefit to sitting in one's own development work with a psychosynthesis coach.

I will now walk through each of the stages of Assagioli's "Act of Will" and offer a brief narrative on how I perceive each stage as being relevant to our work with executive clients.

Stages of the Act of Will – A Useful Coaching Process

Stage 1 – Purpose, based in intention, motivation & evaluation

Stage one begins with a journey into the authentic purposeful and meaningful core of each client. This is often a stage which yields clarification of competing priorities and values for the client. Clients often discover and realize their own patterns of time spent on things more trivial and on the surface. This provides the client an effective way to begin sorting through the clutter and removal of impediments which may have distorted the past and to clarify an authentic personal value's driven direction. This stage of the work serves as a reminder to clients of what they value most and serves to put down anchors to return to throughout the continuum of our work together.

The coach's toolkit in stage one includes personal values exercises, thought provoking questions that illuminate past high points and visualization of a preferred future. Additionally, the identification of past inauthentic behaviors and decisions may emerge for the client in the form of regret. The coach remains diligent in holding this regret and utilizing it as a motivator to more authentic future opportunities. Additionally, subpersonality patterns are identified, and we begin the work of dissipating the hold that these patterns may have on the client. As a previous mentor and coach of mine suggested to me one time, "don't let your past ghostwrite your present or future". The ability of the coach to continue listening for and helping identify these subpersonality distortions is a critical piece of work that will pay dividends for the long term for the client, thus allowing the emergence of clear and authentic purpose from which the act of will unfolds.

Stage 2 – Deliberation

Stage two brings the critical evaluation of potential changes for the client. This is a stage where the coach brings an ongoing curiosity as to what the client is ultimately needing. This curiosity is nuanced with the responsibility to help the client distinguish the real personal narrative (personal stories). This work allows the client the opportunity to tell their story and yet to recognize that they are not their story, but rather so much more than their story. It is also a stage where an empathic assertiveness from the coach to effectively challenge what the true needs are for the client can be critical. This nudge toward a deeper introspection by the client can often contribute to more authentic and purposeful deliberation.

The deliberation stage brings deeper collaboration between coach and client. This collaboration will sometimes include difficult processing of subpersonalities that may be distorting the client's genuine needs. In other words, the deliberation stage brings the opportunity to anchor in authentic personal values while dissipating personal stories that no longer serve the client well.

Stage 3 – Choice and Decision

Stage three brings an opportunity for the client to choose new directions (or stay with old ones), make important decisions, and create goals and actions that are true to the authentic and values-driven work done in stage one and two. The coach holds the pillars of these previous stages for the client, as options are chosen for the move forward. This stage will often bring an energized reaction from the client as new commitments to change are made. This is also a time to review the thoughts and behaviors that the client wants to leave behind as part of their past. For most clients, this stage is a big step toward committing to a preferred future. This is a time where the neutrality of the coach is important as the client chooses a future that resonates with their own sense of "my best and higher Self".

Stage 4 – Affirmation

The affirmation stage is an opportunity for the client to deepen commitments to new direction. In this stage, the client is responsible to begin taking initial actions toward the new desired outcomes and to deepen commitment to making the desired choices a reality. Clients are asked to create images, statements and movements that represent and symbolize the attainment of new purposeful direction. This envisioning process involves both individual exercises as well as guided imagery and other exercises facilitated by the coach. The visualization and imagining of the purposeful vision gives the client the opportunity to further internalize the commitment to these changes. The coach will further the client commitment to the stated changes by reminding them of the values and motivations that were identified in stage one. Affirmation becomes the bedrock for the process of moving into action, as it inspires the client in words, images and experience.

Stage 5 – Planning

The planning stage is a time when the client and coach collaboratively determine a set of actions which will effectively yield the purposeful goal or goals that the client has committed to. This stage illuminates the reality that change is hard work and that new actions and behaviors will be required to accomplish the plan. Clients will often bristle and sometimes regress when the reality check of required new actions and behaviors is more present and pervasive. This is a key opportunity for the coach to skillfully remind the client of why they chose a particular goal. The skillful coach will remind clients of those values and purpose driven anchors that were identified as priorities in stage one and stage two.

It can also be very useful to have a dialog in stage five which asks clients to articulate how they would like to be accountable for the plan and what role the coach can play in supporting or facilitating accountability. It is important to note that most executive coaching clients have evolved to their position out of a willingness to be accountable and an ability to deliver what they are accountable for. Coaches need not tread lightly when discussing and implementing accountability into the process. The bigger challenge, in my own experience, is that executive clients do make significant and rapid change once they have truly committed to it and yet have difficulty acknowledging and recognizing their own progress. This brings in another core opportunity to be the voice of recognition, the proud parent for the client, the affirming ally, the celebratory other.

Stage 6 – Manifestation

The manifestation stage is the execution phase of the client's plan. The client will be making the specific changes that have been defined and committed to. In this stage, the coach will bring the memory of each of the previous five stages and remind the client often of anchors, motivations and commitments that were previously present as the plan was designed. The construction of the client's plan was done with thoughtful and authentic consideration and it reflects the deeper needs of the client. It is imperative that the coach hold the previous stages present for the client as the manifestation unfolds. This will often feel like two steps forward and one step back as the client gets down to the business of plan implementation.

There are certain patterns for the coach to pay close attention to during this stage of the work. Are old subpersonalities showing up again and creating conflict within the client's effort to make changes? Is the client using the demands and busyness of their role as an excuse for not moving forward with the plan? Does the client suddenly decide that while the changes are important and meaningful to make, that now is not the best time to make them? All of the resolutions to these challenges are contained in the work done well in the previous five stages of the defined acts of will. And those stages can be revisited at any time, to re-engage the forward movement of the client's purpose.

Stories Our Clients Tell

Each client comes to us with a very personal and unique narrative. Whether in executive coaching or life coaching the individual narrative will reflect the identifications, subpersonalities and defenses of the individual and their reactions to their own life experiences. For some these stories will be more objective and less distorted than others. For all there will be an opportunity to refine the objectivity of their past stories and to keep the present informed by the past but not owned by the past. In order to move forward with less distorted thoughts, feelings, and behaviors, clients and coaches must recognize that while every client has a story, they are also much more than their story. In other words, a personal narrative which comes from a less distorted place is an opportunity that brings new thoughts, which drive different behaviors and different emotions. Ultimately these less distorted perspectives lead to more productivity and satisfaction toward a life well lived and in service of the client's higher Self.

The executive coaching client works in a complex role and distortions of their story can be prevalent. There is much temptation for these clients to rationalize and compromise their own values in the interest of job security, stockholder value and personal gain. My own experience as a coach has taught me that when these clients experience a coaching process which begins with personal values and anchors in these values, then many positive things happen for the client and those impacted by the client. Additionally, the recognition of over identifications and subpersonalities, in and of itself, will bring the client's story to a more objective place. Once the coach and client begin this work of dissipating limiting identifications and bringing the client to more presence, then the higher Self can reveal itself more fully. I feel strongly that as coaches, we benefit our clients in meaningful ways by developing our skills and understanding of how to more effectively work with the stories of our clients, always directed towards unfolding the story that is most in line with the client's purpose, in life and in work.

Conclusions and Final Thoughts

I hope that this writing has provided the reader with some useful perspective on executive coaching and how psychosynthesis informs effective coaching work. Executive coaching is an underserved field full of significant opportunity for coaches. This opportunity presents coaches with challenging and complex work, influential clients and an opportunity to develop specialization in the field. This specialization requires enhanced skills, understanding, and empathic regard for the client.

In my experience, psychosynthesis brings current and future executive coaches a toolkit that fully equips them for this challenging work. The presence of the coach, a useful and thorough coaching process, and the ability to look more deeply into the stories that our clients bring to their sessions are all core pieces of the psychosynthesis toolkit. These are a few of the core fundamentals that bring about useful and meaningful growth in our clients when effectively utilized. For those who may find themselves interested in a direction forward toward psychosynthesis executive coaching there are more and more programs available to hone the skills and build the toolkit.

The opportunity for impact and meaning is significant as executive coaches. Working with senior leaders who influence other large groups of individuals speaks best to the opportunity that is executive coaching. In my view, there is no other opportunity in professional coaching that can positively improve the lives of so many and so quickly. It is my hope that these leaders will find professional coaches that are ready, willing and able to partner in the growth and satisfaction of the individual executive and the organizations they lead.

Chapter 21

A Model for Psychosynthesis Corporate Coaching

by Julie Rivers and Patricia Elkins

Introduction

Psychosynthesis and Corporate Coaching have distinct histories and have served separate purposes and client bases. In recent years, these fields have begun to come together with psychosynthesis coach training in the psychosynthesis world and corporate coaches expanding their skill set by becoming psychosynthesists. This 'cross-pollination' of skills, concepts, and approaches demonstrates a natural and exciting synthesis and yet, has also created some blurred boundaries around both fields. How can psychosynthesis, a field that deals with self-awareness and an understanding of the psyche and the Self, be integrated into a standard conventional business setting? How does corporate coaching shift when it is informed by the field of psychosynthesis? This chapter will offer some specific suggestions as to how these fields come together optimally and will detail some case studies demonstrating the value that each field offers the other.

We will start with brief backgrounds on psychosynthesis and on the history of corporate coaching.

History

Brief history of Psychosynthesis

Psychosynthesis, a transpersonal psychology, comes from the work of the 20th century Italian psychiatrist Roberto Assagioli. In historical context, Assagioli was a contemporary of Sigmund Freud, founder of psychoanalysis, a psychological model focusing attention on an individual's past through analysis of the past and its effects on the psyche. Assagioli referred to Freud's work

279

as psychological work in the 'basement of the soul' (Keen, 1974). In contrast, psychosynthesis draws its distinction by focusing on a broader lens: Assagioli explored the whole 'house of the soul' and even the neighborhood, country, and planet of its experience. In this broader transpersonal space, psychosynthesis explores that which is beyond the past and the present personality. Who are you, who am I, if we look beyond our personalities? Assagioli was interested in this broader synthesis of Self through self-awareness, self-realization, and, ultimately, through societal integration leading to awareness of our common humanity.

Psychosynthesis has traditionally been the work of psychotherapists and counselors, supporting clients seeking relief from emotional/mental discomfort, pain, diagnosable mental illnesses and trauma, past and present. Clients were therefore motivated to enter into therapy. (In Italy, the founding country of psychosynthesis, this approach was initially employed by psychiatrists and medical doctors, as well). The focus of psychosynthesis therapy may delve into past events that are limiting to the client's present ability to enjoy life, but the sessions are equally likely to tap into the client's strengths, successes, and purpose-driven ideals. As experts in their field of psychology, therapists or counselors typically provide their clients with guidance, insight, and specific suggestions as to how discomfort or pain may be relieved and how happiness, stability and safety can be attained.

In the past 20 years or so, psychosynthesis coaching has evolved within the psychosynthesis psychology space. With the essence of psychosynthesis maintained, the emphasis on healing traumas in the past has given way to focus more on the impact of the past in the context of the present and on the actions that can be taken in the present to create new patterns and to realize goals.

Brief history of corporate coaching

By contrast, corporate coaching emerged in the late 20th century and became mainstream at the turn of the 21st century. It grew out of unmet needs in leadership models and organizational structure as well as self-improvement and human potential movements. Corporate coaching drew from many fields including academia and philosophy, and from work in leadership and supervisory development, sports coaching, and personal development (Brock, 2016). Interestingly, coaching was initially designed as a supervisory function, though it typically is not implemented in that model today. The number of training programs for corporate coaches, professional coaching organizations, coaching conferences and coaching books increased in the 1990s and by the early 2000s, "coaching" was a commonly used term in the business world.

In practice, corporate coaching has been the work of individuals, not supervisors, coming from a range of fields such as Human Resources or Organizational Development, who have found the coaching model an effective approach to help professionals be more effective and fulfilled in their jobs. The focus is often on the future and on taking action, and spends little time on the past unless it informs the client about goals in the present. Corporate Coaching relies on the client's internal resources to achieve meaningful goals by exploring possible options, ways to progress toward desired goals, and action and plans taken to achieve those goals. While many Corporate Coaching models exist, in the authors' corporate experience most strive to align such that the content, direction, and outcome of the coaching work is driven primarily by the client. Client empowerment is a primary goal of the coach, and it is achieved by supporting the client to tap into personal experiences, resources, and gifts to explore and determine optimal ways forward.

A summary of contrasts

The contrasts between the histories of psychosynthesis and corporate coaching can seem broad: the extent and depth of training and content knowledge of the professional role, the dynamic in the professional/client relationship, the varied focus on attending to the past, and the motivation for entering into the relationship on the part of the client. Given these broad differences, you may wonder how they may optimally continue to co-evolve.

To understand this co-evolution, it is necessary to understand a bit more about both of these fields in current practice.

Corporate Coaching Today

Corporate coaching, now a regulated field with internationally recognized organizations, norms, and certification levels, provides well-defined models for how to work with clients. These accrediting organizations provide standards, ethics, and require demonstration of coaching competencies that results in a consistent and rigorous practice of coaching. Corporate coaches tend to be employed after they have been certified by such an international coaching organization.

Models used in the corporate coaching space vary with the most widely referenced model as the GROW model (Performance Consultants International, 2014) described in Sir John Whitmore's book: *Coaching for Performance*(2009). The development and theory around coaching models are described extensively in literature.

Common characteristics of these models include:

+ contracting to understand goals and mutual expectations, discussing the topic and/or underlying issue, a discussion of options, and movement to clarity or action steps
+ a power-free and trusting relationship
+ powerful questioning by the coach for the purpose of increased self-awareness on the part of the coachee
+ action oriented and measurable outcomes

To understand the corporate coaching space more fully however, it is also important to understand what coaching isn't. Corporate coaches are not expected to be specialists or content experts in the field in which they are coaching. Teaching and advising on content is reserved for mentors, consultants, or content experts in a field. The value of the corporate coach is in their objective focus on the coaching process, the client's growing self-awareness and the client's use of their own inner resources rather than a specific outcome of the coach's choosing. While corporate coaches do not provide advice or content knowledge to their clients, they may direct their clients to sources of information.

What do corporate coaches focus on with their clients to establish goals, options, and outcomes? The coach leads the coaching process of contracting, exploring the issue, considering options, and agreeing actions. In this process, self-awareness is fostered through the client's reflection, the coaches' powerful questions, and action-focused accountabilities. The benefits of this approach, as described by the International Federation of Coaching (ICF) includes "fresh perspectives on personal challenges, enhanced decision-making skills, greater interpersonal effectiveness, and increased confidence (ICF, n.d., Benefits of Using A Coach). In addition, ICF indicates that those who engage in coaching can "expect appreciable improvement in productivity, satisfaction with life and work, and the attainment of relevant goals." (ICF, n.d., Benefits of Using A Coach) by accessing their inner resources, building self-confidence, and taking actionable steps with accountability. In summary, corporate coaching work is client centric and aside from process, is client driven.

A Niche for Psychosynthesis in the Corporate Coaching Model Today

How does psychosynthesis 'fit' into the corporate coaching model?

Corporate clients seek out coaching when they are feeling stymied and haven't effectively achieved a goal, created a vision, or overcome a limitation that is aligned to a business objective. For example, corporate clients may be interested in being more effective as a people leader or may struggle in advancing their careers despite concerted efforts. In the process of beginning work with a corporate coach, the coach and coachee overtly discuss and clarify their goals through 'contracted' agreements: discussions at the start of coaching sessions in which a description of the challenge and desired outcomes are made clear. These agreements are then explored by discussing what actions **could** be taken in the present to achieve those goals. Activating a client's vision about what is possible often leads to more understanding of where the client is stuck. A client may not see what appears (to the coach) to be an obvious way forward, the client may know where they are stuck and even why but they cannot unlock their thinking, or the way forward may be clear but the internal resources to implement them seem missing. Often, clients who are aware of their limitations also have many explanations that justify their difficulty in achieving their goals. The result is that forward moving plans become difficult to craft and even more difficult to enact by the clients until they come into greater self-awareness of **why they are stuck** and go through a process of becoming unstuck.

This is where psychosynthesis ideally comes into the blended model of corporate coaching. Psychosynthesis coaching offers many rich maps or frameworks to work in the 'what's possible' space. Some of this work is done in the present, but the true value psychosynthesis brings is in drawing from relevant experiences of the past and integrating into the present the purpose-filled qualities and life experiences that call us into the future. All of this is done in alignment with our values and deeply meaningful truths that begin to come into focus about ourselves. Psychosynthesis helps a corporate coach address past limitations and strengths and draw from the future while keeping a focus in the present.

A foundational construct of psychosynthesis is the wholeness of one's self including our past, present, future, as well as our common humanity and inter-connectedness. The psychosynthesis model includes all these, without bias. We will take a short side-step here to explore the Psychosynthesis Egg diagram, a representation of psychosynthesis psychology, before continuing the discussion of how psychosynthesis supports the corporate coaching model.

Psychosynthesis and the "Egg" diagram

Below is a description of the Psychosynthesis Egg diagram with examples demonstrating the theory of psychosynthesis in practice. Understanding the Egg diagram will help those unfamiliar with psychosynthesis to further explore how it has application to corporate coaching.

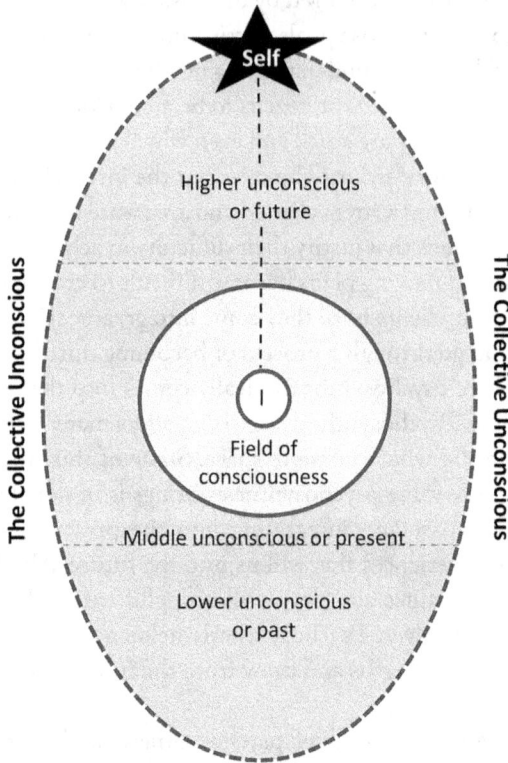

The present or middle unconscious.

The Psychosynthesis Egg diagram shows you, right now, in your current awareness of self in the center "I" sphere. What you are conscious of and what you are thinking about right now is your "Field of Consciousness". The middle unconscious is an expanded set of information available to you but not yet 'booted up' into your active thinking. For example, if I asked you "What is the best way to travel to New York City from your current location?", you would be able to recall from memory enough information to answer the question by bringing known information into your field of consciousness and using that information to answer my question.

The past or lower unconscious

The lower part of the egg represents the past: memories and information that are not called up readily into working memory but nevertheless, may powerfully impact who you are today, how you make choices, as well as the limitations or filters you apply to yourself and others around you. For example, if I said to you "I notice you have a pattern of shying away from writing when given a rich opportunity to write that would clearly benefit you professionally," and I happen to know you have the capacity to write well, I may then ask you, "Can you tell me more about that? Is there something that holds you back?" What may 'come up' from the past or the lower unconscious could be old stories, experiences, feelings, assumptions, and/or beliefs that have a limiting impact on you and drive you to avoid writing, even though you write well, and even when it would be professionally advantageous to do so. You may also neglect opportunities to offer others a chance to write about their experiences because you unconsciously impose your writing 'lens,' whatever it may be, on others. With this information transitioned from your lower unconscious into your field of consciousness, you may explore these limiting thoughts in the context of the present choices facing you, and ultimately you may intentionally make different decisions about writing than you had in the past.

The future or higher unconscious

The upper part of the egg represents the future as well as those purpose-filled qualities that pull you forward and are rewarding for you as a creative, expressive, and unbounded soul. These qualities may not be conscious and yet, they too, like events from the past, may have a powerful impact on who you are today, how you make choices, and the lens or filter that you apply to yourself and others around you. For example, if I said to you, "I've spent 4 sessions working with you in the corporate coaching space, and I've started to notice that you look for situations where you can act as an advocate. You seem to like representing the underdog. What are your thoughts on that?" You may grow in awareness that you feel called to work in this space. With that knowledge and awareness, you may even decide to move with greater intention into this kind of work in the present by becoming an ombudsman, by volunteering at a women's shelter, or by becoming an advocate for a cause that resonates with you.

The collective unconscious

On the upper perimeter of the Egg is the label 'Self' which is directly connected by a line to your "I." This diagrammatic representation indicates two important relationships. First, that your full Self, with the full richness of past, present, and future, is reflected in how you show up in the present. Both your lower and your higher unconscious, as described above, are reflected in who you are today and what choices you make today. In short, your "I" reflects the truths of your fullest "Self." Secondly, your "Self" sits within a broader context of the collective unconscious and is influenced by that. What does this mean? The collective unconscious includes the family, societal, and cultural norms that we know. These are the often-tacit agreements that define what is and is not acceptable in our social systems. The collective unconscious also includes all else that is unknown or unknowable. With awareness of the collective unconscious, you will bring new information into your field of consciousness, and may explore family, societal, and cultural norms, and may intentionally choose differently about the norms and practices you want to perpetuate.

The Value Corporate Coaching brings to Psychosynthesis

We have discussed the psychosynthesis model at a high level and discussed the value that psychosynthesis brings to corporate coaching. We will now explore the inverse relationship: what is the value that corporate coaching brings to psychosynthesis coaching?

As described above, corporate coaching has significantly matured in the past two decades: core competencies are defined, certification processes set a very high bar with required training, experience, and assessment-based criteria, and ongoing development is required. With regard to practices driven by core competencies, these additional distinguishing factors between corporate coaching and psychosynthesis coaching merit mentioning. In corporate coaching, coaches are required to:

- Contract with their clients at every session, to define measures of success and underlying issues
- Ensure the client sets the direction of the session by
  - checking the client's thinking and goals throughout a coaching session,
  - working from the client's perspective more than from the coach's perspective (e.g., using the client's words, orienting from the client's view, and ensuring the client contributes to the coaching method as the session evolves)
  - checking the client's experience within a coaching session (e.g., asking direct progress checking questions like "How are we doing in this session? Are we working in the space that is important to you?")

+ Demonstrate performance against core competencies
+ Ask powerful questions: questions that are short and singular (not stacked), clear, and clean (non-leading)
+ Connect contracting agreements to planning and goal setting during the action discussions toward the end of a session
+ Continue Professional Education to maintain accreditation

The value and importance of conforming to the core competencies is very much aligned to the purpose of corporate coaching: to grow the client's own self-awareness, confidence, and reliance on internal resources. From a business perspective, these qualities help staff to grow in their ability to be self-directed, to work more effectively with others, and ultimately to achieve business goals. Corporate coaching data is increasingly proving to support these objectives.

The level of rigor and specificity of performance required of corporate coaches is currently the biggest differentiator when comparing corporate coaching with psychosynthesis coaching.

Psychosynthesis and Corporate Coaching Come Together

While corporate coaching is now well defined in structure with internationally recognized norms and assessments, psychosynthesis, as a psychology, is somewhat hampered by its own expansive nature. The impact of bringing psychosynthesis coaching together with corporate coaching has the same challenge: Psychosynthesis coaching is focused on meaning, purpose, and looking inward while corporate coaching is focused on outcomes, actions, and awareness of how we "show-up" in our work environment. The challenge in bringing psychosynthesis coaching into the corporate space is in navigating both the level of depth and business-appropriateness of the coaching interaction and the confusion and sometimes incongruity of the psychosynthesis coaching language in the corporate environment.

Psychosynthesis is not prescriptive. The application of psychosynthesis concepts is open to wide interpretation, and it is not structured with clear rules. As a "psychology of the soul," psychosynthesis is as unconstrained by definitions and applications as humans are constrained to prescribed ways of being. The positive aspects of this can be leveraged by giving definition to the application of psychosynthesis maps or concepts in the corporate coaching space. When is it appropriate to connect with the past, the future, or the present? How can someone grow in awareness of limiting beliefs and limiting filters that hamper one's ability to achieve business objectives? How can someone connect to purpose, meaning, and value and then leverage that self-awareness in a business setting?

The defined process steps of the corporate coaching model are specific and repeatable and alignment to the core competencies can be measured and demonstrated. Combining these strengths with the simple yet profound visual framework of the Egg diagram can make it possible for the coach to draw easily on psychosynthesis maps that will be useful to the client while keeping to a standard process.

The coaching model we will use in this chapter blends the corporate coaching process with psychosynthesis: we will reference this as the Psychosynthesis Corporate Coaching model or PCC model.

The following steps represent a generalized coaching process model routinely used in corporate coaching.

- Contracting—coming to a specific understanding of what the coaching will address
- Discovery–discussing the topic and/or underlying issue
- Visioning–exploring options
- Move to Action–a move to clarity or action step

This table presents example questions the coach may ask in each of these steps.

Contracting	Discovery	Visioning	Action
How would you like to focus our session today?	What will this outcome mean to you?	What's possible/What are your options?	What actions will you take and by when?
What outcomes would you like to achieve?	What do you typically do in this scenario?	What could get in your way? / Where might you get stuck?	How will you achieve those goals?
How would you like me to be with you?	How have you been successful in situations like this in the past?	What empowering beliefs do you hold that are as potent as your limiting beliefs?	How will you be accountable to these commitments?

	Explore patterns, beliefs, and emotions that are limiting success.	What's the bigger truth that you sometimes forget?	
	What else?	What resources could help you be successful?	

Merging PCC Steps Into the Egg Diagram

The specific value of the PCC model is seen by mapping the coaching steps into the Egg diagram.

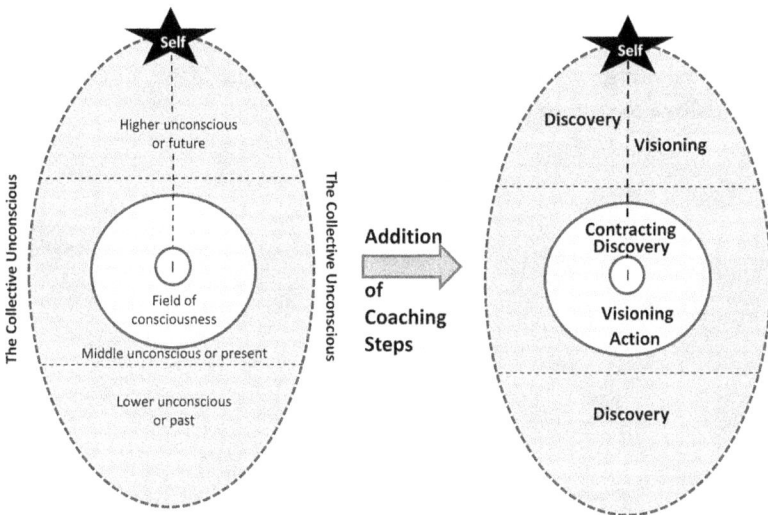

The first and last steps of the coaching process, Contracting and Action, are carried out in the present moment in the current Field of consciousness. While Discovery can happen anywhere, the third step, Visioning or creating options, most often involves work in the upper part of the Egg, helping the client activate qualities from the higher unconscious in opening their perspectives of what is possible.

Coaching in the Egg Diagram

The Psychosynthesis Egg diagram offers a useful aid to the coach in determining where to start the work with a client. We find that individuals seeking corporate coaching are often feeling stuck, as mentioned earlier, and being stuck often has something to do with either the past or future. Are they repeating older patterns? Are they out of alignment with their own purpose? The modified Egg diagram can guide the PCC Coach to explore limiting assumptions, beliefs, emotions, etc., to draw on strengths and alignment to purpose, or to stay only in the practical logistics of identifying and implementing a new way forward in the present.

In our experience, this work often flows as:

+ **Setting a Contract** in the Field of consciousness in the **present**
+ **Discovery** in the Lower unconscious touching on material from the **past**
+ Back to the present to ground new understanding
+ **Visioning** around a desired **future** state in the higher unconscious
+ **Move to Action** back in the **present**

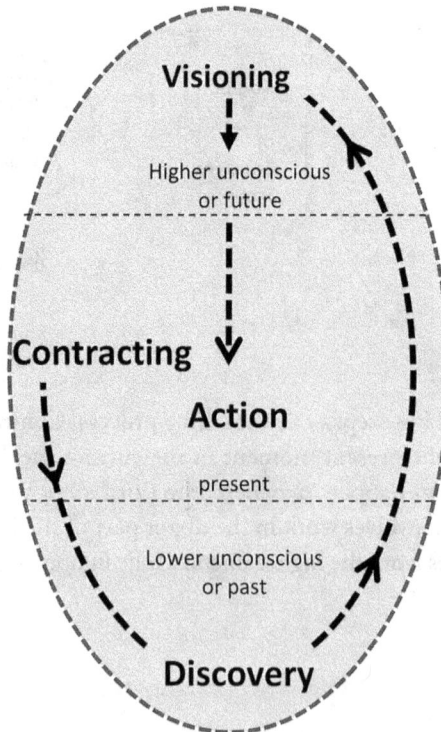

This flow can be followed in a single coaching session or can be carried out over a series of coaching sessions. It follows the arc of building an initial trusting relationship, removing limiting messages due to subpersonalities, exploring purpose and the call to self, and bringing all of these together through concrete action steps to be carried out in the present.

When bringing psychosynthesis and corporate coaching together, PCC Coaches are often guided by a key question: "Where should we be working here? Past, present, or future?" Individual coaching sessions can follow this same process of moving through the coaching steps while doing the majority of the session's work in one part of the egg. For instance, if a session involves work in the lower unconscious, the following questions could move the client to the Visioning and Action steps needed to round out a coaching session:

+ What positive qualities can this part of you bring that can help you with the work we are exploring today? (Visioning—in the higher unconscious)
+ What action will you take when you are aware this personally comes to your attention? (Move to Action—in the present)

PCC Scenarios

The examples provided in the case study descriptions below do not relate to specific individuals, but represent a few typical corporate coaching case studies and how psychosynthesis has application. These examples come from our experiences in working in the corporate coaching space and realizing that taking a psychosynthesis approach would be particularly appropriate.

Communicating with a difficult manager
(an example of movement away from old patterns and toward new, more empowered choices)

Scenario: Client came to coaching seeking strategies to work with a difficult manager.

Angela is a technical expert in a major corporation. For over a year, she has reported to Phil, a middle manager in her department. Angela believes that her manager does not value her work or hear her voice in decision-making discussions. As a result, she has not felt effective in her role or engaged with her work. She researched options around communicating more effectively with Phil, but has not found them useful. Angela now believes Phil has personal issues that complicate working with him.

Possible corporate coaching approach:

A classical business coaching approach to this scenario could have been to work with engaging Angela's ideas around working with difficult people and exploring how she could find acceptance of her work through her own satisfaction with her contributions.

Applying psychosynthesis frameworks:

After contracting around their overall goal, Angela and her coach moved into Discovery. At this stage, Angela's coach was struck most by Angela's levels of frustration and exhaustion about her situation and an emerging theme around needing to please everyone as Angela's most prominent way of working.

Angela's coach moved to work in the lower unconscious in identifying and dialoguing with a part of her that had been assailing Angela with negative self-talk. They then moved into the personal, engaging her will in the area of self-care to combat Angela's feeling of being overwhelmed and lacking in energy. An important element emerged when Angela gave herself "permission" to care for herself. The coaching then went into the higher unconscious. First, in a discussion of her children's beliefs that Angela's work was more important to her than they were, Angela explored ways to be a better parent. Then the coach brought in questions around purpose and meaning: "Where do you want to be in your career? What are your real gifts?" Finally, back in the personal, Angela was able to extend her permission to herself for self-care to giving herself permission for actions she could take around her career. In the end, with a number of obstacles cleared away (negative self-talk, exhaustion, uncertainty as to career direction), Angela gained insight into pervasive management problems in her entire department and began to look for a new job.

Succeeding after promotion to a new role
(an example of supporting the self-awareness and psychological growth needed in new role as a manager)

Scenario: Client's goal for coaching was to develop empathy with new reports.

Matt was recently promoted to a management position from a strong career as an individual contributor. His Type A, drive-for-success, personality did not help him in connecting with the people who now reported to him. He remembered previous managers of his who motivated and supported him in a style he called "hearts and minds." His specific goal for coaching was to develop empathy so that he could connect with his team.

Possible corporate coaching approach:

Typical business coaching might explore the topics of building exceptional teams and how Matt might harness his Type A behavior in the service of connecting with people.

Applying psychosynthesis frameworks:

Matt's coach began in the lower unconscious by exploring dominant subpersonalities. The first was his Type A performer subpersonality which was quite evident through specific language, vocal patterns, and speed of communication. He came to see that this part of him was not welcomed by those he supervised. In classic subpersonality work, he identified and disidentified with the Type A performer and then was able to begin to think about what a different relationship with his employees could look like. An important second subpersonality was identified as his vacation subpersonality. When identifying with this part of him, he was more laid back and super friendly. Moving the work into the personal, Matt then explored how to call on this vacation subpersonality at work and engaged his will to accomplish this. One strategy he used was to put a picture of himself, taken on vacation, next to the door in his office so that he would see the picture whenever anyone came into his office to talk. He also explored how to activate the vacation part of him on specific projects where the Type A part of him had been showing up. Once Matt developed a plan for cooperation with his vacation subpersonality, the work moved to the higher unconscious to explore the qualities of empathy and "hearts and minds" that Matt wanted to embody. Finally, back in the personal, Matt was able to lay out action steps for better interactions with his employees.

Increasing Self-Confidence
(an example of increasing self-awareness and connecting to purpose)

Scenario: Increasing self-confidence.

Linda came to coaching wanting to work on self-confidence. In a development discussion, her manager asked Linda to set a goal of increasing her self-confidence and suggested using a monthly meeting Linda leads as a venue to work on it.

Possible corporate coaching approach:

A conventional business coaching approach might have been to explore how leaders she admired showed self confidence in meetings, what beliefs were holding her back from feeling self-confident in her meeting and how to sharpen the skills to run meetings effectively.

Applying psychosynthesis frameworks:

After contracting in the personal, Linda's coach worked in the lower unconscious, exploring a limiting script from childhood that still played in Linda's mind and developing a powerful antidote message she could use. To increase awareness of Self, the coach moved to the higher unconscious and asked Linda if she would be willing to do a guided visualization. The coach led Linda through a visualization around purpose and meaning, heightening Linda's awareness of what she is proud of in her work and how her work aligns with her values of excellent performance. Then they moved into the present with questions like, "How do people experience you in your leadership role? How do you perceive yourself, and what internal messaging do you hear? How can you replace that with a new story to tell?" Finally, they landed solidly in the present with brainstorming around ways Linda had been running her meeting and what she thought she could bring to it, remaining grounded in the experience of Self she had been generating.

Expressing Psychosynthesis Concepts In Business Terminology

An important aspect of psychosynthesis coaching in this space is the use of business language in working with psychosynthesis concepts.

The table starting on the facing page provides some examples of how to apply psychosynthesis language and concepts into the business world.

Psychosynthesis concept	Business language
Identification/Disidentification/Self-identification (and subpersonalities)	This core concept underpins psychosynthesis and can be brought into the corporate coaching space by recognizing and acknowledging a client's way of interacting in different roles, offering the client the opportunity to step out of that role, and connect with themselves without reliance on it. It essentially asks clients to explore themselves without their roles and/or coping mechanisms. The coach may say, "I am hearing a part of you that sounds like an Inner Critic. Would you like to explore that part of you?" "I think I'm hearing your inner critic again. What is your inner critic's concern?"
Engaging the will	In psychosynthesis, the will is described as having three qualities: good, skillful, and strong. A good will, in the business environment, is one that shows alignment to business goals. A skillful will, is one that demonstrates strategic planning. A strong will is one that that demonstrates persistence. A powerful way to work with will is to ask the client to use the exercise of saying their action step first as "I am thinking of….", then moving through "I want to…", I am trying to …" on through "I will…". Using the word "will" as a verb is more easily understood than using it as a noun.

Psychosynthesis concept	Business language
Purpose, meaning, call of Self	Clients are more familiar with the phrases: "vision for your future," "your mission statement," and "dreams for yourself." Discussion of the spiritual framework of their life can be acceptable in the corporate setting if the coach asks, "Do you have a faith or spiritual dimension to your life that you are in touch with?" If this elicits a positive answer, the word "spiritual" could be used, but be aware that not all clients will be comfortable with it.
Grounding and embodying transpersonal (higher unconsciousness) qualities	Evoking a memory of or using a visualization to bring to mind a scene in which the client was at their best. "How did your body feel in that scenario? How can you bring that body memory to life when you want to feel confident?" "Spiritual" could be used, but be aware that not all clients will be comfortable with it.
Psychological Functions: thinking, feeling, sensing, imagining, intuiting, and impulse/desire	The six psychological functions in psychosynthesis can be incorporated into the business coaching space by affirming them and/or asking direct questions about how someone is thinking, feeling, sensing, etc. It is a technique that helps the client connect with additional sources of information and learn to tap into them.

The Importance Of Training

Corporate coaches can integrate psychosynthesis into their coaching work by the experiential learning of psychosynthesis. There are many psychosynthesis coaching programs, both distance and live learning programs, available across the world. These programs offer the psychosynthesis skills needed to integrate psychosynthesis concepts into the corporate coaching space. It is not enough to read about the concepts presented in this chapter or other literature to grasp fully the value and implications of psychosynthesis practices in corporate coaching. The depth of psychosynthesis work is not intellectual in nature but is experiential and multi-sensory.

Likewise, psychosynthesis practitioners can integrate professionally recognized coaching models from the corporate coaching space. As with learning psychosynthesis, experiential training of formal coaching practices is necessary to truly understand the corporate coaching model in its own right, and then to contrast corporate coaching with a therapeutic or coaching approach of psychosynthesis.

Closing Thoughts

Corporate coaching is strong in process with frameworks that can be applied in the corporate setting and accepted by business clients as relevant to achieving their objectives. Psychosynthesis presents a multidimensional model for helping people move toward wholeness, increasing self-awareness, and personal growth.

As corporate coaches, our work with clients has been irrevocably enhanced and strengthened by our personal immersions into psychosynthesis. This chapter is inspired by our conviction that the integration of psychosynthesis into corporate coaching gives us the ability to take coaching beyond goal achievement to a deeper space that truly awakens the client's own inner resources for achieving their dreams.

References

Brock, V. (2016). *Professional challenges facing the coaching field from an historical perspective*. Available at http://libraryofprofessionalcoaching.com/research/history-of-coaching/professional-challenges-facing-the-coaching-field-from-an-historical-perspective/2/

International Coach Federation. (n.d.). *Benefits of using a coach*. Available at https://www.coachfederation.org/need/landing.cfm?ItemNumber=747&navItemNumber=565

Keen, S. (1974). The Golden Mean of Roberto Assagioli, *Psychology Today*.

Performance Consultants International. (2014). *The GROW model*. Available at http://www.performanceconsultants.com/grow-model

Whitmore, J. (2009). *Coaching for performance: GROWing human potential and Purpose-the principles and practice of coaching and leadership*. Boston, MA: Nicholas Brealey Publishing

Chapter 22

Coaching for Integral Liberation & Transformation

by Raúl Quiñones-Rosado

"The personal is political," says the well-known feminist slogan of the late 1960s, attributed to Carol Hanisch for her essay addressing the debate around the "therapeutic" or "political" nature of women's consciousness-raising groups of the era. While today, some fifty years later, psychosynthesis coaches are not likely to find themselves organizing or facilitating political consciousness-raising meetings (at least, probably not in their roles as coaches), the political, economic, cultural, social and environmental justice issues of the day may well be showing up both in our professional practices and in our personal lives. In fact, these issues are indeed showing up, even when we are not aware of them; even when we may not quite understand how these "external" societal forces effect the "internal," or physical, mental, emotional and spiritual, aspects of our personal lives; even when our education and training may not quite equip us to effectively address the negative impacts of race, class, gender, sexuality and other social power dynamics on our sense of self or on our ability to pursue our life purpose.

Beyond doubt, psychosynthesis coaches tend to be people committed to practices that foster personal growth, spiritual development and the evolution of human consciousness which, in turn, contribute to "transformation" of human culture. The principle of "liberation" abides firmly within our shared values and purpose, even while, given the historical role of the fields of psychotherapy, counseling and coaching, our practice tends to be limited to the individual sphere of experience. In our practice, we tend to give little attention to the collective sphere—the social, cultural, economic or political contexts in which a person's experiences and behaviors emerge and which, in large measure, shape the very identities and subpersonalities, aspects of "self" that, presumably, seek to be liberated.[1] Clearly, the cultural and cognitive biases that minimize the importance of the role of the collective dimension of human experience have serious implications concerning the effectiveness of our coaching practice and, more broadly, our role as agents for the transformation of human consciousness and culture.

Given the historical context and moment in which this is written, as psychosynthesis coaches and members of a community of thought and practice, a key question begs our consideration: Does social justice matter to psychosynthesis coaching? Are matters that involve racism, classism, sexism, heterosexism and other forms of oppression relevant to psychosynthesis practitioners and other helping professionals, particularly at times, such as these, of increasing political turmoil, social unrest, economic uncertainty, and cultural questioning? At times when concerns about climate change and the future of the planet itself, not to mention increased levels of stress, anxiety, personal dissatisfaction and dis-ease seem so commonplace? Often, it seems, these are questions many within the field of coaching may not be very inclined to engage. Though some of us might get "personally" involved, as voters and concerned citizens, or perhaps even as activists, typically "social justice" or "liberation" are simply not considered to be issues within the purview of our work as professional coaches. However, while neither our education nor professional training as coaches includes nor requires us to have, basic knowledge of history, social psychology, sociology, or social identity development, much less economics, societal ethics or critical psychologies, it behooves us to examine the questions and attempt our rightful actions in response.

In this spirit, I share a revised version of a piece previously published by Synthesis Press which, I hope, you may find a useful part of your exploration.

Since the 1960s, there has been an increased interest in relationships between psychology, spirituality, and social action. The spread of psychosynthesis and, subsequently, the emergence of transpersonal psychology as a formal field of study, points to the interest in exploring connections between psychological well-being and spiritual development (Assagioli, 1965/1976, 1973; Walsh, 1980; Wilber, 1977, 1980, 1981). During this same time, interest in examining the role of psychology, psychotherapy and coaching in relation to the sociopolitical well-being of individuals and communities led to the development of various fields, including liberation psychology (Akbar, 1996; Bulhan, 1985; Fanon, 1963, 1967; Moane, 1999, 2003), community psychology (Montero, 2003, 2004; Nelson, 2005; Prilleltensky, 2003; Prilleltensky & Nelson, 1997)

---

[1] For more on identity, social identities, and social identity development, see my paper, "Social Identity Development and Integral Theory."

and critical psychology (Fox & Prilleltensky, 1997; Martín-Baró, 1989, 1994). More recently, a renewed interest in liberation spirituality, or the relationship between spirituality and social action, is also taking place in the form of spiritual activism (Horwitz, 2002; Nhat Hanh, 1992; Sivaraksa, 1992).

Consciousness-in-Action

Consciousness-in-action (Quiñones-Rosado, 2007; Quiñones-Rosado & Barreto-Cortéz, 2002) is an approach that, in some measure, integrates these three orientations to human well-being and development. Drawing from psychology, sociology, critical theory, integral theory, and years of work in communities-of-struggle, consciousness-in-action offers an integral view of well-being and development in the context of social and institutional oppression, of societies in which people's health, educational, economic, social and political outcomes and status can still be predicted by race, class, gender and other social identities. Both a conceptual framework and a practice, consciousness-in-action is a liberatory and transformative process to help people move from emotional and behavioral reactivity rooted in both learned superiority and inferiority to responsiveness. This chapter introduces some of the concepts and principles of consciousness-in-action as they relate to psychosynthesis coaches and the coaching profession.

Personal and Collective Dimensions of Integral Liberation & Transformation

Indigenous traditions inform us that these four aspects—mental, emotional, physical and spiritual—co-exist, inseparably, holistically (Bopp & Bopp, 2001; Bopp, Bopp, & Lane, 1998; Bopp, Bopp, Brown, & Lane, 1984/1989). Individuated spirit, integrally associated with body, mind, and emotions, is understood to be at the core of our humanity. Spirit encompasses our intuitions and values, and is linked to our intellect and creativity, our feelings and beliefs, as well as our desires and drives. Like the Chinese yin-yang, each aspect is contained within the other; like the Yoruba ibeji, the male-female twins, one compliments the other. Further, like a holograph, of which the smallest film fragment contains the whole image, all aspects of our being are ever-present. Together, these four aspects synergistically generate human consciousness and will. It is consciousness and will that allow us to focus our awareness and volition, our attention and intention, for the purpose of our survival, well-being and development as human beings.

301

Spiritual practice, like psychosynthesis and other transpersonal psychologies, often involves ways in which humans seek to reconcile a perceived conflict between individuality and unity. These transpersonal approaches reflect people's impulse to overcome the illusion of their apparent separation and presumed individuality as they move to embrace an intuited Oneness with all other beings and with a Universal All. Within their own cultural context, people who engage this search develop, adopt, or adapt practices or disciplines that move them, consciously and willfully, toward greater personal integrity, self-transcendence, and unity consciousness.

Spirituality, in this broad sense, then, involves the development of the whole being, as all aspects of the personal dimension are impacted by changes in the any one of them (Quiñones-Rosado, 2007).

Obviously, individuals (or more accurately, persons) do not exist alone, separately, in isolation from other people. We are all born into and live within a society, a system that is far more complex than the mere collection of individual persons. This society, with its particular political, social, economic, and cultural structures and institutions, creates laws, norms, rules and traditions, all which serve to regulate relationships among its people. These structures and institutions, in turn, are what provide the context for relationships, processes and dynamics that enable—and often hinder—our survival, well-being, and full development.

Social psychologists maintain that our individual or personal identity, our very sense of self, is socially constructed by our interactions throughout socialization process (Berry, 2002; Gardiner, 2002; Stryker, 2000). Our sense of identity develops, not only because of our particular mental, emotional, physical and spiritual traits, but because much of who we are has to do with our shared experiences with others closest to us and most like us (Jacobs, 2003; Vygotsky, 1978).

At the same time, much of who and how we are has to do with our relationship to others who have a different sense of collective identity, and who also, by virtue of their group membership, exert a different degree of social power and access to the resources needed for their full individual and collective development (Hardiman, 1997; Tatum, 1997). Our very sense of "I am"-ness, therefore, emerges, developmentally in relationship to others, as we learn that "I am not you."

In a society that, both historically and presently, as a general rule grants more social power to men than to women and other-gendered persons, to the rich than to working class and poor people, to white people than to People of Color, to heterosexuals than to gay, lesbian, bisexual, transgender and queer people, and to other dominant group members vis-à-vis subordinated ones, differential social power[2] inevitably plays a central role in shaping our identity, our sense of self—both personal and social.

These dynamics of differential power, within a society that advantages some while oppressing others, have lasting negative impacts on people—both individually and collectively—as people develop distorted (or inflated) self-images, negative (or overly positive) self-concepts, low (or exaggerated) self-esteem, and little (or narcissistic) self-love (Quiñones-Rosado, 2007).

Cognitive Impacts of Internalized Oppression

The effort to equalize the differential power between social identity groups and, moreover, to transform the institutional and systemic forces that perpetuate oppression is, typically, the work of social activism. But if spiritual practice is concerned with our attaining or remembering our inherent unity, then transcending fragmentation of self and overcoming oppositional dynamics within oneself and between social identity groups is also our inevitable task, if not our core human purpose. Spiritual practice and social action, therefore, are essentially two expressions of the same basic human drive: the search for fulfillment of our true humanity, of our divine nature, the evolution of consciousness itself. Spiritual practice tends to be an inward exploration and activity, while social action may well be its outward expression; the first, mostly an individual effort and personal experience, while the latter, a collective effort and shared experience of community, or "common-unity."

The success of these long-term processes might ultimately depend on our ability to: resolve our basic (and subtle) internal contradictions; transcend our felt sense of separateness; experience unity beyond relatedness; realize our True Oneness. Meanwhile, however, both persistent, disciplined spiritual practice and social action, together with other liberatory and transformative practices, may help guide us along the on-going, ever-spiraling process of consciousness-in-action (Quiñones-Rosado, 2007):

+ Perceiving – noticing, witnessing, becoming aware of the contraction, the sense of separation of "I" and "other," of one's social group and another.
+ Recognize – moving beyond ignorance and/or denial of the sense of separation, and the activity of contraction it self, and how this dynamic is played out psychologically within us and sociologically, or collectively, throughout society.

[2]Again, social power is defined as access to and control over resources and opportunities for well-being and development as sanctioned by state authority. This power is not to be confused with either personal or collective power, agency that emanates from within a person or group of organized people, beyond or despite their social status and ranking.

- ◆ Realign – the nature of separate identity, of the contraction of the self, and of the dynamics of differential social power and oppression, its causes, and its consequences.

- ◆ Responding – with full feeling-attention to one's own suffering and to that of others; move toward the transcendence of our socialization—our learned internalized superiority and inferiority—through active engagement with others, non-violent, anti-oppressive, creative and liberating action toward self-determination (personal and collective) and transformation.

Coaching for Liberation and Transformation

Coaching, like social and spiritual activism, aims at helping people move toward greater expressions of well-being in their lives. The major difference, of course, is that the focus of coaches' work tends to be the individual person (or perhaps the couple, the family or specific group), while the focus of activists is the community, institutional policy, or society at large. Coaches mostly address issues that affect the mental, emotional, physical, and spiritual aspects of the person and seek to mobilize their internal resources (both their own and those of clients) to affect positive change and growth. Activists and organizers, on the other hand, seek to address political, social, economic and cultural issues that impact the collective by mobilizing people and other external resources as they seek to effect institutional, structural or systemic changes in the world.

Beyond (and despite) these and other obvious differences, coaching and activism alike respond to the perception, recognition and understanding that the quality of life of too many people is far below what is commonly accepted standards in contemporary US society. Moreover, when examined from a holistic perspective that takes into account the balance and harmony between all aspects at the personal level and within all domains of activity at the collective level, it is not difficult to see just how far people are from enjoying integral well-being.

For people concerned with both personal change and social transformation, an integral perspective of well-being and human development is crucial. Whether we are coaches, therapists, other helping professionals or social activists, our understanding of the dynamic and interdependent relationships between the individual and the collective is fundamental and of utmost importance. Then, as we are able to understand these relationships, we can also begin to recognize and fully appreciate our own personal responsibility to use our professional role in the service of personal and social transformation.

Coaches engaged in consciousness-in-action—a social psychosynthesis of integral liberation and transformation—seek to understand the conflicts, contradictions and incongruities among our many social group identities. Since most conflicts and incongruence tend to become most evident in the midst of intimate relationships, we also work on these with our partners, children, other family members, and those closest to us in our various communities. To all of these relationships (whether our own or our clients'), we seek to bring awareness of social power, and how the dynamics of advantage and oppression (interpersonal, institutional and systemic) come to bear on the particular interaction and upon the relationship in general. Therefore, we strive to further explore how our own thoughts, beliefs, values, attitudes, feelings and behaviors may unconsciously replicate patterns of race, class, gender, sexual, cultural, national, political and other group identities, that would have us collude with the dominant/subordinated hierarchies that are normative in our cultures.

As professional liberatory transformation coaches, psychosynthesis coaches, we are fully aware of, understand and are opposed to oppression in its various expressions:

- Racism: the historical, systematic and institutional imposition of white supremacy—the ideology that presumes the inherent superiority of a socially-constructed "white race"—throughout society for the purpose of retaining State-sanctioned power and perpetuating advantage for white people collectively.

- Eurocentrism: the historical, systematic and institutional imposition of Euro-centered thought and behavior, and white culture, throughout society. The traditional ways of life and collective identities of Peoples of Color are actively sought to be displaced by the ideas, beliefs, behaviors, feeling, attitudes and values shared among people of European descent, a culture presumed to be superior. This is done for the purpose of assimilation, thus establishing internalized self-controls and maintaining compliance among the citizenry within the framework of racism.

- Classism: the historical, systematic and institutional imposition of capitalism—the materialistic worldview of white culture, which objectifies people, other life forms, material and cultural resources, and the natural environment, thus considering all of these "capital" to be invested, exploited, traded and accumulated for personal profit for the purpose of ensuring the privileged status and power of the small owning class.

305

+ Colonialism: the historical, systematic and institutional means of white supremacy, Eurocentrism, and capitalism across national and cultural boundaries for the benefit of the ruling class of the imperial (albeit transnational) power.

+ Militarism: the imposition of colonialism through the use, or threat of use, of the military might of the armed forces, as well as local, state, federal law enforcement, in the US and around the world.

+ Sexism: the historical, systematic and institutional orientation of patriarchy, the ideology of male supremacy, which proclaims men as the standard of humanity (and of divinity in "western" cultures) through systems and institutions that objectify and exploit women by virtue of gender.

+ Heterosexism: the extension of sexism and patriarchy through the exclusive sanctioning of heterosexual relationships which—based upon the presumed superiority of heteronormative identities and behaviors, and the subordinated status of women and LGBTQ persons—are deemed to be the only legal and morally acceptable expression of gender, sexuality and love.

Similarly, liberatory transformation coaches stand opposed to ageism, ableism, anti-Semitism, and all other forms of institutional oppression.

As coaches for **liberation**, our work is about fostering the process of recognizing, embracing, transcending and healing from the negative impacts of oppression, as clients move to restore balance and harmony, or integral well-being, in their lives. We are alert to patterns of implicit bias, of internalized superiority and inferiority, and of exclusion, exploitation and misrepresentation of oppressed individuals and communities.

As coaches for **transformation**, our work is to help people in our larger communities understand the collective human suffering caused by all forms of oppression: those societal forces that hinder our ability to survive and fully develop, the root cause of the social problems we endure. As such, we are ethically committed to counteracting the legacy of systemic advantage of the dominant few.

Psychosynthesis Coaching as a Practice in Consciousness-in-Action

Adoption of this integral liberatory and transformative approach to coaching presumes a commitment to one's own on-going well-being, in which we direct our consciousness and will to all aspects and dimensions of being. In doing so, we can seek greater balance and harmony by continually seeking to resolve internal conflicts between mind (ideas, thoughts, images, dreams), heart (feelings, desires), body (urges, impulses, sensations, perceptions), and spirit (principles, values, meaning, purpose, inspiration, intuition).

Among the most common spiritual or contemplative practices are prayer, meditation, self-observation, and inquiry. For some people, religion-free mindfulness practices and biofeedback techniques are preferred. For others, engaging in physical activities (e.g., taiji, qigong, running, swimming, and other sports) or absorption in music, art, or nature enables them to quiet the mind and experience a similar sense of unity consciousness.

A main purpose—and key benefit—of these practices is to perceive, recognize, and understand the psycho-spiritual nature of oppression: emotional reactivity. Whether we call it ego, self-contraction, the fear of being unloved, the fear of death itself, or all of the above, emotional reactivity leads to the illusion of individuality and a sense of disconnection from others that disrupts our inherent connection and ultimate oneness. Furthermore, emotional reactivity—both cause and consequence of oppression—diminishes our capacity to consciously respond and make appropriate behavioral choices in everyday life, and most certainly in the face of differential social power dynamics.

From the perspective of psychosynthesis coaching, as consciousness-in-action practice, understanding these dynamics allow us, as coaches, to perceive, recognize and address a wider range of manifestations of the psychosocial patterns stemming from internalized oppression and/or associated with institutional, external social forces. This understanding, together with our practiced ability to respond—that is, to catch ourselves emotionally reacting and, then, to relax the contraction—is essential to effective coaching relationships.

Closing Comments

Like many people, my non-religious spirituality leads me to believe that "we are all One in the Divine." And notwithstanding the political stances at stake, I, too, believe that "there is only one race: the human race." But, let me be clear: that we are all One, does not mean we are all the same. Given the reality of our socialization—all the myths, stereotypes, misinformation, and false narratives we were taught as children about one another's identity groups— we cannot ignore or deny that these differences still really do make a difference in our daily lives, to the clear advantage of some and to the utter detriment of most.

In spite of the fact that these differences are socially constructed, their negative impact is real, tangible, measurable and predictable. Thus, we must not believe for an instant that we can merely meditate, counsel or coach away racism, colonialism, sexism, and all the forms of oppression that harm, even kill, and that rob us all of our humanity.

As coaching professionals, each and every one of us is an active participant in our society; there is no such thing as being neutral. Everything we do either supports oppression and suffering or serves to liberate others and ourselves from it. I believe that given the opportunity and the knowledge, psychosynthesis coaches would choose to act against oppression and for liberation. I believe that coaches stand for the positive transformation of our society grounded in a vision of integral well-being and development.

Key to that process of transformation, in personal, professional, and social realms, is to learn to expand our consciousness; skillfully exercise our will; gain control of our attention; and further clarify our intent. We need to develop the ability to see multiple levels of reality simultaneously, and to be able to focus on any one aspect or dimension instantly, to move between foreground and background, without losing the ability to see the "larger picture." By doing this, we can discern where it is that we need to go, and mindfully direct our energy and the movement of a coaching session in that direction.

As coaches committed to liberation from oppression and the transformation of society and consciousness itself, we must "assume our rightful place"[3] as we co-create relationships that are free of the dynamics of dominance and subordination, as we build institutions that fundamentally honor and support our full humanity, and as we deepen our understanding of the Divine and learn to express the best of our divine nature in all contexts. That, I believe, is our greatest challenge.

References

Akbar, N. (1996). *Breaking the chains of psychological slavery*. Tallahassee, FL: Mind Productions & Associates.

Assagioli, R. (1965/1976). *Psychosynthesis*. New York: Penguin Books.

Assagioli, R. (1973). *The act of will*. New York: Penguin Books.

Berry, J. W., Poortinga, Y. H., Segall, M. H., & Dasen, P. R. (Eds.). (2002). *Cross-cultural psychology: Research and applications*. Cambridge, UK: Cambridge University Press.

Bopp, J., Bopp, M., Brown, L., & Lane, P. (1984/1989). *The sacred tree: Reflections on Native American spirituality* (Third, 1989 ed.). Alberta, Canada: Lotus Light Press.

---

[3] A signature phrase of partner and colleague, María I. Reinat Pumarejo, founder and director of Colectivo Ilé: Organizers for Consciousness-in-Action.

Bopp, J., Bopp, M., & Lane, P. (1998). *Community healing and Aboriginal social security reform.* Lethbridge, Alberta: The Four Worlds International Institute for Human and Community Development.

Bopp, M., & Bopp, J. (2001). *Recreating the world: A practical guide to building sustainable communities.* Calgary, Alberta: Four Worlds Press.

Bulhan, H. A. (1985). *Frantz Fanon and the psychology of oppression.* New York: Plenum Press.

Fanon, F. (1963). *The wretched of the earth.* New York: Grove Weidenfeld.

Fanon, F. (1967). *Black skin, white masks.* New York: Grove Press.

Fox, D., & Prilleltensky, I. (Eds.). (1997). *Critical psychology: An introduction.* London: Sage Publications.

Gardiner, H. W., & Kosmitzki, C. (2002). *Lives across cultures: Cross-cultural human development* (2 ed.). Boston: Allyn and Bacon.

Hardiman, R., & Jackson, B.W. (1997). Conceptual foundations for social justice courses. In M. Adams, L. A. Bell, & P. Griffin (Eds.), *Teaching for diversity and social justice.* New York: Routledge.

Horwitz, C. (2002). *The spiritual activist: Practices to transform your life, your work, and your world.* New York: Penguin Compass.

Jacobs, J. E., Bleeker, M.M, & Constantino, M.J. (2003). The self-system during childhood and adolescence: Development, influences, and implications. *Journal of Psychotherapy Integration,* 13(1), 33-65.

Martín-Baró, I. (1989). *Sistema, grupo y poder: Psicología social desde Centroamérica II.* San Salvador: UCA Editores.

Martín-Baró, I. (1994). *Writings for a liberation psychology.* Cambridge, MA: Harvard University Press.

Moane, G. (1999). *Gender and colonialism: A psychological analysis of oppression and liberation.* New York: St. Martin's Press.

Moane, G. (2003). Bridging the personal and the political: Practices for a liberation psychology. *American Journal of Community Psychology,* 31(1/2), 91-102.

Montero, M. (2003). *Teoria y practica de la psicologia comunitaria: la tension entre comunidad y sociedad.* Buenos Aires, Argentina: Paidos.

Montero, M. (2004). *Introduccion a la psicologia comunitaria: Desarrollo, conceptos y procesos.* Buenos Aires, Argentina: Paidos.

Nelson, G., & Prilleltensky, I. (Ed.). (2005). *Community psychology: In pursuit of liberation and well-being.* New York: Palgrave Macmillan.

Nhat Hanh, T. (1992). *Touching peace: Practicing the art of mindful living.* Berkeley, CA: Parallax Press.

Prilleltensky, I. (2003). Understanding, resisting, and overcoming oppression: Toward psychopolitical validity. *American Journal of Community Psychology*, 31(1/2), 195.

Prilleltensky, I., & Nelson, G. (1997). Community psychology: Reclaiming social justice. In D. Fox, & I. Prilleltensky (Eds.), *Critical psychology: An introduction*. London: Sage Publications.

Quiñones Rosado, R. (2007). *Consciousness-in-Action: Toward an integral psychology of liberation & transformation*. Caguas, PR: ilé Publications.

Quiñones Rosado, R. (2010) Social identity development and integral theory. *Integral Leadership Review*, Vol 10(5). Russ Volckmann, Publisher. http://www.integralleadershipreview.com/archives-2010/2010-10/ILRRosado.pdf

Quiñones Rosado, R., & Barreto-Cortéz, E. (2002). An integral model of well-being and development and its implications for helping professions. *Journal of Human Behavior in the Social Environment*, 5(3/4).

Sivaraksa, S. (1992). *Seeds of peace: A Buddhist vision for renewing society*. Berkeley, CA: Parallax Press.

Stryker, S., Owens, T. J., & White, R. W. (Eds.). (2000). *Self, identity, and social movements* (Vol. 13). Minneapolis, MN: University of Minnesota Press.

Tatum, B. D. (1997). *"Why are All the black kids sitting together in the cafeteria?"* and other conversations about race. New York: Basic Books.

Vygotsky, L. S. (1978). *Mind in society: the development of higher psychological processes*. Cambridge, MA: Harvard University Press.

Walsh, R., & Vaughn, F. (Ed.). (1980). *Beyond ego: Transpersonal dimensions in psychology*. Los Angeles, CA: J. P. Tarcher, Inc.

Wilber, K. (1977). *The spectrum of consciousness*. Wheaton, IL: The Theosophical Publishing House.

Wilber, K. (1980). *The Atman project: A transpersonal view of human development*. Wheaton, IL: The Theosophical Publishing House.

Wilber, K. (1981). *Up from Eden: A transpersonal view of human evolution*. New York: Anchor Press/Doubleday.

Part 5

Coaches Evolving: Personal and Professional Perspectives on the Field

Only through an awakening of our deepest souls, only when the sovereignty of the Spirit is recognized and made a reality, will the human race be able to achieve that true power, that secure peace and that divine freedom that is the unconscious goal to which it aspires.
—*Roberto Assagioli*

Editor's Note:
Having had the deep pleasure of working with many, many psychosynthesis coaches, as students, colleagues, guides and teachers, I know that we are each evolving and as we do, we understand better what it is that is important, what rings true, where our Call lies, and what we want to do to live in resonance with our Self. As we grow and mature in our work and in our lives, our perspectives ripen until we have, sitting within us, the clarity of knowing how we will move forward, personally and professionally. We claim what is of value and we have something important to say. We discover what we want to share and we share it. We coach, we speak, we teach, and we write. And the ripening continues in the life long process of psychosynthesis.

Chapter 23

Psychosynthesis Coaching in Action: Case Study: "Alice"

by Cristina Pelizzatti

The Client

 "Alice" showed up in my studio in June 2016 with a clear goal that she intended to reach by the end of the year. Her orientation was specifically towards her professional life. She wanted to devote herself to her new position with an international "natural products" company, which meant she would have to leave her current job. She told me that the problem she faced was very practical: the current job provided her the income she needed to live day by day, but without any personal satisfaction or enthusiasm. The new job, which she was already working on part time, had the potential to provide her with as much income as she could reach by creating a sales network and clientele, but was not going to provide a fixed income. Alice was living in St. Moritz, a beautiful village in the middle of the Swiss Alps, well known as an Alpine ski area frequented by moneyed people, with consequently prohibitive prices.

 The first session was based on assessment by evaluating together the possibility of working together as a guide and a traveler, to manifest her 'Call of the Self' through the chosen goal and therefore understand what work we'll need to do to bring to light what wants to emerge. Through powerful questions we explored our awareness of what brought Alice to me as psychosynthesis life coach. We established the agreement and expectations of the following sessions, and through the transformational coaching conversations we also reflected on the coachee's learning process. We planned a coaching program focusing on her goal as we clarified it.

The Goal

Alice had a clear goal to change her job and start to build a network providing personal satisfaction and income, based in the new job. I sent her my coaching intake form, together with all the references she needed to learn about my coaching approach, as well as the BCC (Board Certified Coach) Ethics Code and my professional affiliations with the Association for Coaching AC, Global.

The Work

The work unfolded in 15 sessions over a time span of 8 months, taking place both via internet and in person. Personal sessions took place in a secluded area of woods and fields in the mountains where I have my cabin studio and where I utilize the natural environment as a setting to experiment with the application of psychosynthesis tools.

These techniques add an additional dimension to the already powerful psychosynthesis process.

From the beginning, I introduced Alice to the tools of psychosynthesis, so that she was comfortable working in this context. The key maps that we focused on were:

- the Egg Diagram
- the Star Diagram
- work with subpersonalities
- the Ideal Model
- identification, disidentification and Self-identification.

Alice "digested" the concepts and practices very well. She was always very excited at the prospect of understanding and experiencing these tools, and found each of them useful in her own work, both during the session and in her personal and professional life.

By "sitting next to her" in a relation between Selves, the transformational process began. The needs of her subpersonalities emerged through recognition of their presence, and Alice's process of self acceptance allowed many parts living within her to integrate into a more complete whole. By coaching the client's process, the transpersonal process of Self-unveiling is revealed. The emerging Self was Alice's Guide along all the sessions.

The Beginning

At the beginning, we clarified some issues that emerged through the questions on the coaching intake form, and then we moved ahead with the Ideal Model exercise to explore the deeper purpose of her stated goal:

Is this goal ideal or idealistic?
How do you see yourself in this goal?
How do you think others see you by reaching this goal?
How do you want to be seen once you reach your goal?
What do you imagine your future to be, by reaching this goal?
What is your: Vision, Motivation, Meaning? Value? Purpose?
Will they be met by reaching this goal?

Following the Guidelines for Goal setting, (a tool from the Synthesis Center) we actively affirmed that:

1. the goal was **conscious** and we could clearly identify the next step needed to start our coaching conversation;
2. Alice **affirmed** the intention and commitment to reach the goal;
3. the goal was **available**, able to be accomplished within the realities of her world;
4. the goal was **controllable/achievable** by Alice, and therefore she could build her team as needed for work in the new job;
5. the goal was **measurable**, with specific outcomes, within a specific time frame;
6. Alice **desired and was willing** to reach this goal. She had already experienced the potential for fulfillment in doing this job and the potentialities of what she wanted to achieve;
7. This goal was very **important** for Alice, both for the money and for her own personal satisfaction, because success in meeting this goal would translate not only into income, but also increased self-esteem and recognition within the new organization.

This action by the "I as observer and willer" potentially resolved the conflict that existed between security (represented by a fixed income), and the purpose, meaning and values (as well as income) that would be derived from building an effective sales force in her new job. During this process we verified that the goal had come from the "I" and not from a subpersonality: the elevated energy and the joy that sparkled from her eyes testified that the goal was aligned with Alice's intrinsic Purpose, Meaning, and Values. We also made sure that the elements in play were aligned with the "I", strengthening them, and that the successes obtained along the way were celebrated, thereby strengthening her self-esteem. Alice worked through small steps, creating desired results characterized by satisfaction and fulfillment, realizing her full potential and ability to assume self-responsibility in the choices she made. I felt in Alice the flow and ease which characterize acting through the "I/Self". The energy level was high and shining, her physical presence was more grounded. She was increasingly able to disidentify from her own story and related subpersonalities and connect to her purpose. Through self-awareness, the larger Purpose emerged and she said: "I'm ready! I can and I will do it! I'm committed to do it!"

The Larger Purpose Emerges

During the first sessions, we brought into awareness the subpersonalities Alice carried around unaware and through a subpersonality questionnaire, we worked on these parts as characters in a play. With powerful questions and the use of art, we grounded the emerging contents and anchored the qualities underlined during the session into actionable steps to be accomplished in between sessions. The dominant subpersonality, the Helper, was found and named during these sessions.

After this process, the next session was dedicated to "the walk into the Egg" using the natural landscape to afford greater access to experiential work. This embodied experience helped to anchor the awareness into the "I" and its closest ally in the subpersonality world, the "Helper". Through the stages of subpersonality work, **recognition** and **acceptance** of the subpersonalities emerge and the **coordination** phase took shape as the "I" started to relate to and communicate with the rest of the personality, and its many subpersonalities.

The Recognition Phase: this work involved repeated visualization exercises consisting of literally walking within the Egg diagram in a quiet, natural

316

setting in a specific, guided manner. The objective is minimum interruption, so I explained the process before she started: it is a systematic and meditative progression between the "I" and upper and lower unconscious levels. The sequence of movements to the upper and lower unconscious is punctuated by movement into the Self, at which point the traveler is encouraged to look at the whole Egg from that vantage point. The sequence is also important: at the end of the progression, the traveler visits the Transpersonal Self, returns to the "I", then the lower unconscious and Lower Self, looking at the whole Egg. The point of this sequence is that the resulting view from the Lower Self contains elements from the Transpersonal Self.

During this process Alice was guided out and back from the "I" by the gentle chime of a Tibetan bell. After about 20 minutes of literally "physically" exploring the levels of the Egg, she would then create a drawing. The energy was palpable during the exercise. I was observing Alice moving into her map of the Psyche, in this setting in nature. It was powerful and useful for her to ground and anchor her awareness toward the "I" as a willer, and as an observer without limiting messages. She experienced the contentless awareness and will that is, in psychosynthesis terms, the Self.

During the 6th session, the drawing which emerged following her walk in the Egg was of a very small girl at the bottom of the lower unconscious, arms extended stiffly downward, crying frantically for help: an image which was linked with a very real series of events in her life. At the same time, the upper unconscious was lit by a radiant sun. The "I" had a smiling face, and there was a strong bond drawn between the "I" and the sun, while rays shone down from the "I" into the lower unconscious.

The creation of this image was accompanied by a cathartic experience—emotional, crying—as it eventually emerged that this subpersonality, which she baptized "The Helper", was her most dominant subpersonality.

Alice was guided through the process of recognition, acceptance, and coordination—she encountered the "Helper", encouraging the child to have trust and self-esteem—to live the life she wanted. She asked the child what the child had done for her (Alice) in all this time. In an attempt to gain respect, the "Helper" had created a series of limiting beliefs that defined what Alice perceived as a "comfort zone". Alice recognized the presence of this subpersonality, her typical behavior, as well as the comfort zone around her. The process of naming her as an existing subpersonality grounded her into the field of consciousness as a real energetic presence, and Alice saw this subpersonality as a limiting facet of her personality. She (the "helper") focused on helping others to the total exclusion of her own needs. We moved along the emerging material with powerful questions. "How do you see yourself?" "How do you think the

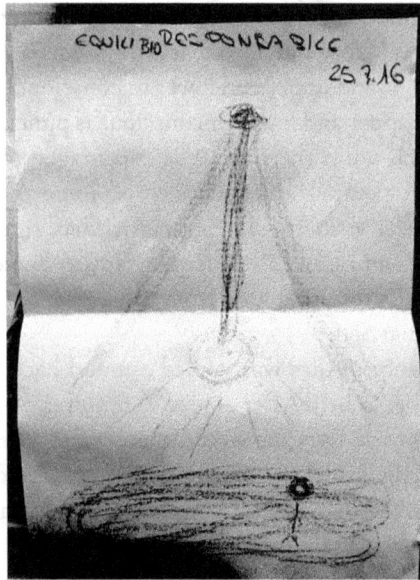

others see you?". "How do you want to be seen?" As part of this process, I suggested that Alice ask the child what she needed. This question, and the subsequent response, established a relationship with the child/subpersonality in which Alice's "I" became a Willer, and at that moment in Alice's mind the image of the child became a heart. I asked her, "Alice, what do you want to say to this heart now?", and Alice said to the heart: "Now I respect you, I trust you, I love you." From that moment, the voice became anchored in Alice's heart: the feeling of separation, of duality, vanished—the voice had become part of her.

From this the flow began. We moved to the **Acceptance** phase, continuing to use the Egg diagram both from a theoretical standpoint and as a practical tool, literally "working inside it". As a result, through the physical experience "within" the Egg, Alice evolved from an unconscious presence of this energy, through an awareness within the middle unconscious of the energetic presence of this "helper" to the appreciation of and access to the qualities of this subpersonality resident in the Transpersonal unconscious, such as courage, humor, determination, curiosity, clarity, premonition, and sense of service.

As a result of the increased awareness and work Alice was doing, she gradually phased out of her old job, devoting more and more time to her new work, with positive results and more income. In fact, she found herself on holiday in a 5 Star hotel in the Mediterranean Sea—all expenses paid by her new company! Each session offered specific next steps and Alice always followed through, because her purpose and goals were strong.

Coaching the whole Egg

Alice offers a good example of working in all areas of the Egg. We discussed her experience in the Egg and she told me, as I could also see from her appearance while she was doing this exercise, that in the lower unconscious she felt heaviness and the presence of a little child, a baby girl—then darkness. She had accessed a core subpersonality, one with deep wounds, but not one we would dig deeply into, as our coaching work did not require this. When Alice was on the Star representing the Higher Self, and in the transpersonal dimension, she saw the little baby girl with her arms stiffly outstretched by her sides, pleading, more clearly, and Alice turned and looked toward her. After she returned to the "I", she described a flow of light from where she was standing (as the "I") directed toward the baby. Alice saw and felt this presence and the strong need to help her. Alice's "Helper" subpersonality carried the deep and true transpersonal orientation towards service, caring and love. At that moment she was experiencing this, realizing that her Purpose was to help others.

Using the stages of subpersonality work to guide and support her in her voyage towards her "I", she was willing to explore the subpersonality. Everything we had done up to that point brought us to the **Coordination phase**. Here, with greater access to her "I", Alice was to able to do deep subpersonality work, aiding the "Helper" subpersonality in freeing her qualities. Alice realized: "I have a story and I'm more than my story" thereby letting go of her old stories.

The Star Diagram comes into play

To better integrate the "Helper" into the "I" we also worked with the Star Diagram in a natural setting in which it was possible to literally "walk" into the diagram as we did with the Egg, thereby exploring and experiencing where the client is dominant and where weak or wounded psychological functions create distortion. The goal of this work is balance and the opening to the last stage of subpersonality work: **synthesis**.

I asked Alice to enter into the Star by choosing a function and becoming aware of anything emerging, pausing for a few moments in the function, rooting into the ground to feel the energy of the function flowing from the earth up into her body. After each pause in the functions, the request was to go back to the I-Self, in awareness and will and from there observe and ground the awareness into the "I". She would then move into the next function, repeating the process. She explored the Star Diagram for at least 10 minutes, accompanied by the Tibetan bell.

Alice discovered that her strongest affiliation in the Star diagram was in being an **Active-Practical Personality Type.** Thinking was also a dominant psychological function and offered the most secure "comfort zone". Alice strongly controlled the **Emotion function** by the **Thought function,** and this was inevitably part of her issue with connecting to others.

At the end of the experience, I asked her to draw her Star.

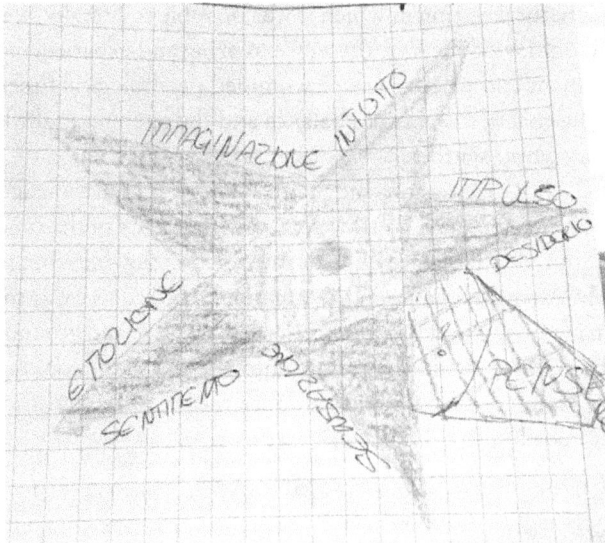

She drew her Star Diagram (previous page), proudly labeling each and coloring it as shown in the photo. When she showed it to me, I said "Nice! What do you see?" She looked at the Star, looked at me, looked at the exercise we'd done previously which highlighted Thought as her dominant psychological function, and then said: "I'd better go outside and check something..."

When she returned she was totally disoriented. She realized she'd completely omitted her comfort zone—the "Thought" point of the diagram! Through this process she realized how, by allowing herself for a moment to be completely present as the Observer, the Thought function was de-activated: completely removed from her Star.

We had a conversation about what was happening and she was very surprised at the result of the exercise, feeling angry at the beginning for being forgetful about her comfort zone. At that point, I explained to her how, during the work with the unconscious, the unconscious then comes into play and it takes the hand in drawing (or writing, or other request from the guide) like a flow, where we allow ourselves to see, write, draw, moving in this particular moment out of the comfort zone—and this is a very powerful moment to ground and anchor what was emerging as a key point in moving forward. Alice realized that her rational mind represented a comfort zone but limited her to a unique way of seeing, feeling, and sensing, therefore relating with the world. With a renewed awareness Alice drew the Thought point back into the Star (the point with hatched filling on the lower right of the star drawing). She experienced her "I" as a willer and awareness and started to cry.

From that moment onward, Alice started to relate to the Thought function with a compassionate attitude, becoming more and more aware, of "who" was carrying the Thought function and "why". The integration phase of "the Helper" began through acceptance and forgiveness and she began using her Thought with more awareness: "I'm using the Thought function therefore I'm thinking that" and "Who's thinking like that and why?" She realized she had the power to direct the awareness, therefore the capability to make choices as the "I".

The Coach

In every session, I celebrated the results obtained by Alice, never letting her ignore her own accomplishments. I congratulated her for the achievements in progress and I maintained a positive attitude oriented towards the larger goals. Being her ally often supported her when she felt less certain, or more engulfed in limiting subpersonality dialogue. I was always working with Alice's will, aligned with purpose, and did this, in part, by assisting her to formulate clearly the issues to be deliberated upon. These included:

+ focusing on problems concerning relationships and partnership with other individuals
+ considering their points of view given their position and orientation in the world
+ bringing awareness to the consequences of possible choices
+ assisting in finding the most meaningful interpretation of the issues
+ seeing, and helping her see, the potentialities hidden by obstacles along the path

Alice's goal then became more directed and morphed into several. Her new goals were to improve her performance at her job, find the courage and the skill to talk in public, and become a more effective manager for her subordinates.

Alice is a very energetic and sensitive person, dominated by the impulse psychological function, helping her to jump into different situations in life and work, but limiting her in being too directive and lacking in empathy in many relationships.

The Ending

Alice made progress toward her goal by giving more and more space and time to her new challenge and letting go of old work. Her self-esteem improved and she became aware of the multiplicity inside herself and recognized this as an asset, as a richness instead of a liability or limitation, and she speaks in public more easily and more often. Through recognition and acceptance of the multiplicity inside herself, by experiencing the "I" as a contentless space of awareness and will, by embracing and nourishing her inner child, and practicing the inner dialogue with a thankful attitude, as a moment of Presence, Alice become able to work in a harmonious way as a whole personality. She realized the commitment with the "Helper" was an empowering part of her, not a disempowering one.

Through the psychosynthesis coaching experience, she realized and came to accept with a more positive attitude that leaving her current job to devote herself totally to the new opportunity would probably put her, at least temporarily, in a more difficult economic situation. Therefore, she chose a more "step by step" approach: to stay in her current job while at the same time increasing her contacts in the wellness arena, improving her profile and visibility in order to develop new contacts and follow with Presence the clients she already had. She's currently working on building up a solid basis of networking in order to accelerate the process of moving completely into an activity which both meets her economic needs and better serves her Purpose: to Help People.

I had a call, after a few days, from another person working for the same organization, referred to me by Alice, wondering what had happened to Alice—they barely recognized her in her new attitude and performance, and he wanted to get there too!

Conclusion

Using the tools and methods of psychosynthesis life coaching, I helped Alice to build a "Context" of a strong sense of "I", the inner Center, which by definition is Awareness, Will and contentless. Through deliberately and consistently holding the space of Presence, being tuned into the inner Center as the Observer and Director, I guided her toward her "I", becoming more and more the "I/Self". I represented an external resource for her (or External Unifying Center), by holding and nourishing Presence, trusting the process and empowering the process inherent in the changes. My role was to facilitate her movement, by trusting in her own inner resources and in her capabilities to create the "New Future" that was seeking to emerge, through a time-based action plan. The role of Purpose as a powerful driver toward her goal and the alignment of Will with the "I" was constantly reinforced during our work through the questions: "Who is the director of this process?" "Who is making this choice?"

Using the psychosynthesis toolkit, I guided Alice in exploring, expanding and empowering the "I" through the "Process" of Knowing, Possessing, and Transforming any "Contents" which emerged during the sessions, representing obstacles to reach the chosen goal. This process helped Alice, as the traveler, to create change in a series of specific, meaningful, and inspired, actionable steps that led to a fundamental shift in attitude, desires, and behavior, thereby fulfilling her dreams and reaching full potential in her life.

Alice's identification with self-images which emerged during the sessions: "the loser", "the victim", "the rejected"—limited her in all the psychological functions, disempowering her, draining her energies down to the point that some days she had to sleep all day because she felt so overtired. Allowing her to see all the contents from the space of the "I", becoming the "Observer and Director", she was able to step out of the comfort zone of well-known behavior to experiment with new ways of doing things. In particular the work within the Star Diagram, in a natural setting, enabled her to experience how things change if we change the "usual way", the "habitual mindset", by letting the intuitive mind work.

Alice realized the power of her own Presence and the empowerment of anchoring her Purpose into the "I", enabling her to begin to take actions toward her goal as a willer and bringing transpersonal qualities into the personal realm. By affirming her intention toward her goal, she allowed the embodiment of the 'Call of the Self' and realized that she could participate actively in the manifestation of the 'emerging Self' through will alignment and the relationship between the 'Call of Self' and the choice to respond.

Through the process of guiding her in exploring more and more of the "I" and through disidentification from story, script, and subpersonalities, the content of her limiting stories and subpersonalities were integrated by recognition and acceptance. By expanding the field of consciousness of the "I", Alice realized the transpersonal qualities of each subpersonality, therefore empowering her "I". She felt stronger and more able to make choices in line with Purpose, Meaning and Values related to her goal, thereby increasing her self-esteem.

Expanding listening, by attentively and appropriately asking for clarifications, deepens the client's ability to listen to themselves fully. The focus on understanding the profound meaning of Alice's goal allowed her to discover what needed to shift to create, by accessing transpersonal qualities, what she wanted most. Listening with a positive attitude toward obstacles and seeing them as opportunities to learn and grow helped build resilience, enabling access to a higher level of awareness, and ultimately to the experience of transformation.

The process of identification, disidentification and self-identification with the "I" brought Alice into progressive reorientation of her awareness of her Higher Self. This increased her ability to direct her energy toward chosen steps. Learning to identify a subpersonality, while, at the same time, being aware of the limitations of over-identification with any part, allowed all of her subpersonalities to be held in a larger whole (I/Self).

Going forward, Alice has learned that her sense of the Higher Self is experienced through the practice of Presence. Through Presence she has learned "Who" it is that does not change throughout the continuous changes in life: The Self.

Chapter 24

Psychosynthesis Life Coaching in the Sciences

by Kevin Harrington

Of real moment is the further factor in the scientific attitude which some of the foremost scientists have utilized, either spontaneously or deliberately. We refer to the creative role of such psychological functions as imagination, intuition, and creativity in scientific research.
                                                   —*Roberto Assagioli*

Having a coach can be a true benefit in one's life. Coaches can help us recognize the choices that exist within the daily patterns and flow of life. Psychosynthesis life coaching in the sciences aims at weaving the broad intent of self-development into everyday tasks and responsibilities, which in turn can motivate scientists to take action upon their heart's desires and be productive in their respective fields. By assuming the expertise is in the hands of the client/traveler (and in this case the scientist), the life coach can assist the person in discovering the possibilities that will help spark the sheer determination, purpose, and initiative that every career needs. When being devoted to looking at the world through the eyes of the researcher, a coach can help guide the navigation of choice points and deadlines, alive-lines and obstacles, all towards opportunities and possibilities.

It makes sense that every scientist could use a life coach—someone to ruminate with from time to time, with whom to constructively converse, and discuss challenges, personal obstacles, goals, and reoccurring responsibilities. A study of over 3,500 Ph.D. students showed that "work-family interface, job demands and job control, the supervisor's leadership style, team decision-making culture, and perception of a career outside academia are linked to mental health problems" (Levecque, Anseel, De Beuckelaer, Van der Heyden, & Gisle, 2017, Abstract). All of these aforementioned links in the chain of mental health must be strong if a coach is to assist in optimizing or maximizing the wholesome scientific work one can do while imparting greater influence as a scientist. For a scientist, coaching is more than just life and work balance. Psychosynthesis life coaching aims to serve the complex experiences of a researcher or supervisor and to regulate actions in the direction of greater purpose and the Call of Self.

Why Bring Psychosynthesis Life Coaching to the Sciences?

Life coaching in the sciences is a natural extension from sports to Fortune 500 companies. It is the art of communication, of instigating change and development while holding a consideration of the visions of that individual (or organization). It is a sequence of efforts to challenge the actions of a researcher while being compassionate to their strengths and weaknesses, beliefs and values. Often times, a life coach may be holding someone accountable for something for which they would like to be held accountable. Through this shared agreement, a life coach helps scientists to actually manifest their scientific ambitions and dreams while taking care of the often tedious and less desirable tasks of their chosen life's work.

By separating the scientist from the lab, a coaching relationship can focus the individual in any given session to what may be most pressing. A Ph.D. candidate or Postdoc may benefit from constructive conversations that spark what it is they really want to be like as a researcher or scientist—in academia or industry. These conversations will lead to discovering what it is they are best at and what they need to do to be the best version of themselves as a researcher or scientist. These engaging discussions can provide the researcher with possible answers to the question of "What type of scientist do I really want to be?" Otherwise, the answer to this question will come too late and most likely at a time of career crisis and low self-esteem.

Through coaching sessions one can experience pivotal reflective periods. By postponing these, all of those insights that would have accumulated over months to years of contemplation and conversation would need to be generated in a stressful time of tough career decisions (…this pressure is likely equivalent to what gives rise to the fusion of hydrogen in stars!). Some people are self-driven and indeed contemplate and develop inner wisdom, but coaching can act as a catalyst to make the most of these in the spirit of what that client is aligned with. Therefore, the coach can stir the pot to manifest these insights and avoid stressful times. If there is no self-care, planning and action, then in

326

those stressful times the answer to the question of "what type of scientist I really want to become" will come at a heavy price, for example: a deteriorating career confidence and reputation by changing fields; a mental/physical health challenge; or the diminished quality in relationships during these transitory times.

If, for example, someone decides shortly after getting a Ph.D. in the sciences, that he or she would rather be a journalist or even a data scientist in the industry, the person would have to accept the preparatory work of becoming familiar with those options beforehand, an action item a coach would surely mobilize the client to work towards. Therefore, this transition time is filled with getting by with the knowledge one can acquire during the commitment phase after deciding to switch fields on an academic path, switch to industry or turn onto the avenue of starting up a company.

With the growing awareness of troubling mental health issues in the sciences, it becomes all the more relevant to consider what the best application is of life coaching tools to serve the entire population of researchers. Many, who are without the benefit of therapy, who have symptoms of anxiety or depression, would profit from healthy discussions about grander things than what one has been absorbed in through the tunnel vision of one's work. Life coaching is a positive resource to prevent the possibility of being trapped by avoidable potholes in work or even mental health disturbances. It helps develop ownership of one's life with purpose and meaning. During research, it can be possible to enjoy the ups and downs of scientific adventures and pursuits, and, as Goethe notes, "When we have done our part within, the exterior will unfold itself automatically" (as cited in Assagioli, 1969, p. 135).

How to Apply Psychosynthesis Life Coaching to the Sciences

A coach aims to foster the quality of a scientist's life as something that can develop and be maintained. Destructive stress only deteriorates the quality and quantity of the science one can do. In some cases, such stress may prevent any further world-changing work from happening. Placing greater emphasis upon empowering and inspiring scientists in their field, ultimately benefits all of humanity. Just as there does not exist a vacuum between the music and the musicians, there is no way to distill the scientist from the science. The quality of life that a scientist experiences, throughout a lifetime, will be interconnected 100% to the actual scientific work one carries out.

One story

Briefly, I highlight here an experience of an anonymous former site director of a significant scientific project. The umbrella organization that hired this director saw that vast developments in his career required significant life processing and management of these career changes. To assist in the increased work demand and responsibilities required as site director, the organization provided a coach. According to this person, as he reflected back on the experience, it seemed that there were always sessions where the coach was trying to help him figure out how to do something or to think of something to solve his problems, personal and professional. In the end, it was quite useful because this scientist, holding an important job within the field, realized that the coach was not there to tell him what to do, but to assist in the important reflection that was necessary in this environment. That work helped challenge the person to commit to the actions that were most relevant for his own growth and development, and then to manifest those actions, making his new, more challenging job, the rewarding career move he wanted, with the impact of increasing scientific work and knowledge in his field. This is the win-win of coaching.

The importance for scientists and science

A coach in the sciences is not going to focus on just getting a researcher to publish more papers, or focus on any "external outcomes" only. Similarly, a coach's role in any athlete's life is more than developing pure athletic ability. As opposed to the level of coaching a scientist receives, an athlete gets daily/weekly/monthly physical treatments and guidance from specialists in general health and fitness, alongside verbal cues from their actual coaches, who have a level of expertise beyond what they have. Ideally, to obtain the best results, the coach does not prescribe or dictate what to do, since the client is on equal grounds with the coach and is in the position of expertise. Coaches will do their best to refrain from giving too many ideas and rather, will work to foster more insight and creative action based upon the ideas that the client has already presented or alluded to during the session. This will be the inevitable course that coaches working with scientists will take.

Each scientist/student/researcher is a unique human being, so the techniques that may be useful will vary. Scientists are, at the very least, logical, critical, and rational human beings given the training they have. Despite the possibility that a more rational, technique-based method may be most effective for a scientist, it is important to avoid dry application of exercises and techniques. A coaching session is collaborative, zeroing in on relevant issues, using individually oriented processes to work on those issues. The coach must gear each response, made in the moment, towards perceiving the abilities and readiness of a client, while challenging each one to stretch and develop. By encouraging thoughtful reflection and non-directed awareness, matched with inquiry into the client's way of being without taking action, a coach can fuel the creative fires to expand the scientist/client's view of excellence and sustainability. Any scientific group or project can benefit directly from these insights, and they will serve **as tangible material to work with once action has begun.**

The rigorous, objective standpoint that science embodies is a blessing and a curse, as scientists may be prone to think only logically and in the insular world of their respective field of interest. They may not reveal to themselves the beauty of the internal and external. The "Both–And" philosophy of psychosynthesis can make a strong contribution to sparking scientific endeavors and understandings. The energy and influence drawn from self-inspiration within the areas of life that are most full of passion and enthusiasm can permeate into the flow of scientists' work, ultimately improving professional career networks and legacy impacts.

This energy of self-inspiration from realms of life that are full of playfulness and pure curiosity can be extremely useful when experienced and channeled, but it is often shadowed by pre-existing obligations to simply carry out the tasks required for a work project. These acts of self-expression and of embodying the inner child are thereby enshrouded like dust clouding the envelope of a newly formed star, creating, for the individual, a blind spot, an inability to feel whole or connected in the midst of their daily work.

It is all the more vital to provide life coaching tools of thought and exercise to support the people who are conducting science—whether under their own supervision, amongst a team or in the larger context of pushing the limits of current human understanding within the scientific community. The leadership required of a supervisor to care for their students' work, to define boundaries and hopes, while communicating enough to guide students without telling them too much, provides rich challenges. The leadership required of graduate students to initiate projects, manuscripts, and proposals of their own volition, and to communicate clearly their needs to a supervisor, also provides an array of complex experiences for a coaching session. From the beginning of a career in science to the winding down into retirement, scientists bring an array of career specific needs, as well as basic human needs, that will all be served by having access to a coach.

Coach and scientist, working together

Coaching can aid those scientists who have been fraught with feeling overwhelmed, helpless, or confused, so they can generate more feelings of

329

solidarity in their work. At every stage of one's career, it is important to understand fully the opportunity one has to influence, advance and shape knowledge within the scientist's field of work. Let us think of Maslow's Hierarchy of Needs. If human beings do not have basic physical and emotional needs met, their higher intellectual capabilities will suffer accordingly. Assuming that it is appropriate to do so, a coach may focus on helping the individual to strengthen the links of mental health and fuse them with the person's scientific career.

To put it simply, imagine the sort of work you would like to see yourself doing when filled to the brim with appreciation and gratitude, with a confidence to grow and to learn. In the natural progression of the coaching session, the coach and client can move forward together in this spirit. By identifying possible hang-ups or required steps that the individual may have just recognized as needing action, one can provide insightful forward thinking to what will need to be done in upcoming situations. It is merely human to get in the way of one's self, so being a few steps ahead can only help to keep things moving. That is where a coach is most effective.

The notion of a work-life balance is also at the crux of why psychosynthesis life coaching is directly relevant for the scientific environment and research atmosphere. Although the ability of a scientist to construct measurable and achievable goals in the three to six-month future will shape any behavior in that time-span, the work-life balance includes more than time management. The work-life balance is a direct manifestation of any individual who can function in a harmonious way with the many aspects of themselves. Coaching aims at developing balance where each person is well centered and grounded, strengthening the stability of both work and life.

Visualizing this together in any coaching session is going to dig into the heart of the client's inner passions and drives. This may result in encouraging scientists to explore in depth the various facets of their lives with presence, honesty, and openness. The scientist, often hyper-focused on work, may need to embrace memorable routines and playful habits, finding inspiration for research in distinctly different areas of life other than science.

Well-centered and grounded **work** may look slightly different from one scientist's perspective to the next, but a coach will likely invite the scientist to uncover, explore and continually develop scientific interests and research skills, helping to open talents and untapped abilities. A coach may remind a scientist that he or she was once a novice and that knowledge of the field and current tools and skillsets do not define one entirely. A coaching session will often embark on various ways to instill a sense of 'Who am I?...as a scientist?' as well as 'How am I?...as a scientist?' so that the individuals feel they are engaging their entire being while addressing these aspects in the broad context of their work.

The unique approach to understanding the **will**, proposed by Assagioli (1974), is arguably where the most dynamic change can take place in the life of a scientist. Too often researchers are employing sheer mental or physical will-power, charging into their tasks without much sleep or care for their physical health and well-being, oscillating stress levels. Any Psychosynthesis Life Coach knows there is more to it than just will power and any wise scientist knows that attempting to solve the same problem with outdated techniques is done only with diminishing returns over time. You have to relax. You have to expand your toolbox. You have to upgrade. You have to care about passing along information to others in a constructive manner.

A well-centered and grounded life, and what that looks like, will differ for each individual. The Psychosynthesis star-diagram, and associated psychological functions, provides an excellent example to describe what it would mean to cultivate a life that is well centered and well grounded.

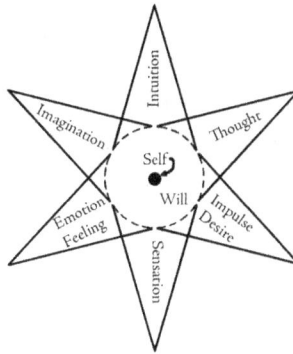

Imagination — Intuition — Thought — Impulse/Desire — Sensation — Emotion/Feeling — Self — Will

As an example, a coaching session could work with the psychological functions of a scientist to identify the areas where there is room for improvement and/or need of integration with another area. For instance, a straightforward application of this in a scientific context would include addressing the details of how an individual scientist, or perhaps research group, overvalues or undervalues each of the psychological functions in the star diagram: imagination, intuition, cognition, feeling, physical sensation, and desire/impulse. One can begin to let go and appreciate each function, realizing they are all of that and more. As foreign as this may seem to a research group, doing this may inspire the group, create leaps in creative ways of working and bring the group together, around new, shared understandings of themselves and each other. Likewise, the individual scientist will draw from a deeper well, when they have explored their own psychological functions.

As there are often conflicts with desire and will for any human being, this may be where most material arises for a coach in the science enterprise. One can picture a coach and a scientist discussing ways to fill the gap between a desire to pursue a certain set of science goals and having the energy and thoughtfulness to write a grant proposal to fund these endeavors. Habitual cognitive approaches to everything may thwart the imagination of scientists, which may give rise to challenging requests by a coach to go daydream or find ways to be creative aside from daily work.

If a scientist has a strong connection to how they are feeling and an awareness of their physical health levels, they may have an advantage in the field, where others may experience burnout and work excessively, not strategically. The intuition scientists have is the key that uniquely defines how they can lead themselves in their chosen field and provide an example for others. It is the flash of insight, an inner knowing, that leads to some of the most remarkable discoveries, but the scientific community does not explicitly cherish intuition. The emphasis on publications, external knowledge, and appearance drowns out the real intuition that often plants the seeds of dreams in the minds of scientists to carry out the work they do. It can be extremely advantageous to have a direct link to one's intuition in the sciences, as there are crossroads and decisions that require an inner sense of where to move in a direction that one feels as the best path forward, not to mention how many insightful discoveries arise (in the past, present and future) from scientists' intuition.

All scientists want to streamline the process of a scientific project efficiently and its associated tasks with quality. While making the most of any data-set and human resource, a life coach can be a catalyst, an enzyme, for a scientist's life and work. As a catalyst raises the energy to overcome the activation energy barrier for a metabolic process to take place, the metabolic process, in this analogy, may come in the form of a scientist needing to acquire a new set of software skills. The client may have a tendency to stick to old, but robust procedures that are less efficient. Therefore, a life coach helps catalyze the types of motivation or visions and actions that need to be cultivated for mastering a new software package, programming new tools and functionalities in order to do calculations at the state-of-the-art level. Of course, a supervisor or research group director may lead in this endeavor, but the life coach aids in fostering the spirit of using these various branches of volition and aspects of will in life, across all spheres on a day-to-day and week-to-week basis. In turn, those goals of making the most out of a scientific project and its team members can be actualized.

One approach would be to use Assagioli's (1974) 'acting as if' combined with effective future pacing. This would allow researchers to step out of their fixed line of thinking and imagine what it would be like to be well past a current roadblock. By envisioning and commenting on the act of stepping into a realm of work and life spheres that they are then experts in, scientist clients may be able to come up with a detailed view of the future. The associated commentary on what it would be like when they realize their goals can motivate daily actions. In turn, this can allow scientists to reach their goals, and achieve a life that is satisfying, in areas that were previously challenging or full of struggles. Looking back after pacing into the future in this way can allow the client to identify actions they took to get there.

Overall, it is desirous to have the ability to balance one's work and life so that a scientist can constantly reinvent the self, as a scientist and as a human being. It is necessary to have the ability to discover and develop stronger connections to what one is doing and who one is. One can think of the analogy of a weight lifter who only works on the upper body and therefore has weak legs. That just won't work. Unfortunately, many scientists live in their heads, and use their bodies to carry their brains around and only focus on their research. Of course, this limits their ability to engage with themselves in dialogue, normal conversations, and creative expression.

Care and Communication is Key

A coaching session places emphasis on self-growth and self-care. At least conceptually, growing and caring for one's self in a holistic manner will aid that person in being able to communicate effectively from their core sense of Self. Every scientist knows how vital it is to a career to communicate effectively. Rather than discussing details of work and ongoing projects, coaching sessions allow for better inter-personal communication skills. The purpose and mission of the scientific work and life career truly can never shine in a standard conversation with a colleague or supervisor. Of course, time is limited, and the most pressing pieces of information to be addressed revolve around the intent of a project, the technical failures and debugging, ongoing progress and results, and the details of the work itself. It may not even be appropriate for a supervisor or colleague to question how others feel about the work they are doing, or if they are emotionally, mentally, or spiritually aligned with their working goals. During a weekly meeting about work, those conversations may simply take away from the research topics that need to be discussed. A coach will therefore serve as the one to build on strengths and characterize weaknesses so the scientist can re-connect to a strong inner self and furthermore have the energy to carry out the work with sustained progress.

It is, of course, easier said than done, especially when there is a feeling of disconnect with respect to the work that must be completed. There may also be a serious need to align one's will with the awareness of why it is one is doing any particular piece of work. Psychosynthesis work may revolve around tapping into the client's potential to challenge what is known in the field. By reconnecting to the contribution to the unsolved problems, the scientist can take a sense of purpose or ownership of the work and imbue it with new energy and commitment.

Nowadays, a Ph.D. may be the result of a team effort, led by an individual, rather than how it was a hundred years ago, when a single individual would make specific and unique contributions to the field. For a Masters or Ph.D. student, the need for transparent communication and guidance can often be the defining factor for the most fruitful projects. However, the personalities of advisors and the students alike may or may not mesh well with one another. Likewise, for the director of an entire research facility, the need for compassionate communication is required so that leadership can be exemplified, as well as adopted, by others.

Homegrown qualities (honesty, dignity, trust, respect) go a long way in strengthening and building the relationships that are close within our lives, but these qualities are significantly more challenging to apply in work conditions because of human awkwardness and miscommunication. Coaching may provide an interesting outlook during rocky communication trails in the hills and valleys of a scientific project. A coach may well be that ideal person to encourage someone purposefully to take interest in courageously embracing a needed, but prolonged and difficult conversation.

Rather than having the scientist focus on the anxiety around communication breakdowns and the administrative concerns with respect to the project, a life coach can help bring the focus of the scientist back to the context of living out the best version of one's self. Many young researchers, at the graduate level, as well as supervisors, professors, and PIs (principal investigators), find themselves lacking the necessary knowledge they may need on a special topic. Additionally, based on their responsibilities to tutor or lecture, they may lack the ability to deviate from their own work in order to teach others to the best of their ability. Working on communicating one's research (through mission statements, elevator talks, or public outreach) is essential and a great example of material that is relevant for psychosynthesis life coaching in the science environment. Too many scientists walk around unable to explain clearly to a layperson what they work on. Over time, coaching sessions will yield scientists who are able to convey the often complex but, nevertheless, important ideas they ponder and research. A coaching session can build upon the good will in the heart of an individual, sparking innovative teaching methods, or inspiring creative public outreach efforts in ways only brought about in the context of these powerful coaching conversations.

Forging a Path Forward

A coach will focus on the development of the individual's scientific career and a healthy life and work experience, never attempting to define or direct the client's life. Even the terminology of 'life coach' may repel many skeptical and trained-to-be-critically-thinking scientists, as it may be off-putting to think of someone teaching them about their life. Nevertheless, in fact, a coach aims at assisting individuals in gaining their own insights and developments towards **what needs to be done, when it needs to be done, and why**. Every psychosynthesis session engages the individual in discovering the direction of unfolding possibilities within life, so that a sense of context and purpose is built and shared. Moreover, the consistency in declaring actions and goals, allows one to stay honest with what the scientist can take on for work, while being in front of deadlines. By creating alive-lines, which are daily or weekly tasks and benchmarks, one can gain control over one's work and choose how to live a meaningful life.

Personal experience shows that many directors or supervisors in the academic/private research setting may not understand the actual application of life coaching, and may misinterpret it as counseling or therapy. A director or supervisor may believe it is simply a matter of the staff scientist or student letting the human resources department or director know when they need to really talk to someone (for example, a mental health professional). In this scenario, perhaps most human resource departments can serve the researcher and find a referral. That means then, that instances of self-growth and development are reserved for sessions in these extreme situations when excess stress piles up, or when things simply become too much for the scientist to handle. This is the wrong approach, however. How does it help to wait until the crisis point comes along? Students and engaged professional scientists, may not need regular scientific supervision, but they would certainly benefit from the connection of talking to another person and the opportunity to schedule last minute, weekly or monthly coaching check-ins to discuss their obstacles and experiences related to the context of their life and their research. The coach is an ally and having an ally along the way may significantly reduce the likelihood of ending up in a crisis.

Psychosynthesis life coaching is about continually inviting in a fresh draft of change, through the window of an individual. Here we examined how psychosynthesis life coaching can empower the scientist to have a growth mindset and to listen to and breathe in, the Call of Self. We explored how coaching can relate directly to the scientist's immediate colleagues and the world at large. In the end, a scientist may become someone who not only exemplifies the work of a scientist, but also the work of a giver, an author, a juggler, a dancer, a musician, a chef, an architect and anything humanly possible.

If a life coach is successful in helping scientists take control over their own inner GPS, then scientists can know what it feels like to do research from the core of who they are. Again, the potential for unexpected life and scientific discovery is what is so appealing in developing this dialogue between coach and scientist. Life coaching in the sciences has now seen the birth of its field, as many human resource departments may seek out professional development workshops, time management training, and other 'soft skills' seminars. Although some call them soft skills, it is not a soft skill to know how to manage your internal and external resources, as negative stress can develop and feed on one's heart and mind to the point of panic, anxiety, and dysfunction. That is a hard fact to deal with, not a soft one. The courage and wisdom developed from the essential skills of utilizing one's inner and outer resources are exactly what one needs to push through and take care of all the myriad components of being a scientist.

It is clear that standard life development workshops/seminars are heading in a positive direction as they address the needs of a scientist/researcher. There is ample evidence to suggest that being able to manage one's time successfully, knowing how to communicate properly with colleagues and advisors, and planning productively for the future are all traits important for the self-defined success of an individual. It is only a matter of time before each scientist has a coach.

References

Assagioli , R. (1969). Symbols of transpersonal experiences. *Journal of Transpersonal Psychology*, (1), 1133-45.

Assagioli, R. (1974). *The act of will: A guide to self-actualization and self-realization*. London: The Psychosynthesis & Education Trust.

Levecque, K., Anseel, F., De Beuckelaer, A., Van der Heyden, J., & Gisle, L. (2017). Work organization and mental health problems in Ph.D. students. *Research Policy*, 46(4), 868-879. DOI: 10.1016/j.respol.2017.02.008

Chapter 25

A Synthesis of Gender

by Leyza A. Toste

What is your personal understanding and experience of gender? How do you define gender identity and gender expression? How has your frame of reference for gender been formed? As a psychosynthesis trained coach the "realization of one's True Self" (Assagioli, 2000, pp. 21-22) is understood as central to the work. As coaches, we must be prepared to coach gender diverse clients towards this "Call of Self". This chapter offers insights and education to prepare you to coach transgender clients—people whose gender identity is different from the gender they were assigned at birth, the primary genitalia associated with male or female reproductive organs, which in some cases, is not as clear as we imagine. Unlike cisgender clients, whose gender identity is the same as the biological sex they were assigned at birth, transgender people are marginalized in society, which leads to a host of issues. As their coach, it behooves you to know as much as you can about what they confront. Everything you can learn about gender identity and what it means to be a transgender person will help you be a better coach and serve your clients more deeply.

I speak to the topic of gender diversity from the heart, having had the privilege of standing by a family member as they came to embody their gender authentically. As well, through my work in human resources, I have experience with what is involved for individuals coming out as transgender in the workplace. Regardless of the setting, being witness to this profound coming to the Self has fundamentally shifted my view of gender. Instead of the rigid, either-or mindset I was raised to believe in, I realize that gender can be fluid and boundless, a synthesis of those qualities defined as masculine and feminine, and that its expression is deeply personal.

It is clear that the polarized (either male or female), view of gender is expanding to encompass a gender spectrum. The current wealth of information on gender identity—as the subject of news articles, magazines[1], films, books, social media, TV shows, and TED talks—has opened the discussion of gender identity and increased the public's awareness that there is more to gender than 'male' or 'female'. At the same time, the official count of adults who identify themselves as transgender has doubled in the past ten years on nation-wide surveys (Henig, 2017, p. 50).

What is less well known is that the concept of a fluid gender identity is nothing new. According to the UCLA Burkle Center,

Lesbian, gay, bisexual, transgender, intersex and related identities have been present in various forms throughout history. All cultures have included, with varying degrees of acceptance, individuals who practice same-sex relations as well as those whose gender, gender identity and gender expression challenge prevailing norms, and many cultures still do. ("Sexual Orientation and Gender identity Throughout History," 2014, para. 1)

However, history and heightened public awareness do not equal acceptance; it is a bitter fact that prejudice against the transgender community is commonplace in our society, affecting all aspects of life, including how transgender people meet their basic needs for survival. "Transgender people are among the most vulnerable communities in the country" ("Transgender Americans Face..." n.d., para 1). This plays out in myriad ways. The difficulties of getting official identification, like a driver's license, passport, or health plan card, to match their expression of gender, opens transgender people to discrimination, whether they are applying for employment, looking for housing, or receiving healthcare. In the workplace, transgender people often face an unwelcome and even openly hostile environment that is replete with micro-aggressions, those subtle ordinary gestures or remarks that leave an individual feeling less than (Nadal, 2013). Transgender people are also at risk for homelessness; one in five will become homeless, either from being denied housing or being at a higher risk for getting evicted ("Issues | Housing," n.d., para 2). Their health care options are absent or limited, since even if they are lucky enough to have benefits-eligible employment, the benefits often do not cover their healthcare needs. To make matters worse, health care providers typically lack the training to manage the specific physical, emotional, and mental health care needs of transgender patients. In short, a transgender person's daily experience of non-acceptance is often so severe that they live in a state of fear for their safety, health, and well-being. Transgender clients of all ages, but especially youth, are not only likely to hear negative remarks about their sexual orientation, but to have been verbally and physically harassed (Kosciw, Greytak, Giga, Villenas, & Danischewski,

---

[1] Two notable sources of information are: *Time Magazine's* March 27, 2017 edition cover story "Beyond He or She" and the January 2017 *National Geographic* issue devoted in its entirety to gender.

338

2016, p. xv). Thus, transgender people tend to be extremely vulnerable and often present as wounded clients. In the United States, the incidence of suicide attempts by transgender individuals is 41%, as compared to less than 5% for the general population (Haas, Herman & Rogers, 2014, p. 2).

While an actively suicidal client will not be a good fit as a coaching client, since they will need a different kind of help (a counselor or psychotherapist, rather than a coach), a transgender client will need your awareness that suicide might be or may have been an issue, as well as your understanding of the other obstacles they expect to encounter in their daily life ("Board Certified Coach Code of Ethics," 2010, p. 3, para 2). Our role as coaches, then, is crucial as we learn **not** to re-traumatize through well-meaning ignorance, confusion, or limiting language.

The core concept of **Presence** in coaching is key to navigating this, as described by Brown (2004) through the coach's development of six qualities that build a "full and facilitative presence" (p.72). Presence embodied in this way shapes the coach's inner knowing and innate confidence in their ability to be there for the client, to guide the client in the emergence of what is fully possible.

At this time about 1.4 million adults report being transgender in the US (Flores, Herman, Gates, & Brown, 2016, para. 1) so you may well have a coaching client who is exploring their gender identity; you may even be the first person they have talked to about it. As a coach, you will be helping them navigate what gender means for them personally as well as in their relationships. You also may be working with people who want to understand and support the journey of a transgender family member, friend, or co-worker.

The question is, how do we, as coaches, support transgender clients in their journey of self-discovery? Specifically, what can we do to strengthen our work as guides and develop greater empathy for our transgender travelers? The rich practice of psychosynthesis offers the groundwork for this endeavor built on a holistic theory brought to bear through a number of maps, co-guiding principles, and techniques, toward the evolution of personal growth and the unearthing of what brings purpose and meaning to life.

Complementary to this, is the need to educate ourselves about what gender means, going beyond a simplistic male or female label. Gender can be scientifically defined as a composite of factors—those relating to genetics and biology that frame gender in terms of chromosomes, hormones, and anatomy—and those relating to the social sciences and psychology, that look at gender in terms of the person's role in society (Henig, 2017, p. 56). Meanwhile, we all experience gender uniquely, both in our internal sense of who we are (gender identity) and in our outward expression of that identity (gender expression). The outward expression of gender can be seen in how we dress and style our hair, in our speech patterns and body language. Even something as simple as what we do with our legs when sitting down can be a form of gender expression.

Our perception of gender is based not only on personal experience, but also on the cultural norms that have shaped us and may determine how we make sense of that experience. While some cultures make room for those who do not fit the cisgender 'norm,' most of us are limited by a cultural idea of male and female as two disparate, fixed, and opposing ways of being. While many people do identify as exclusively male or female, countless others find themselves somewhere in between, or in a place of ongoing movement along a spectrum that is fluid and changing.

Meanwhile most of us have been taught to fear whatever falls outside of the mainstream and to see it as flawed, diseased, deviant, or mentally ill. As research has shown, even those of us who have tried to free ourselves from such prejudices may find we have incorporated them at a subconscious level ("State of the Science," 2015, para 1). Thus raising our own awareness is vital if we are to think more inclusively about gender. We can begin by becoming familiar with the Gender Unicorn (2017) or the Genderbread Person (2012) models, which are used in sensitivity training to help people expand their ideas about gender. These tools illustrate gender as a range of possibilities across the continuums of identity, expression, biological sex assigned at birth, and physical and emotional attraction. This way of looking at gender across a range of feminine and masculine qualities can more truly express a "unity in diversity" that is "harmonious...and complemental" instead of "opposed and conflicting" (Russell, 1982, para. 2c). Those who identify as transgender could be said to embody this unity.

Another step a coach can take to become conversant with this topic entails a self-education process that includes curiosity, the capacity for self-awareness and reflection, and an openness to exploring unfamiliar and, at times, uncomfortable terrain. Educating ourselves is part of our obligation as professionals, to build our capacities is to serve our clientele, but it is also about building trust, the kind that can allow a presenting issue to emerge more easily, and can foster a deeper connection with the client as the coaching engagement unfolds. This continued education can lead to the coach becoming an ally, which means adopting behaviors and practices that actively support the transgender community. In support of this, the following suggestions can be implemented easily in a coaching practice:

+ Become aware of your biases. A good way to start is by taking the Implicit Bias Test ("Project Implicit," n.d.) and familiarizing yourself with the Cisgender Privilege List ("The Non-Trans Privilege," n.d.). An ally is open to broadening their life perspective and becoming aware of deeply-held personal beliefs. If, as psychosynthesis coaches, we trust that presence is the key to our work, then our job is to know how to be present with all people, free from our own limiting, lower unconscious messages and stories.

♦ Information from coaching sessions is confidential ("Board Certified Coach Code of Ethics," 2010, p. 3, para 3). It is unethical and disempowering to disclose a transgender client's change in gender identity unless you have their express permission to do so.

♦ In advertising, identify yourself as an ally by displaying the LGBQ and transgender flags and/or by stating that you are an LBGTQ ally. Noting yourself as a psychosynthesis coach, invites an understanding of your perspective as being transpersonal. Adding the specifics of your alliance to the LGBTQ community focuses your psychosynthesis orientation towards a strong alliance.

♦ On the client intake form, simply ask for the client's 'name,' not their legal or preferred name. The legal name may be different from the chosen name/nickname and if required on the form could 'out' the client, which is not appropriate at any stage. Honestly, you do not even need to know if a client is transgender unless that is part of the presenting issue or story they want to tell. In addition, to ask for a client's 'preferred' name negates its legitimacy; this name is a part of their identity and not simply a preference. If you feel that gender information is necessary in the intake process then allow the client to fill in the descriptor; do not offer a female/male only option. If gender information is extraneous, do not ask for it on the form.

♦ However, use of the pronoun that matches the individual's identity shows respect; therefore, it is appropriate to ask for a client's pronoun on the intake form. Again, do not ask for 'preferred' pronouns since this is a part of the client's identity. Mis-gendering an individual is disrespectful, even if unintended, so do not assume. If you have not asked for this information on a form then ask in person. This can be done with the client by simply identifying your pronoun by stating, for example, "I use she/her/hers pronouns" and then asking what the client uses. (This same principle would be used if the client references people from their lives who are transgender). Going forward, if you mistakenly mis-gender a client, acknowledge this and offer a sincere apology as soon as you catch yourself. The most commonly used pronouns are: he/him/his and she/her/hers. Other terms are known as gender neutral and are used "when someone's gender is unknown or when the individual is neither male or female" ("The Need for a Gender Neutral Pronoun," 2010, para. 1). These are: they/them/theirs, ze (pronounce: zee), xe (also pronounce as: zee), or e (pronounce: ee).

+ The pronoun **they** can be used as a singular, neutral pronoun to describe individuals who don't identify as male or female, and is used that way in publications such as *The Washington Post*, as discussed on NPR's On Air show ("Everyone Uses Singular 'They,' " 2016).

+ Do not refer to a transgender person as **transgendered** or as a **transgender** ("GLAAD Media Reference Guide," n.d.) but as a transgender person. The word transgender "is an adjective [not a noun], and reducing people to just one of their qualities is necessarily reductive and denies their gender and their humanity" ("Transgender is an adjective," 2010, para. 5).

+ Use gender-neutral language in both written and oral expression. For instance, instead of asking, "What is your son's/daughter's name?" ask, "What is your child's name?" Another common example refers to client's partners, friends or family. Do not assume a feminine presenting client has a masculine significant other. Instead, ask, "What is your partner's name?"

+ Seek out further education online or in person. SafeZone training is offered to the public at some local colleges, universities, and LGBTQ organizations. This is designed to raise awareness of gender and sexual, LGBTQ identities and issues, and to "create people who are invested in creating safe and affirming environments wherever they go, and providing those people the skills and knowledge they need to do that" ("Safe Zone," 2017, para. 4.). In lieu of in-person training, the SafeZoneProject web site offers self-guided, online training resources ("The Safe Zone Project," n.d.).

+ Read material that deepens your understanding about the life experiences of transgender individuals and their families. Two best-selling examples are *Becoming Nicole* by Amy Ellis Nut and the memoir *She's Not There: A Life in Two Genders*, by Jennifer Finney Boylan. A good resource for guidance in the workplace is *Allies at Work* by Dr. David M. Hall. In addition, review your understanding of psychosynthesis principles to see where they serve your work with this population. How does Purpose relate to this person sitting in front of me? Is there a way to work with subpersonalities that also includes gender-neutral language? Imagine, even for your own inner awareness, the act of will that every transgender person makes in staking a claim for their own Self, in the face of so much opposition.

+ Being an ally includes active involvement in and/or making a contribution to the work of local or national organizations that support gender diversity equality. Additional support is shown by acknowledging significant annual markers in honor of the transgender communities' struggles. Two of these are: November 20, The International Transgender Day of Remembrance in memory of "those who were killed due to anti-transgender hatred or prejudice" ("The International Transgender Day," n.d., para. 1), and October 11, National Coming Out Day, that "honors all who have come out as LGBTQ or as a straight ally for equality" ("National Coming Out Day," n.d., para. 4).

If adopted, these best practices will go a long way toward creating a welcoming environment and can make a world of difference to someone who often is not seen for who they are.

The work of a coach is multi-faceted. It involves improving the well-being of individuals, building more vibrant and sustainable communities, and increasing societal awareness. Critical to this is work with non-majorative groups, such as transgender individuals, and understanding the synthesis of gender as an essential component of the human experience in the macrocosm of society.

Synthesis, a core concept of psychosynthesis, is described as "movement towards union of the personality" with the "acceptance of differences and tolerance of the tension and conflict that may be caused by these differences" (Firman & Gila, 2007, p. 21). What more essential psychosynthesis concept could guide us towards this work?

A psychosynthesis coach is well positioned to guide transgender clients towards a deepened understanding of **Self**, to know that they are their wounded parts, and that they are more than this; to witness emergence of the Willer "endowed with the power to choose, to relate, to bring about changes in [their] own personality, in others, in circumstances" (Assagioli, 2007, p. 8). What a privilege it is to travel this path with another!

This chapter is dedicated to the courageous, beautiful soul who is near and dear to my heart and has taught me so much. Let their strength and deep connection to the "**Call of Self**" be an inspiration for us all.

References

Assagioli, R. (2000). *Psychosynthesis.* (12th printing) Amherst, MA: Synthesis Center Press.

Assagioli, R (2007). *The act of will.* Synthesis Center Press.

Board certified coach code of ethics. (2010, September 17). Retrieved from Center for Credentialing and Education. http://www.cce-global.org/Assets/Ethics/ BCCcodeofethics.pdf.

Brown, M. H. (2004). *Unfolding self: The practice of psychosynthesis.* New York: Allworth Press.

Everyone uses singular 'they', whether they realize it or not. (2016, January 13). Retrieved from NPR. http://www.npr.org/2016/01/13/ 462906419/everyone-uses-singular-they-whether-they-realize-it-or-not.

Firman, J., & Gila, A. (2007). Assagioli's seven core concepts for Psychosynthesis training. Palo Alto, CA: Psychosynthesis Palo Alto.

Flores, A. R., Herman, J. L, Gates, G.T., & Brown, T. (2016, June). How many adults identify as transgender in the United States. Retrieved from Williams Institute School of Law, http://williamsinstitute.law.ucla.edu/research/ how-many-adults-identify-as-transgender-in-the-united-states/.

The gender unicorn. (n.d.). Retrieved August 24, 2017, from Trans Student Educational Resources http://www.transstudent.org/gender.

The genderbread person v2.0. (2012, March). Retrieved August 24, 2017, from it's pronounced METROsexual, http://itspronouncedmetrosexual.com/2012/03/the-genderbread-person-v2-0/.

GLAAD media reference guide – Transgender. (n.d.). Retrieved August 24, 2017, from GLAAD, https://www.glaad.org/reference/transgender.

Haas, A.P., Herman, J.L, & Rogers, P. L. (2014, January). Suicide attempts among transgender and gender non-conforming adults. Retrieved from Williams Institute School of Law, https://williamsinstitute.law.ucla.edu/wp-content/uploads/AFSP-Williams-Suicide-Report-Final.pdf.

Henig, R. M. (2017, January). Rethinking gender. *National Geographic: Gender Revolution*, 231(1), pp. 50 & 56.

The international transgender day of remembrance [Blog post]. (n.d.). Retrieved September 3, 2017, from https://tdor.info/about-2/

Issues | Housing and homelessness. (n.d.). Retrieved August 24, 2017, from National Center for Transgender Equality, http://www.transequality. org/issues/housing-homelessness.

Kosciw, J. G., Greytak, E. A., Giga, N. M., Villenas, C. & Danischewski, D. J. (2016). *The 2015 national school climate survey: The experiences of lesbian, gay, bisexual, transgender, and queer youth in our nation's schools.* New York: GLSEN. Retrieved from https://www.glsen.org/sites/default/files/2015%20 National%20GLSEN%202015%20National%20School%20Climate%20 20 Survey %20%28NSCS%29%20-%20Full%20Report_0.pdf.

National coming out day – October 11, 2016. (n.d.). Retrieved September 3, 2017 from the Human Rights Campaign, https://www.hrc.org/ resources/national-coming-out-day.

The need for a gender-neutral pronoun [Blog post]. (2010, January 24). Retrieved August 24, 2017, from Gender Neutral Pronoun Blog, https://gen-derneutral pronoun.wordpress.com/.

Nadal, K.L. (2013). *That's so gay!: Microaggressions and the lesbian, gay, bisexual, and transgender community.* Washington, DC: American Psychological Association (APA).

The non-trans privilege or cisgender privilege list. (n.d.). Retrieved August 24, 2017, from University of Oregon, UO Libraries, https://new.ober-lin.edu/dotAsset/ 2012181.pdf.

Project implicit. (n.d.). Retrieved August 24, 2017, from Project Implicit, https://implicit. harvard.edu/implicit/aboutus.html

Russell, D.. (1982). Seven basic constructs of Psychosynthesis. *Psychosynthesis Digest*, 1(2). Retrieved from http://two.not2.org/psychosyn-thesis/articles/pd1-2.htm.

Safe zone. (2017, July 14). Retrieved from University of Alaska Fairbanks Nanook Diversity and Action Center, http://www.uaf.edu/ndac/ events-programs/safezone/.

The safe zone project. (n.d.). Retrieved August 24, 2017, from http:// thesafezoneproject. com/.

Sexual orientation and gender identity throughout history. (2014, May 17). Retrieved from UCLA Burkle Center, http://international.ucla.edu/ burkle/article/139796.

State of the science: Implicit bias review 2015. (2015). Retrieved from The Ohio State University Kirwan Institute for the Study of Race and Ethnicity, http://kirwaninstitute.osu.edu/research/understanding-implicit-bias/

Transgender Americans face staggering rates of poverty, violence. (n.d.). Retrieved August 24, 2017, from Movement Advancement Project, http://www.lgbtmap.org/ news/understanding-transgender-issues-unfair-price-release.

Transgender is an adjective. not a noun. or a verb! (2010, May 24). Retrieved from Feministing Community, http://feministing.com/2010/05/24/transgender-is-an-adjective-not-a-noun-or-a-verb/

Chapter 26

Valuing Self: The Gift of the Cosmos

by Christiana Wall

Recently I experienced a trigger, more than I had in a long time. I have a group of women that I meet with regularly. We support each other in life, share in one another's happiness, and witness and hold each other through the inevitable challenges and losses we face. I was getting ready to set off on a three-month trip about which I had much anticipation and trepidation as well. We were trying to schedule one more meeting before I left, when all of us could be together. One regular meeting did not work for one of us, so I was trying to see if another evening would be better.

During a series of e-mails, there was some frustration over the process and one woman wrote, "Okay this is when I am coming to a meeting!" Another woman could do that too and they scheduled it, even though this was a night when I could not come.

The trigger for me was a powerful one. I suddenly felt a deep emotional disappointment because, I told myself that, even to my trusted inner circle of women, I did not matter. My schedule was not important enough to accommodate, but the schedule of others was. It hit me so deeply that it brought me to tears.

The schedule snafu was done in innocence. No one intended to exclude or hurt anyone else. It was just a simple solution done in haste. I could see this and understand it and still the event struck a chord in me that resonated so powerfully that it overtook me. I brought the upset to the group at the next opportunity, a brief breakfast gathering at a diner. They were apologetic, and compassionate, and surprised. I was surprised myself, because equanimity is my modus operandi.

My emotions were telling me that something was up! The phone was ringing, as Marshall Rosenberg, creator of Non-Violent Communication, liked to say. It was time to pick up the phone and say, "Hello, what have we here?"

What have we here? This is a powerful question because it instantly brings in the "observer self." The Dalai Lama says there is nothing more important for the human being to do than to develop the Observer Self. The Observer Self connects us to that part of us that is the witness of us. This Self, that in psychosynthesis sits in the middle of the egg, is a center of contentless awareness and will. It is not that part of us that gets triggered and has emotional upset. The self is awareness from a larger point of view and the path to a transpersonal perspective on what is going on for us. With the help of the observing Self we can acknowledge the upset and determine what the gift of awareness is that underlies the turbulent emotions aroused when having taken something personally.

When I teach a workshop called "The Art of Not Taking It Personally," I talk about the "Art" as that which allows the invisible to become visible. There are unmet or unprocessed challenges that live in the lower unconscious that can show themselves in surprising ways—suddenly, unexpectedly grabbing our attention. These challenges could be giving us a nudge and saying to us, "Now is a good time to know about this challenge, to become aware of it, and recognize it."

The Course in Miracles validates this. "Beware of the danger of an unrecognized belief." An unrecognized belief can be running the show of our lives, wreaking havoc, causing unhappiness in ourselves that could be making the lives of others difficult as well. The belief or unprocessed challenges of the past will often show themselves as a large emotion that suddenly overtakes us. A deep fear or sadness could show up in the emotions as themselves or as an angry outburst.

The most vulnerable emotions are the ones that come up when our basic safety is being threatened. The feeling of not being valued, being criticized, judged, or blamed for something, being evaluated unfairly, is when our most basic sense of safety comes into question, but not necessarily on the conscious level. When we unpack any of these vulnerable states of being, they all relate to not being seen as valuable, and therefore being potentially discarded or disregarded by our tribe, being left behind, and potentially left to die! These emotions do not reside in the logical reasoning mind. These emotions rest in our physical, in our most primal, biology. Recognizing this is critical to the rebalancing of our Selves.

Roberto Assagioli has outlined for us, in the journey to synthesis of our subpersonalities these five steps: Recognition, Acceptance, Coordination, Integration, and Synthesis. I find these steps equally valuable for the synthesis of the painful experience of having taken something personally, for example, having been powerfully triggered or hooked in our emotions, thinking, and physical sensations. Even the reactive impulses can be hijacked by a particular person, event, or circumstance.

Recognition

The recognition of this most vulnerable place in us is like accepting the invitation to grow. Without the recognition, nothing but remaining stuck in the trigger is possible. There is no freedom possible. The recognition is the portal to acceptance, co-ordination, integration, and the synthesis to who we authentically and wholly are. In the first step, "recognizing" the challenge, helps us to name it. What is its name?

With validation of the writings of Rudolph Steiner and out of Buddhism, I have identified three nearly constant challenges we face just by virtue of being human.

These are:
1. The fear of being **flawed**
2. The need for **acceptance**
3. The fear of **rejection**

I call these challenges the F-A-R challenges. The first, the fear of being flawed comes out of the wisdom of Buddhism and the observation that in the human being there resides the underlying fear of "not enoughness." By recognizing the tendency of acceptance and rejection to have power over our interpretations of events, we have the possibility to be set free from their bondage.

When there has been a trigger to the emotions, such as the phone ringing as we are wrenched surprisingly out of our equanimity, it is the perfect time to ask the questions - "What have we here? Have I been grabbed by any, or all, of the F.A.R. challenges? Have I been taken F.A.R. from my quiet center to discover another part of me that is asking for love?"

For me, it became helpful to acknowledge that my trigger with the scheduling of the women's meeting had to do with all three: the need for acceptance, the fear of rejection, and perhaps even the fear of being flawed in some way. Acknowledging the fear of being perceived as flawed, and seeing the lack of consideration of my schedule as the cause of my fear of isolation, and recognizing my desire to connect with these precious women with a compassionate awareness, is key.

Compassion for self and being tripped up by F.A.R. is a universal challenge for human beings across the globe. Recognizing and accepting it is the way out of the restrictive self-doubt that F.A.R. can cause.

Other questions then arise: how does this connect to a primal wound or core wound of my past? Was it that my brother was the pronounced favorite of our Aunt—a most significant caretaker in our childhood? Was it that the drive-in movie my parents promised me when I was 12 was forgone because I had taken a nap and not woken in time? Was it that my medical doctor mother had gone for house calls when I was two, three and four-years-old just when I needed her most and even though I had expressed this, she still went anyway? Was it also the girlfriends in elementary school who were feeling competitive and trying that on for size? Each of us will have our own set of historical stories that sit at the center of our own wounding.

It appears that as human beings, by virtue of our very design, we are destined to be wounded. It is a rare person that has not had their sense of basic safety breached in some way. Having experienced in one way or another the harsh reality that the people who are our caregivers lack the skill and ability to provide us with a sense of perfect safety at all times, the primal wound is established.

We also have a depository in the lower unconscious for the emotional wounds we are incapable of processing in childhood or adolescence. Carl Jung calls this the shadow and Rudolf Steiner calls this the double. The wound, its emotional effects on us, and the storage of these are all set up to be triggered at some time in the future. The tumult that follows a trigger shows us that there is something in "storage" that wants to be taken out and looked at. Taking the opportunity to acknowledge the "set up" and investigate the trigger more deeply is taking the opportunity to grow.

The personality is the mask through which we meet the world. We develop masks to reach and interact with the world. Some masks are more conducive to meet the world than others are. Often many are needed to meet the multiplicity of circumstances encountered. However, the mask cannot fit the authentic being, and the being must not be mistaken for the mask. The mask gives a particular message but the messenger behind the mask is far greater than the mask.

These masks are congruent with the development of subpersonalities. There are the typical subpersonalities: the inner child or rebellious teenager, the inner critical parent, the professional subpersonality, to name a few. Human beings are not automatically conscious of the masks that we don or the subpersonalities that help us operate, for better or worse, in the "house/car/job" world. Human beings can be most unconscious about them, even whilst the subpersonalities are running the show of their lives. It is also possible for the human being to recognize these subpersonalities as well as recognize when we are functioning through a mask. This recognition happens in the realm of the "I" and out of our distinctly human capacity to observe ourselves.

Acceptance

The first remedy is a moment of reflection that I call the P, M, & S moment.

P– Pause,

M – Marvel,

&

S – Smile!

Pause at the discomfort of disconnection from my centered self, the painful experience of being triggered.

Marvel at the strength and power of the emotion that has grabbed my attention. Match the intensity of "marveling" with the intensity of the difficult emotional reaction being experienced. Wonder about it with openness and curiosity.

And Smile in the most compassionate way at that part of me that has gotten hooked and taken me for an emotional trip.

That last "S" step, the compassionate smile, is where the acceptance happens. Acceptance of the challenge and from whence it comes is the next step. Growth is possible when we can accept the challenge that lives in our as-of-yet unprocessed repository. To first recognize and then accept the challenge, rather than resist and deny it, is essential. In the acceptance of the difficulty, we understand more about the roots of the emotion that has taken us by surprise.

In the example I gave above, I had bumped into an aspect of me that was connected to the primal wound of my past. When in the past had I been discounted, overlooked, not valued, or made to feel second best? I smile at myself in the same way that I would smile at the antics of a small child. The child has just been told not to follow the impulse to do something dangerous or naughty, yet the child does this anyway. The child, not at all deterred, will go with the impulse to the cookie jar and steal a cookie or touch the most breakable thing, or go to the switch of the stove. Seeing this seemingly unavoidable, reactive and impulsive behavior and smiling at it, in the same way we would at the most adorable and naughty child, is the path to compassionate recognition and acceptance.

I accept that there are times when I have acted outside of the integrity of my whole being, when the feelings, physical sensations, thinking, intuition, imagination, and impulse are not working in unity. This is a challenge that human beings face the world over. There are times when I have felt a nudge from the universe and not responded. There are challenges that I may have set before myself that I have not met well, times when I did not avail myself of the authenticity of my being.

The smile can go deep. It is a smile of full love and acceptance, deep into the heart of the recognized fears and longings and missed opportunities. Then bringing that resonance of love and acceptance high into the heavens, holding it within the orbit of the moon, letting it shine softly and gently with the reflection of the sun on what occurs out of disconnection. The love and acceptance moves higher to the level of the rising sun, gradually bringing the warmth and light of love and acceptance ever more strongly. From the perspective of the cosmos, it is my own "I" now joining with the resonance of the spiritual world that is showering the experience of being flawed, or rejected, or isolated, with love and acceptance. Lingering in the acceptance is key. Bask in the golden light of the sun, with the full awareness of the universe, the "I" in the periphery, gradually descending through space, ever moving closer to the earth, to your place on the earth, now joining with the "I" that is here right now, in all its present circumstances, illumined with the acceptance of the valuable Self.

Coordination

Once the challenge is recognized and accepted, it is possible to co-ordinate with it. To coordinate means to bring the different elements of a complex activity into a harmonious relationship, or to organize an activity so that the people involved in it work well together and achieve a good result. To coordinate with a challenge in ourselves means that, once having become newly aware and accepting of it, having become familiar with the challenge and having made "friends" with it, so to speak, it becomes possible to be in a productive and efficient relationship with it. One way to manage coordination is to determine what "need" or "unmet value" have we encountered in the event of getting our emotions hooked? It is helpful to identify the need.

To help with this, I suggest referring to the following list of needs to determine with which one we identify the most strongly. Be aware that not all needs are contained in this abbreviated list, inspired by Marshall Rosenberg, and we could identify others not listed here.

Empathy, Connection, Affection, Warmth, Love, Understanding, Acceptance, Caring, Bonding, Compassion, Communion, Spirituality, Sexuality

Autonomy, Choice, Freedom, Spontaneity, Independence, Respect, Honor

Safety, Predictability, Consistency, Stability, Trust, Reassurance

Family, Mutuality, Friendship, Companionship, Support, Collaboration, Consideration,

Seen/heard, Acknowledgment, Belonging, Community, Appreciation, Partnership

And the need for Purpose, Competence, Contribution, Efficiency, Growth, Learning, Challenge, Discovery

Order, Structure, Clarity, Focus, Information

Celebration, Mourning, Aliveness, Humor, Beauty, Play, Joy

Integrity, Authenticity, Wholeness, Fairness, Expression, Creativity, Honesty

Peace, and the need to be Grounded

As I consider this list of needs, in most cases, they relate to the need to be valued, to be seen as being valuable in the eyes of others, and also to be able to recognize ourselves as being valuable. "To be valued" appears to be the mother of all needs. Stepping back even further in considering needs, I see the need to recognize and value who I fully am. It is possible to have the highest regard for all of who I am, from the most primitive impulses to the divine incarnate. In the loving awareness of this, I begin to have freedom and choice over how I meet the world in my daily life, moment by moment.

Integration
Once identified, ask yourself if this need is familiar to you from sometime in your past. Consider any time from your earliest memories to the recent past. Take time to remember what the experience was. Who was there? What were the circumstances? Where were you? What were the feelings, thoughts, and physical sensations associated with the needs? In the next step of "Integration," you bring things together in order to achieve growth and understanding.

Having made friends with that newly recognized and accepted part of ourselves, it is possible to integrate that part into the already coordinated parts of one's self. Integration calls on the P, M & S (Pause, Marvel, Smile) map. Consciously recognizing the pain of disconnection from the "I," then inviting the "I" in and investigating which need has been discovered, and determining where in our biography this need was not met, it then becomes possible to

353

bring the dyadic dance to this part of our self.

Positive "relationality" begins in the micro relationship, the dyadic dance between parent and child. From baby to childhood, the young human being learns how to connect with other human beings by virtue of the quality of interactions that take place between child and parent. If the child is met with joy, awe, and wonder, it will reinforce the authentic expression in the child. The dyadic dance happens when the loving response of the parent invites the child to dance and delight, and vice versa, the child's loving response to the parent can evoke the authentic expression in the parent. There is a mutual spontaneous authenticity of being. There is a congruence between feeling and expressing, and thereby access to the true, authentic self is developed. There is a relationship of respect and reverence, a witnessing and reflecting back to one another the I/thou relationship. The unfolding of the child is encouraged, rejoiced in, and accepted. If the dyadic dance is impaired or disturbed, this could lead to uncontrolled behavior or regression in the child. What is authentically living in the child will change to evoke a response from the unhealthy environment.

With our imagination, taking our own inner child in our arms, for example, it is possible to give joy, awe, and wonder now. By taking time and imbuing the imagination with feeling and images, it is possible to achieve a sense of ourselves that was not freely given in the course of our biography. We have the ability to dwell and delight in joy, awe, and wonder now. With this imagination comes acceptance and the understanding achieved in the step of coordination. The "woundedness" from the primal wound is integrated into the whole. With the presence of the I affirmed through the tools of meditation, for example, and the support of the spiritual world acknowledged, it becomes possible to integrate an understanding of what steps can be taken to serve the world in my own unique way. I can greet myself in wholeness and meet the world with newly discovered energy to bring my gifts to the world.

At one workshop I was facilitating, a participant became fully aware that the unmet need she had been struggling with for many years in all of her significant relationships was the need "to be valued." She came to the conclusion there and then that, though its absence had been a source of great suffering in her life, she knew that the need to be valued related directly to her higher purpose in life. She realized that she would dedicate herself to not only finding and resting in her value as a human being, but that she would also work to help others do the same. What had been unrecognized in the shadows of her consciousness—that is, her own questioning of her basic value as a human being—had come into the light. As she recognized it, accepted it, and coordinated with it, she began a productive relationship with the importance of being valued, and she began the process of integration: valuing herself as well as seeing the importance to her life's purpose of helping others value themselves.

The "I" is present when it consciously is invited in. There are human beings who meditate and engage in consciousness practices to the point of living in constant connection with their "I." There are initiates who do the same. Then there are those of us who are growing in that capacity. The image of the school bus comes to mind and the question is, "Who is in the driver's seat?" Has the inner teenager grabbed the wheel, and in a fit of rebellion has the bus careening down a dirt road, now going off road with dust flying out in every direction in the path left behind? Then could the consequences of this behavior be painful enough, wakening enough to become fertile ground for the question, "What have we here?" "What have I (or the "not-I") done?" With these questions, comes the possibility of the entrance of the "I."

The following exercise fosters the integration of the "I." Using the "repeated question" approach and working with a partner, with a client, or in writing with yourself, the question is asked, "Tell me, when is your 'I' present?" When the answer comes, the asker says, "Thank you" then repeats the question, perhaps 10 or 20 times. The question can touch into the places in us that know the answer. The "I" itself has the opportunity to express itself. We can remember the times when we have felt whole, when our thinking, feeling, and willing was working in concert with the "I"; when the inspiration has come and we have heard it and known how to respond; those times when we have reached the "zone" in our creative expression or said the right thing at the right time.

This exercise allows us to become more consciously aware of when the "I" has been integrated with the working parts of thinking, feeling, and willing, offering us the possibility of consciously making time for engaging in more of those types of activities.

Synthesis

"Synthesis" can be defined as combining a number of different parts or ideas to come up with a new idea or theory. Here, with synthesis, it is possible to discover the Transpersonal Self. It is, in fact, the Transpersonal Self that can permeate the person and show itself in the whole person in a new way. The integrated, synthesized aspect of us is illumined by the Transpersonal Self. More of who we authentically are shines through, becoming available to us in the daily functioning of the middle conscious. It becomes the truth of who we are. The unmet needs and the new-found awareness of them and their relationship to the associated subpersonalities gathered in the course of our biographies take their rightful place in the integrated, synthesized whole.

It is now possible to have a conscious relationship with the needs we hold most dear. Out of freedom now, and in our relationship to them, we can decide if it is possible to hold that particular need a little less tightly. Perhaps our expectations of how the world should meet us with regard to a particular need, for example the need "to be valued," is loosened. We could begin to make a choice about how much investment we have in the expectation that others should show us our value.

In fact, the fear of isolation is due to being F.A.R. from our centered self. One wisdom is that when we are desperately missing someone or something, it is due to missing the essential connection with one's Self. The painful feeling of disconnection and isolation can be resolved by consciously choosing to be in close relationship with our own "I" being.

These ideas can be applied to the story of my own experience around feeling discounted in the scheduling of the women's gathering, and I can find some clarity and relief. My own "need to be valued" was at stake. These dear women do not define my value. That is the job I do when I make a conscious connection to the whole of who I am. The experience I had was due to the disconnection I had with myself. The pain woke me up to the disconnection and ultimately led me to an opportunity to be more profoundly connected to who I really am. Without the experience, I would still be living with an unrecognized belief that would take me on a ride, holding others responsible for how much I value myself.

From this new vantage point, it can become easier to connect to another source of our value. From the perspective of the benevolent infinite Presence, how could our value be denied? How could the value of any human being be denied or disproven? It could not be. From this place of harmonious inner integration and self-realization that psychosynthesis offers, there is a new possibility of right relationships with others.

The Call of Self in the Call of the Cosmos

If we had a clue about how precious we are, how much Love there is available to us, if we could just get plugged into that, all "things" we hold ourselves back from would be possible. We humans tend to look to others to prove our worth for us. We interpret others' intentions one way or another depending on how we are valuing ourselves at any given moment, often making ourselves miserable. I see many do this. I have done this. Is the primary Call of the Cosmos for us to know our immense value? One that is no greater or lesser than anyone else's value, just all of it incredibly HUGE, unfathomably so, more than we can imagine? The greatest activity of human life could be to know that and to reflect it out to others. The greatest failing may be to deny our worth and see others from this diminished perspective.

All else follows this primary Gift from the Cosmos. Our work is to nurture and allow the Spark of Light that is love, that lives in us, to grow. The rest is details.

Chapter 27

The Call of the Ecological Self:
An Experiential Exploration

by Valerie Silidker

We live in the midst of a deep awakening. In the past century, science has opened our minds to the depth of our interconnection with life and expanded our understanding of evolution and cosmology. We understand that we are part of a complex web of life that has been unfolding within this universe for 13.7 billion years (Swimme & Tucker, 2011). In fact, we are shaped by this journey. Simultaneously, Earth and all living beings are in great peril. It is undoubtedly the most fragile time in the history of the human species physically, emotionally and psychologically. Because, although we have this scientific understanding, our society continues to operate from a limited anthropocentric paradigm that touts separation from the natural world, and in this, we suffer.

Psychosynthesis has the potential to address this suffering and contribute to our collective evolutionary journey through reconnecting us with nature. It is a theoretical point of this framework to form ever-expanding unifying wholes, from the individual Self to the collective Self, by ultimately integrating the ecological paradigm within the psyche and supporting people to care for both themselves and our world. However, what can this actually look like in practice for both coach and client? In this chapter, I will explore this topic and offer several exercises that can support our deepening connection with a greater Ecological Self.

Over the past century, psychosynthesis has contributed to a vast understanding of the many complexities within our psyche as well as our interpersonal relationships. It has supported a deep awareness of Self by shining a light on our personal wholeness and integrating the fragments, or subpersonalities, which can create an identity that is too small. Here is an invitation to bring this profound work of psychosynthesis into an even deeper context. One that includes a rich cosmological and ecological vision of wholeness and interrelatedness; one that expands our perception of Self and inspires greater activation of will both in our individual lives and on behalf of our collective evolution. This is not just about diving into our complex inner world; this is about setting a deeper context for life and taking part in a greater movement, through psychosynthesis and ecological principles, for the healing and "wholing" of our world.

Take a breath.

Breathe into wildness.

In this moment, expand your awareness to be with Earth in its subtle and dynamic beauty and, through this, to experience your own.

At first, the wild movements: the sensation of the wind cooling the fierce sun on your face, tiny red-winged blackbird chasing the vultures away from his tree, tricolored heron hunting for fish. The more you watch, the more you listen, the deeper the subtle rhythms begin to move within you.

You feel yourself deepening, your breath deepening.

Take a moment to become deeply present to what is alive in you now.

You begin to notice an undeniable connection where your internal world expands and your body becomes larger, stretching out beyond your skin.

Feel the sensation; you are expanding, becoming more whole, feeling the world within.

The Earth is moving, and there is a rhythm that moves in you.

Close your eyes. Take a moment to experience the sounds and sensations within you.

Breathe deeply, and slowly open your eyes.

When we tune into the intimacy of nature, the idea of what is inside of us no longer feels like ours alone. We belong to the world. We see and experience our own sense of wildness reflected back to us.

Every cell in our bodies, the animal and mineral ancestors, the information woven into our DNA, the atoms and elements, the billions of organisms that dance in synergy together to make you, you, is of Earth. Beyond our individual self, we are interconnected with life. Everything has come from Earth, and this is not limited to just your physical body. Your emotions and thoughts also exist within this intimate, wild evolutionary dance. It is only in synthesizing these parts together that we recognize our true sense of wholeness.

When we have a thought or an emotion, all of life is participating in creating that thought or emotion along with us. We have been shaped by our entire ecological experience, both within us and outside of us. Our cultural identity, our cultural conditioning, our family dynamic, our empathic ability to feel with our world, our unexamined assumptions about the way we **should** behave or the things we should accomplish, all of these things and more contribute to our identity, our subpersonalities, and our emotional and intellectual response to who we think we are. Sadly, our current state of world has created some devastating effects on our psyche.

The State of our World and the Psyche

There is a movement happening in our world, bringing greater awareness of ourselves and our relationship to life. Though we are experiencing this new level of conscious self-awareness as a positive forward movement, we are also simultaneously experiencing the collapse of certain modern systems and a devastating effect on our psychological and physical well-being. Today, much of the human living environment has become paved over, mechanized, standardized and artificial, alienating us from our basic connection with Earth and suppressing the imagination. Many in Western society live fast-paced, unsatisfied lives, seeking out endless sources of stimulation and distraction leading, ultimately, to an inability to simply be. Depression, addiction, obesity, Attention Deficit Disorder, and more, have skyrocketed in both children and adults. Richard Louv (2008), author of *Last Child in the Woods*, has called this deteriorating psychological consequence from our disconnection with the Earth "Nature Deficit Disorder."

Cultural historian and theologian Thomas Berry said, "We might summarize our present human situation by a simple statement: 'In the 20th century, the glory of the human has become the desolation of the Earth, and now the desolation of the Earth is becoming the destiny of the human'" (Berry, 1978). Our world has become unsustainable and we know that that which is unsustainable, by definition, cannot last. Berry (1988) emphasizes this: "Such an order of change in its nature and magnitude has never before entered either into Earth history or into human consciousness" (p. xiii).

We are, fortunately, in the midst of a paradigm shift, involving a fundamentally new way of perceiving the world, the environment, each other, and ourselves. We are in a transformational moment in the history of the human species referred to by many as The Great Turning: a shift from the Industrial Growth Society to a life-sustaining society. This term was coined by David Korten in his book titled: *The Great Turning* (2006). The shift involves a movement to an ecological postmodern worldview that seeks to incorporate and transform modernist views to align with the evolution of our consciousness. Ken Wilber (1996) confirms this understanding with his view on the development of paradigms. He states:

> As the higher stages in consciousness emerge and develop, they themselves include the basic components of the earlier worldview, and then add their own new and differentiated perceptions. They transcend and include. Because they are more inclusive, they are more adequate. (p. 67)

In essence, the foundation of this emergent paradigm is based on connection and relationships and involves deepening or expanding our perceptions. It encourages us to expand our perception of the whole to be more inclusive and interconnected.

We now live in a period of transformation, when a new world is struggling to be born. The Western world is abounding with possibilities. Deep ecology, for example, provides a philosophical foundation for the formation of an ecological worldview that adequately represents our emerging scientific knowledge. Emerging psychologies, such as ecopsychology, have opened the doorway between nature and the psyche. Within the past few decades, Thomas Berry and cosmologist Brian Swimme claim that modern science has provided the world with a new ecocentric cosmology based on the Universe Story—the scientific understanding of the unfolding universe—within which humans can reconnect with one another and the Earth and find their place and values in an evolutionary/ecological context (Berry & Swimme, 1989). Thomas Berry calls this the New Story or the New Cosmology. This new, more expanded perspective, provides us with a renewed sense of our role as guides in the evolutionary process.

As psychosynthesis practitioners, we know that when we are unaware of certain structures or behaviors, they hold us prisoner and keep us feeling disconnected from our sense of wholeness. Yet, learning to see the structures within which we operate begins a process of freeing ourselves from previously unseen forces and narrow vision, ultimately mastering the ability to work with them and integrate them. This fundamental shift in perspective scientifically, philosophically, emotionally and psychologically, for both coach and client, absolutely is crucial if we hope to contribute to a greater evolutionary movement and support people to reconnect with nature through psychosynthesis. The theory is here; we now need to utilize the practices to incorporate this deeper sense of wholeness into our lives.

Integrating Psychosynthesis and the Ecological Paradigm

Psychosynthesis is an evolving transpersonal psychology. It offers tremendous potential for not only integrating subpersonalities within the whole personality of an individual, but also synthesizing the whole person within a greater ecocentric perspective as part of a more-than-human world. In doing so, it can support people not only in deepening their self-awareness, but the awareness of an Ecological Self and, ultimately, in the conscious participation of our collective evolution. This understanding can set our lives into a deeper context, fundamentally shift our personal meaning, purpose, and values, strengthen the will to act in our own lives on behalf of a larger vision, and, ultimately, contribute to the potential of a more connected, compassionate world. According to the founder of psychosynthesis, Roberto Assagioli (1965a):

> In spite of all contrasts, all oppositions and all negative appearances, the principle of interdependence, of solidarity, of cooperation, of brotherhood —that is, of synthesis—is rapidly gaining recognition. An increasing number of men and women are animated by the will to implement it, and are actively working within different groups and in all fields, outwardly unorganized but inwardly closely connected by a common dedication to the same purpose: the **psychosynthesis of Humanity**. (p. 6)

At its core, psychosynthesis offers maps as guidelines to support this integration. One of these is the Egg Diagram used to illustrate the different aspects of consciousness and the individual and collective unconscious. Our individual unconscious—higher, lower, and middle—is within the Egg and separated from the collective unconscious by permeable dotted lines, illustrating the seamless flow between these states. According to Assagioli (1976), the outer line "should be regarded as analogous to the membrane delimiting a cell, which permits a constant and active interchange with the whole body to which the cell belongs" (p. 21). He goes on to say that the "processes of psychological osmosis are going on all the time, both with other human beings and with the general psychic environment." Within this understanding, we can expand our idea of the collective unconscious to include not only human collective unconscious, but also the ecological unconscious, which contributes to our psychic environment.

From this perspective, we can visually see how our unconscious is interconnected to everything. Information is flowing both into us from our collective unconscious and from us to the collective. Everything is interconnected. This can fundamentally shift our state of conscious awareness to understand how we hold within us not only our own personal pain, but also the pain of the world; not only our own inner wisdom and higher qualities, but also the universal wisdom and intuition from which that springs.

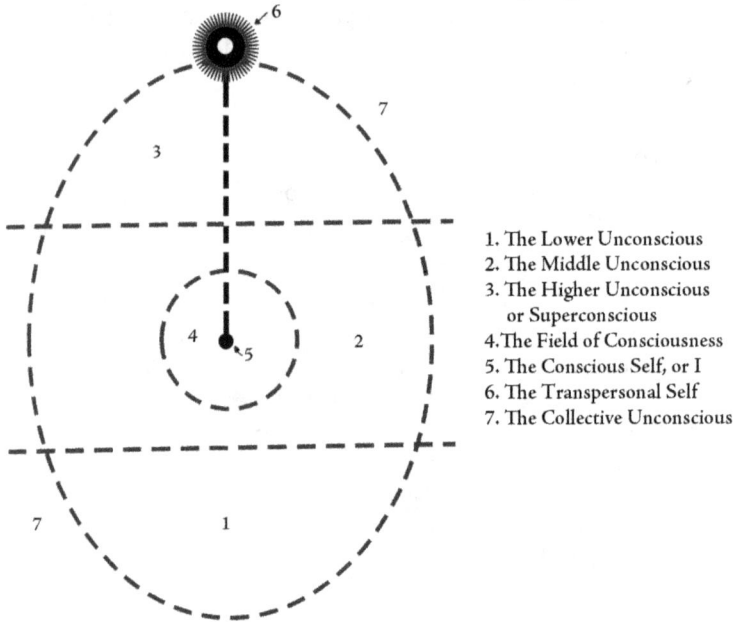

1. The Lower Unconscious
2. The Middle Unconscious
3. The Higher Unconscious
   or Superconscious
4. The Field of Consciousness
5. The Conscious Self, or I
6. The Transpersonal Self
7. The Collective Unconscious

I remember my first big heart-break. It was a paradigm shattering experience in my early twenties of recognizing how we treat other animals in factory farms, circuses, marine parks, etc. and the cruelty we inflict on these helpless ones. I simply had no idea. The truth is, I had never thought about it. Society had shielded me from this recognition until I finally saw the truth, and that reality changed me. My perception shifted, my values shifted, my purpose shifted; everything in my life changed from that moment on. I became a voice, an activist, an organizer, a connector, a lover. I began to feel more deeply with our world and to identify with my Ecological Self as the prime driver in my life. Because I fell in love with the higher quality of compassion for myself as an individual and with a greater vision for the potential of humanity, it led me to study mythology, ecology, deep ecology, ecopsychology, cosmology, and psychosynthesis. I became passionate about understanding our stories, our perspectives, our hearts and widening our vision of what it means to be human in this moment in time.

I believe many of us care about our world. We care about each other and this planet, and we want to make a difference. We are beginning to wake up, yet we can easily become overwhelmed by our personal challenges, our individual wounds, fears, or sense of inadequacy; and we become overwhelmed by the pressures of society and the state of our world. I have found, however, that when we embrace a larger vision of wholeness it can change our relationship to the things that may normally paralyze us or hold us back as individuals. It gives us a different context for living, and this changes our relationship to everything. What we really want are the higher qualities like peace, compassion, connection. When we can experience our pain for the world as our passion for justice, it shifts our perspective.

Feeling with our world is evidence of our interconnection with life. When these emotional responses are understood and experienced as a healthy response, our sense of identity expands and the mind, freed from its cultural trance, retrieves a natural state of clarity. Just imagine the insights and intuition that return once we reconnect to Earth; imagine the shift in our choices, our sense of purpose. We experience our relationship to Self, each other, and our world more clearly and live our lives from a greater vision. Our values become shared values that move us toward a more whole world, and we become part of a positive evolutionary force of collective will.

Insight and Exercises to Support Ecopsychosynthesis

There is much available to us as coaches and group facilitators toward integrating our work with this ecological paradigm. In fact, the work of psychosynthesis is already serving as a base for several ecocentric programs. Deep ecologist and systems scholar, Joanna Macy, founded a body of work called the Work That Reconnects (WTR). Based on ecopsychology, deep ecology, and systems thinking, this experiential group work explores theory and eco-therapeutic practices that move us through the emotional and psychology aspects of this ecological paradigm. Molly Young Brown, author of several books in psychosynthesis, co-authored with Macy the guide to WTR entitled *Coming Back to Life* (2014). Brown merges the work of psychosynthesis and WTR in her practice and for decades has been a huge advocate for bringing the ecological paradigm into the work of psychosynthesis. She pioneered a movement she refers to as ecopsychosynthesis, inviting the community to take a stronger position in this ecological movement in order to create truly meaningful transformation.

In *Reflections on Ecopsychosynthesis* (Firman & Klugman, ed. 1999), Brown invites colleagues to engage in this discussion from various perspectives. She reflects on the limits of psychosynthesis and offers expansive ideas for forward movement. She proposes that the "Self" described in psychosynthesis is related closely to the "Ecological Self" coined by founder of Deep Ecology,

365

Arne Naess. This Ecological Self can be understood as "a sense of self encompassing all of nature, all of life, and acting from this very inclusive perspective" (p. 8). Molly argues that psychosynthesis, even as it aims to bring together the spiritual and psychological dimensions, suffers from an anthropocentric perspective. She said, "The spiritual has often been treated as a transcendent aspect removed from the material world, rather than immanent within all creation..." (p. 9).

Another prominent voice in this movement is eco-depth psychologist "gone wild," Bill Plotkin (2013). Plotkin founded Animas Valley Institute, which wilds the work of psychosynthesis and ecopsychology through theoretical and experiential nature-based practices of wholeness. He incorporates subpersonality work as he guides people into the inner wilds of the soul with his work of Soulcraft. He also created the Nature-Based Map of the Psyche as a guide to becoming fully human. Plotkin adds his voice to the ecopsychosynthesis conversation.

My own experience as a Deep Ecologist and psychosynthesis guide focuses on group and individual coaching and weaves into psychosynthesis powerful tools from the Work That Reconnects, Soulcraft and ecopsychology. I have experienced profound breakthroughs with my clients using nature-based visualizations, experiential wilderness work, and deep self and collective inquiry based in ecocentric perspectives. I have found that the inner desire to engage the will and bring about personal change becomes magnified when it is done on behalf of a larger calling. It is fueled by a collective will sparked by the Call of the Ecological Self. This Call that whispers, nudges, and screams for us to awaken into a deeper awareness, invites us to do our inner work so that we can fully align our will with this collective evolutionary will and recognize our unique purpose toward the whole.

We are in a unique position as coaches, to work with those who are called to this inner journey of self-exploration and integration into wholeness. In psychosynthesis, we understand the Self as a center of contentless awareness and will, and just as we know our Self beyond the stories, we also get to know our Self through the stories that shape us in our own lifetime and beyond. The greatest evolutionary story of our time, The Universe Story, brings with it an expanded vision of what is possible when we align our self with our higher Self, which includes the Ecological Self, and live a life that is deeply meaningful, purpose-driven, and part of a greater vision than we may have even realized. We are called upon now to support the collective movement needed to take part in the Great Turning and consciously move us forward in our planetary evolution. In this way, psychosynthesis can fully support the individual, groups, and the planet in their process of unfolding.

Journey Deeper into this World

To support our work in bringing theory into embodied practice, it is important to deepen our own awareness. I have included several exercises and visualizations to support us. It is important that we experience them first as guides and coaches, so that we may become more present to our own connection with our Ecological Self. From this intimate understanding, we are better able to use these tools with clients.

These exercises are a great way to begin. They are sourced from psychosynthesis, the Work That Reconnects, and my own experience. May they support you personally in your life and in your role as a guide for others. As you step powerfully into this world, may you, too, be inspired to create your own.

The Blossoming of the Rose

This is a classic psychosynthesis visualization and, in my opinion, one of the best invitations from our field to presence ourselves as nature as well as universal energy. I have included it here, because I feel it is relevant to this particular focus.

1. Sit quietly and comfortably. Close your eyes, take a few deep breaths, and relax your body.

2. Imagine a rosebush, with many flowers and buds. Now turn your attention to one of the buds. The bud is still enclosed in its green leaves, or sepals, but at the very top, a rose-colored point can be seen. Focus on this image, holding it in the center of your awareness.

3. Now, in a slow movement, the sepals start to separate, turning their points outward and revealing the rose-colored petals, which are still closed...The sepals continue to open until you can see the whole bud.

4. Next, the petals also begin to unfold, slowly separating...until a fragrant, fully opened rose is seen...At this stage try to smell the perfume of the rose with its characteristic and unmistakable scent.

5. Now, imagine that a ray of sunlight shines on the rose, giving it light and warmth...Take a few moments to experience the sunlit rose.

6. Look at the very center of the rose. You will see appearing there the face of a wise being, full of understanding and love for you.

7. Talk to him or her about whatever is important in your life now. Feel free to ask questions about what is meaningful to you: life issues, direction, or choices you may need to make. Take the time you need to communicate in this way. (If you like, you can pause at this point and write down what happened, amplifying and evaluating further

whatever insights were gained.)

8. Now, identify yourself with the rose: imagine that you become the rose, or that you take the whole flower inside yourself...Be aware that the rose—and the wise being—are always within you and that you can get in touch with them and draw on their qualities whenever you choose...Symbolically, you are this flower, this rose. The same life that animates the universe and has created the rose is enabling you to awaken and develop your innermost being and all that radiates from it.

9. Now, imagine that you become the whole rosebush...Be aware that you are firmly planted in the earth, drawing nourishment from it...Your leaves and flowers are growing upward, nourished by the energy and warmth of the sun's light.

10. Become aware of other rosebushes, other plants and trees—all animated by the same life energy, all part of the same planet, of the greater whole. Take some time to experience this...Then, whenever you like, open your eyes.

11. You may want to write about what happened or draw a picture, paying special attention to your dialogue with the sage, and to any insights that the exercise brought you.

(Assagioli, 2000, pp.188-190)

Self as Earth

This simple visualization, written by me, invites us into an expanded sense of Self and allows us to experience the rhythms of life within us. Though you have read it earlier in the chapter, take time now to fully experience it.

Take a breath.

Breathe into wildness.

In this moment, expand your awareness to be with Earth in its subtle and dynamic beauty and, through this, to experience your own.

At first, the wild movements: the sensation of the wind cooling the fierce sun on your face, tiny red-winged blackbird chasing the vultures away from his tree, tri-colored heron hunting for fish. The more you watch, the more you listen, the deeper the subtle rhythms begin to move within you.

You feel yourself deepening, your breath deepening.

Take a moment to become deeply present to what is alive in you now.

You begin to notice an undeniable connection where your internal world expands and your body becomes larger, stretching out beyond your skin.

Feel the sensation; you are expanding, becoming more whole, feeling the world within.

The Earth is moving, and there is a rhythm that moves in you.

Close your eyes. Take a moment to experience the sounds and sensations within you.

Breathe deeply, and slowly open your eyes.

What did you notice?

Reference: Written by Valerie Silidker

The Web of Life

This practice is an invitation to reconnect with the interconnectedness of life. It was written by Joanna Macy for the Work That Reconnects.

Lie down, stretch out. Relax into the floor.

Feel your breathing in your lungs, abdomen. Notice how it glides in and out. The oxygen ignites each cell, stirs it awake as it burns in the metabolism of life. Extend your awareness deep within to feel this energy.

It is all around you, too, weaving you into the web of life.

Imagine you can see interlacing currents, like threads of light. See how they connect you with others. Experience the great multiplicity of strands, formed by countless relationships, woven of the work and food, the laughter and tears you've shared with others. They shape what you are, they hold you in place. Sense those interwoven threads, rest into them.

The web sustains your bones and blood and skin, concocted so intricately out of the food you have eaten, out of grains, vegetables, fruit, nuts. The soil that yields the grain for your bread, the boughs of the tree that bear apples for you. The hands that plow, sow, reap, gather. They all are of your body now.

Back through time this web extends: mothers, fathers, great-grandmothers and great-grandfathers, giving you your coloring and features, your gestures, your tone of voice.

The web extends back through countless generations, through numberless ancestors we share, all the way back to those with gills and wings. For it is of star stuff evolving that we all are made in the flowing of time. We are each a jewel in this vast net, that called us into being. Each of us an irreplaceable gem, sparkling with awareness, reflecting the world. Sound of gull crying over the sea, sight of mountain rising, colors of sunrise, scents of pine and loam, the excitement of a new idea, the melody of a half-forgotten song.

There is pain, too, coming in along the strands of the web: a friend with cancer, an oil spill coating the beach, an Iraqi mother weeping for her lost children. Do not shut them out, they live in the web of this planet time. Open to these sorrows, breathe them in, so the channels may stay open for the flow of energy and life and change. If we block the pain, we block the joy as well.

369

There is power in the flowing of this fluid net, love that has enriched us, and love that we give. Feel the caring and love that flow through you.

Open to the pulsing of the web, its murmurs, whispers, tugs. Through that vast network all forms arose, intelligence arose. It shaped you as it shaped the mockingbird and the deep-diving trout. You are of it, of it, even to the terrors we've unleashed now. Open to it all, unafraid, relaxed, alert. You are the universe knowing itself.

To all our brothers and sisters, open now, in this time of great hardship. You go now through a dark place, but you do not go alone. And you do not go without your own timeless knowledge of the dark. You come from it, it is behind your eyes, and we will look into it, together, until the dark itself is clear...and home. There is nowhere you can go where you're not held in the web that sustains us all.

Still sensing these connections through space and time, stir and stretch now, open your eyes.

(Macy & Brown, 2014, pp. 270-271)

Breathing the Tree

This guided visualization gives us an experience of interdependence as an evocative way to tune into connection with and gratitude for our world.

Take a deep breath and close your eyes.

Imagine that you are stepping into a lush forest.

Notice the smell of the damp soil and other earthy scents that fill the air.

See the sunlight dancing on the leaves, the depths of colors. Listen to the sounds of birds singing, the wind whispering through the trees.

As you step deeper into this forest, notice the way the soft earth embraces your step, the sensation of the ground beneath your feet, calling you deeper.

Allow yourself to wander, taking in the world around you.

As you find yourself entering deep into the heart of the forest, you come to a large old growth tree.

Take in the presence of this ancient One, several hundred years old.

You cannot see the top of this tree as it extends into the sky. You expand your arms and the base of the trunk is far wider than your reach.

You step forward and gently place your hands upon the rough textured bark. Deep grooves caress your hands and you tune into the energy of life flowing through this living being.

You become aware of your breath.

Inhaling and exhaling, you begin to feel as if you are being breathed.

As you exhale, you are aware that this tree is breathing in your carbon dioxide, you are breathing into this tree. And as you inhale, this tree is breathing into you; you are breathing in the oxygen of this tree's breath.

Stay present to this exchange of life. Breathing into the tree and being breathed into, the tree's breath filling your lungs.

Inhale...exhale...together. This interdependent dance of life.

You exist as one being mutually dependent upon the other for your life.

Take a few moments to breathe, together.

Staying with your breath, you gently bow to honor this exchange and give thanks to this tree for your life.

You slowly make your way out of the forest, feeling deeply connected and aware of your interconnectedness and interdependence with life.

Gently coming back to your body, your present awareness in this moment.

Open your eyes.

Write down any insights that you received from this journey.

Reference: Written by Valerie Silidker

The Council of All Beings

This ritual sparks the imagination, intuition, and other psychological functions to reconnect with the more-than-human world and remember our interconnection with life. It was originally written by Joanna Macy and John Seed. The Council allows us to break free from our anthropocentric cultural views and embrace and embody a wider vision of our Ecological Self.

The Council of All Beings is described below by Joanna Macy.

1. Participants begin by letting themselves be chosen by another life-form, be it animal, plant, or natural feature like swamp or desert. We use the passive verb, be chosen, in order to encourage people to go with what first intuitively occurs to them, rather than selecting an object of previous study. This way our minds are more receptive and humble, more open to surprise. When out-of-doors, we can wander off alone to happen on the identity we will assume. When indoors, some quiet moments suffice, as we relax and wait with an open, non-discursive mind for the imagined presence of another life-form. Then we take time to behold this life-form in our mind's eye, bestowing upon it fullness of attention, imagining its rhythms and pleasures and needs. Respectfully, silently, we ask its permission to speak for it in the Council of All Beings.

2. If time allows and supplies are available, we make simple masks, working together in companionable silence with paper and paints, twigs and leaves. Then, briefly clustering in small groups, we practice taking on the identity of our chosen life-form. This helps us let go of our self-consciousness as humans, and become more at ease in

imagining a very different perspective on life.

3. Then, with due formality, the participants assemble in a circle and the Council of All Beings commences. To create a sense of sacred space, prayers and invocations are spoken. Native American practices, such as smudging with sage or cedar, and calling in the blessings of the four directions, are often used here to good effect. When I am the guide, and speaking, of course, as my adopted life-form, I like to begin the proceedings by inviting the beings to identify themselves in turn, a kind of roll call: Wolf is here, I speak for all wolves. *I am Wild Goose; I speak for all migratory birds.*

4. Welcoming them all, I thank them for coming, and, with some solemnity, set the theme for our deliberations. *"We meet in council because our planet is in trouble; our lives and our ancient ways are endangered. It is fitting that we confer, for there is much now that needs to be said and much that needs to be heard."*

5. The council unfolds in three consecutive stages. First, the beings address each other, telling of the changes and hardships they are experiencing in these present times.

a. "The shells of my eggs are so thin and brittle now, they break before my young are ready to hatch."

b. "I'm tightly crowded in a dark place, far from grass and standing in my own shit. My calves are taken from me, and instead cold machines are clamped to my teats. I call and call for my young. Where did they go? What happened to them"

c. "As Lichen, I turn rock into soil. I worked as the glaciers retreated, as other life-forms came and went. I thought nothing could stop my work; but now I'm being poisoned by acid rain."

6. The second stage of the Council begins after most have spoken, and the guide invites humans into the center. Since it is clear that one young species is at the root of all this trouble, its representatives should be present to hear these testimonies. So, a few at a time, the beings put aside their masks and move to sit for a while, as humans, in the middle of the circle. The other life-forms now speak to them directly.

a. "For millions of years we've raised our young, rich in our ways and wisdom. Now our days are numbered because of what you are doing. Be still for once, and listen to us."

b. "See my possum hand, humans? It resembles yours. From its print on the soft soil you can tell where I have passed. What mark on Earth will you leave behind you?"

c. "Humans! I am Mountain speaking. For millennia your ancestors venerated my holy places. Now you dig and gouge for the ore in my veins. Clear-cutting my forests, you take away my capacity to hold water and release it slowly. See the silted rivers? See the floods? In destroying me, you will destroy yourselves."

7. In the third stage of the Council, the other life-forms offer gifts to the humans. Recognizing how dependent they have become on humankind, they would help this young species deal with the crisis it has created. As ritual guide, I might cue this stage by saying, *"Many humans now realize the destruction they are causing; they feel overwhelmed and powerless in the face of the forces they have unleashed. Yet our fate is in their*

hands. O fellow-beings, what strengths of ours can we share with them, what powers can we lend them?" With this invitation, the beings in the Council spontaneously begin to offer their own particular qualities and capacities.

a. "I, Lichen, work slowly, very slowly. Time is my friend. This is what I give you, humans: patience and perseverance."

b. "I, Condor, give you my keen, far-seeing eye. Use that power to look ahead beyond your daily distractions, to heed what you see and plan."

8. One after another, the beings offer their particular powers to the humans in the center. After speaking, each leaves its mask in the outer circle and joins the humans in the middle, receiving the gifts still to be given.

a. "As Mountain, I offer you humans my solidity and deep peace. Come to me to rest, to dream. Without dreams, you lose your vision and hope. Come, too, for my strength and steadfastness, whenever you need them."

b. "As Leaf, I would free you humans from your fear of death. My dropping, crumbling, molding allows fresh growth. If you were less afraid of death, you would be readier to live."

9. These gifts reside already in the human spirit, as seeds within the psyche; otherwise, they could not be spoken. Their naming brings forth a sense of wholeness and glad possibility. When all of them have been offered, the Council of All Beings is formally concluded. Then the assembled often break into singing, drumming, exultant dancing - releasing energy after the long, attentive listening. Sometimes the group just sits in stillness, silently absorbing what has been learned or writing in journals.

10. Care is taken to thank the life-forms, who have spoken through us, and to dispose of the masks in a deliberate fashion. The masks may be formally burned, or hung on a tree or wall, or taken home with us as symbolic reminders of the ritual. On occasion, at the close of a Council, wanting to stay identified with the other life-forms, we fancy that we are putting on human masks, the better to work for them as we re-enter the world of the two-leggeds.

Reference: (Macy, 2005)

Joanna Macy (2005) invited us to consider the Council of All Beings as a way of connecting with, and accessing insight into, our Ecological Self. As we come to a close, I invite us to consider that as well. What other-than-human being might choose you to speak on its behalf at the council? What would you represent of our larger world, and what gifts would you offer humanity in support of The Great Turning?

The part of us that allows us to be chosen by and speak on behalf of other-than-human beings is guided by our imagination and intuition, two powerful psychological functions for moving us beyond anthropocentrism and into the wisdom of our Ecological Self. You see, everything that we create in this world must first be imagined. To take part in the healing of our world, we must first imagine what that might look like.

In the council, when we speak on behalf of another being, we also access our intuition through our imagination as wisdom from the collective unconscious. This wisdom is always present within us, for we have been shaped by the same mystery that gave birth to the universe. In this way, the Council of All Beings is a profound invitation to tune us into our Ecological Self and receive guidance from our collective unconscious. When we cannot physically access the natural world or take part in a group ritual however, guided visualization offers us access to our inner world in very similar ways. Either way, these exercises help us remember our potential as human beings and see with new eyes a more whole and inclusive world.

Together, we can imagine a more connected and compassionate future, and listen more deeply to our collective calling. As we ignite our hearts and spark our vision, we become inspired to respond to this ecological call and take action on behalf of life. With greater awareness comes greater will. Psychosynthesis can help lead the way.

References

Assagioli, R. (1965a). *Psychosynthesis: Individual and social.* Synthesis Center. Available at http://synthesiscenter.org/articles/0116.pdf.

Assagioli, R. (1976). *Psychosynthesis.* New York: Penguin.

Assagioli, R. (2000). *Psychosynthesis, A collection of basic writing.* Amherst, MA: The Synthesis Center, Inc..

Berry, T. (1978). The new story: Comments on the origin, identification, and transmission of values. *Teilhard Studies,* (1), 1–13.

Berry, T. (1988). *The Dream of the earth.* San Francisco: Sierra Club Books.

Berry, T., & Swimme, B. (1989). *The universe story.* Clinton, WA: New Story Productions.

Firman, D., & Klugman, D. (Eds). (1999). *Conversations in psychosynthesis: An AAP monograph: Reflections on ecopsychosynthesis.* Amherst, MA: Association for Advancement of Psychosynthesis.

Korten, D. (2006). *The great turning: From empire to earth community.* Bloomfield, CT: Kumarian Press.

Louv, R. (2008). *Last child in the woods: Saving our children from nature-deficit disorder.* Chapel Hill, NC: Algonquin Books of Chapel Hill.

Macy, J. (2005). *The council of all beings.* Available at Rainforest

Information Centre, http://www.rainforestinfo.org.au/deep-eco/Joanna%20 Macy.htm.

Macy, J., & Brown, M. Y. (2006). *Coming back to life: Practices to reconnect our lives, our world.* Canada: New Society Publishers.

Macy, J., & Brown, M. Y. (2014). *Coming back to life: The updated guide to the work that reconnects.* Canada: New Society Publishers.

Plotkin, B. (2013). *Wild mind: A field guide to the human psyche.* New World Library, Novato, CA: New World Library.

Swimme, B. & Tucker, M. E. (2011). *Journey of the universe.* New Haven, CT: Yale University Press

Wilber, K. (1996). *A brief history of everything.* Dublin: Gill and Macmillan.

Chapter 28

The Bump-Set-Spike of Being a Psychosynthesis Coach: Lessons from the Sports Coach to the Life Coach

by Karen Herold

I am five feet four inches tall. There is nothing about my physical stature that would make you think I have springs for legs and can jump high enough to spike a volleyball let alone get my fingers over the net to block a kill from an opposing hitter. Volleyball showed up in my high school during my senior year, and of course I played, since I played every sport I could in high school. I was fortunate to have had a coach who had played college volleyball and I learned quite a bit over the course of that one season. I played rec ball through the local parks department for many years before my family came along. I would not describe myself as a high-level player, nevertheless, I spent fifteen years of my adult life coaching volleyball.

I coached many teams during that time, probably twenty-five or thirty. I began coaching in the CYO (Catholic Youth Organization) league for the school where my three daughters attended grade school. After a few of years of coaching CYO I was invited to coach Club Volleyball. I coached mostly girls, but also snuck in a few boy's teams. I coached all ages, from fourth grade, raw beginners to 18-year old's who were playing their final club season before heading off to play college ball. But my favorite age, by far, was coaching Girls' Club volleyball for 13 and 14-year-old young women.

Club volleyball is a youth competitive sports system that helps players to develop their playing skills. The club I coached for focused on working with highly competitive players who were interested in playing volleyball at the college level. Most coaches, as well as many sane adults, avoid coaching 12 to 14-year-old girls like the plague. The hormones are pumping, and the insanity can be real. But I loved coaching this age so much. At the time, I would explain that it was so interesting to see them trying on different personalities throughout the season, now I see that they were trying on **subpersonalities** to find those that would carry them through the teenage years and further. I felt honored to be allowed to be a part of a team with them. Even though I was the coach, I had an important position in their lives and I was allowed to see and hear about parts of their lives that they were not sharing with their parents at that point. I was often a listener, a shoulder to cry on, a guide.

It has only been recently that I have begun to see the training for **psychosynthesis coaching** that I received as a volleyball coach for 12 to 14 year-old- girls. It is not at all surprising to me that life coaching grew out of the field of sports coaching. Perhaps the first person to highlight the connection of a person's inner dialogue and their outer success was Timothy Gallwey. In his 1974 book *The Inner Game of Tennis* Gallwey talks about how in the game of tennis, the person on the other side of the net isn't the only one you are working against. Gallwey talks about the inner opponent, or inner critic, as the loudest voice that judges, criticizes and second guesses every move you take. Gallwey goes on to say that instead of helping you to play better, this inner critic voice creates a greater challenge by questioning every single play you make.[1]

In the state where I live, the Club Volleyball season begins with tryouts the weekend after the high school state volleyball tournaments, usually the first or second weekend in November. The tryout weekend is crazy. Each club has a tryout school gym and the goal is to form a team that includes experienced players in each position: setter, outside hitters, middle blockers, right side hitters and liberos (liberos are the defensive player that wears the off-colored jersey and plays back row only). The parents are shepherding their daughters from school to school, sometimes making it to four or more 3-to-4-hour tryouts in a single weekend. It is usually very stressful for all parties; the coaches, the players and the parents. What adds to the stress is that there are diverse goals for each party. The clubs want to field the best team possible. The players want to play for the right coach in the right club, but mostly they want to play with their friends. The parents want the players to either (a) have the best coaching to help them get the golden egg... "The College Scholarship" or (b) to play for a club that isn't horrible, but which also doesn't cost too much. Clearly there is a challenge here, there is a lack of alignment of **purpose**, and many un-named and conflicting goals and needs.

The team coaches watch the players as they are run through drills and through careful observation and presence to each girl, the coaches decide which girls would be the best fit for their team. They negotiate with players towards a

---

[1]https://www.lifecoachhub.com/beginners-guide-to-life-coaching/history-of-life-coaching pulled 6/4/18

very strong alignment of purpose, inviting the player to see this particular team as the player's best choice. The player then decides where she would like to play and must often convince her parents why this is the best choice, even in the face of parental obstacles, often involving the very real circumstances of financial viability for the family. The parents want what is best for their daughter but may have a different perspective on what that looks like.

Bringing all the parties to a shared understanding and commitment to purpose can be very challenging for any coach. Sound familiar? It sometimes seems like finding clients and having them commit to you as their coach is like fielding a volleyball team of teenage girls, especially when we are starting out our coaching career. Finding alignment, shared values about how to work together, but most importantly arriving at a shared understanding of the **Purpose** of your relationship is vitally important in the beginning of the coaching relationship. The Life Coach needs to know who can be part of the team: which clients will be a good fit, which are ideal clients, which clients will not work for this coach at this time. And certainly, the coach needs to know when the client should not be in coaching but is better off in psychotherapy. It's not often that a gymnast tries out for volleyball, but if she does, the coach will know to direct her towards a better fit.

The coaching staff at the club I coached for often laughed, pulled their hair out, rolled their eyes and shook their heads, as we all realized that we were at the mercy of teenage girls. While we were glad they were aware of their value and their power, it was also always a crazy week as we finalized the team. We took the team we were blessed with and, soon after, the season started. Similarly, in the coaching relationship we often have an interview session where the coach and client meet and assess each other. If we decide to work together we discuss all the details: the contractual details, the payment process, the appointment requirements. Then the first session arrives, and it is time to start, with coaching skills at the ready and a game of answering The Call of Self to play and win.

Perhaps one of the best coaches I ever had the pleasure of working with always said "I don't care who's on my team. Give me a team and I am going to coach them." That is the reality of the coaching relationship. We do screen our clients, but once we have agreed to work together, we get our clients right where they are. They may not be the (imagined) perfect client and we know they aren't a perfect human being, but they are **your** client and now it's time to start coaching. The lack of perfection (the client's and yours) is what creates the field, right?

The club volleyball season is long. The playing season starts in January, but practices start in December. There are three-hour evening practices, two nights each week and generally two weekend tournaments each month. The tournaments last one, two or even three days over holiday weekends. The last tournament is late June or early July. Deciding to coach a team is a big commitment. It means that you will invest your time and your mental, emotional and physical resources in the team and in each individual girl for seven months. It means that you will do your very best to help each player to grow individually and as a member of a team.

The similarity to psychosynthesis coaching is clear. When you commit to working with a client you bring "all of you" to the relationship. You bring the wisdom you have gained through experience, the knowledge and skills you have gained through training and education, and the unique attributes that make you the right coach for this person into each appointment. You commit yourself to working alongside the client to help her or him reach their goal and to live their purpose. You prepare for each session by checking notes from previous sessions, thinking about possible coaching tools that might be useful in the next session and then coming into Presence and allowing whatever needs to come into the session the space to arrive and be held. Whether it is seven months or seven sessions, you are present, fully, to the unfolding of the client and to the shared goal of a victory—whatever victory the client has set as a healthy and purpose-filled goal.

Every club season and each team is unique in many ways, but there are also similarities. One of the things I could always count on was what I named the "Do or Die practice". The beginning of the season is like a honeymoon. During this phase of the season the girls really like everyone on the team, the coach is the best they have ever had, the practices are fun and always exciting, and it is a "given" that this team is going to be really successful and go to the National tournament and probably be in the top ten teams in the country at the end of the season.

Then the first tournament arrives and reality sets in. Some girls play more than others, some players are getting annoying on the court, some players are getting annoying off the court, the coach is sometimes not-so-nice, the drills are getting old and maybe the team is not top-ten material after all. The players start showing up to practice unprepared to practice at their full capacity for the entire three hours. Practices always begin in the same way, with warm up and ball control drills. All drills have a focus and goal, which means the team continues in a drill until they achieve the goal. In this way, the girls are always playing under some pressure to become comfortable in a highly competitive environment.

There was a warm-up ball control drill that we did at the beginning of each practice. The drill included all the players on the team passing (bumping) the ball in a controlled way to other players and moving in prescribed patterns. The goal of the drill was to keep the ball in play for two minutes. This may sound like a big challenge but for these players it was an easy goal to reach… until the "Do or Die practice". The challenge of the drill was not passing the ball in a controlled way, as all the players were able to perform that skill. The challenge was for everyone on the team to stay focused until the goal was met. If the players attempted to perform the drill and they were not completely engaged and focused, and if they were subconsciously testing the coach to see if she was really committed towards reaching those goals, the drill could become challenging. How many times does a client focus on a change, only to be sabotaged by inside and outside obstacles? How often as coaches do we feel that shift with our client when they start to realize "oh, I may have to change in some way or confront something about myself, and that is hard?" How many times might we, as coaches, have to review the goal, evoke the will, and confirm the purpose, so that once more the client can step into their power in moving towards their ultimate goal.

For one team I coached, a team that usually met the two-minute goal for this drill the first or second time they tried at each practice, we ended up doing the same drill the entire practice because they could not reach the goal of keeping the ball in play for two minutes. That means three hours of the same drill. And then we started the next practice doing the same drill. Thankfully the team met the goal within five minutes at the second practice. As a coach, it was one of the hardest practices I ever ran. I **wanted** to give in, my heart was crying out to let it go. The voices in my head were clamoring to make me give up and it took all my **Will**, strong, good and skillful to continue to hold to our goal throughout those three hours. And throughout, I focused on the stated purpose of the client, in this case a team of girls. They wanted to be better volleyball players. I took a strong stance to remind them of that, by staying right where they were stuck, until they no longer were.

As hard as it was, it ended up being the best thing I ever did for that team. By holding them accountable to a goal we had all agreed was fair and within their abilities, I communicated to them that I believed in them, that I knew they were capable of it and that I cared enough to make sure that they believed they were capable of it. As a team, we talked about it extensively afterwards and it led to an informed decision on their part. When they first joined the team they all said "yea, we wanna go to Nationals! Sure, we'll work hard. We wanna win." After this experience, they realized the level of hard work and commitment it would take to reach their goal and with that knowledge they recommitted to their Purpose, this time with full knowledge of what they were committing to. It was a perfect example of turning their desire for a successful season into a Will-full decision. A decision that was fully informed by knowledge rather than an idealistic image of what they would like. They did in fact have a great season, went to Nationals, and ended up a top team.

The parallels of this story to psychosynthesis coaching are clear. Our job as a coach is to see our client as healthy, able, fully-functioning and with all the necessary abilities to take the steps needed to reach their goal, their **Purpose**. Having confidence in your client is vital. Communicating it in every interaction is vital. Believing that they can "get there" and reinforcing their belief in their ability is one of the most important tools we bring to the coaching relationship. Using accountability in a wise and thoughtful way reinforces for the client that the coach cares enough to make sure that the client also believes they can reach their goal. My commitment to "showing up", to my Presence, called forth that same act of Will by my players. The goals we ask our clients to commit to are the building blocks of reaching towards their goals. Each time a client faulters on meeting an agreed upon goal there is opportunity for deeper understanding and a stronger and more fully informed commitment towards Purpose.

Back to the 12-14-year-old volleyball players; What did these young women respond to? Truth telling and honest positive regard and kindness, the same as most adults. Teenage girls are usually a lot more unguarded about letting you know if they are not seeing these attributes, and they usually don't have the skills to say so in a kind way. Warren W. Wiersbe said "Truth without love is brutality, and love without truth is hypocrisy." Teenage girls can be brutal, but they do speak truth! As coaches, we strive for love with truth.

Sometimes it is **so** easy to see what a client should do. It would be great if you could just say "you know if you would just step up and do what you said then you would be living your Purpose right now". Sure, it may be true, but will the client hear it? And if the client hears it will she or he be able to make the change, or will they be devastated because it was said in way that didn't honor and respect the fact that they are trying? Clients come to coaching because it is **not** easy to make the change and/or meet the goal they have set. Sometimes the progress is painfully slow as baby-step by baby-step they chart a new neuropathic pathway through the brain and the emotions. Every volleyball player I coached had challenges, or rather opportunities for improvement. If they didn't they would have been representing our country playing on the National Team! They came to our club because we had a reputation for developing players through good consistent coaching. We kept coaching throughout the long 7-month season, year after year, never giving up on finding the opportunities for improvement and offering the steps for it. But in the end, just like in psychosynthesis coaching, it was always up to the player to decide whether they would accept the opportunity and take the steps to reach for what was possible. Our positive regard for our clients, our unfailing trust in their knowing the answers to their own questions, and our absolute belief in their ability to reach their goals along with our skills and the tools of psychosynthesis are the foundation that encourage our clients to reach towards their Call of Self.

As you can probably imagine, a team with 12 girls includes 12 distinct personalities and 12 different learning styles. One of the biggest challenges a coach deals with is figuring out how to communicate with each of the girls in a way that they can not only hear but can use to make the desired change in their playing. I intuitively understood that some kids were more cerebral, auditory, verbal, visual or kinesthetic when it came their learning style. And that made the difference for most of the kids. But there was always that other kid that I could just not figure out how to say something to in a way that would allow them to understand it and make the desired change.

Coaches have a name for this, we call it "coachability". There is the kid who you can give a coaching direction to, who seems to be very "coachable". She can hear it one time and immediately make the adjustment. And then there is the kid that you spend the entire season trying to get them to make a single change. As I look back from this vantage point of psychosynthesis coaching I can see that understanding the psychological functions would have been **soooo** helpful. I had some understanding of learning differences that I gained on my own by being aware of different learning styles. But my coaching was always based on the psychological functions that I had access to, the ones that I was most comfortable with. The players who could access those same psychological functions as I could were the ones who were able to learn from me. The **psychological functions** that I had no awareness of were the ones that probably would have helped me the most with those kids who couldn't "hear" me. The players I struggled with the most were the ones who understood and wanted to discuss the emotional aspects of everything. I couldn't connect with them in that way because that was not a strong psychological function for me. I could see how these players would lose interest when I couldn't "hear" the language that they were talking from. When these players would move on to a coach that was more adept at speaking the language of the emotional psychological function these players would often flourish.

There is another familiar way that life coaching feels like volleyball coaching. When I was coaching volleyball the team was always near to my conscious awareness. I was always thinking about what was working for the team: what we could work on in practice, how I could teach something that wasn't working well in tournament play, or how I could help a specific player to move to the next level in a specific skill. At the same time, I was also keeping in mind the team goals for the season, developing systems to make sure that all the players were getting tournament playing time, thinking about how much physical conditioning was needed, questioning the amount of rest the players needed and tracking the many school and social life influences. I was looking at the small picture of each practice and each player and at the same time the large picture of the team and the season. I was keeping bifocal awareness throughout.

I often feel that same awareness with my clients. They pop into my conscious awareness, along with some thought or exercise or tool to share at the next session and then they go back underground to my middle unconscious. It is like the egg diagram with the dotted lines between the middle unconscious and the conscious where ideas and thoughts bleep back and forth and along with them creative concepts, memories of tools and exercises, and new connections. All of them constantly moving into and out of the conscious mindspace. I always have an idea of what could happen at an appointment with a client, but it rarely happens the way I have tentatively planned. The process is very similar to volleyball coaching; the engagement with, listening to, responding to and questioning the client and at the same time the bifocal vision that leads to the inner voice questioning "is this working, is she engaged, what is her energy level today, do we need to increase or decrease tension, is she dialed-in and focused or is she struggling?" Always keeping in mind, the guiding star of Purpose, and then adjusting, listening, considering, creating, questioning, moving from one vision to the other, from one level of awareness to another, from one level of engagement to…Presence.

A word I would use now to describe the type of relationship my players responded to is Presence. At the time I would probably have described it as "all-in" or "completely invested" but those terms don't reach the depth of being-ness that Presence describes.

Almost all athletes have experienced the time-altering experience of "being in the zone". The experience is described as a deep sense of connection, a lack of awareness of anything else but you and what you are connecting to, a flow state where everything happens with ease and no struggle, like you know where the ball is going before it goes there, and your body just moves on its own, a feeling of calm and no worry. Artists describe the same experience when they enter in to the creative flow. There were times when I was coaching volleyball, more with some teams than others, when I felt that same flow state. I knew the players were in the right place at the right time and I had no worries about the outcome of the game or match. The feeling of rightness was more important than the result of a game, although I cannot think of single game that was lost when the team was in that flow state. I didn't know how to create that flow state, either as an athlete or as a coach. It just happened sometimes, and I could never predict it or plan it. But our practice and the movement of "bump-set-spike" was the form in which that flow was invited in. And I wonder, now, if this "flow state" is the effortless will in action.

Many years later I now can create the flow state, that effortless will, much more easily when I am working with a client. My meditation practice is immensely helpful in this, and I also know that my belief, my intention, my practice and my conscious seeking of "flow" has contributed to greater ease in reaching it. I don't have all the answers, but I do know that the interaction with a player or with a client is richer, deeper, more constructive and healing when it comes from this place of Presence.

In the club that I coached for we spent a lot of time and energy focusing our awareness on the fact that what we were teaching our players included lessons that were more important than learning how to bump, set and spike a volleyball. We realized that the true gift of a team sport was the life lessons that were learned from playing a team sport: lessons like the value of hard work, being a member of a team, becoming a great teammate, putting the needs and goals of the team before your own, as well as responsibility for time management, goal setting and focus, and becoming a good communicator with teammates and coaches. These lessons are the most important gifts we gave to our players; the ones that will benefit them for their entire lives. Our clients often receive the same type of gift. As they work towards their goals they learn about themselves and what limits them from accomplishing their goals. What are the habits, the self-limiting thought patterns and the subpersonalities that have impacted them in limiting ways? Working with a psychosynthesis coach leads to life lessons for each of our clients, life lessons that can help them to live a life of Purpose and Meaning.

So, what exactly is the "bump, set and spike" of volleyball and how does it relate to psychosynthesis life coaching? The Bump is the most basic method of moving the ball, and we practiced it over and over in every single practice. Passing the ball, more or less gently, from the forearm to set it up for the setter to have the opportunity to have the best chance for a perfect set, and then the spike, the vertical leap and full force swing that whacks the ball so hard and with so much velocity into the other team's court that a point is scored! Goal attained!!! Psychosynthesis life coaching's "bump" is many things, the creation of the alliance between coach and client, the movement of deliberation, in the act of will, after purpose has been established, working through the best way to get to that goal. It is presence and bi-focal vision. That was why we practiced this so often in volleyball. It leads to everything else. The "set" is just that, and in this analogy, it may be done by coach or client. It is the moment when choice gets made. The coach may set the ball, just when the client is ready to receive it and take that next step. The client may set it for themselves, moving into choice with a clear set up, ready to take action. The "spike" is the action: the leap and the use of strong force to get the ball over the net to score a point, passing through any obstacles that may be trying to block that shot. This is the client in manifestation, fully engaged with good, strong and skillful will. This is the moment of success: the next step; another point; the will in action, in service of purpose; the client directing the movement.

I am grateful that I realized early in my club coaching career what the most important thing I had to offer my players. What I realized is that the most important task I had as a coach was to love the girls no matter what. To love them in their junior-high hormone fueled exasperating-challenging-fun-craziness no matter what. The players who haunt me are the ones that, for whatever reason, I couldn't accomplish that goal with. My goal, my Purpose, is to never let one of my psychosynthesis clients have reason to believe that I don't love them. For me, Love is the Purpose.

Chapter 29

Psychosynthesis and The Martial Way

by William Burr

The Beginning

Outside, a soft rain began to fall, with a slow drip, drip from the eaves of the ancient training hall. The dim shapes of the nearby temple and archery court faded into the darkness, and a lost autumn moth, seeking shelter from the rain, fluttered around the single lantern, casting flickering shadows into the corners. Disturbed by the movement, my consciousness shifted briefly in amazement at my surroundings. Was I really here, with three other candidates for trial at the Great Shiai in Mitō, citadel of Japanese swordsmanship? The impassive features of our teacher Saito Sensei ("Sensei" – teacher) and the Master of our dojo, Aoyagi Shihan ("Shihan"–Master Swordsman) bore grim testimony to the fact that it was all very real. Sensing a disturbance in my zanshin (literally "situational awareness" or presence), Aoyagi Shihan's hands made a slight movement. The hiss of his sword as it cut a lethal arc toward my temple was accentuated by the stamp of his foot as he rose from the "seiza" kneeling/sitting posture into one of combative engagement, right foot forward.

Yes, it was real, all right.

These were the beginnings of a journey of over thirty years through the many pathways of the martial arts, ranging from "jutsu" forms—purely applied combat techniques such as street fighting, ninjutsu, krav maga, and Paul Vunak's (disciple of Bruce Lee/Dan Innosanto) Progressive Fighting Systems, through popular Japanese forms such as karate and aikido, to the lesser-known fringes of Chinese-style wushu such as Vietnamese viet vo dao.

The Martial Way

A brief word on terminology: The martial arts in Japanese are described by the term "budō", literally "martial way". "Bushidō" means "the way of the warrior"("bushi"). The Chinese term for martial arts is "wushu", while the popular term "kung fu" (or "gong fu") literally means "acquired skill", i.e. a skill which is acquired over time through consistent, repetitive effort or training. One of my favorite examples is the "kung fu" of sweeping the floor!

These martial traditions can be further broken down into "external" and "internal" styles. External styles emphasize muscular strength, speed, and endurance: The spectacular displays of Karate or Korean Taekwondo are excellent examples of this, as is Brazilian jujitsu or Muay Thai, the Thai sport of kickboxing. Internal styles, among the best known of which are Japanese Aikidō and the Chinese art of T'ai Chi Ch'üan, utilize the flow and interplay of energy in a combat situation: while attack techniques involving punches and kicks are still found, the emphasis is on defense through sensitivity and application of "Chi" or "Qi"—internal energy—to deflect an opponent, using their own energy and momentum to disrupt their attack, preventing further aggression through application of joint locks and holds.

In martial arts circles, it is said that an external practitioner can defeat an internal style when both are in the early stages of training, but over time the internal practitioner will gain the advantage. From my experience as a Psychosynthesis Life Coach, why this happens involves psychosynthesis.

Evolution of "The Way"

Proficiency in fighting technique was essential for survival in the constant civil wars of pre-Edo era Japan, with the concept of the classical warrior reaching its height during the reign of Minamoto Yoritomo, first shōgun of the Kamakura shogunate (1192-1199). However, the advent of the Tokugawa shogunate (1603 - 1868) unified the country under a single military ruler, imposing peace on the warring clans. In the process, society was placed into a straitjacket of strict social order, with clear and inviolable class distinctions between farmers, tradesmen, warriors, the clergy, and nobility. In this context, fighting men were bound to service of the daimyō, the regional lords, and were known as "samurai", literally "one who serves". In this peacetime environment the warrior class, prohibited from doing anything else and at the same time privileged guardians of an ancient martial tradition, suffered from prolonged inactivity. This began to lead to a general breakdown of warrior ethics and gave rise to an urgent need for balance between the civil and martial aspects of society. Unless the warrior fulfilled the role of moral guardian he was, in the opinion of the leading Zen, Tendai and Shinto thinkers of the time, an idler and a social parasite. A similar situation had occurred in China centuries earlier, where a succession of strong imperial dynasties and a flowering of various schools of thought dedicated to the search for appropriate principles and systems for living led to the evolution of a profoundly moral vision of the warrior's role in society and of martial arts in general.

The outcome of these processes was the transformation of the martial arts from a set of combat techniques into a "way" (Japanese "Dō", Chinese "Tao", 道) dedicated to upholding a moral society and, in the process, furthering the spiritual evolution of practitioners. In this form the martial arts have a number of intersections with psychosynthesis which are the subject of this chapter.

The Way of the Flexible Mind

The focus will narrow to Japanese Budō, and Iaidō in particular, as I have studied this path since the early 1980s. Although I gained black belts in other arts, "iai" (pronounced "eeyaee"), the art of swiftly drawing the deadly curved longsword of the samurai, the "katana", to cut down an opponent or opponents in the same motion as the draw, has always remained a centerpiece of my martial arts training. The reason for this lies partly in the fact that many arts or "dō" have evolved here in the West into competitive sports, such that tournaments and training more closely resemble those of purely combative forms. In contrast to other weapon arts (nunchaku, sai, Chinese broadsword, lance, etc) iaidō has as its basic premise the use of a lethal weapon to achieve "one strike, one kill" results. This therefore involves subtle concepts of timing based on an acute awareness of one's surroundings and the opponent's intentions, and the mental and physical flexibility to adapt to an emerging situation in either a pre-emptive or reactive manner. The characters for "iai" (居合) are interpreted to mean "a state of mental presence characterized by flexibility". Although less lethal substitutes for the katana are available in the form of "iaitō", or practice swords, the true art is the skillful use of a "Nihontō", or edged sword. A mistake with one of these in drawing or sheathing can mean the loss of a finger.

As a result, the practice of iaidō in its purest form is solitary, consisting of a series of actions and techniques forged over centuries in the desperate circumstances of actual combat and brought together in a simulated fighting sequence termed a "kata". In contrast to, for example, karate, where kata are also a fundamental part of training, the iaidō practitioner never confronts a physical or manifest opponent: the confrontation is always internal, between action and tension, between the practitioner's own "monkey mind" and the attainment of a state of wushin, "no-mind", where technique dissolves into a fluid reality consisting of what I call "dynamic immobility". The objective is to heighten awareness and skill to the point where the sword need never be drawn: moving toward the ideal of the internal martial arts that the "best fight is no fight".

While the proficient use of a deadly weapon may seem an odd way towards alignment with a harmonious and ethical state of society, the skilled iaidō practitioner is effectively confronting and challenging themself morally every time the sword is drawn. The exponent of iaidō does not view their sword as merely an extension of their hand. Such an approach would be simplistic, limited to a focus only on technique and to subsequently low levels of personal evolution. In classical budō the sword is seen as an extension of the mind, and in this way becomes an instrument which can lead to higher character development: when the mind and body are united harmoniously through the process of austere training called "shugyo" there is a development of personal character which manifests itself in terms of courage, patience, and dignity whether one is at rest or engaged in furious action. Training in this way to follow the path of self-realization reflects the primary purpose of the classical martial arts.

Psychosynthesis and Martial Training

Returning to a more general view of the subject, there are several aspects of martial arts training which may be viewed through the lens of psychosynthesis.

In most Eastern martial traditions with which I am familiar or have studied, the place of practice, whether it be a Japanese dōjō, a Vietnamese vo quan, or Chinese wuguan, holds an altar. In iaidō (and other Japanese classical martial traditions) this is termed the "kamiza", or "spirit seat", where the traditions of the school or "ryu" and the deity are resident and respected. In classical forms the entire dōjō and the relationships and movements within it are all relative to the kamiza. Where the layout of the dōjō permits, the kamiza is opposite the entrance, reflecting the concept that, "inside" the dōjō a subtle evolutionary process is underway. This process is further reflected in the tendency of most ryu to divide techniques into a series of phases of advancing difficulty and skill. The highest levels are the "okuden"—the "inner teachings".

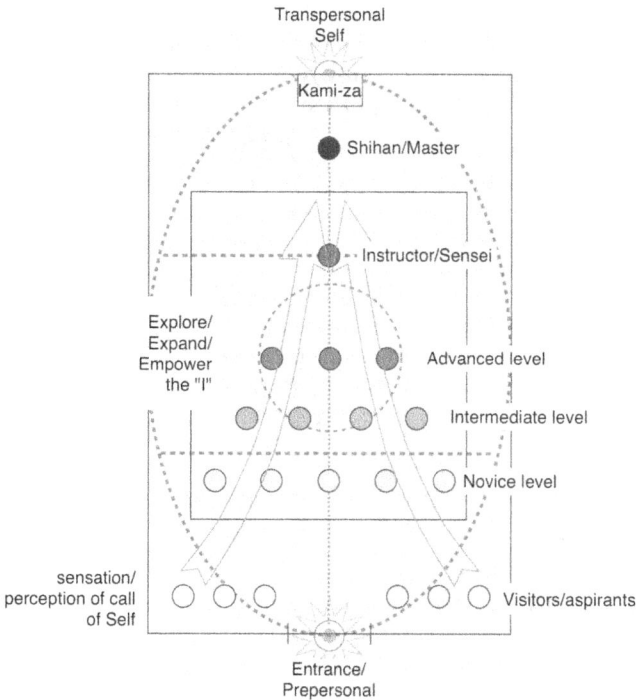

Parallels with psychosynthesis are found not only in the mental evolution of practitioners, but also find synchronicity with other elements of the dōjō: visitors, practitioners, instructors, and, on particular occasions, the

Master of the school who may be accompanied by advanced practitioners or master swordsmen/women (shihan). As seen in the illustration, the journey towards proficiency mirrors the cyclical evolution portrayed by the Egg Diagram. I clearly remember the struggling, awkward phases not only in the beginning of training, but at intervals thereafter: as my skills advanced, the depth of my ignorance increased, much as the higher you fly, the farther away the horizon is. This inner struggle would be mirrored in the actual setting, where beginners were in the back of the training hall, advancing only as their proficiency increased.

Some of the most arduous and effective training would take place in the center of the dōjō, corresponding physically and figuratively to the Middle Unconscious. Here the instructor would work with students individually in front of the class, as rote movements would begin to blend and flow harmoniously with practice, moving from conscious to unconscious, leading towards the state of no-mindedness— "wushin"— mentioned earlier, which is a pure state of content-less awareness and will. And it is here that the psychosynthesis concepts of the personal self (the "I") and subpersonalities are so pertinent to the martial arts. If we are still dominated by the drives of reactive, angry, analytical, aggressive, proud, etc. subpersonalities, the probability of a positive outcome in a fight diminishes. There are several reasons for this. The actions/reactions of the subpersonality are energy sinks: while adrenalin gives us a momentary kick, if the fight lasts longer than that it becomes a matter of strength, stamina, and skill, and as every martial artist will tell you, there's always someone stronger. A subpersonality gets in the way—the emotions involved cause us to "tighten up" to the point where antagonist muscles (for example, the triceps in an upper-body technique) are actually working against the protagonists (pectorals and biceps). This not only slows us down, all this conflict tires us faster. Modern biomechanical analysis of the role of "Qi" (bioenergy) in projecting force (Friedman, 2005) has shown that, in addition to whatever extracorporeal effects are manifested, such as the classic demonstration of blowing out a candle placed on the other side of a sheet of paper with a punch, a state of "no-mind" during the performance of techniques substantially removes the antagonist/ protagonist conflict. The potential this represents can be seen in cases where impossibly heavy weights are moved during crisis situations. Another potential liability presented by an active subpersonality in a fight is the "cookbook" response: "ah, he just launched a frontal kick at me, waddoIdonow?"

For these reasons classical martial arts de-emphasize lengthy, analytical explanations. The arduous training regimen is designed to foster a state of no-mindedness ("wushin"), consisting of situational awareness ("zanshin") and will ("tai no zen"/interception), but totally without contents (Warner & Draeger, 1982) that would only get in the way of the split-second actions necessary to survival: corresponding precisely to the concept in psychosynthesis of "presencing into the 'I' with pure awareness and will".

The Coaching Component

Drawing parallels between martial arts training and Psychosynthesis Life Coaching (PLC) is straightforward. I hold instructor's ratings in several arts, and the essence of this process is coaching. Students came to the school with greatly varying levels of awareness of why they were there, ranging from a simple desire to "learn the moves", through the enthusiasm of a recent viewing of Bruce Lee or Jackie Chan, to an inexplicable attraction to the nebulous concept of the "martial arts". It is relatively easy to begin martial arts training in the West: the student arrives, pays their subscription, buys the uniform, and receives instruction. The result at our school was a widely varying range of subpersonalities entering the dōjō: the hard case, the dreamer, the underdog, the top dog, etc., with a correspondingly varied degree of commitment to the process.

When I started training in Japan 35 years ago, the initial phases were designed to weed out any candidates not manifesting the qualities of determination, courage, and commitment necessary to show respect for the martial traditions of the ryu. After going through a series of introductions and interviews, I was accepted on a trial basis and spent the first month learning the various stages of pain as I sat in seiza on a hardwood floor for what seemed an eternity at a time and watched the class practice under the stern eye of Saitō Sensei. If I was still there after that, it was because all the menagerie of subpersonalities which had influenced the decision in the first place had receded into the background ("you gotta be kidding!...".."this hurts like no tomorrow!"..."where's the action??!!"). The toughness of the training was making it clear that my own expectations and visions of prowess meant absolutely nothing, dropping away to leave simply an intense focus on the present and the will to carry on. In the process my relationship with my classmates and my teachers deepened: humility, constancy, consistency and dedication to arduous training were met with commitment and loyalty.

The lack of stringent trials for applicants prior to the beginning of training meant that part of my job as an instructor in the West was sorting out the motives of my students. In our school, this process was "tough love"—while there was a commercial side to it (I remember my partner observing dryly that presenting the Master of our school with a chicken and a bottle of wine wasn't quite going to cut it...) we ran a program that included not only the expected external technique, but severe, classical internal discipline. The result was the initial dropout rate every season was almost a third of the class. But for those who stayed, the growth in mind, in body, and in moral fiber was...typical of a classical martial arts education.

Nurturing the student's belief in themselves and their ability to confront the severe physical and emotional challenges of arduous training was fundamental to this process. Most students arrive, as do clients in a coaching setting, with "presenting issues" typical of the problems and inhibitions associated with subpersonalities and general life patterns that may be helpful or dysfunctional. The capable instructor finds themself unconsciously and naturally in a role well-known in psychosynthesis life coaching—that of the external unifying center. The Psychosynthesis Life Coach consciously fulfills this role utilizing a broad array of tools and techniques to help the client claim their own essential internal unifying center, their Self. The effective martial arts instructor, displaying, what in psychosynthesis coaching is termed "congruence" by setting both a technical and behavioral example, follows a similar path, adopting an approach that is both directive (teaching and training of technique) and receptive, opening space, through meditation and emphasis on "wushin", for the true Guide—the Self of the student, to emerge and express itself.

The student, like the coaching client, has to be continually invited into an ever-expanding series of emerging challenges. Meeting these challenges, overcoming fear and resistance, quieting the "monkey mind", and building physical and mental prowess in martial arts training are a process of exploring, expanding, and empowering the "I". Where exceptional instruction in the martial arts stands out is recognition of the existing dignity and potential of the student, while constantly moving the "horizon" farther out. The exceptional coach embodies this same orientation.

Another trait very commonly found among high level practitioners and teachers, coaches, and other helping professionals, is humility. Whether martial arts instructor or psychosynthesis coach, the qualities of presence, simplicity, humility, commitment, consistency, courage, and wisdom will all contribute to the formation of the internal unifying center in our students and clients, as they internalize and strengthen, within themselves, these same values.

Epilogue

Inherent in this description of skills and traits is the fact that the process of growth, in any field of endeavor, is open-ended: there is no point of arrival. Whereas my progress was driven by technique and stamina years ago, the inevitable limits of physical development prompted a shift in emphasis from external styles dominated by speed, power, and timing, to the internal world of sensitivity, flexibility, and energy. Metaphorically, it's as if a passage through the turbulence of a raging waterfall has now entered a deep, quiet pool. Subpersonalities continue to be an issue with demands and expectations, but the quiet space inside where technique dissolves into awareness and will is growing with practice, constancy, and commitment. Another fascinating aspect is the feeling of living the Way, whether donning the uniform and practicing as the sun sets behind the Western mountains, sitting in presence with a coaching client, or living the small events of everyday life. The Way may have been that of the sword, the staff, or the empty hand: the attainment, through the martial arts, of a state of dynamic immobility, a state of pure awareness and will, without content, the experience of self—is yet another waypoint on the journey of self-realization.

The road goes ever onward. While the true Grand Masters I have known have come from different cultures and followed different paths on the Way, the one comment they all made which was identical was simply: "I am merely a student of the martial arts".

Part 6

Past, Present & Future

From the Eternal
Out of the past
In the present
For the future
　　　—Roberto Assagioli

Editor's Note:

As we come to our last section, I invite you to touch the deep well of psychosynthesis through getting to know Dr. Roberto Assagioli. His life's story is also the story of everything he created and of his intention to "seed" psychosynthesis into a future that he would not see. As psychosynthesis moves firmly into the field of life and business coaching, and its many variants, we see the essential truths held in psychosynthesis theory and practice. And they take us into this new work, with a "reverence" that we see expressed in our last chapter.

Chapter 30

Roberto Assagioli: A Multifaceted Life

by Catherine Ann Lombard

When World War I erupted, Roberto Assagioli (1888-1974) had recently graduated as a medical doctor and was living in Florence. Not long afterwards in 1915, Italy reluctantly entered the war, one of the bloodiest and deadliest conflicts in history, and the 28-year-old was called into military service as a medic. As a lieutenant-doctor, Assagioli served at the military hospital in Ancona, Italy, as the vice-director of its neurological center. However, he was required to periodically venture into the field where doctors were typically supplied with the minimum of provisions—gauze, some surgical instruments, grappa and cognac as anesthetics, and morphine to relieve the pain of only the most desperately wounded (Bonetti & Nataloni, n.d.).[1] To protect himself, Assagioli carried a gun—but, one that would never fire a shot—as his "pistol" was carved out of soap and painted black (Giovetti, 1995).

Twenty-five years later, Assagioli would face yet another World War. Instead of a young man, he was nearly 53 years old, married and a father. As one of the first psychoanalysts in Italy, Assagioli had established himself as medical doctor in Rome, specializing in nervous disorders, and was known as "the doctor who performs miracles" (Lunelli, 1991). For the preceding decade, Assagioli's vision of the human psyche, one that included a spiritual dimension, had successfully been promoted through his first Institute of Psychosynthesis, established in 1926. His work was being published in Italian, German, French, and English, and he had traveled for the first time to the United States. During the 1930s, the threads of Assagioli's life seemed to have synthesized into a fine tapestry of personal authenticity and professional success, enabling him to employ his multiple skills and talents while simultaneously providing the highest value and service to others (Esposito, 2008).

---

[1]Note that all translations from Italian are mine.

At the same time, political darkness and uncertainty was looming over Europe. Jewish-born, Assagioli was soon subject to Mussolini's racial regulations, modeled on the Nazi Nüremberg laws, which limited him and his work in countless ways. After nearly 35 years of participating in its meetings and writing for its various publications, Assagioli chose to resign from the Italian Theosophy Society hoping that the organization might avoid retaliation from the fascist regime (Esposito, 2008). But this act was to no avail. In 1938, the society was dissolved by the regime for refusing to adopt its imposed racist laws. That same year, Assagioli's own institute was also shut down (Rosselli, 2012).

Then one August evening in 1940, while Assagioli was quietly working in the study of his country villa, aptly called "Villa Serena," three policemen arrived and entered his home. Briefly questioned, Assagioli was handed papers that stated his crimes and he was whisked away in a police car (Lunelli, 1991). After traveling all night by train to Rome, upon his arrival, he was interrogated, handcuffed, strip-searched, and ultimately imprisoned for "praying for peace and inviting others to join, along with other international crimes" (Assagioli, 2016). In the end, Assagioli was placed in a solitary cell, without knowing when, if ever, he might be released.

And yet he decided there and then to assume an attitude of:
wholehearted, generous acceptance. Not a passive, sad "resignation," but a positive/serene acceptance of an unavoidable condition—an active search of the best way of utilizing in the fullest measure the opportunities offered by the new situation. (Assagioli, 2016, p. 21, emphasis in original)

Despite his frail health, the poor food, his barred cell, and the uncertainty before him, Assagioli came to the clear realization that he was actually free. Later in his book, *Freedom in Jail* (Assagioli, 2016), he eloquently wrote about having the freedom to choose which attitude to take—from self-pity to passive vegetation, martyrdom to consuming anger, humor to experimental inquisitiveness. Perceiving and accepting the power of his inner freedom, Assagioli (2016) wrote about the inherent privileges and responsibilities this freedom held—for himself, others, life itself, and God.

When finally released after spending a month in jail, Assagioli would describe his time in prison as "very interesting and useful" (Lunelli, 1991). He never uttered one word of bitterness even after he and his family were forced to "play hide-and-seek" in the Catenaia Alps from Nazi persecution for several months, his beloved Villa Serena was ransacked and damaged by canon fire, and many of his personal notes, writings, and books were destroyed. Instead, Assagioli (2016, pp. 83-87) described his trials in humoristic footnotes in a collective letter to friends, including Carl Gustav Jung.[2] In this same letter, written soon after the war, Assagioli said he had "an inner calling to carry out my small part in the big and joyful task of individual, national, and worldwide renewal" (2016, p. 87).

These stories about Roberto Marco Grego Assagioli anchored in the last century's World Wars perhaps best exemplify his visionary genius. Throughout his lifetime, Assagioli was able to live creatively while expertly holding, balancing, and ultimately synthesizing the polar tensions that life continually presented him. Not only did he envision a truly open model of the human psyche that included all aspects and dimensions of humanity, but his own life exemplified the synthesis of difference. One of his favorite sayings was "never **either/or** but **both/and**" (Rosselli, 2012, p. 16, emphasis in original).

Assagioli considered psychosynthesis to be an attitude of integration and synthesis of all fields of life, with the aim to harmonize the conflicts within and between our body, emotions, thoughts, will, and spiritual experiences. We live in a world that consists of a multitude of polarities that we all need to learn to bring into balance and ultimately synthesize. By definition, a polarity implies two items that are different to the point of being opposite. How well we balance these opposites—in our outer and inner worlds—is fundamental to our subjective experience, physical and spiritual energy, and inner peace. Assagioli (2011) stated that:

> Psychosynthesis…is above all a dynamic, one could say a dramatic, concept of the psychic life as a struggle between the multiplicity of rebellious and contrasting forces and a unifying Center that tends to dominate, harmonize, and employ them in the most useful and creative ways. (p. 15)

The previously mentioned stories about his attitude during both World Wars demonstrate Assagioli's ability to manage a number of deeply profound polarities: war and peace, external activity and inner serenity, life and death. Perhaps one of his favorite techniques for synthesizing opposites was humor. Talking about his arrest and imprisonment in a 1960 interview, Assagioli said that being put into a solitary cell greatly pleased him because the privacy offered "a welcome opportunity for a spiritual retreat." He then recalled: "When three times each day the guards came to inspect carefully my cell and find out whether I had tried to saw the bars of the window, I could scarcely refrain from laughing" (Medlock, 1960). His singular use of humor is well documented in his beloved essay, "Smiling Wisdom" (Assagioli, 1946) in which he describes the spiritual value of laughter.

---

[2] This letter is dated September 1944.

Clearly, balancing polar energies, both inwardly and outwardly, is essential to psychosynthesis. Assagioli (1965) wrote that the human personality has a number of principal polarities, including: body–soul; conscious–unconscious; lower unconscious–superconscious; extraversion–introversion; aspiration–inspiration; and "heart" (Eros)–mind (Logos). The process of balancing and synthesizing opposites is a method of psychosynthesis, which he described as:

> …analogous in a certain sense to a chemical combination: for example, the absorbing of two elements into a higher unity endowed with qualities differing from that of either of them. For the individual, it amounts to the formation or reconstruction of a new personality—coherent, organized and unified—around a higher center. (Medlock, 1960)

Figure 1.
Spiritual Acceptance

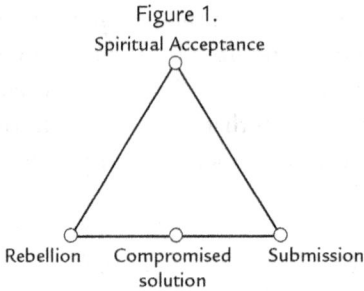

Rebellion   Compromised   Submission
              solution

Assagioli (1965) often used triangular diagrams to depict how synthesis "transforms, sublimates and reabsorbs the two poles into a higher reality" (p. 11). Figure 1 is a diagram in which Assagioli (1965, p. 13) shows a polarity that perhaps best depicts his experience once conscripted into war and later sent to jail. On the right side is the act of 'submission' and on the left 'rebellion,' the former being a passive loss of will and the latter a willful act of aggression. In the center sits a 'compromised solution'—a legitimate field of action that combines and neutralizes each opposite in which neither one is dominant. In both World Wars that Assagioli faced—the first as a military medic needing to carry a gun and the second as a political prisoner—he sought a 'compromising solution' that is, a soap pistol and the decision to use his time in jail as a retreat. Beyond these compromised solutions, we also know from his personal reflections in *Freedom in Jail* that Assagioli (2016) was able to transmute and transform these opposite poles into the higher unity of 'spiritual acceptance.'

Synthesizing Western and Eastern Philosophy

While dramatic, Assagioli's two war experiences only reflect a single facet of his life's journey towards synthesis. As evident in some of his earliest writings, he believed that the convergence of Western and Eastern philosophy was paramount to the development of human consciousness. Brought up in Venice in "a cultured upper-middle-class Jewish family," Assagioli received a full classical Western education, including five years of Greek and eight of Latin (Hardy, 1987, p. 11). He was fluent in French, English, and German and studied Russian irregularly "during boring university classes" (Assagioli, 1992, p. 13). Assagioli recognized the influence of Platonic ideas on his formulation of psychosynthesis, including Plato's discourses on awakening, the context of the soul, and the possibility of harmony within the individual and the world (Hardy, 1987).

Besides Plato, Assagioli was greatly influenced by (as well as fond of) Dante Alighieri's *Divine Comedy*. Dante, according to Assagioli, was "one of the greatest poets, but also one of the most aware, the most fully conscious" (Caldironi, 2004, p. 127). Like most Italians, he would have grown up studying the epic 14th century poem in school, and Assagioli's archives clearly indicate that he studied the *Divine Comedy* in great detail. Later in life, he would sometimes quote certain Cantos to his own psychosynthesis students (P. Ferrucci, personal communication, 2016).[3] Moreover, in his writings about polarities, he cites Dante's famous expression Canto: *"Luce intellettual, piena d'amore"* ("The intellectual light, full of love;" *Paradise* XXX: 40) as an example of the synthesis of Eros and Logos (Assagioli, 1965). One can easily align Dante's literary, philosophic, and theological masterpiece to Assagioli's own vision of the human psyche, better known as the "egg diagram" (See page 8). Dante's pilgrimage through Hell is a symbol of his analytical exploration of the lower unconscious, his ascent up the mountain of Purgatory indicates the process of purification and the gradual raising of consciousness, and his visit to Paradise depicts various superconscious experiences towards the alignment of the I-Self connection (Lombard & den Biesen, 2014). As Assagioli (2000) wrote: "the central symbolic meaning of the *Divine Comedy* is a wonderful picture of a complete psychosynthesis" (p. 186).

These great Western writers and philosophers—Plato and Dante—were only two of the many dozens of writers, poets, scientists, and mystics that Assagioli studied, contemplated, savored, and felt inspired by. He was a great scholar, and approximately 3000 of his books are now curated in his former Florentine home where the Psychosynthesis Institute of Florence operates today. Assagioli loved his books, and when he and his wife would escape Florence during the summer for cooler temperatures at their country villa, he would often fill up his car with so many books that his wife barely had a place to sit (R. Giacomini, personal communication, June 2012). Leafing through his books today, one can see that they are well studied. Many pages are marked

---

[3]According to Piero Ferrucci, Assagioli would often cite one particular line to his students: *"Messo t'ho innanzi: omai per te ti ciba"* ["I put the food out; now you feed yourself."] (*The Divine Comedy, Paradise* X: 25).

with underlined and circled words, and penciled notes appear in the margins. In the back of his books, Assagioli would often make his own index of topics that he found pertinent to psychosynthesis.

In addition to Western thought, Assagioli notably studied and was influenced by Eastern culture, philosophy, and religion. His earlier articles in *Leonardo* (founded in 1903) and *La Voce* (founded in 1908), two prominent literary journals to which he contributed (also financially), reveal his wide breadth of interests, including the American New Thought movement, Hindu as well as Catholic mysticism, Romantic poets, and the works of psychologist Edward Carpenter and French poet philosopher Han Ryan. The notes he made for his book *Freedom in Jail* (2016) alone cross countries, topics, and religions to include an impressive array of psychological and spiritual literature, such as: Count Hermann von Keyserling, the founder of the School of Wisdom; theosophist Alice Bailey; psychiatrists Carl Gustav Jung, Ferdinando Cazzamalli, Francesco de Sarlo, Alfred Adler and William James (to name a few); Christian mystics Jean Pierre de Caussade, John Chapman, and Evelynn Underhill; Buddhist mystics Dwight Goddard and Bhikshu Wai-Tao; esotericist P. D. Ouspensky; and classical writers such as Epictetus, Augustinus, and Luke the Gospel writer.

Assagioli also explored Jewish mysticism including the writings of Martin Buber, with whom he corresponded regularly, and Gershom Scholem. Similar to Dante's *Divine Comedy*, the Kabbalistic diagram of the Sephirot, which represents humankind's relationship to God, can also be aligned with the 'egg diagram' in psychosynthesis (Hardy, 1987). Other Kabbalistic thinking that parallels psychosynthesis theory is the fact that they both emphasize the Will and are concerned with developing personal self-knowledge and awareness. In addition, both approaches urge us to ultimately synthesize Love and Will. In one of the thousands of notes curated in Assagioli's archives, he cites United States Orthodox Rabbi Leo Jung: "One of the fundamental doctrines of the Kabbalah is the miraculous power of love" (Assagioli, n.d.b).[4]

In Assagioli's personal life, one can also see the influences of Eastern and Western perspectives. He was Jewish-born, but his mother was a theosophist, allowing him to encounter spiritual and esoteric knowledge early in this life. In 1922, he married Nella Ciapetti (1893-1973), who was Roman Catholic and also an active theosophist, writing articles for the journal *Ultra* (to which he also contributed) and lecturing on "Maternal Spirituality." From 1926 to 1930, the Assagiolis held theosophical meetings in their private home in Rome (Esposito, 2008). While at first it may seem as if Assagioli's varied interests

---

[4]His citation is from Leo Jung, Ed. *Judaism in a Changing World*, The Jewish Library Series. 4. New York: Oxford University Press, 1939, p. 263

were a mélange of beliefs, he was able to unite them through psychosynthesis into a unified vision. While he believed in karma and reincarnation, he often referred to stories about Francis of Assisi (Lombard, 2016), and always remained interested in Jewish culture, subscribing to Jewish newspapers and belonging to Jewish organizations during most of his lifetime (Hardy, 1987). He was known to practice hatha yoga, raja yoga, and various types of meditation, and for many years, Assagioli held lectures and led group meditations in his Florentine home. He published articles in both Italian and English about accompanying Rabindranath Tagore, the Bengali poet and Nobel Prize winner, during his visit to Italy in 1926. Photographs show him conversing with Lama Govinda in Sardinia in 1972 (Berti, 1988) and visiting with the Benedictine monastic community of Camaldoli in the Casentino mountains outside of Florence (Maraghini, 2016). Perhaps Assagioli's personal and spiritual synthesis of his myriad of beliefs is best summed up by his statement: "Psychosynthesis has elements of oriental thought, but does not adhere to any specific oriental doctrine. It also derives much from Christianity…and the ideas of Plato. The range of psychosynthesis extends to all that is good, wherever it might be" (Caldironi, 2004, p. 53).

Synthesizing Science and Spirituality

As a medical and psychiatric doctor, Assagioli was a trained scientist, receiving his degree in 1910 from the University of Florence. Having studied neurology and psychiatry, Assagioli included in his dissertation a critique of psychoanalysis. While no letters between Assagioli and Sigmund Freud remain, we know that they did correspond based on a letter Freud wrote to Carl Gustav Jung noting that the young scholar's German was "impeccable" (McGuire, 1974). Between 1907-1909, Assagioli spent time at the Psychiatric Clinic at Burghölzli, University of Zürich, where he came into contact with psychoanalytic theory and worked directly with Jung and Eugen Bleuler, famous for his discovery and work on schizophrenia (Rosselli, 2012). Assagioli met with Jung several times over his lifetime, during which they had "delightful talks." About Jung, Assagioli said in an interview in *Psychology Today*, "Of all modern psychotherapists, Jung is the closest in theory and practice to psychosynthesis" (Keen, 1974).

Like Jung, Assagioli was a scientist and, at the same time, an esotericist. Both had interests in astrology, alchemy, telepathy, other paranormal activities, and symbolism. Assagioli repeatedly stated that his principles and methods were based on solid personal experience and that the superconscious does not need to be demonstrated but is a fact of consciousness that contains its own evidence and proof within itself (Haronian, 1976). His explorations, even his most esoteric, were viable approaches to understanding the structure, dynamics and contents of the unconscious psyche, and hence, all pertinent to his professional work as a psychosynthesis psychologist and scientist.

One of the distinguishing concepts of psychosynthesis is that spiritual drives and urges are viewed as being as real and fundamental as, for example, sexual and combative drives. This idea is far removed from Freud's belief that spiritual experiences are merely repressed sexual urges or a regression to the postnatal stage of development. Another unique concept of psychosynthesis is that it can develop along two distinct paths as **personal psychosynthesis** or **spiritual psychosynthesis**. The ultimate goal of personal psychosynthesis is to continually harmonize and integrate all contrasting, partly undeveloped, and uncoordinated conscious and unconscious functions to the point where we fully recognize our responsibilities in this world and appreciate others. Spiritual psychosynthesis aims to integrate material from the higher unconscious into aspects of our personality. Persons who undertake spiritual psychosynthesis begin to transform their behavior and attitude, becoming more compassionate and inclusive and less controlled by unconscious drives such as greed or rage. It is important to note that personal psychosynthesis alone can be satisfactory for many individuals and a worthy endeavor in itself. For some, however, personal psychosynthesis is not enough. These individuals also long for spiritual psychosynthesis, which allows them to relate to their higher urges and grow toward greater realization of their spiritual essence.

Throughout his life's work, Assagioli insisted that psychosynthesis is both scientific and spiritual. For Assagioli (2000), the word "spiritual" means "all states of awareness, all the functions and activities which…[possess] values such as the ethical, the esthetic, the heroic, the humanitarian, and the altruistic" (p. 35), and by "scientific," he means that such spiritual experiences, as well as all psychosynthesis concepts, can be investigated scientifically. In fact, many of his principles and techniques, based on his own personal subjective experience, are being (re)discovered to precisely correspond with current data and models of neuroscience (Ferrucci, 2012). For example, only since the 1990s have scientists changed their ideas concerning the brain's structure; in particular, they no longer believe that the brain remains fixed once it achieves maturity. Instead, "brain plasticity"—the extraordinary ability of the brain to modify its own structure and function—is now commonly understood as a fundamental and significant lifelong property of the brain. More than a century ago, Assagioli spoke of the "plastic unconscious," the area of our unconscious that gives us an indefinite capacity to learn, elaborate, and create. In his book, *The Act of Will*,

Assagioli (2002) provides us with seven laws (appendix) that actually work with this idea of brain plasticity, helping us to direct our will to modify our behavior, attitude, and mindsets.

While psychosynthesis can be viewed as a foundational bridge between psychology and spirituality (Lombard, 2017), Assagioli (n.d.) wrote that psychosynthesis "is independent from, and neutral towards all religious creeds and metaphysical doctrines, but is compatible with any of them." He also insisted that the spiritual dimension of the human being is not only religious or mystical, but can also be a manifestation of higher qualities aligned with the individual's life, including: "the scientific line (concrete knowledge), the philosophical line (abstract knowledge), the artistic line (beauty) and the activity line (concentration on practical problems – service)" (Assagioli, n.d.c).

As a scientist, Assagioli wrote and edited more than 150 articles and essays during his lifetime and founded the scientific periodical *Psiche* (*Psyche*, 1912-1915, 1973-1974). He is the author of numerous books on psychosynthesis, most notably *The Act of Will* (2002), which he wrote after a near-death experience at the age of 77 (Giovetti, 1995). Assagioli served on the editorial board for both the *Journal of Humanistic Psychology* and the *Journal of Transpersonal Psychology*. Besides Jung and Maslow, his scientific colleagues included outstanding figures like Albert Einstein and logotherapy founder Viktor Frankl. Throughout his entire life, Assagioli created and participated in international congresses on psychoanalysis and psychotherapy. He was one of the 53 founding members of the Italian Society of Psychology (1910), and personally founded the Florence Circle of Psychological Studies (1913) and the Institute of Psychic Culture and Therapy (1926) which, in 1933, became the Institute of Psychosynthesis in Rome. In 2012, there were more than 100 psychosynthesis centers worldwide, including 26 centers in Italy (Directory of Psychosynthesis Centers Worldwide, 2012). Today, psychosynthesis is practiced in more than 60 countries.

Many of Assagioli's ideas, that were novel during his lifetime, have become part of mainstream psychology. Humor has always played a part in his life and work. In 1906, his article "The effects of laughter on pedagogical applications" was published in the *Journal of Applied Psychology*. In the 1920s, he was already discussing the benefits of music therapy, color therapy and psycho-energetics. In the 1960s, he expressed ideas about bio-psychosynthesis, defining it as "the inclusion of the body in all processes of human development," and he was one of the founders of the Italian Society of Psychosomatic Medicine (Rosselli, 2012). Not unlike today's popular mindfulness meditation, a fundamental psychosynthesis technique is a 15-minute meditation that allows you to dis-identify from your body, feelings, and thoughts, allowing you to more easily connect to your real, authentic self. As pointed out in his eulogy, Assagioli "was very early. Who was there to hear such a large and balanced statement? Not many... Almost sixty years needed to elapse, so far was he ahead of his time" (Firman & Gila, 2002, p. 14).

Synthesizing Relationships with Others

Assagioli always carefully delineated his scientific work from his personal and spiritual life. According to Assagioli's niece, Donatella Ciapetti Assagioli, "esotericism formed his basis [for psychosynthesis], but he always separated his interests in esotericism from his scientific work, because he did not want to be misunderstood" (Giovetti, 1995, p. 103). He was also discrete concerning his personal life; for example, in *Freedom in Jail*, he writes about his reticence to publish his prison experiences (Assagioli, 2016). Susanne Nouvion, French socialist and founder of the French Institute of Psychosynthesis (*l'Institut Français de Psychosynthèse*), noted that Assagioli never wanted personal power, often repeating: "The personal 'I' must diminish, the Higher Self must grow" (Giovetti, 1995, p. 103)[5]. Further evidence of his longing to dis-identify himself as a person from his psychological insights is noted in the fact that he chose not to attach his name to his vision. Unlike Freudian or Jungian psychology, the surname Assagioli remains distinctly separate from 'psychosynthesis.'

While Assagioli remained a private individual, he was, nevertheless, deeply devoted to establishing authentic relationships with others. Interpersonal synthesis is a process that begins with the harmonization and cooperation of the couple and family, then moving outward to include a synthesis of nationals, internationals, and all planetary life. According to Assagioli, synthesis of the couple is fundamental to achieving the psychosynthesis of humanity. He wrote: "When talking about the consciousness of a group, talk above all about the human couple: ...their synthesis, and about their central importance as a fundamental basis and model of inter-psychics at its most vast and complex" (Assagioli, n.d.e). He noted that a couple can take different forms, including: doctor–patient, teacher–pupil, master–disciple, author–reader, and coauthors of a work of art such as a book, music, or opera (Assagioli, n.d.d, n.d.f).

Assagioli stated that individuals should not "lose" themselves completely when in a couple, which he then extended to the process of inter-individual groups. He wrote that we need to "resist the tendency to throw ourselves completely into the group, as it may be a form of evasion from individual

---

[5]This quote actually derives from the Gospel of John 3:30 (NIV): "He must become greater; I must become less."

responsibility to one's Soul" (Assagioli, n.d.a). Once again, we return to the triangle depicting the synthesis of polar opposites. This time, each individual in the couple is positioned at the polar points at the bottom of the triangle. Assagioli insisted that the mid-way point between two opposites is not static inside us, but is rather in "a state of continuous oscillation." This back and forth can create a lot of tension! Consequently, persons in relationship must learn to balance the principles of "distance" and "tension" between themselves and the other in order to maintain an equilibrium in the relationship. The goal is to achieve a synthesis of each separate individual into a third entity that holds "a higher unity endowed with the qualities which transcend those of either" (Assagioli, 2002, p. 101).

Assagioli's entire life was devoted to intra-personal psychosynthesis. As a good friend of the family, Luisa Lunelli knew the Assagiolis for many years, and wrote about them as a couple: "Their relationship was the best. They were different, but they complemented each other and communication between them was easy and continual. Indeed, you could see their understanding and love only increase every day" (Lunelli, 1991). They had one son, Francesco Ilario, who at the age of 15 became ill with pulmonary tuberculosis, which would cause his death 12 years later. During these years, Assagioli sought help from the best specialists in Italy and Switzerland along with the latest curative medicines and methods. At the same time, Assagioli encouraged Ilario to read the great works of philosophers, writers, and poets, "standing beside him with his affectionate presence, serene, available, helping him to quietly feel his love" (Giovetti, 1995, pp. 52-53). Throughout this great suffering, Assagioli helped his son to accept and spiritually prepare for his imminent death. A few days after his son's funeral, Assagioli said, "His eyes now see a more glorious Sun!" (Lunelli, 1991).

Assagioli had many devoted students whose testimonies verify his astute educational skills, profound humility, constant goodwill, and deep spirituality when forming relationships. Through his mere presence, he was able to convey deep personal and spiritual wisdom. Assagioli was a "gentle synthesizer who left things open" (Rosselli, 2012). As his niece, Donatella Ciapetti Assagioli, said:

> He gave much and did not judge others. No matter what happened, he always remained serene… He taught his students without words, without imposing his ideas, only by personal example. He used humor to spread his important seeds… He was very wise and profoundly good. (Giovetti, 1995, p. 73)

Sergio Bartoli recounted one occasion when he adamantly defended Assagioli's writings before their psychology and psychoanalytic colleagues. The next day, Assagioli slipped "one of his famous notes" into Bartoli's pocket that said, "Correct your impulsiveness!" (Giovetti, 1995, p. 78). Another student, Andrea Bocconi, recalled an instance that particularly revealed Assagioli's character. Assagioli was leading a meditation when a knock came at the door and a tailor entered to ask what material Assagioli wanted his pajamas made of. Assagioli selected a sample, thanked the man who then left, and then, completely unperturbed, closed his eyes and returned to the meditation. Meanwhile, Bocconi had experienced the tailor's entrance as a frustrating interruption. "I never saw him angry or irritated," said Bocconi. "He was stable, very serene, …free of his emotions…We knew when we were with him that we had an authentic and true gift!" (Giovetti, 1995, p. 96). It was Assagioli who suggested that Piero Ferrucci, one of his students, assistants, and co-workers, write about psychosynthesis, a process that would ultimately become fundamental to Ferrucci's life. He said, "Assagioli gave me a profound sense of love, joy, [and] will" (Giovetti, 1995, p. 87).

With regard to developing national and international inter-personal synthesis, Assagioli was instrumental in establishing psychosynthesis institutes and organizations around the world. In 1956, he created the Psychosynthesis Research Foundation in the United States and during the 1960s organized centers in India, Paris, Athens, and California. In the 1970s, centers continued to open in London and Canada.

Assagioli was not limited to working with groups that focused specifically on psychosynthesis. In the early 20th century, he played a fundamental role in Florence's literary scene. As part of the movements that were emerging in philosophy, art, and literature, he was a close friend with Giovanni Papini. Together they collaborated and wrote for the Florentine journal *Leonardo* (1905–07). Later, he became friends with Giuseppe Prezzolini, writer, cultural organizer, and director of the *La Voce* (1908–12), to which Assagioli also contributed. In the 1950s, he founded the Italian Union for Progressive Judaism, which was based on "an attitude of openness and understanding and collaboration with all peoples and religions" (Giovetti, 1995, p. 61). During the same decade, he initiated and led creative meditation groups with his collaborators at the Sundial House in Tunbridge Wells (UK), which remains active today. Throughout the 1960s, he contributed to international conferences including: the International Congress of Psychotherapy in Vienna (1961), with a research paper on "Psychosynthesis and existential psychotherapy"; the International Congress of Psychotherapy in London (1964), where he presented a paper on "Synthesis in Psychotherapy"; and First International Psychosomatic Week at the Catholic University of Rome (1967), with a presentation on "Psychosomatic Medicine and Biopsychosynthesis."

As his reputation grew later in life, Assagioli dedicated himself to training

410

and referred to his patients as "collaborators." In 1973, he formed a small group of young students, many of whom became instrumental in creating the Società Italiana di Psicosintesi Terapeutica (SIPT), a school of psychosynthesis psychotherapy that provides the accredited formation of professional doctors and psychologists in Florence, Italy. During the last years of his life, he continued to receive international guests and to hold lectures, gaining in popularity to the point where young people would queue outside his home to obtain a place, squeezing into the room and hallway to hear him speak (Rosselli, 2012).

Synthesizing with the Stars

Assagioli was notoriously deaf in his old age, which he did not regret, and would even joke about. His student at the time, Dr. Giacomini, remembered how the telephone in Assagioli's studio would ring and ring, but he would act as if unable to hear it, leaving it for the secretary downstairs to answer. "Yet, he always seemed to be able to hear whatever question you had," said Giacomini (personal communication, June 2012).[6] In 1972, despite his wife's loss of memory and declining health, the Assagiolis celebrated their 50th wedding anniversary in their summer house in Capolona, which they had named 'Villa Ilario.' That evening Assagioli recited a poem by Trilussa about being together through all that is joyous and all that is painful. The next year, Nella Chiapetti died, leaving Assagioli a widower (Giovetti, 1995).

Three months before his death, he specified seven core principles for "Training in Psychosynthesis": (a) disidentification, (b) personal Self, (c) the will, (d) the ideal model, (e) the synthesis in its various aspects, (f) the superconscious or transpersonal conscious, and (g) the transpersonal Self (Assagioli, 1974). At the same time, he was interviewed by Sam Keen for *Psychology Today* and at the end of the interview was asked about how he viewed death at the age of 85. Assagioli responded with:

> Death looks to me primarily like a vacation. There are many hypotheses about death and the idea of reincarnation seems the most sensible to me... Death is a normal part of a biological cycle. It is my body that dies and not all of me. So I don't care much. I may die this evening but I would willingly accept a few more years in order to do the work I am interested in, which I think may be useful to others... Also humor helps, and a sense of proportion. I am one individual on a small planet in a little solar system in one of the galaxies." (Keen, 1974)

While Assagioli spoke about death, Keen (1974) noted: "there was no change in the tone or intensity of Assagioli's voice and the light still played in

[6]Piero Ferrucci said in a personal interview, June 2016, that Assagioli was, in fact, telepathic.

his dark eyes, and his mouth was never very far from a smile."

Surrounded by his students and his secretary, Ida Palombi, Roberto Assagioli died at 86 years of age from a strong heart attack at Capolona on August 23, 1974. The last word he spoke was "Ilario." Cremated a week later in Arezzo, his remains are interred with his mother's in the Trespiano Cemetery, Florence. Assagioli's death notice read: "Roberto has seen the day of his Liberation" (Giovetti, 1995, p. 114).

A Brief Chronology of Robert Assagioli's Life[7]
1888: On February 27, Assagioli is born in Venice, Italy.

1904: Moves with his family to Florence and enrolls in the Faculty of Medicine at the Institute for Advanced Studies.

1907: Frequently visits and studies at the Burghölzli Psychiatric Clinic at Zürich University where he works with Carl G. Jung (1875-1961) and Eugen Bleuler (1957-1939). Becomes a member of the Freud Society in Zürich.

1906-1909: Publishes his first scientific article in the *Rivista di Psicologia applicata* (*Journal of Applied Psychology*) entitled "The effects of laughter and their pedagogical applications." In Rome he attends theosophical meetings and begins studying Indian philosophy.

1910: He receives his doctorate degree in medicine under Prof. Eugenio Tanzi (1856-1933). In his thesis, he discusses psychoanalysis and expounds for the first time his conception of psychosynthesis.
He participates in Florence at the First Italian Conference on Sexual Issues with the report "Transformation and sublimation of sexual energy." Publishes his article, "*Le idee di S. Freud sulla sessualità*" ("S. Freud's ideas on sexuality"), a commentary on the "Three Essays on the Theory of Sexuality" by S. Freud.

1912: He founds and finances the publication of *Psiche*, a magazine of psychological studies. In its second issue, for the first time, Freud's article "The psychoanalytic method" appears in Italian translation.

1917-1919: During World War I, he is called up as a medical officer, and in 1919 he is vice-director of Ancona Neurological Centre at the military hospital.

1920: He opens an office in Florence. He founds the group "Florence" of the Independent Theosophical League, and becomes its president.

1922: On August 12, he marries Nella Ciapetti in Florence.

<u>**1923**</u>: On September 12, his son Francesco Ilario Assagioli is born.

[7]For a more extensive chronological biography, see www.archivioassagioli.org/strumenti_pub.php

1926: The Assagioli family moves to Rome, and their house becomes the meeting place of the Independent Theosophical League, group "Rome." He founds the Institute of Psychic Culture and Therapy in Rome. In 1933, it becomes the first Institute of Psychosynthesis.

1927: Publication of *A New Method of Healing: Psychosynthesis* (in English).

1926-1938: He travels throughout Europe and to the United States, expanding his network of international relationships. At the same time, he intensifies the development, formulation and spreading of psychosynthesis.

1938: The fascist regime closes the Institute of Psychosynthesis under an accusation of pacifism.

1939: As a Jew, he resigns from the Theosophical Society. Soon afterwards, the society is closed by the regime.

1940: He is arrested on charges of pacifism and spends one month in at Regina Coeli prison in Rome. Afterwards, he is released with confinement.

1946: He relocates his family to Florence, where he reconstitutes the Institute of Psychosynthesis. At the end of the 1950s, via San Domenico, 16, Florence, becomes the Institute's definitive location.
He begins to travel in Europe and the U.S. for cultural, psychological and spiritual contacts. Activities intensify through new initiatives, publications, lectures, conferences, and his participation in national and international meetings.

1949: He founds the Italian Union for Progressive Judaism, adhering to the "World Union for Progressive Judaism." He forms a group of Creative Meditation with collaborators at the Sundial House in Tunbridge Wells (UK).

1951: His son Ilario dies of pulmonary tuberculosis.

1956: He creates the Psychosynthesis Research Foundation in the United States at Valmy, Delaware. Later, the Foundation will move to New York City, N.Y.

1959: He opens the Centre de Psychosynthèse in Paris.

1960: The psychosynthesis center in Athens is constituted. Writings on psychosynthesis are translated and published in Greek.

1965: He publishes his book *Principles and Methods of Therapeutic Psychosynthesis* (in English).

1966: A collection of a series of lectures that Assagioli gave at Rome is published (in Italian only) as *Psicosintesi – Armonia della Vita* (Psychosynthesis – Harmony of Life).

1967: Assagioli holds a presentation on "Psychosomatic Medicine and Biopsychosynthesis" at the First International Psychosomatic Week in Rome.

1969: The Psychosynthesis Centre in California is constituted.

1973: The Canadian Institute of Psychosynthesis in Montreal, Canada, is officially constituted.
His wife Nella Ciapetti dies.
The Act of Will is published in English.
The Società Italiana di Psicosintesi Terapeutica (SIPT; The Italian Society for Therapeutic Psychosynthesis) is created in Florence.

1974: The Center of Psychosynthesis in London opens.
On 23 August, Roberto Assagioli dies at dawn in Capolona, at the age of 86.

1988: A collection of articles written about the transpersonal dimension of the human psyche, is published posthumously as *Lo sviluppo Transpersonale*. In 1991, the book is published in English as *Transpersonal Development*. Numerous other collections of his articles and lectures are published as books (in Italian only).

2016: His reflections on his time in jail are posthumously published as *Freedom in Jail*.

References

Assagioli, R. (n.d.). Archivio Assagioli: Florence, Italy, Archivio Studio, 996. [Manuscript note]. Retrieved from www.achivioassagioli.org

Assagioli, R. (n.d.a). Archivio Assagioli: Florence, Italy, Archivio Studio, 9207. [Manuscript note]. Retrieved from www.achivioassagioli.org

Assagioli, R. (n.d.b). Archivio Assagioli: Florence, Italy, Archivio Studio, 5330 [Manuscript note]. Retrieved from www.archivioassagioli.org

Assagioli, R. (n.d.c). Archivio Assagioli: Florence, Italy, Archivio Studio, 11454. [Manuscript note]. Retrieved from www.achivioassagioli.org

Assagioli, R. (n.d.d). Archivio Assagioli: Florence, Italy, Archivio Studio, 15509. [Manuscript note]. Retrieved from www.achivioassagioli.org

Assagioli, R. (n.d.e). Archivio Assagioli: Florence, Italy, Archivio Studio, 16168. [Manuscript note]. Retrieved from www.achivioassagioli.org

Assagioli, R. (n.d.f). Archivio Assagioli: Florence, Italy, Archivio Studio,

16194. [Manuscript note]. Retrieved from www.achivioassagioli.org

Assagioli, R. (1946). Saggezza sorridente [Smiling wisdom]. *La cultura nel mondo, 1.*

Assagioli, R. (1965). *L'equilibramento e la sintesi degli opposti* [Balancing and synthesizing opposites]. Florence, Italy: Edizioni Istituto di Psicosintesi.

Assagioli, R. (1974). *Psychosynthesis training.* Florence, Italy: Istituto di Psicosintesi.

Assagioli, R. (1992). *Come si imparano le lingue con l'inconscio* [How to learn a language with the unconscious]. Florence, Italy: Istituto di Psicosintesi.

Assagioli, R. (2000). *Psychosynthesis: A collection of basic writings.* Amherst, MA: The Synthesis Center.

Assagioli, R. (2002). *The act of will.* London, UK: The Psychosynthesis & Education Trust.

Assagioli, R. (2011). *Dalla coppia all'umanità. Introduzione alla psicosintesi interindividuale* [From the couple to humanity. Introduction to inter-individual psychosynthesis]. A. Alberti (Ed.). Florence, Italy: L'Uomo Edizioni.

Assagioli, R. (2016). *Freedom in jail.* C.A. Lombard, (Ed.). Florence, Italy: Istituto di Psicosintesi.

Berti, A. (Ed.). (1988). *Roberto Assagioli 1888-1988.* Florence, Italy: Centro di Studi di Psicosintesi.

Bonetti, O., & Nataloni, A. (n.d.). *L'odio e la pietà: La sanità militare italiana durante la grande guerra.* [Hatred and pity: Italian military healthcare during the Great War]. Retrieved from zioni/L'odio%20e%20la%20piet%E0.pdf

Caldironi, B. (2004). *L'uomo a tre dimensioni: Colloqui con Roberto Assagioli* [The man of three dimensions: Conversations with Roberto Assagioli]. L. Oretti (Ed.). Ravenna, Italy: Edizioni del Girasole.

Directory of Psychosynthesis Centers Worldwide (2012). Cheshire, MA: Association for the Advancement of Psychosynthesis. Retrieved from http://docshare01.docshare.tips/files/13219/132193495.pdf

Esposito W. (2008). Introduzione. In Assagioli, R. (2008). *Il mondo interiore* [The interior world] (pp. 35-46). W. Esposito (Ed.). Vicenza, Italy: Edizioni Teosofiche Italiane.

Ferrucci, P. (Sept 2012). Psychosynthesis in the light of neuroscience, *Psychosynthesis Quarterly, 1*(3), 4-14.

Firman, J. & and Gila, A. (2002). *Psychosynthesis: A psychology of the spirit.* Albany, NY: State University of New York Press.

Giovetti, P. (1995). *Roberto Assagioli: La vita e l'opera del fondatore della Psicosintesi* [Roberto Assagioli: The life and work of the founder of psychosynthesis]. Rome: Edizioni Mediterranee.

Hardy, J. (1987). *A psychology with a soul.* London: Routledge & Kegan Paul.

Haronian, F. (1976). Psychosynthesis: A psychotherapist's personal overview. *Pastoral Psychology,* 24(1), 16–33.

Keen, S. (Dec 1974). The golden mean of Roberto Assagioli. *Psychology Today,* 97–107.

Lombard, C.A. (Dec 2016). Assagioli's reflections on the poor man of Assisi, *AAP Newsletter,* 5(4), 10-16.

Lombard, C.A. (2017). Psychosynthesis: A foundational bridge between psychology and spirituality. *Pastoral Psychology.* doi: 10.1007/s11089-017-0753-5.

Lombard, C.A., & den Biesen, K. (Sept 2014). Reading the Divine Comedy from a psychosynthesis perspective: The beginning of a spiritual journey. *AAP Newsletter,* 3(3), 5-11.

Lunelli, L. (1991). *Roberto, Nella, e Luisa.* Retrieved from www.psicoenergetica.it/thesaurus_assagioli.htm.

Maraghini, F. (2016, Nov 7). Assagioli al Monastero di Camaldoli (Arezzo). [Web log post] Roberto Assagioli: Lo scienziato dello spirito: IL FILM. Retrieved from http://www.robertoassagiolithemovie.com/2016/11/07/assagioli-al-monastero-di-camaldoli-arezzo/.

McGuire, W. (Ed.). (1974). *The Freud/Jung letters, The correspondence between Sigmund Freud and C. G. Jung.* Bollingen Series, 94. Princeton: Princeton University Press.

Medlock, J. (Nov 1960). Personal glimpse of Dr. R. Assagioli. *The Hindu Weekly.*

Rosselli, M. (2012). Roberto Assagioli: A bright star. *International Journal of Psychotherapy,* 16(2), 7-19.

Appendix: Psychological Laws (Assagioli, 2002, pp. 51-61)

Law I – Images or mental pictures and ideas tend to produce the physical conditions and the external acts that correspond to them.

Law II – Attitudes, movements, and actions tend to evoke corresponding images and ideas; these, in turn (according to the next law) evoke or intensify corresponding emotions and feelings.

Law III – Ideas and images tend to awaken emotions and feelings that correspond to them.

Law IV – Emotions and impressions tend to awaken and intensify ideas and images that correspond to or are associated with them.

Law V – Needs, urges, drives, and desires tend to arouse corresponding images, ideas and emotions.

Law VI – Attention, interest, affirmations, and repetitions reinforce the ideas, images, and psychological formations on which they are centered.

Law VII – Repetition of actions intensifies the urge to further reiteration and renders their execution easier and better, until they come to be performed unconsciously. (Conscious creation of habits.)

Law VIII – All the various functions, and their manifold combinations in complexes and subpersonalities, adopt means of achieving their aims without our awareness, and independently of, and even against, our con-scious will.

Law IX – Urges, drives, desires, and emotions tend and demand to be expressed.

Law X – The psychological energies can find expression: 1. directly (discharge – catharsis) 2. indirectly, through symbolic action 3. through a process of transmutation.

Chapter 31

Your Call of Self: Strategies for the New Coach

by Dorothy Firman

Coming to the field of coaching is a process of evolution based in an individual's own experience of purpose, meaning and values. A career choice to work so closely with other people is inevitably guided by an inner calling for deep and meaningful work. The early days in the field are the ground upon which each coach builds a professional identity. When consciousness is brought to bear in creating a new identity (in any endeavor) that identity will likely be a closer reflection of what is deeply true. A good actor is not just a skilled technician. A good parent is not one who has read all the books. A good coach is not just one who has been well trained. One of the gifts of the profession of coaching is that it is, in fact, an invitation to be true to your own values and beliefs. In fact, the invitation is even more expansive, as being a coach really does offer a place to be authentic, to be the person you are, to do work that is a fit, both at the level of skill and training and at the level of purpose, meaning and values. Coaching is, for many, a path of right livelihood.

The building of this new identity, like any building, requires a blue print of sorts. A first consideration will wisely be connection to purpose. Checking in for that connection is worth doing as a beginner...and often along the way of maturation in the field.

It is an easy exercise to trace the **coaching inclination**, if you will, to the affairs of childhood. Were you the child who talked to everyone? The one who wondered about the world? The rescuer of small animals? Did you notice kids in need? Were you the puzzle solver? The explorer of nature? The creator? Inventor? There's no formula, of course, but it is worth taking the time to find out a bit about how you got where you are today. Think back to books you loved, heroes you had, games you played. What was the role you played in the

419

family, in the school community, with grandparents, siblings, friends? Where, in your young life, did you experience resonance, that sense that we all have from time to time, of being meaningfully connected…to what you are doing, to the environment, to yourself, to another person?

Purpose, meaning and values define a life, as woven threads of your uniqueness, threads that begin young, and continue to be woven throughout life: A tapestry that, at its best, is a deep reflection of the call of Self. To help connect to the purpose that has moved you to become a coach, you might just ask:

- What attracted me to coaching in the first place?
- What is the meaning it has for me?
- What is my vision for myself as a Coach?

The answer to these questions assures a deep will alignment as you step into this new professional identity. There is nothing more crucial than staying connected to purpose. From this source derives our very will to be the best we can be. "The chief characteristic of the volitional act is the existence of a **purpose** to be achieved; the clear vision of an aim, or goal, to be reached" (Assagioli, 2010, p.99). In the early stages, the purpose is to gain the skills to fill up the toolkit that will be with us throughout our careers. But by the time we work with another human being, the purpose will have changed. We will be there to help, to serve, to offer support, to challenge, to care. We will also be there to have a profession, to earn a paycheck, to be a contributing member of our society. But really each purpose will be different.

As these answers connect the coach to a sense of purpose, they will strengthen the move into an identity that is new in form, but feels like home, because in fact, the new professional identity will be a set of clothes that fits you perfectly. After all, you've been shopping for quite awhile. Staying connected to deeper meaning and purpose while stepping into the coach role, into that new set of clothes, invites you to know yourself—in a profound way.

How does one optimize that move into being a coach? Good training, skilled teachers and mentors, successful practice sessions and putting your coaching practice out in the world, all help! And yet even with that, the inner voices that may have troubled you, in past work, in life, even as a child, will still be there to offer a challenge. These voices can become blocks to a healthy professional identity. We come to the field with a call, a longing, a belief, a fair amount of faith and a lot of not knowing. Each positive experience helps us build an identity that is stronger and more comfortable. Each set-back feeds our own voices of doubt. "Can I do this?" "Am I good enough?" These inner saboteurs are blocks to developing a strong and authentic professional identity, a deep sense of "I". Thus, they need to be challenged, understood and healed.

It is a mandate to coaches to do the work that they will ask their clients to do. It is the work of self-discovery. In claiming the right and the deep need to know ourselves, in this professional identity, we must face our own limiting conditions, blocking beliefs, old messages and personal demons. In the end, what we don't want is for the inner judge or scared child to be running the show: not in our personal lives and not in our professional lives. But to be sure, the pull of this dynamic is strong. Even the seasoned veteran will come away from work on a bad day, full of the voice of self-criticism. And surprise of surprises, that voice will be very much the same as it was when that now-adult coach was a young child. And on another, not so good day, that mature individual, well trained, highly acclaimed, grey hair and all, will **feel** like a child. This is to be expected and we would set ourselves up for a fall if we thought otherwise. What will serve us throughout our career, though, is having such a strong professional identity (Kottler, 1987; 2004) anchored into the best of who we are, that it is this **self** that shows up for work, sees clients, gets supervision and monitors the shenanigans of our old, deeply embedded, still wounded subs.

The good coach has plenty of bad days and hears old inner voices, feels young inner feelings, and visits self-doubt regularly. The danger (and it is dangerous for both coach and client) is that these experiences are unconscious, unmonitored, taken as the whole truth, repressed or projected or otherwise included in dysfunctional and dangerous ways: Thus, the importance of creating, early on, that professional identity whose foundation is built on purpose, meaning, values, skills, unique attributes of the coach-to-be and a deep sense of Self that is more than our conditioning.

- ♦ What are the limiting beliefs that hinder me professionally?
- ♦ What subpersonality steps in when there are challenges in the work?
- ♦ Am I still trying to be something to someone from my past?
- ♦ Who am I beyond any limiting conditioning from my life?

As you work to uncover the wounds and reclaim the essence of who you are, you will be able to build a professional identity that is truthful, authentic and unique to you. And you will become, then, an honest and available model for your clients.

Finding Self

More than half a century ago, Abraham Maslow (1968) brought the field of psychology to a new consideration of what human beings are, essentially.

The work of humanistic and transpersonal psychology paved the way for seeing humans beyond conditioning. The very basics that most coaches so often take for granted, now, about those that sit facing them, are basics that tell us about ourselves, as people and as professionals. A piece of Maslow's advice about human nature bears repeating.

5. Since this inner nature is good or neutral rather than bad, it is best to bring it out and to encourage it rather than to suppress it. If it is permitted to guide our life, we grow healthy, fruitful, and happy.

6. If this essential core of the person is denied or suppressed, he gets sick sometimes in obvious ways, sometimes in subtle ways, sometimes immediately, sometimes, later.

7. This inner nature is not strong and overpowering and unmistakable like the instincts of animals. It is weak and delicate and subtle and easily overcome by habit, cultural pressure, and wrong attitudes toward it. (p.4)

Inner nature, essential core, innate presence, self, I, center are among the many phrases used to describe the **who** that each of us is, before, or beyond, or in spite of, our conditioning. And it is our job to bring it out, nurture it and finally become it. Become our Selves.

Without trying to answer the biggest questions about these lofty ideas, it is clear enough, that we can become more authentic people and professionals through our own work and through our own commitment to being true to ourselves. Another early voice in the field, Clark Moustakis (1956), offers a broad description of this process of becoming self. "True being is self and other, individual and universal, personal and cultural. It cannot be understood by comparison, evaluation, diagnosis, or analysis" (p. 4).

What then are we looking for? In a very simple way we are always looking and listening for cues, insights, felt-senses and intuitions to guide us. In the theory of psychosynthesis (Assagioli, 2000) this is referred to as an internal unifying center: That is the experience of self that is steady and timeless, around which we can build or refine our personalities, make choices, honor values and move in the world through deeper relationship to who we are. More simply stated we are talking about **the who that I am**. This sense of "I" is a balance of how we have always known ourselves, what makes each of us unique, the still calm center that we sometimes find inside and the ways we are part of a larger whole.

The self can also be defined as the only part of us which remains forever the same. It is the sameness which, once found and fully experienced, acts as an ever-present pivot point for the rest of the personality, an inner stronghold to which we can always refer in order to regain a sense of poise and self-consistency. Then we can see that self remains the same in ecstasy and despair, in peace and turmoil, in pain and pleasure, in victory and defeat. (Ferrucci, 1982 p. 61)

The fields of psychology, as well as philosophy and religion are full of thoughts and theories about this concept. Definitions are not, in the end, needed. People who are self-reflective will know, intrinsically, when they are operating from center, being true to themselves, and living authentically. They will know when they are not. Anchoring back into that knowing of Self will stand the coach in good stead, for the journey is not easy. It will take us through all of the feelings that humans can have. It will feed every old wound that we have. It will make us feel great and lousy. And yet, if we are not at the mercy of every passing experience, but know ourselves in that "inner stronghold" we will not be tossed about on the waves so easily.

It is assumed that coaches will be self-reflective and so this work is a given as we train in, step into and live through the field we have chosen to be in.

+ Who am I?
+ How do I know my own inner nature?
+ How will I support myself in being true to myself?

A seasoned psychosynthesis practitioner offers us a frame of reference for the asking of these questions.

Perhaps the notion of becoming, then, is a better road to walk; that is, instead of seeking a static, formulaic answer to the puzzle of "Who Am I?" we might view the questions as demanding more of us than that. Certainly, it is closer to our experience that being a person is a **process** of some sort, regardless of how we respond to the anxiety that this process involves us in from time to time. (Klugman, 2007, pp 163-4)

And anxiety is inevitable. How we respond to it and other tumultuous experiences is the key. And how we know ourselves will give us the stance from which to encounter everything that comes our way.

No one does well as a round peg in a square hole, but unless we know a fair amount about who we are, we will truly not know where we fit. It is a worthwhile reminder for the beginning coach that the work will unfold more seamlessly if it is work that is right for you. And you will better know what work is right for you, when you know more about who you are. A professional identity can be bought off the rack at your first job. It will look, more or less, like everyone else's. If you're not careful, the identity you assume will look like a favorite teacher's or an old role model's, though it won't fit you nearly as well

423

as it fitted them. You want a designer outfit. It will be made just for you. And it will fit perfectly. This new identity will just be you, dressed for work.

The Unique Coach

Professional identity formation and development are individual matura-tion processes that begin during one's training for the profession, evolve during entry into the profession, and continue to develop as the practitio-ner identifies with the profession. These processes can be viewed as the ex-periences that help the practitioner wed theory with reality in the direction of greater flexibility and openness. (Brott & Kajs, para.7)

In order to move towards an identification that is a good fit, the begin-ning coach will need to know a lot about themself. Doing some work on mean-ing and purpose and checking into those old, family-of-origin issues that are the bread and butter of our field begin this process in a healthy fashion. At the same time, the new coach will want to assess his or her own personal realities.

+ What's in that toolkit that I have?
+ What styles, skills, strategies am I really comfortable with?
+ What am I missing?
+ What do I deeply believe that is important to my work?
+ Where do I want to head now that I'm in the field?

Staying in touch with one's strengths and weaknesses, preferences, skills, and best practices is a lifelong task. This is a good thing and allows the new coach to enter the field fully equipped to work with the people who come to the office. Not only training, but personality and style, have some bearing on who each of us can and should work with and how we will work. New coaches will be more ready to work with that first round of people who come into the office if they have taken stock. If I have easily available qualities of humor and com-passion, then I will have solid strengths to start out with. If I am uncomfortable with certain techniques I've been taught, I will be in better shape, knowing this and taking it easy as I start out. If I have sensitivities or my own wounding, preferences or judgments, I want to know them. The more I know, the more I can choose, appropriately, how to work with each person who comes to me. Our first clients are our rite of passage, and even now, looking back many years, I can remember them fondly and with appreciation for how I worked with them, as new as I was to the field. At the same time, any coach who has been in the field is likely to look back on their early days with a note of wonder. "How did I do that?" Of course, each helping professional will learn more, become more skilled, be more comfortable and ultimately find more and more out about the field and about their own uniqueness in the field, as the years progress. But one doesn't wait for yet more training, more books read, more theories understood, to step up and do the work.

> ...learning the art of helping is a journey. It is described as a journey with a beginning but no real endpoint. Those who embark on this course find it to be a lifelong process of discovery rather than a destination. (Young, 2001, p. v)

Walking in to that first day on the job and every one of those early days in the early years is an opportunity to anchor into the strengths and gifts that are immediately available. And first and foremost is the gift of Self. Young notes: "A client will have a relationship with you, not a set of skills" (Young, p.18). What an essential reminder this is. As you come forth into the field, you are the helper. You are not a set of theories or skills. These will be in your toolkit and they will serve you well. But also in that toolkit will be a lifetime of experience in the world, your own struggles and hard-won successes and the very core of your purpose for being in the helping professions, however you may know that. And you will be the helper sitting in the seat opposite your client. Whoever you are, with strengths and weaknesses alike, is who will be in the chair. And that is a great start.

"Genuine helpers are non-defensive. They know their own strengths and deficits and are presumably trying to live mature, meaningful lives" (Egan, 1998, p. 50). Being in this field is part of the meaningful life you are carving out for yourself. Training, study, self-reflection and on-going work are the tools that mature people use to be good at what they do. This is what showing up, as a coach, is all about. And each coach is unique. For this we can be grateful. As every client is unique and should be seen that way, so are we.

To honor that which is unique about you promises the ability to be genuine, to show up with skills and authenticity and to be that coach who knows how to do this work over many years, without illusion or pretense, knowing the ups and downs and coming to work, with all of who you are.

There is not a right set of skills or theories. There is no assumption that coaches need to be a specific way. We all know the guidelines, ethical mandates, legal requirements and basic training that are the foundation of our work. Beyond those, it's just a single person, bringing whatever they have to offer, in service of a personal, meaningful and clear purpose to help other human beings. The authenticity that you bring to bear on your work will make all the difference in the world... to you, to your clients, to your family and community and to the field itself. You are the coach.

Bouncing Back

"It was difficult to embrace a professional identity that had been in place only 48 hours. I reacted with an acute bout of indigestion" (Bender & Messner, 2003, p. 9).

No matter how well we build a professional identity, it will be challenged, both in the beginning of our careers and from time to time throughout. Early on the voices of doubt will make every minor challenge into a big deal and coaches who are paying attention will notice how often they stretch too far to accommodate a client or hold boundaries too tightly in order to feel "professional" or stick too closely to the rules in order to be safe or some such unconscious strategy to help transition into this new world. That's all fine. Having some safety mechanisms, some healthy defense structures in place is a good idea. What we want, though, is not to get stuck in rigid roles or ideas about who we should be. And in that opening to more authentic ways of being, defenses are lessened. That's good and bad news. Truly authentic people; open, caring people are relatively undefended. This allows deeper empathy, clearer access to intuition and the profound possibility of the I-Thou relationship. The bad news is that letting go of defensiveness creates vulnerability in ways that may leave us open to wounding. Tough choice. But the really good news is that over time and with practice, in life and in the profession, each of us can become both more "defenseless" and "safer". True safety lies not in a good shield, but in an openness, that needs no defense. And then, from this ideal model of a place we'd like to be, comes the invitation to let it be ok to make mistakes. Because, okay or not, we will.

Everyone makes mistakes. No matter how "together" we are, how "with it," how well-prepared for any particular moment, at times we all stumble, blunder, unwillingly expose our uncertainties, imperfections, and shortcomings. There are times for all of us when, unpleasantly taken by surprise, we are exposed as momentarily unable to cope. All it takes to feel overwhelmed is a situation that has become too much to handle. It is then that we feel helplessly foolish and embarrassed. If we have been exposed to excessive shaming as children, we may also experience the needless pain of feeling deeply ashamed. At such moments, it is hard to remember that this happens to everyone, that the awful sense of ineptness and confusion will soon pass. Most of us do not understand how to go about making new space for ourselves. We can be needlessly hard on ourselves, slower to forgive than we would be with another. (Kopp, 1976, p. vii)

Bouncing back is a skill to be learned and one that will be strengthened by the very nature of our professional identity. If the coach defines themself with the undertones of childhood wounding, unrealistic cultural expectations or any other perfectionist, "should" based, defensively-driven mandate, that coach will fall harder and bounce back less easily than the one whose professional identity is defined from within a deeper core truth and a lot of self-understanding. The less-defended coach will bounce back more easily, knowing, both cognitively and in the heart of hearts, that to be human is perfectly acceptable. It is one of the gifts of this field. Our very humanness, in its very real imperfection is part and parcel of who we **should** be. Or else how could we ever relate to the other in front of us?

There are some guidelines to help. Note the risk for the beginner of being performance driven…or even more basically of thinking that there is a right way (and then of course a wrong way) to do coaching.

The first stage is the dualistic or absolutist position that can also be called the "right/wrong" stage. It s characterized by the belief that a helper's responses to a client are either right or wrong… This black/white, success/failure way of thinking increases internal pressure and makes the helpers overly concerned with their own performance. (Young, 2001, p. 6)

Of course, there some basic rights and wrongs but these aren't the ones that are likely to trip us up. What will trip us up are the things that already lurk inside as doubts and fears, old messages, too high expectations and the like. Better to go in knowing you will trip…and fall…and get up again. We all do.

This is the key. We will have many experiences, some good, some bad. So much will transpire in our sessions. Some of it will help another human being. Some of it will not. But we will live in this world and feel the feelings that are in us and some of those that come at us. Our job is to be aware and to know how to behave. That's why we have done our own personal work. That's why we've been well trained in the profession. We'll get mad, but will likely never scream. We'll get sad and we'll have to choose whether to let our sadness show. We'll get scared and we'll keep right on working.

+ What's likely to trip me up?
+ What do I know that will help me bounce back?
+ Am I willing to be human?

Going Forward

The field of coaching is open and continues to grow. New coaches will carry the field forward and will become the wise elders of the future. There is opportunity and responsibility in this role. When we know ourselves deeply, even as we step into new and unknown worlds, we step in on solid footing. Any illusion we have that we will know enough, have the answers, solve the problems, cure the client, will drag us down. Knowing who we are and why we are doing this work, will enter us into a powerful world of transformation and of mystery.

One of our oldest and wisest voices in the field of psychology, James Bugental (1985), reminds us of this. He invites us *To Seek a Wild God*.

The wild god is the god of mystery. And mystery is a word too seldom found in psychological writing or psychotherapeutic discourses. We deny mystery; we pretend it exists only in the minds of children, authors, and mystics. And we fool ourselves and blind ourselves when we do so.

Mystery enfolds knowledge, contains knowledge. Mystery is infinite, knowledge finite. As knowledge grows, mystery grows even more. Mystery is the latent meaning always awaiting our discovery and always more than our knowing. (p.273)

And Assagioli agrees: "Psychosynthesis does not aim or attempt to give a metaphysical or a theological explanation of the great Mystery—it leads to the door, but stops there (2000, p.5)." Thus, the great adventure of life. Training in psychosynthesis has already taught us this, by opening us to the wide world of all that we are, in all levels of the unconscious, with all our many parts, with the depth and height of our Self, through our awareness and will, the psychological functions that give us our wide range, through presence, that most basic assumption upon which all helping is founded and finally through our deep connection to the Call of Self. There is no piece of psychosynthesis theory or practice that does not remind us to be open, to seek discovery, to expand, becoming more of who we are, at every turn. "...we must have the courage and the will to throw ourselves boldly and joyfully into the adventure which the future holds" (Assagioli, 2010, p. 120). This adventure is the life-long work and play of Self-Realization. The process of Self-realization is psychosynthesis.

Welcome to the new professional identity that you are claiming. It is a gift, a challenge, a responsibility, and a long learning curve. It is your home away from home, your job, your calling. It is a mystery and it is a chance to be alive and to live in your own deep truth.

References

Assagioli, R. (2010). *The act of will.* Amherst, Ma: Synthesis Center Press.

Assagioli, R. (2000). *Psychosynthesis: A collection of basic writings.* Amherst, MA: The Synthesis Center Press.

Bender, S & Messner, E. (2003). *Becoming a therapist: What do I say, and why?* NY: The Guilford Press.

Brott, P & Kajs, L. (ND) *Developing the professional identity of first-year teachers through a working alliance.* retrieved Feb. 20 from www.alt-teachercert. org/Working%20Alliance.html.

Bugental, J. (1987). *The Art of the Psychotherapist.* NY: WW Norton & Co.

Egan, G. (1998) *The skilled helper: A problem management approach to helping.* Pacific Grove, CA: Brooks/Cole Publishing Co.

Ferrucci, P. (1982). *What we may be: Techniques for psychological and spiritual growth. through psychosynthesis.* Los Angeles, CA: JP Tarcher Inc.

Klugman, D. (2007). *The feeling life: Reclaiming your emotional vitality and purpose.* NY: Feeling First Publications.

Kopp, S. (1976). *The naked therapist: A Canterbury Tales collection of embarrassing moments from more than a dozen eminent psychotherapists.* San Diego, CA: EdITS Publishers.

Kottler, J. (1987). *On being a therapist.* San Francisco: Jossey-Bass Publishers.

Kottler, J. (2004). *Introduction to therapeutic counseling: Voices from the field.* CA: Brooks/Cole-Thomson Learning.

Maslow, A. (1968). *Toward a psychology of being.* NY: Van Nostrand Reinhold Company.

Moustakas, C. ed. (1956). *The self: Explorations in personal growth.* San Francisco: Harper & Row.

Young, M. (2001). *Learning the art of helping: Building blocks and techniques.* 2nd ed. Upper Saddle River, NJ: Merrill Prentice Hall:

Chapter 32

Future of Psychosynthesis in Life Coaching

by Ewa Danuta Białek

Psychosynthesis has entered an extremely important, thriving period in terms of its use in personal and transpersonal development in various aspects of the human experience. Looking back over the last 20 years, and taking the perspective of time and culture, we can notice a marked trend among people desiring to transcend personality and pursue spirituality. People, at much younger ages than in past generations, are starting to look for a deeper sense of meaning in their lives. A stronger need for personal development is crystallising and calls for attention, as it always has. At the same time, there are many people who feel that there is something more than personal growth that they are being called towards. This is the spiritual aspect of life, not bound by a cultivated religion or a particular worldview, but held as the deepest level of development of Self.

Psychosynthesis is a unique philosophy and psychospiritual psychology, based on the synthesis of experiences, both personal and spiritual. It is also an extraordinary set of techniques, allowing us to work with all areas of life, by ordering them in harmony around the entire Self, that is, one's personal, physical and spiritual nature. My individual experience of psychosynthesis, over nearly twenty years, grows out of self-education, and has made me aware of how true the following proverb is: "The more you get into it, the more complicated it gets!" This points to the life long quest for continuous progress and evolutionary movement, a process that is natural, essential **and** complicated! What emerges for psychosynthesis life coaches, from this developmental mandate, is the necessity to "dig deeper and reach higher", in supporting each individual in their own unique evolution. As coaches, we are inspired by the need for understanding who each person (client or coachee) is and where they are going, in their quest for a purpose filled life. As we understand the client's purpose, we are able to bring the full power of psychosynthesis into the coaching environment, to support this desired manifestation. Connected to purpose, anchored in presence, we support the movement of the client's will.

There is also a budding sensitivity, by both coaches and clients, to the problems of the world and the crisis of civilization, in which we participate as humankind, as well as to civilization illnesses, environmental threats, **and the** inner Call related to these. This Call of Self, demands the identification and activation of one's gifts and talents, to be put at the service of the public and all of humanity. Pending civilization problems must be effectively dealt with so as to not repeat past mistakes of the world history once again. Thus, the development of coaching is an historical necessity for building a spiritual partnership oriented towards evolution, with global awareness as part of the core of psychosynthesis coaching actions.

Right now, we need to return to individual responsibility for ourselves and the state of the world. These are times when we pay dearly for carefree and careless activities which pose a threat to individuals and the planet. These emerging needs, of responsibility, awareness of the larger experience of humanity, and inner connection to personal values and purpose, can be addressed by a number of psychosynthesis applications, not so much in therapy, but more in spiritual development, whereby each person, not only becomes a more human, but also a more mindful and spiritual being. The "man-as-machine" paradigm, deprived of a soul, is becoming slowly, but surely, replaced with a larger paradigm: that of "being a spiritual being in a human experience."

Victor Hugo once said: "Nothing is more powerful than an idea whose time has come." With its holistic approach to mental, physical and spiritual health and sustainable development, psychosynthesis is the idea for the new millennium, as was, in fact, announced by the title of an international conference in San Diego in 1996, "Psychosynthesis for the Next Century." It is now that next century, and nearly twenty years into it, the work of psychosynthesis is more important than ever.

Although psychosynthesis can have a number of therapeutic applications in treating mental and physical health problems, including psychosomatic disorders, the versatile nature of its influence on various levels of human development makes it a perfect tool both for individuals as well as professional and social groups in terms of personal support and transpersonal development of healthy people, in what is called, most universally, the field of life coaching.

Psychosynthesis offers an exceptional space for the development of self-consciousness. It embraces a philosophy of life that promotes well-being in many areas of life. Internal harmony (equivalent to homeostasis), at all levels of the self, is a key defining principle of this work. Will and the action of pursuing one's life mission is another. In these processes, every client discovers hidden talents and the invitation to offer them to the world, in service of other people. In this process, many people begin to feel the need to free themselves from systems which fix them on a particular and limiting mind set, representing herd mentality instead of individuality, and beyond that collective consciousness. Given so many limiting messages, finding a true calling and finding the way to live that calling is difficult for most everyone. Psychosynthesis, with its emphasis on awareness of life purpose, proves very helpful in finding the will to create a meaningful life.

With many different techniques available, concerned with thinking, emotions, impressions and intuition, it is possible to make adjustments to one's own mind set using the relevant questions and perspective. Owing to this, psychosynthesis enables one to trespass limiting barriers and find inner harmony, moving towards the creation of mindfulness in every moment. One's own observer (director), based in the disidentified "I", is capable of making ongoing, personal changes in the "here and now." And it is this, that allows for evolution. These self-awareness techniques teach us how to empower movement in the direction we pursue. This work gives an insight into a vision that transcends everyday reality and the five senses. It allows us to see, hear, and feel the soul, whose experiences are rich and resonate deeply with the inner calling towards life purpose.

Becoming open to this communication and guidance leads to a deeper relation with oneself and the surrounding world. The support, guidance and alliance, offered by a psychosynthesis coach is derived from the personal Call of Self, and therefore allows one to reorder oneself, starting from the very core of one's being, the transpersonal or spiritual Call of the Higher Self. As a result, one understands much more of who they are and where they are headed. Such a deep insight gives a client the opportunity to discover profound relationships with the surrounding reality and helps each individual to find a unique place in the life of society or even the world, which leads to inner harmony, health and external well-being.

Psychosynthesis, enabling the observation of growth, allows for taking actions based on pure intentions, resulting from pursuing transparent values in one's own life. This deep need for Self-fulfilment will keep on surfacing in each individual, and the psychosynthesis coach, rooted in the spiritual Self, will help this person bring their deepest callings to life.

The transpersonal perspective of the Self as a human and the world as a place where one pursues passion and calling, is a foundation of psychosynthesis practice and gives clients the strategies and support to transcend limitations, seek continuous fulfilment and identify the next steps of Self-realization.

The transpersonal, or spiritual, stage of development, gives a direction to life and helps clients to see themselves as a part of a greater whole. This higher development (spiritual psychosynthesis) is a key orientation in psychosynthesis coaching. Coaches and clients, alike, are able to render this very aspect of development through broadening the vision beyond the personal, by entering into a transpersonal perspective of meaning and purpose in our lives—into the essence of the psychosynthesis of this age, as postulated by Roberto Assagioli, who himself could see quite clearly how people needed to evolve, personally and globally.

As psychosynthesis experts, we have a great vision of our contribution to the world and humankind, taking into consideration the individual **and** the global realities. Thanks to this broad and deep perspective, coaches are able to support a growing number of people in seeking their place in the world, finding the meaning of their lives and living the experience of offering their gifts to the world.

The world is awaiting solutions to the problems haunting it, in every area. We are ready, as psychosynthesis specialists, to offer our talents to the world as it actually needs them. We are, therefore, filled with power, combining the spiritual and personal nature of each one of us, and, simultaneously, we are empowered with the strength of the international community we create. We are deeply convinced that psychosynthesis is an idea whose time has come.

Chapter 33

Reverence for the Process of Psychosynthesis

by Amy Spalding-Fecher

When I came to psychosynthesis, I was looking for a way to integrate my personality as well as my professional aspirations. I had recently moved back to the US after 16 years living overseas and was feeling distinctly dis-integrated. For a few years prior to leaving South Africa, I had practiced and eventually trained in a process-oriented art program called "Bridging Polarities through Art." Process art puts the emphasis on what we experience while making art, rather than the end product. I had become fascinated in creating space for the unconscious to emerge through this process, but was not quite sure how to bring this offering into the world. Psychosynthesis seemed to be a good partner in this process so it made sense to enroll in the course and see where it took me.

Each step of my journey with psychosynthesis since then has unfolded in a way that has felt inevitable–organic and natural, and frankly somewhat mysterious. I have not always known why I was taking the next step, but I trusted when the way opened up in front of me. I did not embark on the psychosynthesis training with the clear intention of becoming a Psychosynthesis Life Coach, and in some ways I am grateful for that. This open attitude of curiosity and possibility has made the journey that much more intriguing and helped me to see that the many threads in my life. Architecture, teaching, process art and coaching all stem from the same source: facilitating the manifestation of spirit into form, either in myself or in another. When we coach, we hold the space for meaning, resonance and insight to emerge for the client. I believe good architecture can do this—it is both an expression of the designer's inner landscape, as well as a holding environment for the occupant. The art making process embodies this as well.

My deep reverence for Psychosynthesis continues to evolve through study, teaching and professional and personal association. I know I have only scratched the surface of all it has to offer and may well feel this way all my life. For me Psychosynthesis is not just a tool, but like the process of making art, it is an endless experience filled with the wonder of living as a human being on earth. The eternal question is, how do we live our lives so that our choices support us in manifesting our unique, authentic selves? What guides us and supports us in making those choices?

Assagioli's concept of the Will, so central to his work, fascinates, challenges and perplexes me all at the same time. When something unfolds naturally with a certain inevitability, what role does the Will play? Given that the "I" is composed of Awareness and Will, is this unfolding just an example of the "self" living life, aligned with one's purpose, whether conscious or not? I often ponder the nature of Will—is the Will an action? Is it an impulse? A resonance? Is it a thing ("the Will"), a verb ("I am willing"), a function of the personality ("I have a Will" and "I am a will")? I continue to explore these ideas as I slowly move away from my cultural conditioning, in which the Will is what is imposed on recalcitrant beings resisting what is "good" for them—the Victorian Will. I have come to understand that what matters is an attunement to what is emerging, and that one chooses to live and act in a way that supports and furthers the unfolding self.

What I love about Psychosynthesis is that it so boldly and unapologetically claims the role of the transpersonal in our evolution. Who are we, as unique beings, and what is our essence wanting to be released in to the world, just as a rose's scent is released into the ether? I have long felt the presence of the transpersonal through art and architecture, in relationships, in nature, and have known it within myself. Yet I have spent much of my life with my authenticity and aspirations trapped and thwarted by subpersonalities and limiting beliefs. Am I free of them? Of course not, but the knowledge that I am more than them is a game changer. I was only dimly aware of the choice point, rarely stopping to step out of reactivity or behavior with a simple choice—the choice to anchor into the "I" and live in a way that contributes to the evolution of my higher Self, not against it. This is the freedom bestowed by an act of Will.

More than this, it has been revolutionary for me to turn towards my subpersonalities, my limitations, and embrace them with acceptance and curiosity, and discover the sweet beauty that lies beneath them. Who knew? I have discovered parts of myself that hid their tenderness and wonder behind a strong intellect and well-defended fortresses, thereby mistaking the shell for the creature. Although process art helped bring this part of me to the surface, it was Psychosynthesis that helped me to understand and celebrate these parts of me as essential to my very being.

How do I ground all of this in my work? Well, when I sit down to engage in an art process such as painting on wet paper with liquid watercolors, or shaving powdered chalk pastels onto paper, I center in a place of Presence—a place of stillness into which I allow an impulse to emerge. Sometimes it is a color, an intuition, a thought, or an image. Most of the psychological functions are at play when I am engaged in the art making process. Sometimes it is the will of a subpersonality that makes the first few marks, but eventually as I drop into the process and guide my awareness continuously back to what is happening in front of me, I connect with a timeless place that has no agenda, no content. I allow the process to lead me—as in coaching, where the coach often leads by following. The use of Will in this process is similar to meditation—repeatedly and without judgement bringing one's awareness back to the present moment and disengaging from strong identification with content.

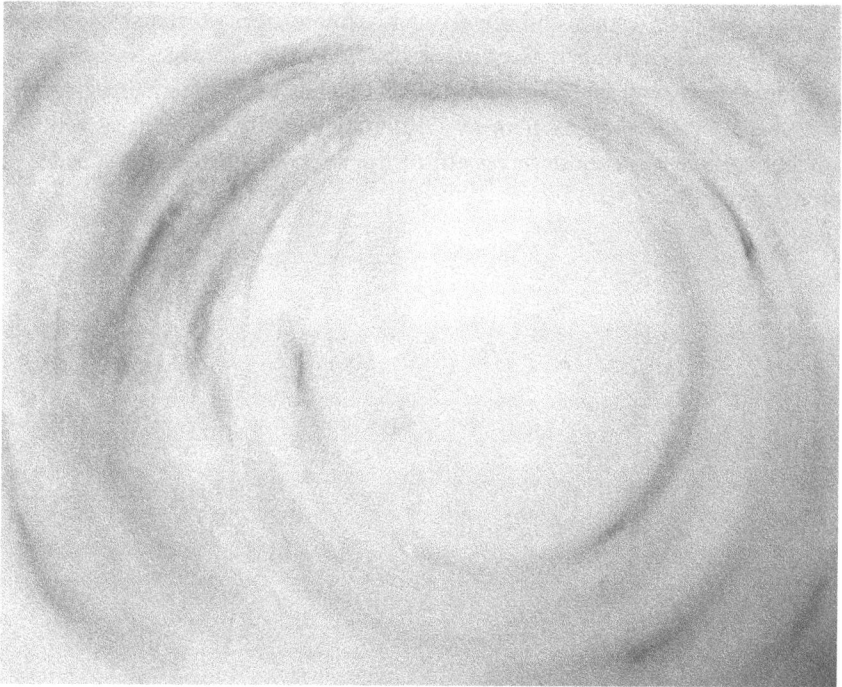

My gratitude towards this process, which fits so well with the psychosynthesis of the human being and the planet, is immense. The more I read and listen and learn, the more appreciation I have for Assagioli and the people who continue to sow the seeds of his wisdom in the world. We are at a time when fragmentation of self is evident all around us; it is vital that people have a way to harmonize their personality into an integrated whole in order to heal our communities. It is easy to despair when looking around at the state of the world. For me the antidote is to practice inner peace, and psychosynthesis and coaching are a perfect vehicle for this. If we cannot find peace and integration within us, we cannot create it in the world around us. And just as there is a need for activists out in the world fighting for democracy, fairness and justice, we need advocates for inner justice, coaches who will help us to drop into a space of stillness and kindness where we can "put out the welcome mat" and skillfully explore whatever emerges within ourselves. The practice of Presence is one of the strongest ways of becoming an advocate for oneself and for others.

During my training I repeatedly heard the refrain "don't mistake the map for the territory" or "don't mistake the finger pointing at the moon for the moon itself". The open-endedness of the field of Psychosynthesis is one of its greatest assets. The study of Psychosynthesis is the finger pointing at the limitless space within and between all beings. It is what allows each of us to apply the various maps to our own terrain, and travel to and explore areas previously wounded, misunderstood and exiled. The process opens the door to what is resonant in the inner recesses of our psyche. At the same time, it points to a universal terrain shared by all beings in all its mystery and richness. Indeed, this is evolution in action, if we can choose to get out of the way and let the natural order of things unfold.

Part 6

Author Biographies

But at times the conscious self rises or is raised to that higher region where it has specific experiences and states of awareness of various kinds which can be called "spiritual" in the widest sense. At other times it happens that some contents of the superconscious "descend" and penetrate into the area of the normal consciousness of the ego, producing what is called "inspiration." This interplay has great importance and value, both for fostering creativity and for achieving psychosynthesis.
—Roberto Assagioli

With deep thanks for the many "inspirations" that our authors have brought to this book, to their work and to the world.
—Dorothy Firman, editor

Chapter Author Biographies

Susan Jewkes Allen is the founder of Synthesis San Francisco, offering training and programs in psychosynthesis for professional and personal growth. After more than two decades as a therapist and community development consultant, she now has a global coaching practice. She is the co-founder of Life + Work, and specializes in career transition. Susan is a member of the Istituto di Psicosintesi in Florence and is committed to bringing the theory and tools of psychosynthesis to a new generation of practitioners. www.SynthesisCenterSF.com

Dr Ewa Danuta Białek is a life-long scientist in the field of medicine. She completed postgraduate studies in psychology and a number of courses in Psychosynthesis. In 1997, she founded the association, "Education for the Future" and in 2004, the Institute of Psychosynthesis in Warsaw, Poland. She is an author of 40 books and 60 scientific articles. She is passionate about well-being education, creating systemic solutions for raising healthy children, health education, and well-being work throughout adult life. Her work focuses on practical applications www.psychosynteza.pl or ewa.bialek@psychosynteza.pl

William Burr, FInstCT, PLC is a former President and Vice-Chairman of European electronics industry associations, and has a background in oceanographic engineering and microelectronics. After postings in Hawaii, Japan and the United States, Bill accepted the position of CTO of an Italian SME, driving a subsequent MBO and introducing innovations that powered the business to a turnover of over $120 million. A certified Psychosynthesis Life Coach, his C-level executive experience has subsequently been applied in coaching and mentoring start-ups in fields as diverse as "digital creative" and "More than Moore". An active investor, Bill continues to closely monitor emerging technologies and, when not doing that, keeps fit practicing martial arts and managing an Alpine property in Italy's Valtellina.

Martha Crampton, PhD (1933-2009) was the founder and director of the Canadian Institute of Psychosynthesis, and a leading teacher of psychosynthesis in North America and internationally. She was trained by Roberto Assagioli and brought her experience of psychosynthesis into the fields of psychotherapy, training and, in her later years, into the field of life coaching, as one of the earliest advocates for the field of psychosynthesis life coaching. Martha was a

441

remarkable thinker, a loving and compassionate teacher and a strong writer, whose work is to be found on many psychosynthesis sites throughout the world, touching on guided imagery, work with the unconscious, life coaching (appearing, with permission, in this book) psychoenergetics and more. For more of her writing, visit www.synthesiscenter.org and view the "PDF Downloads" page.

Patricia (Trissa) Elkins, Ph.D. is a business and group coach in an ICF Prism award winning coaching program in an international corporation. She teaches a number of internal coaching training programs as well as programs on corporate and personal resilience and brings the life affirming positivity she has developed from her psychosynthesis practice to corporate life. Trained in psychosynthesis at the Synthesis Center, Amherst MA, Trissa runs workshops on psychosynthesis and coaching in the Philadelphia area. www.synthesiscoachingphiladelphia.com or synthesiscoachingphiladelphia@gmail.com.

Roger Evans is the co-founder, in 1973, with his wife Joan, of The Institute of Psychosynthesis, a Psychotherapy, Coaching and Counselling Training School in London, UK. He is also Managing Director of CLC, a management consulting practice that works with boards, CEOs and senior leadership teams on issues of leadership transformation and change. He is an accredited psychotherapist and has been training and supervising coaches for the past 35 years. He is the co-author, with Peter Russell, of the book *The Creative Manager* (1989) and is about to publish his new book *5DL Five Dimensions of Leadership* in September 2018.

Dorothy Firman, Ed.D, LMHC, BCC is the founder and director of the Synthesis Center and its 40 year-long training program. She is currently a consulting faculty for many of the psychosynthesis life coach training programs that have grown from the Synthesis Center Training. She has been a psychotherapist and is a retired professor of psychology. Dorothy (Didi) has authored many books, including her most recent, *Engaging Life: Living Well with Chronic Illness*. She has practiced psychosynthesis her entire adult life, having come to the field in her early twenties. Her current work involves supporting the movement of psychosynthesis life coaching, offering coaching and coaching supervision, and living gradually into retirement. She continues, as president of the Synthesis Center, offering occasional workshops and trainings. Didi@synthesiscenter.org

Alan C. Haras is the founder and director of The Cardoner Institute for Contemplative Leadership and the owner of Hamsa Yoga Center in Lake Orion, Michigan. He is a board certified coach, trained spiritual director and retreat guide, 800-hour Dharma Yoga teacher, and a speaker on various dimensions of spirituality and contemplative practice. With a Master's degree in Religious Studies, Alan's classes, seminars and workshops are suffused with a deep appreciation for the world's wisdom traditions—joyfully drawing upon a host of stories, anecdotes and teachings from various lineages to illustrate shared themes. www.alanharas.com.

Kevin C. Harrington, received a B.Sc in Astronomy and B.Sc in Psychological Brain Sciences at the University of Massachusetts, Amherst. He has a professional life coach certification from the Synthesis Center, and is deeply interested in the development of his own and others' potential to pursue their goals and dreams with passion and purpose. Currently a Ph.D. candidate at the Max Planck Institute for Radio Astronomy in Bonn, Germany in the field of galaxy evolution, Kevin believes that one of the next frontiers in coaching lies within the science/research environments. He enjoys traveling and playing percussion worldwide as a semi-professional hobby. LinkedIn (https://www.linkedin.com/in/kevin-harrington-80a15092/) or kcorneil1223@gmail.com

Karen Herold, worked for 30 plus years in the business world She considers herself a recovering CPA, finance and business executive. She left her business career to pursue a master's in transpersonal psychology followed soon thereafter by certification as a psychosynthesis coach. She is a yoga teacher, creative expression arts facilitator and a life transition coach. Karen is also a member of the faculty at Sofia University where she teaches the practicum courses. Karen loves to support students as they begin the process of bringing their dreams for sharing their transpersonal education and their unique skills and gifts into the world. Karen is the mother of three adult daughters and three grand children. All three of her daughters played club volleyball, and were coached at one time or another by their mother...which is a future chapter in a book! karen@wise-transition.com or www. wisetransition.com

Mark Horowitz is a leadership and organizational development consultant, an experienced educator, and board certified coach. He trained in Humanistic Psychology with Abraham Maslow, Ph.D. and in Psychosynthesis with Roberto Assagioli, M.D. He has studied the field of human systems for over thirty-five years as a licensed individual and family therapist and as a management consultant and coach for businesses in the United States, Europe, Scandinavia, and Russia. He is a faculty member of the International School of Psychotherapy and Group Counseling in St. Petersburg, Russia, and has been an adjunct faculty member at John F. kennedy University and Antioch

San Francisco in California, and at Suffolk and Lesley Universities in Boston. Mark has taught Psychosynthesis at many centers around the world, including the Psychosynthesis Institute in San Francisco, The Synthesis Center and the Institute of Psychosynthesis, London. He lives outside of Boston with his wife, Abby Seixas. mark@newcontextcoaching.com or www.newcontextcoaching.com.

Aubyn Howard is the co-founder (with Paul Elliott) of Psychosynthesis Coaching Limited, which runs the Post-Graduate Certificate in Psychosynthesis Leadership Coaching Programme twice a year in London. A version of the programme runs in Italy in partnership with IIPE and an international version will start in 2019. Aubyn holds an MA in Psychosynthesis Psychology with the London Institute of Psychosynthesis and an MSc in Change Agent Skills and Strategies at Surrey University. He draws upon more than 30 years' experience as a consultant, facilitator, educator and coach, bringing about transformational change and leadership development. He is an APECS Accredited Executive Coach. aubyn@psychosynthesiscoaching.co.uk or www.psychosynthesiscoaching.co.uk

Kirsten Ireland, MSc, is a certified Psychosynthesis Coach and Hypnotherapist and the Director at Meadow. Kirsten has worked for over 20 years in transformation, working with individuals to support them coming into wholeness and aliveness, and at organizational and systems level to deliver social and environmental change. Meadow is a purpose-driven organization dedicated to catalyzing possibilities for change. We do this through 1:1 coaching and guiding; partnering with organizations; tackling global challenges using a living systems and warm data approach; and producing tools and information to support new ways of perceiving and acting in the world. www.meadowonline.org

Richard Lamb practices out of Nottingham in the East Midlands of England and from London, UK. Richard's life story took a challenging turn in February 2001, when he fell from Tower Ridge, a winter mountaineering route on Ben Nevis, Scotland. In time, he came to understand this experience as his own 'initiatory event', and in hindsight, led him to answer the Call of Self as a Psychosynthesis Coach and Hypnotherapist working with trauma survivors, including fellow amputees. www.truenorththerapy.co or richard@truenorththerapy.co

Catherine Ann Lombard is a Psychosynthesis Psychologist, Counselor and Researcher. She received her MA in Psychosynthesis Psychology from the

Institute of Psychosynthesis, London, affiliated with Middlesex University, London. Catherine is also a writer and has had numerous scientific articles published on psychosynthesis as well as personal essays about international travel and spirituality. She lives in Umbria, Italy with her husband, dog, and cat where they grow their own vegetables and live quietly in nature. To learn more about her, the Italian tours to poetic places she and her husband lead, and to read her bimonthly blog, please visit: www.loveandwill.com.

Blake McHenry, PLC, has an extensive and successful background in business, having held roles as a senior executive in both sales and human resources for Taylor Made Golf Co. and for YETI Coolers. Today Blake spends his professional time coaching senior leaders as well as doing coaching and supervision of professional coaches. His work is devoted to deep support of his clients, both in their personal and professional lives. Blake loves spending time with his wife, granddaughters Caroline and Annemarie and their Siberian huskie Rex. mchenryblake@gmail.com

Alejandro Negrete has a BA in East-West Philosophy from Colorado College. He is a board certified Transpersonal Coach specializing in Psychosynthesis, as well as a teacher and astrologer. Since 2004 he has devoted himself to the study and exploration of Transpersonal Psychology and spirituality through the lens of the Perennial Philosophy. His primary passion is helping others to develop a conscious relationship to their True Self through which they can fulfill their unique calling and achieve lives of greater purpose, happiness and fulfillment. www.perennialself.com

Cristina Pelizzatti has been a guide for over ten years, supporting people through Psychosynthesis and Ecopsychology towards achievement of personal and professional well-being and activation of their highest potentials. Her Purpose is to help people reach excellence, living a satisfying and meaningful life in line with their "Call of Self": reconnecting with Purpose, Meaning, and Values, developing awareness, activating Will. She is a Certified Psychosynthesis Life Coach PLC; Psychosynthesis Coach Trainer; Supervisor Counselor in Psychosynthesis; Certified Resilience Practitioner; Transpersonal Counselor; Psychoenergetic, Ecocounselor, Ecotuner, Green Coach; with specialization in Foundations of Positive Psychology, MBSR and an MA in Indovedic Psychology. cris@criscoaching.com or www.synthesis-coaching.com

Raúl Quiñones-Rosado, PhD, is a social psychologist, social justice educator and Psychosynthesis coach. He is founder of c-Integral, LLC, a social enterprise that conducts leadership development, antiracism organizing and other decolonizing efforts. His book, *Consciousness-in-Action: Toward an Integral Psychology of Liberation & Transformation,* is required reading in graduate programs in psychology, counseling and social work, and is cited by leading international scholars in the fields of critical and liberation psychology. His writings on racism, race policy, Latino identity, integral well-being, counseling and coaching appear in academic and professional publications. Raúl currently lives between Greensboro, North Carolina, and Cayey, Puerto Rico. raulquinones.com

Wilka M. Roig Rivera holds a Master of Arts in Transpersonal Psychology, and a Master of Fine Arts. She is a professional dream worker, Biomagnetism therapist, Psychosynthesis coach, Integrative Grief Therapy and Archetypal & Cross-Cultural Psychology practitioner. Wilka is an end-of-life doula, educator, facilitator, consultant, ordained minister, Tai Chi instructor, writer, musician, artist, designer, silversmith, baker, and mythmaker. Her professional interests include Transpersonal & Somatic Psychology, Neurobiology of Trauma, Loss & Grief, Neurobiology of Relationships, Taoist Inner Arts, Tibetan Buddhism, Mindfulness, Dream Work, Transformative Storytelling, Feminist & Gender Studies, Visual & Expressive Arts, Confectionery & Culinary Arts, and Wine Culture. www.wilkaroig.com or info@wilkaroig.com

Julie Rivers is an ICF and BCC certified coach working at an international corporation as a learning professional and corporate coach. She began working as an ICF certified corporate coach and then deepened her coaching work by studying and then integrating psychosynthesis coaching practices into the corporate coaching environment. Julie enjoys blending her love of learning with coaching and coach training programs. Trained in psychosynthesis at the Synthesis Center, Amherst MA, Julie runs workshops on psychosynthesis and coaching in the Philadelphia area. www.synthesiscoachingphiladelphia.com or synthesiscoachingphiladelphia@gmail.com.

James Rogers lives in the Hudson Valley with his wife and two daughters, Ella and Summer, where he spends his time swinging in the hammock, watching the fireflies and strumming on his guitar. He is an attorney, government official, advocate for justice and a poet, song-writer and musician. He completed Psychosyntheis Training Levels I and II as well as the teacher training. Jamrogers@gmail.com

Paula Sayword is on the Board of Directors of the The Synthesis Center and is the author of 2 books of poetry, *What Sleeps Inside* and *Canticle of Light and Dark*. Her poems have appeared in numerous journals and anthologies. She lives in Western Massachusetts with her longtime woman partner.

Valerie Silidker MS, BCC is co-founder of Psychospiritual Coaching and founder/director of Inspired Life Workshops. She is a Deep Ecologist, Evolutionary Activist, Board Certified Mindset and Leadership Coach, and Coach Trainer in the work of Psychosynthesis. Val works with changemakers, emerging leaders and visionaries to inspire the highest level of mindset, connection and creativity in their lives, and has inspired the transformation of thousands of people over the past few decades. Val is passionate about rewilding our hearts and believes that through love and connection we are inspired into sacred action toward a more compassionate and whole world. val.silidker@gmail.com or www.psychospiritualcoaching.com/

Barbara Veale Smith, M.Ed., wanted to change the world. Supported by her spiritual teachers, she discovered a few simple and surprising truths: change comes through constancy; awareness is always present, it accepts everything, doesn't have any content, and yet attending to it, allows contentment to flourish. At ContentmentCoaching.com, Barbara now helps people make changes that allow peace and joy to blossom in their lives, and thus in the world. In addition to coaching, she directs the nonprofit, Undefended Heart.org. Barbara is a two time graduate of Boston College and a Board Certified, Open Focus™ and Psychosynthesis Life Coach. bveale.smith@gmail.com

Amy Spalding-Fecher is a Psychosynthesis Life Coach, a trainer at The Synthesis Northeast Training Program, an Artist and a registered Architect. Her coaching approach combines Psychosynthesis with process-oriented art in a gentle path of insight and transformation. Her practice also draws from her background in design, construction and coaching to help clients explore and articulate what is meaningful about the spaces in which they live. She believes that transformation in our society and in our world begins with transformation within each individual. amy.spaldingfecher@gmail.com

Leyza A. Toste, BCC, is a life synthesis coach, Reiki master, astrologer, and founder of Sundara Pathways, LLC. 'Sundara (Sanskrit for beautiful) Pathways' speaks to the beauty in every life path, and the understanding that no two are the same. Leyza's client work blends complementary techniques in a welcoming space for all. She trusts in the power of what is possible when an individual aligns with their truth and she is passionate about helping others experience that joy. www.sundarapathways.com/

Ilene Val-Essen, P.hd., has been passionately serving parents for decades. An innovator in the field of parent education, she blends Western psychology with Eastern philosophy, bringing a unique voice to the global community. Her books, *Bring Out the Best in Your Child and Your Self* and *Parenting with Wisdom and Compassion*, along with the Quality Parenting programs, invite parents to enter a new paradigm. Family life becomes so much easier and more rewarding. Her materials have been translated into Spanish, Dutch, and Swedish. Val-Essen practices as a MFT in California. www.BringOutTheBest.com or IleneValEssen@me.com.

Sara Vatore is a Board Certified Life Coach, Somatic Experiencing® Practitioner, Certified Nia® White Belt Instructor, MELT Method® Instructor and a Peak Performance Coach. Through her understanding of the nervous system and the body, Sara helps her clients build capacity and resiliency in their systems, to more dynamically and easily negotiate life challenges, overcome fears and blocks and set and manifest goals. From Olympic athletes, to entrepreneurs, to coaching professionals, to the mom next door, Sara is passionate about supporting others on their journeys towards health, resilience and deep transformational growth. www.saravatore.com.

Christiana Wall is a Psychosynthesis Life Coach specializing in Relationship Coaching and Counseling dedicated to helping individuals, couples, groups and organizations live and work in alignment with what brings them meaning, purpose, value and joy. She teaches workshops entitled "The Art of Not Taking It Personally" and "The Art of Letting Go of Resentments." She brings insights and practices to her work from her training in Non-Violent Communication, Restorative Justice, Spatial Dynamics, Anthroposophic Psychology and Dynamic Facilitation. c.wall.email@gmail.com

About The Synthesis Center

The Synthesis Center is a non-profit corporation founded in 1976 and dedicated to the dissemination of psychosynthesis theory, practice and experience. The Center has helped in the formation of five new training Centers, throughout the US and in Italy. We currently operate as a support for these Centers and a resource for the public. The Synthesis Center offers occasional workshops, life coach referrals, and graduate training offerings. The Center continues to offer Independent Study programs in Psychosynthesis Life Coaching. We are accredited as a Board Certified Coach training center. As part of our offering to the public, we continue to make psychosynthesis materials available, in print, on the web and in newsletters. To join our mailing list or for any inquiries, contact: admin@synthesiscenter.org

About Synthesis Center Press

The Synthesis Center Press started in 2000 with the publishing of Dr. Assagioli's seminal book, *Psychosynthesis: A Collection of Basic Writings*. We continued with the publishing of other related books in the field and Dr. Assagioli's second book; *Act of Will*, in cooperation with AAP. *The Call of Self: Psychosynthesis Life Coaching* is the latest in our offerings related to psychosynthesis.

Other books by Synthesis Center Press:
Psychosynthesis: A Collection of Basic Writings by Roberto Assagioli
Counseling in a Complex Society: Contemporary Challenges to Professional Practice, Edited by Nicholas Young and Christine Michael
Counseling with Confidence: From Pre-Service to Professional Practice Edited by Nicholas Young and Christine Michael
Act of Will by Roberto Assagioli
Canticle of Light and Dark by Paula Sayword
The Dance of We: The Mindful Use of Love and Power in Human Systems by Mark Horowitz

Other books authored and co-authored by Dorothy Firman:
Daughters and Mothers: Healing the Relationship
Chicken Soup for the Mother & Daughter Soul
Daughters and Mothers: Making it Work
Chicken Soup for the Soul: Celebrating Mothers and Daughters
Chicken Soup for the Father and Son Soul: Celebrating the Bond That Connects Generations
Brace for Impact: Miracle on the Hudson Survivors Share Their Stories of Near Death and Hope for New Life
Engaging Life: Living Well With Chronic Illness

www.ingramcontent.com/pod-product-compliance
Lightning Source LLC
Chambersburg PA
CBHW071727270326
41928CB00013B/2592